Teaching and Learning with Technologies in the Primary School

This fully updated third edition of *Teaching and Learning with Technologies in the Primary School* introduces practising and student teachers to the range of ways in which technology can be used to support and extend teaching and learning opportunities in their classrooms.

Newly expanded to include 50% brand new chapters reflecting the abundant changes in the field since the last edition was published, it offers practical guidance underpinned by the latest research and teaching in the field. The authors draw on the extensive experience of educators in Australia, England, Ireland, Scotland, South Africa, the U.S.A. and Wales to provide local, national and international examples of the application of digital technologies to teaching and learning across the primary curriculum.

Illustrated throughout with case studies and examples together with a glossary explaining key terms, chapters focus on how technology-based practices can support the teaching of individual subjects, as well as a range of teaching and learning styles. Key and new topics covered include:

– Supporting reading and writing with technology
– Technology in the early years
– Developing e-skills of parents
– Use of Virtual Reality in learning
– PedTech
– Resilience in the digital world

Written for all training primary teachers, as well as more experienced teachers and technology co-ordinators looking for guidance on the latest innovative practice, *Teaching and Learning with Technologies in the Primary School, 3rd edition*, offers advice and ideas for creative, engaging and successful teaching and learning.

Sarah Younie is Professor in Education Innovation at De Montfort University, UK. Her primary research is in translational research in education, that is, the application of research in practice. Sarah is editor-in-chief of the journal *Technology, Pedagogy and Education*.

Marilyn Leask is visiting Professor of Education at De Montfort University, UK, co-chair of the MESH Guides knowledge mobilisation initiative and has been a teacher, researcher, secondary school assistant head, local authority policy officer and university dean. She has had policy roles in two UK national agencies.

Teaching and Learning with Technologies in the Primary School

Third edition

Edited by
Sarah Younie and Marilyn Leask

Routledge
Taylor & Francis Group

LONDON AND NEW YORK

Designed cover image: © Getty Images

Third edition published 2024
by Routledge
4 Park Square, Milton Park, Abingdon, Oxon, OX14 4RN

and by Routledge
605 Third Avenue, New York, NY 10158

Routledge is an imprint of the Taylor & Francis Group, an informa business

First edition published by Routledge 2000
Second edition published by Routledge 2015

British Library Cataloguing-in-Publication Data
A catalogue record for this book is available from the British Library

Library of Congress Cataloging-in-Publication Data
Names: Younie, Sarah, 1967- editor. | Leask, Marilyn, 1950- editor.
Title: Teaching and learning with technologies in the primary school /
edited by Sarah Younie and Marilyn Leask.
Other titles: Teaching and learning with ICT in the primary school
Description: Third edition. | Abingdon, Oxon ; New York, NY : Routledge,
2024. | Revised edition of: Teaching and learning with ICT in the
primary school. 2nd edition. 2015. | Includes bibliographical references
and index. | Identifiers: LCCN 2023047738 (print) | LCCN 2023047739
(ebook) | ISBN 9781032528823 (hardback) | ISBN 9781032528847
(paperback) | ISBN 9781003408925 (ebook)
Subjects: LCSH: Education, Elementary—Great Britain—Computer-assisted
instruction. | Internet in education—Great Britain. | Telecommunication
in education—Great Britain.
Classification: LCC LB1028.5 .T382 2024 (print) | LCC LB1028.5 (ebook) |
DDC 372.133/40941—dc23/eng/20231109
LC record available at https://lccn.loc.gov/2023047738
LC ebook record available at https://lccn.loc.gov/2023047739

ISBN: 978-1-032-52882-3 (hbk)
ISBN: 978-1-032-52884-7 (pbk)
ISBN: 978-1-003-40892-5 (ebk)

DOI: 10.4324/9781003408925

Typeset in Galliard Pro
by codeMantra

Contents

Contributors

Many thanks to the teachers, teacher educators and researchers who contributed to this book, many of whom are members of the Technology, Pedagogy and Education professional subject association www.tpea.ac.uk.

Dr. Fiona Aubrey-Smith is Associate Lecturer supporting postgraduate programmes at the Open University, and an independent strategic education consultant supporting schools. Her work focuses on the relationships between digital technology, pedagogy and education.

Jon Audain is the PGCE Primary Programme Co-Leader at the Institute of Education, University of Winchester. He is also the Past Chair of the Technology, Pedagogy in Education Association (TPEA), a national subject association for evidence-informed research and education technology.

Daniel Ayres is a Senior Lecturer in Initial Teacher Education at the University of East London. Before joining UEL he taught children across the primary age range at schools in the London Boroughs of Tower Hamlets, Newham and Redbridge.

Professor Gary Beauchamp is Professor of Education in the School of Education and Social Policy at Cardiff Metropolitan University. His research interests are interactive technologies in teaching and learning, especially in the primary school.

Jeffrey Beaudry is a Professor in the Educational Leadership program at the University of Southern Maine. He has research interests in visual learning, concept mapping, and critical thinking, with more recent work in data visualizations of diversity and equity.

Graham Bell is a teacher educator at Sheffield Hallam University. His particular interests are in the fields of creative approaches to teaching and learning, and pupil engagement.

Dr. Karen Blackmore is a Principal Lecturer in Science Education at the University of Worcester. Her particular interests are in deploying mobile technologies in the classroom to support the acquisition of scientific inquiry skills and enable positive learning relationships.

Susan Borland is a Specialist Leader of Education and Lecturer in Teacher Education at Sheffield Hallam University. Her particular interests and research are in the fields of Primary and Early Years computing and literacy.

Dr. Nina Bresnihan is an Assistant Professor in the School of Computer Science & Statistics, Trinity College Dublin. Her particular research interests include computer science education, technology and learning and gender and computing.

Paul Brooks is a Senior Lecturer in Education at Cardiff Metropolitan University. His interests are in the fields of global and comparative education, immersive technologies and environmental education.

Dr. Helen Caldwell is an Associate Professor at the University of Northampton where she is a specialist in educational technology, teacher education and online learning. She co-leads the Centre for Active Digital Education.

Louise Caldwell is the Programme Manager for OurKidsCode in the School of Computer Science and Statistics in Trinity College Dublin. She is responsible for the roll-out of family creative computing coding workshops and clubs in rural and urban communities across Ireland.

Sammy Chapman is an educator and researcher at Cardiff Metropolitan University. His particular research experiences are in the fields of Technology in Learning Design and Expressive Arts.

Rachael Coultart is a Teacher and Computing Subject Leader from Stevenage St Nicholas Primary School and Nursery. Her particular interests include the effective use of technology in the Early Years.

Jean Edwards is a Senior Lecturer in the Faculty of Education, Health and Society at the University of Northampton. Her fields of interest are art education and using digital technologies in primary art and across the curriculum.

Josephine Farag is a Senior Lecturer at Cardiff Metropolitan University. Her research interests are Decolonising the Computer Science Curriculum and Digital assessment and pedagogical practice.

Warren Fearn is Associate Professor in Design at York St John University. His particular experiences and interests are in augmented reality, 3D graphic motion and educational technologies.

Emma Goto is a teacher educator at the University of Winchester. Her particular experience and interests are in primary computing, computational thinking, early childhood education, philosophy for children and education theory.

Kirsten Gould is an RTI Coach at Sacopee Valley Elementary School. Her particular interests are in the fields of educational neuroscience, high-impact strategies for teaching and learning, and the science of literacy instruction. She is a specialist in neuro-positive teaching and learning and she has received awards for her work in elementary science education.

Dr. Marian Henry is a primary teacher in Dublin. She has a Doctorate in Education and MA in Media Studies. Her research interest is in developing children's digital media literacy.

Dr. Wayne Holmes is an Associate Professor in the UCL Knowledge Lab at University College London. His research takes a critical studies perspective to the teaching and application of Artificial Intelligence in educational contexts (AI&ED), and their ethi-cal, human and social implications. Wayne is leading the Council of Europe's project: *Artificial Intelligence and Education. A critical view through the Lens of Human Rights, Democracy and the Rule of Law*; he is also Consultant for the *Technology and AI in Education* unit at UNESCO, for which he co-wrote AI and Education: Guidance for Policy-makers.

Professor Jonathan Hook is at the University of York. His research is in the field of Hu-man-Computer Interaction and explores the design and development of new interactive media content forms and tools to support their creation.

Paul Hopkins is subject leader for primary science at the University of Hull. He has re-search interests in technology-enhanced learning, nationally and internationally.

Dr. Kristina Kelly is a lecturer in Teacher Education and Professional Learning and an early career researcher at Cardiff Metropolitan University. Her research interests include play pedagogy, Additional Learning Needs (ALN) and outdoor learning.

Professor Marilyn Leask has forty years' experience of teaching and researching in schools and universities, nationally and internationally, and special research interests in teacher development and the use of digital technologies to support teaching and learning. In 1984 her classroom was connected via an early form of Internet with other schools. As a UK public servant she had responsibility for working with teachers, teacher educa-tors and researchers to put the research knowledge base underpinning teacher training online. However, the incoming UK government in 2010 took offline all the resources paid for by the taxpayer, many of which were integrated into teaching programmes. To protect teacher access to research-based knowledge, with Professor Younie and others she established the Education Futures Collaboration charity which co-ordinates the creation of the freely available MESHGuide research summaries for teachers (www. meshguides.org), which are used in over 200 countries.

Dr. Diane Levine was a teacher and public servant before doing her PhD at the University of Warwick. She is currently a lecturer/researcher at the University of Leicester. Di's particular research interests are in the ways in which children and young people survive and thrive when life is challenging, especially in a digital world.

Sarah Lloyd is a primary music specialist with significant experience supporting teachers to deliver musical learning with their classes. She leads sessions for ITT trainees, sup-ports leaders and teachers in schools and is a learning resources producer for Aurora Orchestra.

Damian Maher is Senior Lecturer in the School of International Studies and Education at the University of Technology Sydney (UTS). His research focus is on the use of digital technologies in school and tertiary settings to support teaching and learning.

Dr. Louis Major is a Senior Lecturer in Digital Education at the University of Manches-ter. Working in the Manchester Institute of Education, he co-leads the Digital Technol-ogies, Communication and Education (DTCE) Research and Scholarship group. Louis' research focuses on digital technology's role in the future of education, in particular, how this can help to address educational disadvantage and support effective dialogue and communication.

Dr. Mario Marais retired from the Council for Scientific and Industrial Research (CSIR) of South Africa in November 2022 as a Principal Researcher in the e-Government Impact Area. His research is mainly in the domain of sustainable development of rural communities, especially regarding education, using a social capital perspective to evaluate and foster collaborative sustainable development via social community mapping, Social Network Analysis (SNA) and network weaving.

Beth Mead is a secondary school Computer Studies pupil, who has published several international papers on the creative use of IT and Computing, including original work in Scratch and Python. She has presented her work to teachers at several international conferences.

Helen Mead is a freelance primary music specialist. She is currently working with Winchester University, Awards for Young Musicians and Aurora Orchestra.

Dr. Richard Millwood is a Research Fellow at Trinity College Dublin. His particular experience is in educational technology applied to learning at all levels.

Dr. David Morris is an education consultant with a Doctorate in Education. He was previously a Senior Lecturer in Initial Teacher Education at the University of East London. He has over twenty-five years' experience in the education sector.

Dr. Deborah Outhwaite is the Director of DTSA, and an EdD Supervisor in the Centre of Higher Education Studies (CHES) at the University of Liverpool. She has thirty years of experience in education and is the Chair of BELMAS.

Rachael Peckover is a former Deputy Headteacher and now an Assistant Professor in the School of Education at the University of Nottingham. Her interests are school governance, leadership, continuing professional learning and primary maths.

Professor Christina Preston is the Founder of MirandaNet. Her research interests are in the value of collaboration in the creation of knowledge about education in the context of education innovation.

Dr. Marnie Seymour is Senior Fellow Knowledge Exchange (CPD) and Academic Lead for NPQ and ECF programmes at the University of Winchester. She is a primary modern foreign languages specialist.

Glenn Strong is an Associate Professor and researcher at Trinity College Dublin. His particular interests are in the fields of computer science education.

Rachael Summerscales is a Senior Lecturer in Initial Teacher Education at Sheffield Hallam University and an Independent Trainer and Advisory Consultant in Early Years. Her particular interests are in children's learning dispositions and inquiries, social and emotional development and early literacies.

Professor Linda Theron is a full professor in the Department of Educational Psychology at the University of Pretoria. Her clinical and research interest is in child and adolescent resilience, with a special interest in how situational and cultural context shapes the resilience of African young people.

Philippa Thompson is a Principal Lecturer in Early Childhood Studies at Sheffield Hallam University and co-chair of the Early Childhood Studies Degrees Network.

Her research interests include the well-being of young children, families, practitioners and undergraduates through participation and advocacy.

Sharon Tonner-Saunders is a lecturer at the University of Dundee. Her particular interests are intercultural learning and digital technologies to promote inclusion and diversity in schools.

Gurmit Uppal is a senior teacher who works in the London Borough of Havering. She divides her time between teaching computing to primary-aged pupils and supporting early-career teachers. She also works with trainee teachers and lectures on undergraduate and post-graduate education courses.

Emma Whewell is an Associate Professor in Learning and Teaching at the University of Northampton. Her research centres around teacher training, mentoring, identity, digital pedagogies and access and participation.

Amber Williams is a teacher with a specialism in teaching special education needs and information communication technology and computing at St John's School.

Lawrence Williams is an experienced classroom practitioner and teacher trainer, who has received many national and international teaching awards for his work in the creative use of IT and Computing. He is TPEA Specialist Leader in EdTech Education, an Associate Member National Conference of University Professors, and is a member of the IFIP Technical Committee 3: Education.

Dr. Nick Young is a senior lecturer within the School of Education at Cardiff Metropolitan University. Nick is a former primary school teacher with a particular interest of technology use within the primary classroom.

Professor Sarah Younie is a Professor in Education Innovation at De Montfort University and visiting Professor at Chichester University. She has taught in schools and universities for over thirty years and after obtaining a Ph.D. in Education, she has undertaken international and national research. She is the BERA (British Education Research Association) national convenor for the 'Educational Research and Policy Making' Special Interest Group. She is a Trustee and founder member with Professor Marilyn Leask of the Education Futures Collaboration (EFC) charity and MESH (Mapping Education Specialist knowHow) project, which provides research evidence to inform teachers' professional practice, and she represents MESH on the UNESCO International Teacher Task Force (ITTF) panel; MESH contributes to UN SDG4. As the UK Chair of a national subject association, she has submitted evidence for Parliamentary Select Committee Inquiries into Education. Professor Younie is the editor-in-chief of the journal *Technology, Pedagogy and Education*. Her primary research interest is in translational research in education, that is how research can be applied to practice.

Case studies

Figures

Tables

Tasks

Foreword

I am delighted to write the foreword to this informative textbook. The day after my elder daughter was born, twenty years ago, the pediatrician came to do her newborn health check. She passed her back to me, and said 'Look after this one well, she may live to be 140 years old!'

Technology and education go hand in hand, some people are more interested in technology than others, but what we are all now aware of is that this is something that cannot be ignored in our teaching in primary education. The way in which children learn has altered immeasurably over the last few decades, and this trend was exacerbated by the Covid-19 pandemic.

I know that our Early Years and Primary Beginner Teachers in our PGCE programmes and our mentors and leaders in schools will benefit tremendously from this book.

Those who have engaged only superficially with how technology has an impact on learning in the digital age will perhaps be surprised by the content of the chapters. Specific chapters on resilience, pedagogy, SEND, assessment, Early Years, Art, dialogue, storytelling and film cover areas important to the well-being of children in a digital world.

Those engaged in the curriculum areas of English, maths, science, STEM, MFL and computing have a great deal to learn here.

The chapters on augmented reality, interactive technologies, outdoor learning and videoconferencing are illuminating in a Primary context.

The chapters on neuro-positive strategies, global citizenship, school policies in online safety and family learning all enable us to think more widely about the impact of technology.

The concluding chapters on sustainable uses of technology, and how we can support CPD, are invaluable for those of us engaged in developing the teaching profession moving forward.

Whatever your particular area of interest, this textbook enables our steps forward in teaching and learning with technologies in the primary school to be both acknowledged and better understood—enjoy!

Dr. Deborah Outhwaite FCCT
Director
Developing Teachers Schools Academies (DTSA)

Introduction

"If we teach today as we taught yesterday, we rob our children of tomorrow"

(Dewey, 1944: 167)

You will be teaching young people many of whom can expect to be alive in the 22nd century. The changes they will face in their lifetime are unimaginable, so it is essential that pupils are prepared to be resilient, to be adaptable and to understand and protect themselves against online risks.

An openness to learning about emerging advanced technologies and an awareness of how to use technologies effectively for a wide range of purposes are part of the toolset they will need to be effective citizens, family members and employees over their lifetime.

However, teachers need to teach children how to protect themselves from manipulation. Teachers also need to be aware of the dark web. There is a lack of moderation of material on the web which means your pupils can come across harmful material. We expect during the lifetime of this book that increasingly countries will pass legislation and control access to the web. For further information see the work of Professor Kathleen Richardson, from the Centre for Computing and Social Responsibility at De Montfort University on 'cyber ethics,' who critically examines the role and use of robots and artificial intelligence (AI). For children and young people, we hope for a set of protocols that might provide standards for web content that content producers might sign up to that are robust in protecting children from harmful content.

Emerging Trends: Watch Out for Artificial Intelligence (AI)

To write this section on AI we asked an AI driven chat bot to define the term. Here is the response:

"What is AI?—Artificial Intelligence involves using computers to do things that traditionally require human intelligence. AI can process large amounts of data in ways that humans cannot. The goal for AI is to be able to do things like recognize patterns, make decisions, **and judge like humans** (our emphasis).

There are several approaches to creating AI, including rule-based systems, machine learning and deep learning. Rule-based systems use a set of predefined rules to make decisions and perform tasks. Machine learning involves training a machine to use a large amount of data so that it can learn to perform a task without being explicitly programmed to do so. Deep learning is a subset of machine learning that involves using artificial neural networks with multiple layers to learn from data.

AI has a wide range of applications, including speech recognition, natural language processing, computer vision, robotics, autonomous vehicles, and more. It has the potential to transform many industries and improve our lives in numerous ways."

In education, one of the biggest challenges is the language/text-generated answers AI can provide for assessment.

We think this area of technological development is most likely in the short term, to bring significant changes to teachers and pupils' daily lives and teachers' practices. There is, for example, current discussion about whether the school sector can assess coursework through independent study following the release of AI text/content generators such as ChatGPT. Current plagiarism software is not sophisticated enough to pick up whether an essay has been generated using text-generated AI.

However, beyond the challenges of AI for assessment are wider ethical questions about AI, as AI is amoral—it has no conscience, it can provide wrong answers and fake references. Furthermore, who owns the copyright of the generated text? Chapter 2 provides advice about how to raise issues of ethical use of data with your pupils and safeguarding issues.

How to Use This Book—Further Resources

During your career you can expect to find that education attracts a lot of attention from politicians and, in some countries, there are no checks and balances to protect educators from politicians keen to create a headline by imposing change. But the politicians have no long-term responsibility for educational outcomes in the way that educators do.

So, depending on the context in which you work, you may find you have to accommodate political objectives in your professional practice, which may be contrary to the professional values and knowledge about effective teaching outlined in this book.

There is, however, a world-wide collaboration of educators building a research-informed evidence base for practice, which we are part of and which we hope will provide you with evidence-informed professional support during your teaching career—see MESHGuides on www.MESHguides.org. These guides present research that outlines the value to learners of the technology tools which are mentioned in this book. If you register to receive the MESH Guides newsletter you will be kept abreast of new developments. Sign up on www.MESHguides.org.

We would like to thank all the authors who have shared their research and their ideas through this book. We hope that you find the ideas stimulating and that your pupils learn more than they would do otherwise from your implementation of at least some of the suggestions outlined.

Marilyn Leask and Sarah Younie
March 2024

Reference

Dewey, J. (1944) *Democracy and Education*, New York: The Macmillan Company.

1 Learning in the digital age

Developing critical, creative and collaborative skills

Marian Henry

Introduction

There are many compelling reasons to use digital technologies in our classrooms from motivating pupils and enhancing their learning experiences to facilitating planning and the organisational elements of education. All of these are significant, but the focus of this chapter is broader and deals with the complex relationship between education, changes in society and children's lives. The chapter is in three parts. The first is an overview of literature and research relating to the concept of the Digital Age and education. We then look at how pupils are understood within the Digital Age, research on their engagement with digital technologies outside of school and how this relates to technology use in school. The third section focuses on how you can foster children's critical, creative, and collaborative abilities as these are seen as crucial in ensuring that pupils flourish in the Digital Age.

Objectives

By the end of this chapter, you will be able to

- critically reflect on literature and research relating to the Digital Age, digital technology and education
- think in a deeper way about the digital generation and how we understand their existing digital skills
- recognise the importance of fostering children's critical, creative and collaborative skills
- develop strategies for putting this knowledge into practice in your classroom.

The digital age, technology and education

The term 'Digital Age' describes how society, culture, politics and economics are increasingly suffused with digital technologies. In this way, the term is closely linked to other popular concepts such as the 'Information Society' or 'Knowledge Society'. What these titles have in common is that they place information at the heart of contemporary life. In *Theories of the Information Society* (2006), Frank Webster highlights that 'information' became a distinguishing feature in discussions of the modern world over the past thirty years. He points out that while theorists and scholars take many different views on how our world is changing and developing, there is some level of consensus about the salience of 'information' in contemporary society. The centrality of information is closely linked to the continuing development of digital technologies. It is against this backdrop

DOI: 10.4324/9781003408925-1

of the growing significance of information, and the tools that promote and sustain it, that twenty-first-century education finds itself.

Education and society have a dynamic and interactive relationship. This means that they influence each other. What happens in education has an impact on how society, the economy, culture and politics develop. The reverse is also true because changes in society, culture and politics have a bearing on what is expected of education. Digital technology in education is a clear example of this interactive relationship. The significant investment in, and promotion of, technology in education is not limited to particular schools, districts or countries. Nearly every country in the world, regardless of geopolitical, economic or social circumstance, has implemented an educational technology strategy (Selwyn, 2011). Towards the late 1990s in many Western countries, the industry around information and communication was seen to have taken over from the more traditional manufacture of goods (Webster, 2006; Selwyn, 2011). This shift was perpetuated by the development of digital technologies and the use of these technologies in education was important in developing the information economy within a country. What is common among these policies is a close interlinking of education with employability, productivity and the wealth of the nation. In 1999, Stephen Ball was writing about how investing in digital technology for use in education was a core element in investing in the future of the national economy. This was seen by nations to be especially important as the world moved towards being a global competitive economy.

We are now more than two decades into the significant investment in digital technology across society, including education, and this is an interesting point in time to reflect. Selwyn and Aagaard (2021:8) write that in the past we had 'largely uncontroversial support for technology use in education' but that at present, there is a growing worldwide trend, for example, for mobile phones to be banned from classrooms and schools in various regions and nations such as France, Israel and various states in Canada and Australia. They question if this signals a decline in the overall digitisation of schools. Reflecting on views of digital technologies in society and education, David Buckingham (2020) wrote that digital technologies promised a world of infinite knowledge, promoting new forms of creativity, encouraging small-scale business, reviving democracy and leading to more active, creative, pupil-centred forms of learning. This democratic dream, he writes

> has a very bitter taste today: far from promoting deliberation and informed debate, social media are arguably contributing to their demise; and the digital world is increasingly dominated by a small number of commercial companies that are unaccountable to nobody but their shareholders.
>
> (Buckingham, 2020:231)

In recent years, we have seen growing concern over fake news and disinformation, the potential to incite radicalism and hatred over social networking sites, cyberbullying and hate speech. We also, no doubt, experienced the potential of digital technologies to keep us connected in new and interesting ways during the global pandemic of 2020, whether it was hosting Zoom get-togethers, playing games like Uno and charades on apps such as Houseparty, or having a watch party where people in different locations could view a movie 'together' chatting in real time while watching a synchronised stream. For many people, the lockdowns propelled forward their use of digital technologies for work, education, shopping and leisure. For teachers, there was a need to upskill in terms of providing and creating digital content and finding new ways to communicate with and engage their pupils. As the old saying goes, necessity is the mother of invention (Leask and Younie, 2022; Hordatt Gentles and Leask, 2021).

What we can see as we reflect on the Digital Age thus far is that evolution brings both opportunities and challenges for society, education and our personal lives. Within education, we have the opportunity to help pupils develop their digital skills while supporting and enhancing their learning across other curricular areas. We must also recognise the challenge of encouraging them to reflect on their digital technology use, and on how they access and interpret information. It is easy to get swept up in the idea that technology will or has changed learning. As was stated in a NESTA report 'Technology has no impact on its own—it all depends how we use it' (Stokes, 2012:8). Technology is part of the story, but in order for digital technologies to have a positive impact on learning, we need teachers to be informed users of it in the classroom. While digital technologies may be 'widely present in the domestic environment and pupils often have great confidence in using them' there is an important role in the education setting to support greater criticality and explore functions and applications that at home can be 'quite often poorly understood or used' (DiBari, 2019:181). The role of the teacher, as a knowledgeable facilitator of children's interactions with digital technologies cannot be underestimated. As Buckingham writes: 'where we have inspiring teachers, they can use technology in inspiring ways' (2020:231).

Children in the digital age

Good pedagogy builds from what pupils already know and understand. When it comes to the pupils we are now teaching, some may refer to them as 'digital natives'. This term was coined by Marc Prensky in 2001 to describe pupils who have spent their 'entire lives' surrounded by digital technologies. His claim was that due to their interaction with technologies digital natives 'think and process information fundamentally differently from their predecessors'—digital immigrants (2001:1). The problem for education, according to Prensky, was that teachers were trying to teach digital natives in an outdated language. According to Prensky, digital natives are wired differently and learn differently and, therefore, both the methodology and the content of our teaching need to change.

The concept of the digital native is now over twenty years old. It was, and still is, problematic. It assumes that *all* pupils grow up surrounded by technologies but to what extent can we be sure this is the case? International research undertaken during the Covid lockdown period starkly revealed children's different levels of access to, and use of, digital technologies (Hordatt Gentles and Leask, 2021; Leask and Younie, 2022) which depended on national infrastructure and their socioeconomic status. Earlier research showed the impact of their parents' attitudes to the use of technology (Livingstone and Boville, 2001) and their own preferences (Livingstone and Helsper, 2007a). This gap between children's use of digital technology is referred to as the 'digital divide' and giving pupils access to technology in schools and libraries is presented as an answer to bridging the divide. This assumes that access to technology solves the problem, but research has shown that there are very few pupils who do not use the internet, in contrast to adult populations, undermining an understanding of a clear divide between users and non-users. The digital divide in relation to pupils is less about *if* they use digital technology and more about *how* they use it. Livingstone and Helsper (2007b) argue that there is a 'continuum of digital inclusion'. This describes children's use of technologies from basic activities of information-seeking to more sophisticated uses such as interactive and creative activities. They point out that there is not one digital divide; rather there are a number of divides that are based on gradations of inclusion. There can be divides between pupils of different age groups, genders and socioeconomic classes and these divides are evolving over time (Tsatsou, 2011). Research shows that pupils with access to computers and the internet at home gain more from their experiences of digital technology when they are in school and so instead of ameliorating a divide, schools may exacerbate it (Meneses and Mominó, 2010). Furthermore, the Covid-19 global pandemic that forced long-term school closures in 2020 highlighted how digital divides further marginalised large numbers of learners such as those without home access to digital technologies or reliable internet connections and also pupils with special needs (Leask and Younie, 2022). In their blogpost report based on the *Global Connectivity Report 2022*, Livingstone, Helsper and Rahali reported that when looking at connectivity among children and young people around the world crucially 'the more societies become connected, the more a lack of connection presents a problem for those who are excluded'. They add that it is also clear that access does not ensure that children benefit from the digital age.

The report *EU Kidslonline 2020* (Smahel *et al.*, 2020) compiles findings from surveys of 9–16 year-olds across 19 European countries about their experiences and practices online. This followed a report on children's activities published in 2010 (Livingstone *et al.*, 2010). While there were some differences in the countries that participated, it is useful to look at some of the broader themes describing how pupils in Europe are participating in the online world and how this engagement evolved between 2010 and 2020. The authors state that there has been a major shift between 2010 and 2020 in how pupils access the internet with the widespread use of smartphones now being integrated into different social contexts and activities. While the 2020 report acknowledges that the internet has become more embedded in children's lives, the range of online activities they take up has not changed significantly despite many more digital technologies being used in education and at home. The authors state that 'the same pattern can be observed as in 2010, whereby the majority of pupils engage in communication and entertainment activities, along with schoolwork, whereas content creation or seeking news is taken up only by a minority of children' (Livingstone *et al.*, 2010:25). It was found that information navigation skills are unevenly distributed across countries, including the ability to choose the right keywords in an online search and the ability to assess the reliability of online information which varies between 36% and 75%. This evidence counters the 'digital natives' rhetoric and celebratory discourses about web 2.0 users as producers in that there was a significant variability across countries in terms of the level of creative skills (p. 35). This is not to say that some pupils are not developing digital skills, rather it highlights that simply being born at a particular time does not guarantee that pupils are 'digital natives'. The *EU Kidsonline* report (Smahel *et al.*, 2020) was conducted before 2020 and therefore it doesn't indicate to what extent children's digital skills may have been enhanced due to their increased learning via digital technologies and platforms. The Covid-19 pandemic accelerated the use of digital media and platforms for use in education. The lockdowns that were experienced around the world had a profound effect on education and its need to use technology and digital platforms to communicate and educate their pupils. Livingstone *et al.* (2022) write that today's youth are the most connected generation, but less is known about the *quality* of digital experiences and outcomes. The *EU Kids Online* report asserts that digital skills are a 'fundamental precondition of children's successful engagement with the world through the internet…relevant for young people's participation in society, education, employment and their general well-being' (p. 35). The final section of this chapter is designed to support you in ensuring that you give pupils the opportunity for meaningful learning experiences with digital technologies that lead to their development of digital skills. The lessons and tasks aim to give pupils opportunities to develop their critical, creative and collaborative skills in relation to digital technologies.

Fostering critical, creative and collaborative skills

Critical skills

Digital technologies are often presented as a 'tool' for learning – a technology. These technologies shape how we access and share information and how we communicate. As such, they are more than simply tools; they are *media*. As David Buckingham writes, media do not '...offer a transparent window on the world...media *intervene*: they provide us with selective versions of the world, rather than direct access to it' (2003:3). When we interact with media – from websites, social media and YouTube to newspapers and books – we are not looking through a transparent lens; the information has been selected and edited. The information has been *mediated*. As pupils navigate the World Wide Web, they are interacting with 'digital texts'. Enabling them to interpret and create meaning in relation to these digital texts is closely related to the teaching of literacy and the following sections essentially are about how we can apply the deep engagement with text that you are encouraged to have in relation to books and print and to apply it to the full range of digital media.

Children need to learn with and through technology, but they also need to learn *about* digital technologies. This enables them to develop the critical, higher-order thinking skills to engage with the full range of media they encounter both in school and at home. The extent to which they are encouraged to develop these critical skills through using media as a teaching aid—i.e. using a website about animals in a science lesson – is questionable. This is because when technologies are an aid to learning, the focus is on the content as opposed to developing the child's understanding of who made the website, who funds its development, how certain animals or issues are presented, and so on. Learning about digital media develops critical skills because pupils are encouraged to question and make judgements about the quality and trustworthiness of the information they are accessing. In this way they are learning how to be discerning and judicious digital media users. While pupils may come to school with confidence and competence in using technologies, they do not necessarily come with fully developed analytic and evaluative skills. In an era where there is an abundance of information, misinformation and disinformation, one of the most important things we can do in education is develop children's critical skills.

A good way for pupils to learn to be critical is through small group interaction with a teacher guiding the process. Reflecting on her own experiences of fostering critical literacy in primary school pupils, Swain reflects 'I would argue that in order for pupils to adopt critical perspectives independently, they first need opportunities to explore this with an experienced reader, so that they can understand the principles involved' (2010:135). In relation to still images, moving images, sounds and websites, pupils can be asked to discuss the authorial intent, to develop an alternative perspective, or to read against the given interpretation. The discussion should be open-ended and while the teacher can lead the discussion, it is best if the pupils discuss the topic without feeling that the teacher has an ultimate 'right answer' in mind. The teacher's questioning style is therefore very important. Questions should be open and begin with statements like 'I wonder why the author said...' Space needs to be made for deliberation and discussion. The challenge for you as a teacher is that you have to have some sense of where the discussion may go, but at the same time, if you steer it in that direction, you are stopping the pupils from having their own authentic reactions. Through critical discussion, pupils learn to listen to their own interpretations and they also learn to listen to others.

Content creation

We would never teach pupils to read but not to write. Teaching pupils to 'write' using a range of digital media, is an integral part of helping them to learn in a digital age. It is important for a number of reasons. Firstly, creating their own content enables them to see themselves as creators of content and not simply consumers. Creating content in the form of a digital video, a photograph with a caption or contributing to a class wiki is empowering for pupils as it lets them be in control of the production process. It gives them a sense of agency also as they can represent their views, experiences, concerns and interests. In essence, giving pupils the opportunity to create content is about encouraging them to find their voice in the Digital Age. You may also like to allow the pupils to use a generator such as Break Your Own News where pupils can generate their own fake news stories and can see how easy it is to make content online that appears realistic and trustworthy. (Web links are listed at the end of the chapter.)

How do I enable pupils to learn critically and creatively?

When you want to foster children's critical and creative abilities in relation to their use of digital media there are two key things to remember. The first is that critical and creative activities are closely related. As pupils analyse digital texts, it helps them understand the choices they make when creating their own digital texts. Similarly, when pupils are creating content, they learn about how to communicate with their audience and about the vast range of choices made by producers of content they enjoy. Secondly, developing critical and creative abilities is not about having a body of information you want pupils to learn. Nor is it about a list of skills or tasks you want them to complete. It is about developing their understanding. We want pupils to understand the digital world, how it works and how they can engage with it in ways that are rewarding and fulfilling for them. For this, you want them to develop understanding of four key concepts—production, language, representation and audience (Buckingham, 2003). Each of these concepts is described below and strategies that you can use over a series of activities to create a series of class blogs are outlined. Now consider Tasks 1.1 – 1.4.

Creating a class blog

Creating a class blog is a large-scale and ongoing task. It will develop as you and the pupils learn more and add and take from the content they present. The emphasis here is on the process of working critically, creatively and collaboratively. Encouraging the pupils to reflect on their work and to improve it is an important part of the process. Over time, you want to ensure that you are addressing each of the four concepts: production, language, representation and audience. Also, the critical and creative processes do not need to be limited to the class blog or internet, they can also be developed in relation to other curricular areas such as visual arts, music and civic and ethical education.

Task 1.1: Critical analysis of the production stage

Production: Studying production with pupils involves helping them to understand that there are many interests at stake in media production such as understanding the role of public service broadcasters, private companies, the use of advertising and media regulation.

Critical

- Look at other class blogs or children's websites and ask the pupils 'Who made this?', 'Why did they make it?', 'What information do they want the reader to gain?', 'Have they left out any information?', 'Why would they do that?'
- You can also get the pupils to see if there are any advertisements. They could discuss why this is and how the ads are chosen for the medium or content.

Creative

- When you begin to create a class blog with the children, encourage them to think about what their key message(s) are, how much information they want to communicate and what the best way to communicate it is. As pupils discuss their choices and reasons for these, you can encourage them to reflect on the choices made by other producers of media. Children should also have plenty of time to edit and rework their ideas over time.

Task 1.2: Critical analysis of the language stage

Language: Different media and different genres use different forms of language. Each language has its own codes and conventions. For example, a television programme makes use of certain conventions in relation to the opening credits, the types of camera shots or music used. A soap opera will have slightly different codes and conventions to a sitcom or current affairs programme.

Critical

- In the case of a class blog, the languages we have are print, sound, still images and moving images. Children can decide what is best for the information they want to impart.
- Encourage the pupils to look carefully at other blogs and at the images or text used.

Creative

- Children also need to decide if they want the content to be funny, serious, emotive and so on, and how different modes of communication may help this.
- They can choose fonts and colours and discuss their choices.

Task 1.3: Critical analysis of the images presented

Representation: Media products invite us to see the world in particular ways and not others. Studying representation may prompt questions about positive or negative images, bias, stereotyping and realism. The pupils could be asked how a blog depicts the topics that are shown. How are the female/male, young/old, good/bad characters portrayed?

Critical

- Compare two versions of the same story.

Creative

- When pupils have some experience of creating digital content, you can ask them to represent it for two different audiences. This helps them to think about how different people have different perspectives. Media content is not a 'transparent window on the world'.
- Ask pupils to tell a well-known fairy-tale from the perspective of another character.

Task 1.4: Critical analysis of written texts

Audiences: Studying audiences means looking at how audiences are targeted and addressed.

Critical

- Children can discuss what they think the target audience for different websites is. Would they choose to look at this website? What do they think of the content and who do they think it is aimed at? Advertising is also relevant for discussion in relation to audiences.
- Considering audience also involves reflecting on one's own media use, habits and patterns of use in everyday life. What or who influences their choice of media? What do they really enjoy, or not enjoy? How do they find out about new content—websites, films, television shows?

Creative

- Creating content for two different audiences (as above).

Collaborative learning

The critical and creative ideas above require that pupils work well together. It is important as teachers that we don't assume that pupils can collaborate. Group work, even for adults, can be challenging. Therefore, as part of your planning, you will need to have some strategies to help the pupils work together such as assigning clear roles. Learning to collaborate is about more than just working with others, it is about seeing others as a source of knowledge, as people we can learn from and also as the sum of the parts being greater than each individual (Poore, 2011; Lau, Lui and Chu, 2017).

One of the key elements of the Digital Age is the idea of many people working together to create something. A good example of this is Wikipedia. Pupils need to be taught and guided through content creation using digital tools. Creating a class wiki can give the opportunity to discuss and discover the advantages and disadvantages of communicating through these media. In this way pupils learn how to share information in a responsible way. It may also be upsetting for pupils if someone edits or changes what they have written on a class wiki but this provides an opportunity to introduce the idea that even experienced authors produce many drafts before their work is ready for publication. Working on collaborative projects can be challenging, but these are important lessons for pupils to learn as they are relevant to the Digital Age. Teaching and reflecting on these challenges with pupils are valuable in enabling them to participate in the digital environment.

Summary and key points

The overall aim of this chapter was to broaden your understanding of changes and developments in the Digital Age, in pupils' lives and in their learning with and about digital technologies. The key points we covered are

- While access to digital technologies has improved and this generation is the most connected generation, international studies and reports point to gaps in terms of variations in access to digital technologies but also variations in the quality of interactions pupils have with digital media.
- There is a significant role for teachers to play in nurturing children's digital skills through lessons that are critical, creative and collaborative.
- How you can foster critical lessons in your class in relation to story, news stories and digital media.
- How you can encourage pupils to create and understand the elements of creating digital texts, perhaps also exploring the creation of 'fake news'.
- How you can use the ongoing development of a class blog to foster additional critical and creative abilities while giving pupils a longer-term experience of collaborative creation.

Further resources

Break Your Own News: https://breakyourownnews.com/. Accessed 5 February 2023.
   This is a news generator where children can input their own headlines, ticker (the text that rolls across the bottom of the screen) and images. It allows children to create what appear to be realistic news stories. The app comes with a disclaimer that it should be used for fun, humour and parody and that care should be taken about what is shared.
Buckingham, D. (2020) Rethinking digital literacy: Media education in the age of digital capitalism, *Digital Education Review*, 37, June 2020. https://revistes.ub.edu/index.php/der/article/view/30671. Accessed 5 February 2023.
   This article is an excellent review of how we understand developing digital literacy in light of the positive and negative developments that have evolved in the area.
Cyber Academy https://www.trendmicro.com/internet-safety/for-kids/cyber-academy. These cyber-academy short lessons are aimed at 7–10 year-olds. They include lessons on passwords, misinformation and kindness online. Accessed 5 February 2023.
Cybersafe kids Year in Review 2022: https://www.cybersafekids.ie/resources/#research.

This is a review of pupils aged 8–12 in Ireland and how they are participating in the online world. The research is conducted in 2021–2022 and, therefore, gives unique insights into children's digital lives post-pandemic. Accessed 5 February 2023.

EU Kids Online 2020: https://www.lse.ac.uk/media-and-communications/assets/documents/research/eu-kids-online/reports/EU-Kids-Online-2020-10Feb2020.pdf. Accessed 5 February 2023.

Survey results from 19 countries. This report maps the internet access, online practices, skills, online risks and opportunities for pupils aged 9–16 in Europe. Teams of the EU Kids Online network collaborated between autumn 2017 and summer 2019 to conduct a major survey of 25,101 pupils in 19 European countries.

Selwyn, N and Aagaard, J. (2021) Banning mobile phones from classrooms-An opportunity to advance understandings of technology addiction, distraction and cyberbullying, *British Journal of Educational Technology*, 52, 1: 8–19.

This article looks at some national and regional governments that are banning mobile phones from school settings. This is an interesting examination of some of the concerns relating to young people's use of technology and the implications for policy and practice.

Topical Talk: https://economistfoundation.org/topicaltalk/. Accessed 5 February 2023.

Topical Talk provides a library of world-class resources on big issues in the news. The resources are trustworthy and made by teachers in collaboration with world-leading journalists and fact-checkers from *The Economist*. A new topic that is relevant to the current news is published each week.

References

Ball, S.J. (1999) Learning and the Economy: a "policy sociology" perspective, *Cambridge Journal of Education*, 29, 2: 195–206.

Buckingham, D. (2003) *Media Education: literacy, learning and contemporary culture*, Cambridge: Polity.

Buckingham, D. (2020) Rethinking digital literacy: media education in the age of digital capitalism, *Digital Education Review*, 37, June 2020. https://revistes.ub.edu/index.php/der/article/view/30671. Accessed 5 February 2023.

DiBari, C. (2019) Digital technologies in the 0–6 years educational services: a Media Education experience in nursery school and preschool, *Studi sulla Formazione*, 22: 177–186.

Hordatt Gentles, C., and Leask, M. (2021) *Teacher experiences and practices during Covid-19*, International Council for Education of Teachers and MESHGuides. https://www.icet4u.org/docs/ICET_MESH_REPORT_AUGUST_2021.pdf. Accessed 5 February 2023.

Lau, W.W.F., Lui, V., and Chu, S.K.W. (2017) The use of wikis in a science inquiry based project in a primary school, *Education Tech Research Dev.*, 65: 533–553.

Leask, M., and Younie, S. (2022) *Education for all in times of crisis: lessons from covid-19*, Oxon: Routledge.

Livingstone, S., and Bovill, M. (Eds.) (2001) *Children and their changing media environment: a European comparative study*, London: LEA.

Livingstone, S., and Helsper, E.J. (2007a) Taking risks when communicating on the Internet: the role of offline social-psychological factors in young people's vulnerability to online risks, *Information, Communication and Society*, 10, 5: 619–644.

Livingstone, S., and Helsper, E.J. (2007b) Gradations in digital inclusion: children, young people and the digital divide, *New Media and Society*, 9, 4: 671–696.

Livingstone, S., Haddon, L., Gorzig, A., and Olafsson, K. (2010) *EU kids online: final report*. http://eprints.lse.ac.uk/39351/. Accessed 5 February 2023.

Livingstone, S. Helsper, E., and Rahali, M. (2022) *Digital skills in the lives of children and young people*, London: London School of Economics. https://blogs.lse.ac.uk/parenting4digitalfuture/2022/06/29/digital-skills-itu/. Accessed 5 February 2023.

Meneses, J., and Mominó, J.M. (2010) Putting digital literacy in practice: how schools contribute to digital inclusion in the network society, *The Information Society*, 26: 197–208.

Palmer, S. (2006) *Toxic childhood: how the modern world is damaging our children and what we can do about it*, London: Orion.

Poore, M. (2011) Digital literacy: human flourishing and collective intelligence in a knowledge society, *Literacy Learning: the Middle Years*, 19, 2: 20–26.

Prensky, M. (2001) Digital natives, digital immigrants, *On the Horizon*, 9, 5. Available online at https://www.marcprensky.com/writing/Prensky%20-%20Digital%20Natives, %20Digital%20 Immigrants%20-%20Part1.pdf. Accessed 4 February 2023.

Selwyn, N. (2011) *Education and technology: key issues and debates*, London: Continuum.

Selwyn, N., and Aagaard, J. (2021) Banning mobile phones from classrooms-An opportunity to advance understandings of technology addiction, distraction and cyberbullying, *British Journal of Educational Technology*, 52, 1: 8–19.

Smahel, D., Machackova, H., Mascheroni, G., Dedkova, L., Staksrud, E., Ólafsson, K., Livingstone, S., and Hasebrink, U. (2020) *EU Kids Online 2020: Survey results from 19 countries*, eukidsonline. net, London: London School of Economics. Doi: 10.21953/lse.47fdeqj01ofo.

Swain, M. (2010) Talking it through: languaging as a source of learning, *Sociocognitive perspectives on language use/learning*, 112–130.

Tsatsou, P. (2011) Digital divides revisited: what is new about divides and their research? *Media, Culture and Society*, 32, 2: 317–331.

Webster, F. (2006) *Theories of the Information Society*, 3rd ed., Oxon: Routledge.

2 Teaching and learning for resilience in a digital world

Diane Levine and Linda Theron

Introduction

Political, environmental, social and economic difficulties impact on everyone involved in school life in many deep and different ways. Making sure that pupils and the people who work with them can survive and thrive when life is tough is therefore an essential part of personal development in our century. This chapter begins by helping you to understand that resilience is a set of connected processes that works across many aspects of a pupil's life. Resilience pathways in a digital world specifically are then considered. You are invited to think about your own resilience as a teacher, and the kinds of school policies that are best placed to support safe and resilient digitally mediated activities for everyone in a school community. This chapter offers a number of tasks to help you translate the material here to your own setting, and a case study to offer some guidance as to the ways in which pupils can be taught to be resilient in a digital world.

Objectives

At the end of this chapter you should be able to:

- understand the multisystemic resilience model underpinning best school practice in a digital world
- identify the risk and protective factors at play in your digitally mediated classroom
- have developed a range of ideas about how you and your pupils can use technologies to build and reinforce your resilience pathways.

Introducing multisystemic resilience

Resilience is the capacity to function well when exposed to significant stress (Masten, 2014). In the context of education, pupils demonstrate a capacity for resilience when they experience challenges to their learning or wellbeing but still manage to be engaged in school, make academic progress, or achieve academic success (Martin and Marsh, 2006). Positive outcomes such as academic success can be difficult to achieve for pupils living with a significant challenge, because they may be less likely to be school-engaged or learn well when they are exposed to high levels of stress at home (e.g., parental illness; domestic violence; food insecurity; abuse/neglect), in their neighbourhood (e.g., crime; violence; structural disadvantage; negative peers/bullies) or in the digital world (e.g., cyberbullying). Positive education outcomes are also unlikely when pupils attend schools that are poorly resourced in comparison with others in society, staffed by teachers who are significantly stressed or often absent or do not protect pupils from harmful experiences at school.

DOI: 10.4324/9781003408925-2

Importantly, resilience is not a 'DIY endeavour' (Ungar, 2019). Said differently, the capacity of any pupil to cope well with high levels of risk exposure is rooted in resources that are distributed across multiple systems. Some of these systems, like biological and psychological ones, are found in pupils themselves (i.e., they are personal resources). For instance: good health, physical fitness, the ability to regulate emotion or behaviour, effective concentration skills or a sunny personality are all personal resources that support pupils' capacity to function well when they are exposed to significant stress. However, many resilience-enabling resources are not personal and are instead found in the social, institutional, and ecological systems that pupils are connected to (Ungar and Theron, 2020). For instance: supportive parents, competent and caring teachers, and a well-resourced school environment were associated with the school engagement of a sample of vulnerable pupils in South Africa (Theron *et al.*, 2022). Similarly, a study with a large sample of fourth grade pupils and their teachers from the European Union showed that feelings of belonging at school, support from family, teacher competence (including keeping order in the classroom), and a safe school environment mattered for pupils' academic resilience (García-Crespo *et al.*, 2021). Some studies have also reported that pupil access to green space supports academic resilience (Browning and Rigolon, 2019).

In summary, a multisystemic understanding of resilience teaches us that resilience to the challenges that threaten successful learning is about more than a pupil's motivation to learn, intelligence or any other personal resource. While personal resources are important, they must be complemented by resources (such as emotional or psychosocial support) in pupils' families, communities, and schools. As the next section shows, the same is true for resilience in a digital world.

Task 2.1: Strategies for managing concerns in a digital world

Observe your class for one day. Make a note each time you or one of your pupils:

- Are exposed to risks – these could be in their learning, during social interactions, emotionally or in their practical day-to-day activities.
- Takes an opportunity to use their resilience systems or pathways.

Now make a list of the circumstances that facilitated any moments of coping. Bear in mind that coping can look like both positive and negative outcomes. Coping that can lead to negative outcomes is called 'maladaptive coping' (Wadsworth, 2015). For example, a child who is experiencing bullying online might refuse to engage with the problem – they are coping by pretending the problem is not happening, but the outcome is not likely to be positive.

Childhood resilience in a digital world

In recent years we have seen a shift in language away from the idea of 'digital resilience', towards the idea of 'resilience in a digital world'. This is helpful because it enables us to:

- Move away from arguments about definitions of 'digital resilience', and think in more practical and useful ways about how to help our pupils cope well when using digital technologies, and when online.

- Think about the resilience pathways that pupils need in online settings, and our role as educators in facilitating these, rather than placing all of the responsibility for their resilience with the pupils alone.
- Acknowledge the need for teaching practices that are culturally sensitive to the role and function of the 'digital' in different pupil's lives.

The risks pupils face in a digital world

In response to changes in the digital environment, and the increasing power afforded to technology developers and large data companies, Livingstone and Stoilova revisited their original typology of risks faced by pupils in a digital world (2021). They called the revised typology the '4Cs', namely Content, Contact, Conduct, and Contract. For each 'C', they then thought about types of risks pupils might face and classified these as 'aggressive', 'sexual', 'values', or 'cross-cutting'. For example, exposure to Aggressive Content might comprise witnessing violent or extremist material. Aggressive Contact might comprise being cyber-stalked. Aggressive Conduct might comprise bullying others online. Aggressive Contract might comprise exposure to a gambling game or phishing scam.

Promotive and protective factors for pupils in a digital world

While the risks pupils face online seem enormous and intimidating, as a teacher you are in a unique position to help your pupils build and maintain the systems that promote and protect their resilience to risk exposure. This includes mobilizing their personal resources (e.g., supporting pupils to learn protective skills) as well as supporting resilience-enabling changes in the family and school systems that pupils are connected to (e.g., advocating for parental control or protective school policy). In short, you should be prepared to help your pupils recover well and move forward if they have a bad experience in the digital world. Table 2.1 builds on Livingstone and Stoilova'a 4Cs and explores some of the promotive and protective factors *you* have the power to seed, maintain, or influence in your classroom.

Table 2.1 Promotive and protective factors teachers can introduce in their classrooms to counteract pupils' online risks

Example risk	Promotive and protective factors and values in the classroom
Values-based risks	
Persuasive design (Contract)	Young pupils are unlikely to be able to identify elements of problematic design. Reinforce messages surrounding age limits for common software and explain the implications of a digital footprint. Use software in the classroom built using 'humane design' principles.
Harmful user communities (Conduct)	Create opportunities for building self-esteem in the classroom. Play team collaborative games and celebrate mutual successes.
Mis/Dis-information (Content)	Draw on examples around the curriculum (e.g., Literacy, History) to teach pupils to be critical of the content they consume.
Radicalization (Contact)	Ensure pupils have access to resources (e.g., books or toys) that counteract negative stereotypes, and promote tolerance.
Aggression risks	
Graphic content (Content)	Expose pupils to a wide range of positive or constructive content and a focus on building criticality. Encourage and highlight parental and school controls (such as filters).

(Continued)

Table 2.1 (Continued)

Example risk	Promotive and protective factors and values in the classroom
Harassment (Contact)	Create spaces and ways for pupils to disclose safely, such as personal desk notes.
	If a pupil reports aggressive contact, restore safety for them as quickly as possible. Thank them for telling you. Make sure they know they have done nothing wrong. Keep a written record of what has happened.
Cyberbullying (Conduct)	Teach pupils how to report abuse, and make sure they know that reporting poor conduct is okay.
	Work to build a robust school cyberbullying policy that focuses on restoration rather than solely punishment.
Phishing (Contract)	Teach pupils about the signs of online scams of all sorts, and how to report these.
Sexual risks	
Body image norms (Content)	Use the PSHE curriculum to focus on healthy body representation and self-image.
Grooming (Contact)	Professional multi-agency working and intervention is fundamental to countering the risk of grooming. Talk with your school safeguarding lead to find out about relevant school policies and teacher responsibilities. After a pupil reports sexual risk exposure, restore safety for them as quickly as possible. Thank them for telling you. Make sure they know they have done nothing wrong. Keep a written record of what has happened.
Non-consensual sexual communication (Conduct)	Professional multi-agency working and intervention is fundamental to countering the risks of non-consensual sexual communications. Talk with your school safeguarding lead to find out about relevant school policies and teacher responsibilities.
Trafficking (Contract)	Professional multi-agency working and intervention is fundamental to countering the risks of trafficking. Talk with your school safeguarding lead to find out about relevant school policies and teacher responsibilities.
Risks cutting across all of the 4Cs	
Privacy/data protection abuses or discrimination	Ensure pupils know and appreciate the value of their name, location, likes/dislikes, and movements from a young age. The Information Commissioner's Office in the UK has generated lesson plans, posters, and worksheets that you can use in your classroom (see Resources).
	There are strict laws governing what happens in the aftermath of a data breach or an experience of discrimination. Talk with your safeguarding lead about school policies in this area. Think about possible impact on the mental health and wellbeing of the pupils in the school, as well as staff and school families.

At an appropriate time, undertake Task 2.2.

Task 2.2: Understanding pupils' concerns

Ask your pupils to write a short letter to you, or share a drawing with you, that shows what makes them worried when using technology. Categorise your pupils' worries using the 4Cs. Use a collective group lesson such as circle time or a Personal, Social, Health, and Economic lesson (sometimes called 'citizenship' or 'life orientation skills') to talk about strategies for managing these worries. Help your pupils to understand that they do not have to manage their worries alone.

Building personal resilience as a teacher

So far in this chapter we have mainly talked about what you can do as a teacher to ensure the pupils in your class can recover well when things go wrong in their online lives. However, the evidence tells us that teachers' lives are also challenging: work-life imbalance, feeling overwhelmed, lack of adequate resources, or absence of necessary school-level support are all common themes that emerge in the literature focusing on why teachers leave the profession or experience burnout (Beltman, 2018). As a result, we suggest that you should also take the opportunity to care for your *own* resilience in a digital world, particularly in your early career, without feeling that resilience is your sole responsibility.

A study by Drew and Sosnowski (2019) found that teachers who were able to recover well when things went wrong had three common aspects to their practice. They:

- Developed a strong sense of purpose rooted in the day-to-day context of their class-room work, which enabled them to make their way through constraints, and make the most of enablers.
- Reframed challenges or problematic experiences into learning experiences or opportunities for growth.
- Drew on their relationships with other staff, pupils, and leaders to cope with challenges.

Strangeways and Papatraianou (2019) added deeper insights into the teacher resilience picture in their study of the resilience narratives of Aboriginal beginning teachers in Australia. Their findings reinforced the idea of resilience as a set of processes, rather than a trait or something we are or are not. They encourage us to think of resilience as something that enables us to think about how we sit as individuals in a wider ecological context, in time, and in place. In practice, and for you as a teacher (perhaps at the beginning of your career), what this means is that when you work on your own resilience, you do that in the context of your classroom, your school, your location, your home, *and* the digital technologies that you use to do your job and live your life.

Protective and promotive factors for teacher resilience in a digital world

Just like thinking about the ways you can embed promotive and protective factors as practices in your classroom, you can think about promotive and protective factors for you as a teacher. Here are some examples for you to consider:

- What support networks do you draw upon that rely (at least in part) on digital technologies? Are these social, familial, or professional networks, or a combination of these? How do you draw strength from these networks, and how do you contribute to them?
- How do you build and maintain relationships using technologies? Does your team use technology to communicate during school hours, after/before school hours, or both? What impact does this use have on your resilience?
- What strategies do you use to manage your own technology use? Do you know about technology designs that emphasise people's emotional and physical needs and wellbeing (sometimes called 'humane design')? Do you feel able to make choices about your technology use that protect you from risks becoming issues? Are you aware of your school's social networking policy, and does it fit your own use of social networking? How do

you use technologies to help you both make best use of your time in the classroom and also to help you address particular challenges faced by pupils who are disadvantaged or struggling?

Now undertake Task 2.3.

Task 2.3: Creating a protective environment for yourself

What do *you* need in order to cope when life in your classroom is challenging or when the school's, or parents', online demands on you become overwhelming? Talk with a mentor or experienced, trusted colleague about how to create and maintain a protective environment for yourself, both online and offline.

Resilience and internet safety in school

Different countries have different forms of legislation relating to online safety (sometimes called internet safety or e-safety) and child protection. Globally, however, schools have two key roles with regard to internet safety. First, they must make sure that the school's own online practices keep pupils safe. Second, they must teach pupils about being safe online, both in and out of school.

Good school policies ensure both of these things happen, and are an intrinsic part of school safeguarding and child protection policies. They consider internet safety and resilience as part of a wider suite of measures that are taken to ensure pupils are able to survive and thrive as a result of their educational experiences, as well as problematic or high-risk encounters online. In Case Study 2.1, we share an example of how a whole-school approach to thinking about promotive and protective factors was co-created with pupils in primary schools, leading to changes in policy and practice.

Case Study 2.1: Digital ethics of care

A team of teachers, researchers, and pupils in primary schools in Northamptonshire, UK, wanted to help pupils develop their capacities for being kind to themselves and others online (O'Reilly *et al.*, under review). The team wanted to build kindness as a promotive/protective factor in the pupils' resilience pathways. To do this, they built on the idea of 'ethics of care', which tells us the human capacity for empathy is an important part of helping us be responsible for our behaviours. The pupils interviewed one another and participated in focus groups that created the concept of a 'digital ethics of care'.

Table 2.2 sets out the ethical code the pupils devised.

Table 2.2 Digital ethics of care – developed by pupils

This digital version encouraged the pupils to:
- feel like they could take healthy actions online
- understand that they had some responsibility for their own content
- promote empathy and care for themselves and others in digital spaces
- bring together their understanding of their rights.

The pupils recognised that they were, on occasion, exposed to unkind behaviours on-line, and that those unkind behaviours led to negative emotions such as sadness, fear, and stress. They also told the researchers that they believed that there was a great variation in the functionalities of different gaming and social media platforms that facilitated both exposure to unkindness, and also opportunities to be kind. The pupils had ideas for how they could be taught good and bad behaviour online; they actively wanted adult guidance in learning these things and made these suggestions for teachers:

> 'Create a scenario with, um, so the person that's being mean and the person that has received the comment and everything but swap it round, see what…how the person that's being mean, see how – understand, so they can understand how the other person felt'.
>
> 'Going over, like, safety online, and doing maybe like text messages and say what's wrong and what's good about this'.

You have already thought about some of the things you can do in your own classroom to support your pupils' resilience pathways. However, Professor Angie Hart and her colleagues (e.g., Kara *et al.*, 2021) have found that whole-school resilience-based approaches are more likely to make a longer-term positive difference than short-term interventions (although these can also be effective for some pupils, some of the time). This may be in part because significant mental health or special/additional needs interventions can take a long time to put in place, whereas if a whole school is adopting a practice that has been found to be effective, then everyone will likely get at least a little bit of benefit from those practices. For this reason, having some consideration of resilience in your school's policy on online safety can be a helpful tool to make change happen across the school.

Task 2.4: School e-safety policy and resilience

Does your school have a policy focused on ways of keeping pupils safe online? Evaluate the policy for its potential in building resilience in more than one system. What changes could be made to create a more robust set of systems for supporting pupil and teacher resilience in a digital world?

Summary and key points

Pupils demonstrate their resilience when they experience challenging experiences, but still manage to cope well with their school life. A multisystemic understanding of resilience teaches us that resilience to the challenges that threaten successful learning is about more than a pupil's motivation to learn, intelligence, or any other personal resource. While personal resources are important, they must be complemented by resources in pupils' families, communities, and schools. Teachers need to have the tools and frameworks to be able to maximise pupils' chances of successful recovery from difficult experiences in a digital world.

In this chapter, you have learned about this type of multisystemic resilience in a digital world. Specifically, you have been invited to think about:

• The Content, Contact, Conduct, and Contract risks pupils and teachers face in a digital world.

- Effective teaching practices, such as thinking about the protective and promotive factors that can be put in place in a classroom to address the 4Cs across resilience systems.
- The importance of building protective and promotive factors for your own resilience.
- Making the most of the safety policies and practices in your school in building resilience pathways for yourself and the pupils with whom you work.

The tasks have encouraged you to reflect on both your pupils' wellbeing and development and your own wellbeing as a teacher. This is an important practice to adopt – both for your pupils and yourself – to help you to grow into the reflective, resourceful, and resilient practitioner you want to be.

Further resources

BoingBoing, https://www.boingboing.org.uk/. Accessed 6 February 2023.
BoingBoing works across schools and wider communities to facilitate and promote socially-just approaches to resilience research and practice. Their website includes guides, toolkits, video resources, workbooks, and training opportunities.

Information Commissioner's Office, School Resources in support of the Children's Code, https://ico.org.uk/for-organisations/posters-stickers-and-e-learning/school-resources/. Accessed 6 February 2023.
The Information Commissioner's Office has produced a set of free, downloadable lesson resources including worksheets, presentations, and plans focused on helping pupils learn about their data, data privacy, personal privacy, and keeping safe online. The resources are available in English and Welsh, and are personalized for England, Northern Ireland, Scotland, and Wales.

Internet Matters. Digital Resilience Toolkit. https://www.internetmatters.org/resources/digital-resilience-toolkit/. Accessed 6 February 2023.
Internet Matters supports parents and carers in navigating the complex world of child internet safety. Despite reliance on the slightly outdated term 'digital resilience', their Digital Resilience Toolkit may offer some helpful insights into age/development-focused resources, to suit the age of the pupils with whom you are working.

NSPCC Learning, Example online safety policy statement and agreement, https://learning.nspcc.org.uk/research-resources/templates/online-safety-policy-statement-and-agreement. Accessed 6 February 2023.
The NSPCC has a range of useful e-safety/digital safety resources available on their website, including a good practice example of an online safety policy statement and agreement for use in schools.

Ungar, M. (Ed.). (2021). Multisystemic resilience: Adaptation and transformation in contexts of change. Oxford University Press, USA. https://academic.oup.com/book/41117?login=false. Accessed 6 February 2023.
This free book download offers perspectives on resilience from many different disciplines. It also includes case studies from around the world, some of which might be applicable to your context, or offer you a new way of thinking about resilience in your classroom.

References

Beltman, S. (2021) Understanding and examining teacher resilience from multiple perspectives. In C. Mansfield, ed., *Cultivating teacher resilience*, Springer, Nature. https://doi.org/10.1007/978-981-15-5963-1_19.

Browning, M. H., and Rigolon, A. (2019) School green space and its impact on academic performance: A systematic literature review. *International Journal of Environmental Research and Public Health*, 16(3), 429. https://www.mdpi.com/1660-4601/16/3/429.

Drew, S. V., and Sosnowski, C. (2019) Emerging theory of teacher resilience: A situational analysis. *English Teaching: Practice and Critique*, 18(4), 492–507.

García-Crespo, F. J., Fernández-Alonso, R., and Muñiz, J. (2021) Academic resilience in European countries: The role of teachers, families, and student profiles. *Plos One*, 16(7), e0253409. https://journals.plos.org/plosone/article?id=10.1371/journal.pone.0253409.

Kara, B., Morris, R., Brown, A., Wigglesworth, P., Kania, J., Hart, A., and Eryigit-Madzwamuse, S. (2021) Bounce forward: A school-based prevention programme for building resilience in a socio-economically disadvantaged context. *Frontiers in Psychiatry*, 11, 1–13, https://doi.org/10.3389/fpsyt.2020.599669.

Livingstone, S., and Stoilova, M. (2021) *The 4Cs: Classifying online risk to children.* (CO:RE Short Report Series on Key Topics) Hamburg: Leibniz-Institut für Medienforschung | Hans-Bredow-Institut (HBI); CO:RE - Children Online: Research and Evidence. https://doi.org/10.21241/ssoar.71817.

Martin, A. J., and Marsh, H. W. (2006) Academic resilience and its psychological and educational correlates: A construct validity approach, *Psychology in the Schools*, 43(3), 267–281. https://doi.org/10.1002/pits.20149.

Masten, A. S. (2014) *Ordinary magic: Resilience in development*, Guilford Publications, New York.

O'Reilly, M., Levine, D., Batchelor, R., and Adams, S. (under review) *Exploring the value of a Digital Ethics of Care approach for teaching primary school children digital citizenship: A child as co-researchers study.*

Strangeways, A., and Papatraianou, L. (2019) Remapping the landscape of resilience: Learning from an Arrernte teacher's story. *Journal of Intercultural Studies*, 40(1), 16–31.

Theron, L., Ungar, M., and Höltge, J. (2022) Pathways of resilience: Predicting school engagement trajectories for South African adolescents living in a stressed environment. *Contemporary Educational Psychology*, 69, 102062 https://www.sciencedirect.com/science/article/pii/S0361476X22000212.

Ungar, M. (2019, May 25) Put down the self-help books. Resilience is not a DIY endeavour. *The Globe and Mail*, https://www.theglobeandmail.com/opinion/article-put-down-the-self-help-books-resilience-is-not-a-diy-endeavour/. Accessed 6 February 2023.

Ungar, M., and Theron, L. (2020) Resilience and mental health: How multisystemic processes contribute to positive outcomes. *The Lancet Psychiatry*, 7(5), 441–448. https://doi.org/10.1016/S2215-0366(19)30434-1.

Wadsworth, M. E. (2015) Development of maladaptive coping: A functional adaptation to chronic, uncontrollable stress. *Child Development Perspectives*, 9(2), 96–100.

3   Pedagogy and technology

Fiona Aubrey-Smith

Introduction

As you read through the different chapters of this book you will discover the many ways in which technologies can enhance learning. Yet the most important tool in your teaching toolbox is you. Your understanding of what it means to be a teacher and what it means to be a learner will define which technologies you choose to use, and how you then use them in your classroom (Aubrey-Smith, 2021; Selwyn *et al.*, 2020; Twining *et al.*, 2017). This chapter about Pedagogy and Technology will guide you through research about the relationship between pedagogy and technology, what exactly we mean by pedagogy when thinking about technology and the choices that you will be making about technologies (including some that you might not realise that you are making!).

Objectives

At the end of this chapter you should be able to:

- explain the relationship between pedagogy and technology
- understand with greater precision the different forms of pedagogy
- recognise the influence of pedagogy within decisions that you make when using technology.

Why focus on pedagogy?

As you read through this book, you will discover the many different ways that technology can be used in order to support, enhance or extend learning. Each of the chapters in this book will share research evidence reflecting the positive and often transformational impact of purposeful technology use. However, the most important tool in the technology toolbox is you. Your understanding of what it means to teach and to be a teacher, and what it means to learn and be a learner, will define which technologies you choose to use (or not use), and importantly, how you then use them in your classroom.

The use of technology in schools is often referred to as EdTech (Educational Technology). This term encompasses many things that provide features and functionality to support learning, teaching, management and administration. However, for the purposes of this chapter, we are focusing specifically on digital technology supporting learning and teaching through classroom application. You may hear colleagues talking about this as pedagogically led uses of technology, or 'PedTech' for short.

DOI: 10.4324/9781003408925-3

When we think about the use of digital technology to support learning and teaching there are a number of international trends that are helpful for us to be aware about. Notably, one of these includes a sustained increase in levels of financial investment by schools reflecting a global assumption about the potential of technology to positively impact learning outcomes (e.g. IMARC, 2022; EEE, 2021). For example, in 2022, digital technology in education represented about 5% of global education expenditure – a significant $6.5 trillion (HolonIQ, 2022). Specifically across the UK, and despite complex budgetary pressures, a majority of schools continue to invest strategically in ways to improve teaching and learning through the use of digital technology with an assumption that such investment will create a significant impact on learning (e.g. BESA, 2022; CooperGibson, 2021).

Additionally, both quantitative (measurable) and qualitative (descriptive) research has shown that teachers and leaders worldwide see digital technology as a vital tool to support learning and to address some of the significant barriers caused by social, cultural and economic inequalities (e.g. OUP, 2022; OECD, 2022; UNESCO, 2021).

However, despite financial investment and a belief in the beneficial effects of digital technology, many teachers are still not quite sure what digital technology to use and when, neither are they sure precisely how to use it to ensure an impact on learning. This creates,

> *...a repetitive cycle of technology in education that goes through hype, investment, poor integration, and lack of educational outcomes. The cycle keeps spinning only because each new technology re-initiates the cycle.*
>
> (Kasinathan, 2021, p. 25)

In other words, there is a familiar pattern seen across schools where there is investment in new technology, only to see very little impact on learning. Indeed, it can sometimes be more troubling than this with a very real risk that the use of digital technology can *prevent* effective learning. For example, the Organisation for Economic Co-operation and Development (OECD) ran an international teaching and learning survey of teachers (TALIS) which found that,

> *...inadequate use of digital technology is a hindrance to quality instruction.*
>
> (TALIS, 2018, p. 23)

So, it is important that we think carefully about what we are doing when using digital technology. However, historically, the focus has been on the technology itself and how to implement it into classroom practice. This has encouraged teachers to focus on the technology first and the details about learning second. Yet research about the use of digital technology in education consistently tells us that it is not the technology itself that has an impact on learning but the way in which digital technology is used (Aubrey-Smith and Twining, 2023; Luckin, 2018). For example, the Education Endowment Foundation (EEF) published a report synthesising existing literature about using digital technology to improve learning, which stated a key finding that,

> *...technology must be used in a way that is informed by effective pedagogy.*
>
> (EEF, 2019, p. 3)

But what do we mean by *effective pedagogy*?

What do we mean by pedagogy?

In the UK school sector, the term pedagogy is generally used to refer to strategies or methods used by teachers in their teaching practices. However, as teaching has become more informed by research, the use of the word pedagogy has been increasingly adopted as a general term to incorporate a number of things, including those identified in Table 3.1.

It is important to be aware that pedagogy is about how learning is supported in its broadest sense – not just about the role that teachers and teaching play in that process (Aubrey-Smith and Twining, 2023).

Table 3.1 Definitions of pedagogical terminology

Pedagogical *theories*	academic theories (explanations) about what it means to be a teacher and to teach
Pedagogical **beliefs**	personal, deep-seated views about what it means to be a teacher and to teach
Pedagogical **approaches**	processes and procedures that implement particular pedagogical theories
Pedagogical **intention**	how we intend for learning to be supported through a particular approach
Pedagogical **practices**	the practical actions that we use to implement a pedagogical approach
Politicised pedagogy	approaches that we are encouraged to use to conform to local or national policy or expectations

*For more detailed definitions and explanations, please see Aubrey-Smith and Twining, 2023.

As you will see from the definitions set out above, there are subtle but important differences about precisely what is being referred to with each of these phrases. Some of these phrases refer to surface-level actions (pedagogical practices) – the things that we do in our classrooms every day, whether we are early career teachers or senior leaders. Other phrases refer to overarching ideologies (academic pedagogical theories or personal pedagogical beliefs) – things which we don't often think about unless studying at university or reading academic texts. Finally, there are phrases that refer to biased views or those with a particular agenda (politicised pedagogy or pedagogical intentions) – aspects which we may or may not agree with.

The point is that the word 'pedagogy' should be considered as an umbrella term – one that incorporates a wide range of ideas about different aspects of supporting learning (commonly oversimplified by just referring to teaching). This means that when we are thinking about improving our teaching practice, using a generic phrase such as 'effective pedagogy' becomes rather problematic. The phrase 'effective pedagogy' is too vague, which means that we don't necessarily know or fully understand precisely what to focus on improving (Aubrey-Smith and Twining, 2023).

Theories of pedagogy

In your professional development as a teacher you will have learned about different academic theories relating to pedagogy. You may have heard about the Soviet psychologist Lev Vygotsky and the Zone of Proximal Development (Vygotsky, 1978), and the Swiss psychologist Jean Piaget's Theory of Cognitive Development and the four stages of learning (Piaget, 1952). You may also have heard about the American psychologist Burrhus Skinner and the theory of behaviourism, where we are conditioned to do certain things based upon stimulus, reward and punishment (Skinner, 1968). There are many academic theories about pedagogy which each draw on theories spanning across psychology, sociology, anthropology, ethnography, biological sciences to name a few.

These different theories each provide a different explanation of how learning happens and therefore how learning should be supported (which is what we are referring to in the study of pedagogy). Each of us will most likely align with one of the four main theories summarised in Table 3.2. (For a comprehensive explanation, please see Aubrey-Smith and Twining, 2023).

Table 3.2 Summaries of the main theories of pedagogy

Traditional Views on Pedagogy	Where learning involves acquiring information. Learners are extrinsically motivated and their potential for learning is innately determined.
Individual Constructivist Views on Pedagogy	Where learning involves the individual construction of a mental model of reality guided by the teacher. Learners are intrinsically motivated, and learning is limited by age or stage.
Social Constructivist Views on Pedagogy	Where learning involves the co-construction of social reality through interactions with 'more knowledgeable others'. Learners are intrinsically motivated, and learning is not limited by age or stage.
Sociocultural Views on Pedagogy	Where learning involves becoming a member of a community who has shared purposes and valued ways of working. Learners are intrinsically motivated and are not limited by age or stage.

Now consider Task 3.1.

Task 3.1: Surfacing your pedagogical beliefs

You may find it helpful to consider which of these theories your beliefs most closely align with. A short activity that will walk you through this process can be found at www.onelifelearning.co.uk/resources.

What is effective pedagogy?

All of these theories and terms mean that referring to 'effective pedagogy' can be rather problematic because the term 'effective' is dependent on the values of the belief system from which it emerges. In other words, what you think is important will define whether you think something is good. Thus, one person's view on whether pedagogy is effective will be different from another person's view. This applies, even within the same national policy framework, the same school and sometimes even when teaching from the same lesson plan. We can have more in common (pedagogically) with a teacher sharing the same specialism than a teacher in our own school (Karaseva *et al.,* 2015).

We therefore need to be very precise when we think about pedagogy and what we want to do in our classrooms if we are to create meaningful experiences for our learners – both with and without the use of digital technology. This is about your own unique classroom practice and recognising that it is influenced, but not defined, by other people, policies and expectations (Aubrey-Smith, 2021).

Effective pedagogy happens when the pedagogical belief systems of the teacher are aligned with the pedagogical practices that are taking place in their classroom. If we are clear about our pedagogical beliefs, we are more able to define appropriate pedagogical intentions and choose the most relevant pedagogical approaches. This will result in clear and coherent pedagogical practices.

If there is a lack of clarity about what we believe, or about how we translate our beliefs into practice, it can result in mixed messages for our learners. This was famously summarised by Hamachek (1999, p. 209) who said that,

Consciously, we teach what we know. Unconsciously, we teach who we are.

Now go on to the next task 3.2.

Task 3.2: Surfacing embedded pedagogical messages

Carefully observe a colleague interacting with their class, a group or an individual learner while they use digital technology, once you have gained consent and agreement.

Watch your colleague's body language and the power dynamics that it creates – looking at how the learners respond accordingly.

Listen to the volume or tone of voice that the colleague uses and how it affects what learners consequently do.

What kinds of embedded messages are being conveyed from the teacher to the learners? To what extent do you think your colleague is aware that they are communicating in this way? (We are rarely completely aware!)

Now reflect on your own practice when using digital technology – you may wish to video yourself so that you can watch yourself back. What is your tone of voice and body language that you are conveying to your learners? To what extent are these messages reinforcing or contradicting your pedagogical intentions?

It's all about you: the teacher

While school context and expectations from leadership, colleagues and pupils act as an important influence, ultimately it is the teacher's own pedagogical beliefs that shape *how* digital technology is used or not used. Furthermore, the way that a teacher incorporates digital technology into learning amplifies the teacher's underlying pedagogical beliefs – whether they are aware of that or not (Aubrey-Smith, 2021).

There is an important but very subtle detail within this research finding from Aubrey-Smith (2021), which is that it is entirely possible for a teacher to adopt digital technology and use it based upon instruction from a third party – perhaps a colleague, leader, trainer, digital champion or social media voice. Many teachers use online and offline networks and resources to source ideas recommended by other teachers – often preferring suggestions that can be immediately replicated (e.g. 'best practice ideas' or 'top tips'). What we need to be aware of is that every idea – however good it is – emerges from a particular set of pedagogical beliefs held by the person who created or defined that idea. Those beliefs may or may not align with your own. Therefore, the 'idea' may or may not align with your own pedagogical beliefs, even if the action itself is appealing, achievable and actionable. This can result in very mixed messages for the pupils in our classrooms. If we believe that learners should be autonomous – making meaningful decisions about their own learning, and then assign them a prescriptive activity with little choice within it (e.g. AI-driven, self-marking, online learning activities), our actions are contradicting our beliefs. If our beliefs prioritise learner choice, then we need to ensure that the activities that we plan also prioritise the provision of meaningful choice.

Let's unpack an example of a common use of digital technology in more detail. There are lots of online concept mapping tools available that allow learners to add virtual sticky notes (or similar) to a shared space. Many digital champions encourage the use of these tools because they allow learners to use a range of ways to contribute their ideas (e.g. voice-notes, weblinks, drawings, typed text, etc.), and these tools also allow a wide group of learners to see or hear the ideas from their peer group. There is a constructivist pedagogical *belief* (about the interaction between learners being valuable) embedded within this pedagogical *approach* (of using a collaborative concept mapping tool). The pedagogical *intention* of using a collaborative concept map may be for all learners to be facilitated to contribute to a discussion, and for all learners to be able to access and engage in that discussion. However, for this to happen, the experience is completely reliant on the nature and quality of interactions between the learners, which may not necessarily be carried out through the digital technology itself. The role of offline interaction and conversation may well determine whether our pedagogical intentions have been achieved. Therefore, if we adopt this digital technology (collaborative concept mapping), but without considering how we facilitate meaningful social interactions between those using it, our learners may be left wondering what the benefit of using that digital technology really is.

It is important to note that sometimes we hear enthusiasts talk about one of the benefits of technology being that it 'engages' learners. The nature of visual and audio stimulus along with the real-time responsiveness within digital technology can be very appealing to all of us. However, we must be cautious about the short-term mindset of valuing engagement as the main benefit of using digital technology. This is now seen by many as an old-fashioned way of thinking because it positions digital technology as a novelty experience. Pedagogically-led uses of digital technology can offer far greater benefits beyond 'engagement', most importantly – supporting, enhancing and extending learning (Luckin, 2018).

Same tech, different pedagogy

We all need to remember that we must not use any kind of digital technology (or indeed any kind of resource or tool) unless we have a clear understanding of how it will enhance teaching and learning in our classroom. The easiest way to do this when planning specific learning experiences (e.g. lessons or activities) is by asking questions that surface what Twining *et al.* (2017) identified as the four aspects of pedagogy (Views on Learners and Learning, Views on Teachers and Teaching, Views on Knowledge, Views on Schooling).

These are complex ideas, and so a simplified set of four questions might be:

• How will the experience of this activity result in learning?
• What role do I want my teaching to play in supporting that learning?
• How will new knowledge be formed (by or with learners) through this experience?
• How does this experience connect to the learner's life beyond school?

When we make lesson or activity plans, we will be creating pedagogical intentions whether we are aware of it or not. The next task, 3.3, will help you to surface these intentions.

Task 3.3: Surfacing pedagogical intentions

Think about an activity that you are currently planning for your class. Make some notes that respond to each of the four questions above. Which aspects of your planning become clearer or more precise as a result of thinking through these four questions?

Let's look at some illustrated examples.

Four different pedagogical views on digital collaboration

A common classroom activity involving digital technology is to ask learners to work in pairs or small groups to create a shared artefact that reflects their learning. When using digital technology this might be a cloud-based document, online presentation slides, concept map or thought board. Often teachers will assign this kind of activity because they are keen to promote collaboration – learners working together as part of their learning. However, teachers with different pedagogical beliefs will have different views on what collaboration looks like in practice. Table 3.3 shows us the following example.

Table 3.3 Different pedagogical interpretations of collaboration when using digital technology

View on Pedagogy	*Collaboration is often interpreted as...*	*An example of what this looks like when using digital technology*
Traditional	Completing the same task, in parallel to each other, while seated in a group	A group is assigned the same online worksheet. Learners sit together and complete the task at the same time – each with their own version.
Individual Constructivism	Completing the same task, with a sub-section assigned to each learner, seated as a group	A group creates a shared online document. Each learner completes their own section but has visibility on the whole document.
Social Constructivism	Completing the same task, providing feedback and challenging each other	A group creates a shared online concept map. Learners discuss what the key components are, each learner drafts a first version and then provides recommendations to each other to edit and improve.
Sociocultural	Connecting meaningfully with people who have a shared interest in a particular real-world issue or problem	Identifying an expert and arranging a video-call to discuss a real-world issue which then becomes the start of an online group project with a tangible, real-world outcome.

Read the descriptions again and notice how the nature of the interaction between learners differs with each view of pedagogy. In some cases the activity could not take place without other learners being in direct contact with each other (e.g. sociocultural example). In other cases the activity could be completed just as easily in complete isolation.

True collaboration in learning happens when two or more people interact in such a way that knowledge and/or outcomes are developed that would not otherwise happen. The interaction extends the thinking of each peer involved in the interaction. The emphasis is very much about socially situated cognitive challenge – in other words, people proactively learn *because of* the specific stimulus provided by peers. Collaboration is therefore arguably aligned with socially oriented forms of pedagogy – social constructivism and sociocultural views. The other forms of pedagogy described as collaboration are likely to instead be parallel learning or groups co-operating to fulfil a task.

The key point to remember is that if your pedagogical beliefs are that social interaction is an important part of learning, then it is vitally important to plan for meaningful social interaction at a granular level. What interaction will take place, how, and why?

The reason for highlighting this example is because when using digital technology, teachers often focus on the processes or outcomes achieved through its use, rather than considering the holistic experience that the learner will have. Let's use the example of collaboration above to illustrate the difference between an individual constructivist and a social constructivist approach (arguably the two most common pedagogical beliefs held by classroom teachers).

A common example of collaboration when using digital technology is for a group of learners to produce a shared online document – where each learner chooses, or is allocated, a section to complete. As a group, the outcome is therefore a document that is more substantial than what an individual learner may have produced on their own. Let's imagine a group of learners are tasked with producing a slideshow about the planets.

An individual constructivist approach would allocate each learner within the group one of the planets (or may allow learners to choose themselves). Each learner would then use suggested or assigned materials (e.g. ebooks, websites, videos, infographics) to find out facts about that planet and to summarise those facts on their slide in the shared slideset. Each learner will be able to clearly identify their own research and their own written-up findings through their allocated slide. When each of the learners has completed their slide, the final slideset may be reviewed by the group to check the task had been processed correctly, before being handed in for the teacher to mark.

A social constructivist approach would start in a similar way, but the group would initially form a concept map together, sharing their existing knowledge, and then identify what they wanted to find out. Each group member may work individually or in pairs to respond to those knowledge gaps or questions, returning their findings to the whole group for discussion. These cycles of identifying knowledge gaps, seeking out findings and then sharing through discussion would happen many times during the activity, with agreed key points about any of the planets being captured on slides step-by-step throughout. Learners would collectively produce a final piece of work by reviewing each slide before discussing and implementing improvements. The final piece of work would include ideas and perspectives that individual learners may not have thought of or considered were it not for the insights from other peers. This could include an interactive image or timeline taking account of the whole solar system rather than just each planet in isolation. Consequently, the learners are able to meaningfully assess changes to their collective understanding.

In both of these examples, a group is working together to produce a shared outcome. The role of digital technology is to give visibility to the whole project while allowing each individual learner to contribute to a shared document simultaneously. However, it is the interaction between those learners – which may well take place offline and away from the digital technology – that highlights the different pedagogical approach.

Before you start using any kind of digital technology (or any kind of resource or tool) you need to have a clear understanding of how it will support the learning in your classroom. The sequencing of this thinking is important because it must be the learning that is considered first – precisely what are you trying to achieve and why? Only when you are clear about that should you begin to consider which digital technology (or other resources) will be most appropriate to help you to achieve those intentions.

Pedagogical trends for effective classroom digital technology

Digital technology can (but doesn't necessarily) change power relationships in the classroom, giving more autonomy to learners. This better prepares learners to be proactive and responsible citizens and to develop the skills that they need to become lifelong autonomous and effective learners. However, it can be intimidating for some teachers and even for some learners – particularly in schools where there is a lack of trust (of learners, and/or of teachers). However, there is a correlation between the level of trust between teacher and learner, and the level of impact seen when using digital technology in that classroom (Twining *et al.*, 2017).

In classrooms where digital technology is making the greatest impact on learning it is because digital technology has become a deeply embedded part of learning experiences. Digital technology in these classrooms is no longer a novelty, used simply to 'engage' learners but a practical tool that encourages metacognitive processes (Maher and Twining, 2016). In these classrooms, digital technology is seen as a tool that makes it possible to achieve particular pedagogical beliefs. For example, making learning:

- More autonomous, with learners able to access relevant support resources on demand (e.g. online folders containing instructional videos, wordbanks, scaffolds).
- More inclusive for all learners (e.g. sub-titles during inputs, screen masks for reading, picture dictionaries, auto-translate, talk-to-text).
- More sensitive to cognitive load (e.g. interactive images, individualised feedback and pacing, bitesize resourcing).
- More creative (e.g. use of audio, video, image, animation, publishing and audience).
- More responsive through real-time whole-class formative assessment during teaching (e.g. quickfire online forms during inputs) and individualised activities during learning (e.g. AI-driven adaptive software).
- More interactive, more collaborative, more social, more precise, more community-minded … the list goes on.

Sometimes, teachers are concerned about how this can be achieved in the context of existing school systems, which can occasionally be interpreted as constraining what is possible within classrooms. However, as teachers we often have far greater choice about our practice than we realise – if we think very carefully about what we are really trying to achieve.

Summary and key points

By sharing insights from international research, this chapter has drawn your attention to the relationship between pedagogy and technology. The chapter began by drawing out the importance of effective pedagogy and encouraged you to reflect precisely on what we mean when we use the word pedagogy. Definitions were provided for terms including pedagogical beliefs, pedagogical approaches, pedagogical intentions and pedagogical practices. You then read examples illustrating how different pedagogical beliefs result in quite different ways of using the same digital technology, and you have read about how important precision is when thinking about exactly what we want our learners to experience.

As you consider the ways in which you use digital technology in your practical teaching in future, you are encouraged to continuously return to two key points:

- Ensure that you have very clear and **very precise pedagogical intentions** that set out (i) **what** learners will be learning, (ii) **how** they will be learning, and (iii) **why** particular approaches have been chosen.
  This ensures coherent learning experiences for your learners.
- Be forensically precise about **how** and **why digital technology will add value to your pedagogical intentions**, making the most of new ways of working, but not being distracted by novelty technologies and ideas.
  This ensures a focus on meaningful learning experiences rather than task-oriented 'doing' or learners being 'engaged'.

Further resources

Aubrey-Smith, F. and Twining, P. (2023) *From EdTech to PedTech: Changing the way we think about digital technology.* London: Routledge.
In this book, the research and ideas addressed in this chapter are set out in detail.

Short videos addressing key points discussed in this chapter, illustrated by examples of classroom practice can be found at http://pedtech.lgfl.net/.

For the latest resources to support pedagogically led uses of digital technology please see www.pedtech.org.

References

Aubrey-Smith, F. (2021) *An exploration of the relationship between teachers' pedagogical stance and their use of ICT in classroom practice.* Doctoral Thesis. The Open University. https://oro.open.ac.uk/75001/.
Aubrey-Smith, F. and Twining, P. (2023) *From EdTech to PedTech: Changing the way we think about digital technology.* London: Routledge.
British Educational Suppliers Association (BESA) (2022) *Insights Archive.* Available at: https://www.besa.org.uk/insights/?category=research.
CooperGibson (2021) *Education technology (EdTech) survey 2021.* DfE: London. https://www.gov.uk/government/publications/education-technology-edtech-survey-2020-to-2021.
EdTech Evidence Exchange (EEE) (2021) *U.S. K-12 public education technology spending.* https://edtechevidence.org/wp-content/uploads/2021/07/FINAL-K12-EdTech-Funding-Analysis_v.1.pdf.
Education Endowment Foundation (EEF) (2019) *Digital technology to improve learning: An evidence review.* London: EEF.

Hamachek, D. (1999) 'Effective teachers: What they do, how they do it, and the importance of self-knowledge', in Lipka, Richard, P. and Brinthaupt, Thomas, M. (eds) *The role of self in teacher development.* New York: State University of New York Press.

Holon Education Intelligence Unit (HolonIQ) (2022) *Sizing the global EdTech market.* https://www.holoniq.com/notes/sizing-the-global-edtech-market.

IMARC (2022) *Digital classroom market: Global industry trends, share, size, growth, opportunity and forecast 2022–2027.* IMARC: New York.

Karaseva, A., Siibak, A. and Pruulmann-Vengerfeldt, P. (2015) 'Relationships between teachers' pedagogical beliefs, subject cultures, and mediation practices of students' use of digital technology'. *Cyberpsychology: Journal of Psychosocial Research on Cyberspace, 9*(1), Article 6.

Kasinathan, G. (2021) 'National educational policy 2020: Imagining digital technology as a resource to achieve educational aims'. *Voices of Teachers and Teacher Educators*, Vol. X, Issue II, December 2021, pp. 20–28.

Luckin, R. (ed) (2018) *Enhancing learning and teaching with technology: What the research says.* London: UCL Institute of Education Press.

Maher, D. and Twining, P. (2016) 'Bring your own device–a snapshot of two Australian primary schools'. *Educational Research, 59(1)*, pp. 73–88.

Organisation for Economic Co-operation and Development (OECD) (2022) *Education policy outlook 2022: Transforming pathways for lifelong learners.* OECD: London. https://www.oecd-ilibrary.org/education/education-policy-outlook-2022_c77c7a97-en.

Oxford University Press (OUP) (2022) *Addressing the deepening digital divide.* OUP: London. https://oup.foleon.com/report/digital-divide/cover/.

Piaget, J. (1952) *Origins of intelligence in the child.* London: Routledge and Kegan Paul.

Selwyn, N., Hillman, T., Eynon, R., Ferreira, G., Knox, J., Macgilchrist, F. and Sancho-Gil, J. (2020) 'What's next for Ed-Tech? Critical hopes and concerns for the 2020s'. *Learning, Media and Technology, 45(1)*, pp. 1–6.

Skinner, B.F. (1968) *The Technology of Teaching.* New York: Meredith Corporation.

Stringer, E., Lewin, C. and Coleman, R. (2020) *Using digital technology to improve learning.* London: Education Endowment Foundation.

TALIS (2018) *Teaching and learning international survey: Insights and interpretations.* https://www.oecd.org/education/talis/TALIS2018_insights_and_interpretations.pdf.

Twining, P., Browne, N., Murphy, P., Hempel-Jorgensen, A., Harrison, S. and Parmar, N. (2017) *NP3: New purposes, new practices, new pedagogy: Meta-analysis report.* London: Society for Educational Studies.

UNESCO (2021) *Reimagining our futures together: A new social contract for education.* https://unesdoc.unesco.org/ark:/48223/pf0000379707.

Vygotsky, L. S. (1978) *Mind in society: The development of higher psychological processes.* Cambridge, MA: Harvard University Press.

4 Special educational needs and technology

Amber Williams

Introduction

This chapter introduces ways that digital technologies can be used to develop inclusive practices and argues the case for a social rather than medical model through which to view pupils' learning needs. The chapter begins with a discussion surrounding key terminology and proceeds by examining how technology can support the particular needs of pupils with special needs and disabilities.

Objectives

At the end of this chapter you should be able to:

- critically analyse the potential for technology to enable learning for all pupils with special educational needs and disability (SEND)
- select appropriate technology-based tools to support the needs of pupils
- identify resources to keep up to date in the field of SEND and technology.

Background: definitions and statutory requirements

Although the definition of an inclusive curriculum often encompasses those with English as an additional language (EAL), gifted and talented (GandT), looked after children (LAC), transient population and other minority groups, this chapter focuses on pupils with SEND who have a learning difficulty which calls for a special educational provision to be made for them. Pupils have a learning difficulty if they:

(a) have a significantly greater difficulty in learning than the majority of others of the same age, or
(b) have a disability which prevents or hinders them from making use of facilities of a kind generally provided for others of the same age in mainstream schools or mainstream post-16 institutions.

(UK Government, 2014: 1)

DOI: 10.4324/9781003408925-4

In England, government guidance in 2001 set out three principles for developing an inclusive curriculum:

(a)   setting suitable learning challenges
(b)   responding to pupils' diverse learning needs
(c)   overcoming potential barriers to learning and assessment for individuals and groups of pupils.

(DES, 2001)

However as inclusion, inclusive practice, SEND and learning difficulties hold different meanings for different people, it is important for you to explore your interpretation of the terms, taking account of the political and professional context in which you work. We suggest that at this point you undertake Task 4.1.

Task 4.1: Defining inclusion

Ask a range of peers and professionals for their definition of inclusion across the whole curriculum. Using the term 'inclusive curriculum' browse some of the government guidance, academic literature and support organisation websites (see Further resources and Websites at the end of this chapter) and develop your own personal definition of inclusion.

Breaking down barriers

According to the British Educational Communications and Technology Agency's (BECTA) (2003) literature review, technology can benefit pupils, teachers and parents/carers. Some specific benefits identified are greater learner autonomy, communication support, personalised learning opportunities, attainment, motivation and engagement with learning. Florian and Hegarty (2004) suggest six ways in which technology can be used to meet the needs of pupils with a SEND. Table 4.1 sets these out. Though this research was carried out 20 years ago, these basic advantages stand the test of time.

Table 4.1 Six ways technology can be used to meet the needs of pupils with SEND

Technology can be

- used as a tutor
- used for exploration
- applied as a tool
- used to communicate
- used for assessment purposes, and
- used as a management tool.

There are many specialised assistive technologies and this chapter introduces a range of these that support an inclusive curriculum and inclusive teaching.

Attitudes and beliefs

E-Inclusion or digital inclusion can be accomplished by addressing attitudes and beliefs (Glazzard, 2011; Sze, 2009) and addressing clearly the needs of individual pupils by selecting the appropriate technology. The two main ideological frameworks used in this field are the medical and the social model of disability. The teacher needs to adapt their teaching and access methods to the pupil's abilities e.g. the fact that a pupil cannot use a mouse does not prevent them from using a computer, so the teacher may for example, then get the pupil to use eye gaze technology.

The medical model of disability (also referred to as individual tragedy, within-child, or deficit model) views disability or persons with a disability as 'faulty' and in need of 'fixing' from their limitations' (Barnes *et al.*, 2002). Those holding this viewpoint do not see a need to adapt the environment or personal views of practitioners and wider society to be inclusive but imply the problems and responsibilities lie with the person with the disability. This model seeks to return the person to 'normal' on the basis of identification of symptoms, diagnosis and cure (Johnstone, 2001).

In the UK the medical model was originally challenged by the disabled people's movement through the proclamation from the Union of Physically Impaired Against Segregation (UPIAS) in 1976 which states that 'it is society which disables physically impaired people. Disability is something imposed on top of our impairments by the way we are unnecessarily isolated and excluded from full participation in society' (UPIAS, 1976: 14). This counter argument is now known as the social model of disability (Oliver, 2004). The social model of disability proposes that disability is constructed by those that are nondisabled who create environmental barriers, socially stigmatizing attitudes and discriminatory behaviour. Now undertake Task 4.2.

Task 4.2: Understanding your views

Reflect on the following question:

1. What are your personal views on special education and disability?
2. Are your views similar to those of colleagues/family around you?
3. What are the advantages and/or disadvantages of differing views?
4. Consider the likely lived experiences of pupils in your school who have a special educational need or disability. How might you and your pupils act to ensure their right to education is respected and supported?

Addressing the needs of the individual pupil

Technology can usefully support the identification of some needs – for the English National Curriculum and pre-key stage standards for example, the Evidence Me software from 2Simple allows the teacher to record evidence of an individual pupil's attainment and then design lesson objectives to support progression/scaffolding in learning.

Technologies may also help you with designing assessment materials, researching SEND or computer-based assessment (CBA). One example of CBA is Lucid Ability – a computerised system for assessing verbal and non-verbal abilities. (Many of the pre-made CBA used for the identification of a SEND should not be used independently without a thorough evaluation of the whole pupil.) In addition, merely using ready-made online resources or CBA does not create an enabling environment. The tools must be individualised to assess the needs of the pupil and then support and create personalised learning opportunities during whole class instruction, independent work and social activities. However, as Bower *et al.* (2010) state, the intricate relationship between technology, content and pedagogical knowledge is complex.

The SEND Code of Practice for England identifies four principal areas of need:

- communication and interaction
- cognition and learning needs
- social emotional and mental health needs, and
- sensory and/or physical needs.

(DfE, 2015: 97)

Each of these areas is now addressed individually in relation to supporting the pupil's needs with technology. The areas are of course interrelated.

These are the headings used for all assessment and planning with pupils with SEND and are the headings used in the Education Health Care Plans for individual pupils (DfE, 2015).

Communication and interaction (autistic spectrum conditions, speech, language and communication needs)

Technology creates opportunities to aid, develop or teach communication e.g. in the form of augmentative and alternative communication (AAC) which includes all forms of communication except oral speech and provides pupils with a means of communicating or interacting with others. Examples of AAC include body posture, gestures, signs, symbols or written words and include but are not limited to aided modes such as communication books and tablets which include speech output.

The ability to adapt personal mobile devices to suit the needs of individuals is expanding. The number of applications (apps) to support pupils with SEND has flourished and specific programs such as Proloquo2go which is a symbol-supported communication app providing a voice to all users. Proloquo2go covers all users from early use of SGDs (speech generated devices) to advanced communicators. Language skills can be expanded and built upon as and when needed. There are, however, barriers to the use of single apps such as Proloquo2go such as being restricted to Apple devices such as iPads.

The world of AAC and technology is rapidly developing and there are several companies which provide bespoke hardware and software for the user such as Tobii Dynavox and Jabbla. These devices have more benefits such as cases that allow for a louder output and accessories that support access such as eye gaze. Software can vary for users and is not strictly set to a specific type. Examples of AAC software are TD snap which is a symbol-supported AAC software, TD talk a simple text-to-speech app that enables natural conversation using just your eyes or hands and Mind Express, Grid and Board Maker which cover several parts of AAC.

There are limitations to implementing AAC including the ability of pupils to operate effectively, technical problems, slowness, attitudes from others towards AAC, communication limitation of the equipment and complexity of the device (Hodge, 2007). When selecting communication tools considerations must be given first to the physical and cognitive abilities of the pupil, the capability of the technology, and the types of communication that will occur (Blackstone *et al.*, 2007). Each selected AAC tool should be easy to operate, require limited training, be of limited cost and be personalised or adaptable. The challenge here is not to replace current methods of communication but to use technology alongside other communication systems (Hodge, 2007). This can reduce or possibly eliminate the communication barriers faced by pupils and begin to place the pupil and not the learning difficulty at the forefront of education.

Furthermore, technology has the potential to teach and aid the development of social skills for pupils that may find it difficult to socialise with peers or adults. For example, apps such as ConversationBuilder and Kloog social skills series (http://kloogsocialskills.com/) teach specific social skills, remind pupils of social behaviours and encourage or develop social interactions. Apps can allow the pupil to easily use reference material without feeling alienated from their peers and can promote greater inclusion.

Some applications are preloaded with stories to teach social skills but they may not address the immediate needs of the pupil. However, apps such as Stories2Learn (https://edshelf.com/tool/stories2learn/) allow you or parents to create individualised programmes.

Cognition and learning needs (specific learning difficulties, moderate learning difficulties, severe learning difficulties, profound and multiple learning difficulties)

Cognition and learning refers to a continuum of needs ranging from pupils who occasionally need 1 to 1 support to pupils who may need 24 hours of constant 1 to 1 support. This section briefly examines some key design features that you should consider when using online learning for pupils with cognition and learning needs. The Web Accessibility Initiative (WAI, https://www.w3.org/WAI/) provides in-depth guidance on creating and ensuring accessibility for all (see http://www.w3.org/WAI/demos/bad/). See also Kuegel (2013) for further details.

Accessing learning online for pupils with special educational needs has to be taken into consideration and made suitable for all, 2Simple education provides educational software for schools since 1999 and has a range of products to help teachers tick all the boxes – not only in the computing curriculum, but across all subjects. Purple Mash is a software provided by 2Simple which allows the teacher to create specific learning tasks for all differentiation needed within a classroom. Purple Mash also includes schemes of work for the computing curriculum and phonics which can be set for individual learners to achieve. Whether it's inspiring your writers, extending your coders or boosting the creativity in your pupils, Purple Mash has everything you need to deliver a unique EdTech experience which is simple to use and loved by all.

Help Kidz Learn is a website which is designed to support learners with their early computing skills such as cause and effect, they have several parts to the website which allow learners to play games and activities that are organised into meaningful learning objectives, beginning at a cause and effect level and early interaction, through the range of skills required to be able to make independent choices. This type of platform allows for accessibility for all as it can be used alongside some hardware such as switches and touchscreen therefore allowing users with physical barriers to be able to access the same platform as other learners in the classroom.

Hardware can be taken into consideration with learners with cognition and learning needs as this can open up more opportunities to overcome barriers to learning such as engagement and participation. Where a pupil is identified as having SEND, schools should take action to remove barriers to learning and put effective special educational provisions in place. This SEND support should take the form of a four-part cycle through which earlier decisions and actions are revisited, refined and revised with a growing understanding of the pupil's needs and of what supports the pupil in making good progress and securing good outcomes. This is known as the graduated approach. It draws on more detailed approaches, more frequent review and more specialist expertise in successive cycles in order to match interventions to the SEND of children and young people. (DfE, 2015: 100) A successful way to remove barriers is the correct hardware provided for all learners. Schools should take into consideration the strengths, needs and motivators for pupils prior to deciding what hardware to use. Hardware which encourages more engagement and participation could be the use of interactive floor projectors, adaptive mice and keyboards, light boxes, switches and tools such as Bee-Bots and early programming devices. Many of these can be found using the inclusive technology website, which provides a range of devices and adaptations to support learners with cognition and learning.

Augmented Reality (AR, see Chapter 18) can connect the pupils' virtual worlds and the real world through the use of a webcam with GPS, compass and object recognition and create occasions to develop authentic individualised learning. In addition, AR can provide pupils with some control of the pace which their learning occurs and create possibilities to engage, stimulate and motivate pupils (Yuen *et al.*, 2011). A few tools currently available include StreetMuseum (free iPhone app that allows the user to blend history and reality while on the streets of London), and Google Sky map (free for android and lets the users interact with the stars in the sky). See also the AR tools from String (http://www.poweredbystring.com/).

Social, emotional and mental health (SEMH) needs

The SEND Code of Practice defines SEMH as "Children and young people may experience a wide range of social and emotional difficulties which manifest themselves in many ways. These may include becoming withdrawn or isolated, as well as displaying challenging, disruptive or disturbing behaviour. These behaviours may reflect underlying mental health difficulties such as anxiety or depression, self-harming, substance misuse, eating disorders or physical symptoms that are medically unexplained. Other children and young people may have disorders such as attention deficit disorder, attention deficit hyperactive disorder or attachment disorder." However specific characteristics associated with behaviour are well contested in the literature (Frederickson and Cline, 2010). Strategies to use include, but are not limited to, teaching pupil behaviour, positive reinforcement, matching curriculum and ability, ensuring high rates of success, structured transition between activities and also self-regulation (Sugai and Horner, 2002).

Self-regulation can be quickly and inexpensively supported by technology. It is about encouraging pupils to take control of their learning (Cooper *et al.*, 2007, as cited in Joseph and Konrad, 2009: 246). E-tools include reminder and organisational tools such as Iprompts developed by handholdadaptive (https://www.autismeye.com/handhold-adaptive/) which provides picture schedules, visual countdown timers and choices between images. Many silent reminder/stopwatch/clock functions or specific apps (Motiv®Aider) on a mobile phone can be set to vibrate at given intervals to remind pupils to complete a self-regulation task. Organisational tools such as Evernote can be used for setting goals, graphing performance or recording written information regarding behaviour. Verbal recordings on apps such as Voice Notes or iTalk Recorder can help pupils to make verbal records of their on-task and off-task behaviour. These are a starting point for you to examine methods to support the specific needs of pupils with SEMH needs.

Sensory and/or physical needs (visual impairment, hearing impairment, multi-sensory impairment and physical disability)

There is a plethora of assistive technologies to support pupils with additional sensory or physical needs that create enabling environments. A majority are free to download or are built into many websites, PDAs and apps. Examples include large keyboards, a simple-to-operate computer mouse, a virtual magnifying glass, text-to-speech programmes and speech-to-text programmes. However, with so many different resources available, all of them in a state of constant change and development, there is understandably a limited body of literature evaluating the 'success and performance' of assistive technologies (Jutai *et al.*, 2009: 219). Physical adaptations may need to be purchased and modified to support pupils with physical challenges such as switches which give pupils the opportunity to choose between different items on the screen and support with cause and effect. There are many different forms of switches and choosing the correct one can depend on the needs of the pupil. For example, some pupils may need a tactile switch if they have a visual impairment or some pupils may have a physical impairment which would require head switches.

Teachers must also take into consideration the possibility that technology can also become a barrier to accessing the curriculum and create further tensions. Slobodzian (2009) explains how the use of YouTube in the classroom has been seen as one method to bring the larger world into the classroom. However, teachers must realise that many aspects may not be accessible to pupils with visual or hearing impairments. YouTube has made closed captioning an option for those creating videos and, in the search options, teachers can filter results that include videos with closed captioning. For full details see (https://support. google.com/youtube/answer/100078?hl=en&sjid=17518188639469643160-EU).

To keep up to date, you can follow disability support organisations such as Autism Speaks at https://twitter.com/autismspeaks or British Dyslexia at https://twitter.com/ BDAdyslexia.

Online safety and SEND

Online safety for SEND pupils has to be explicitly addressed. In a survey of over 2000 secondary schools conducted by BeatBullying, the charity suggests that overall incidents of cyberbullying are not different among those with and without statements of SEND. However, pupils with SEND are 16% more likely to be persistently cyberbullied. The charity defines persistent as 'happening day in, day out, over a period of months or sometimes years' (Cross *et al.*, 2009: 5). Incidents reported included hoax mobile calls, hurtful text or emails and unkind messages on social networking profiles (Cross *et al.*, 2009). Furthermore, Childnet International describes specific risks for pupils with SEND and these include difficulties with terminology due to language delays, interpretation of content or interactions, understanding of safe and acceptable information to share. One further risk described is that some pupils may not realise that their behaviour online might be viewed differently by the receiver and therefore may be interpreted as bullying or even sexual harassment.

To address these highlighted issues with online safety, the Keeping Children Safe in Education team (DfE KCSIE, 2022) updated their policy to include the following statement:

> It is essential that pupils are safeguarded from potentially harmful and inappropriate online material. An effective whole school and college approach to online safety empowers a school or college to protect and educate pupils, and staff in their use of technology and establishes mechanisms to identify, intervene in, and escalate any concerns where appropriate.
>
> (DfE KCSIE, 2022: 35)

Online safety can be challenging to teach and comes with its own difficulties such as many SEND learners needing learning as and when it occurs which cannot always be done with online safety. Childnet have included a feature on their website called STAR SEND tool kit which covers SEND online safety resources and teaching and learning plans. STAR SEND Toolkit | Childnet. Now undertake Task 4.3.

Task 4.3: SEND online safety

Read the KCSIE document and make notes about how you will embed online safety across the curriculum including, for example, helping all pupils distinguish fake news and evaluate the reliability of information they may come across on different websites as well as protecting their personal information.

Summary and key points

This chapter has outlined how enabling environments can be created by addressing attitudes, clearly identifying the needs of the individual pupils and using appropriate technologies to meet their needs. It has looked into statutory guidelines put in place by the DfE to support learners with SEND and suggestions on how to overcome barriers within classrooms and learning. The chapter has included the following key areas of learning for pupils with SEND:

- Cognition and learning.
- Social, emotional and mental health.
- Sensory and physical needs.
- Communication and interaction.

It has also outlined the importance of online safety in all pupils' learning, keeping up to date with the current accessibility tools for all pupils and the dangers of online safety through the use of documents such as KCSIE.

Acknowledgements

The contributions of Yota Dimitriadi, Nick Peacey and Christina Keugel to earlier editions are acknowledged.

Further resources

Cheng, S.C. and Lai, C.L. (2020) Facilitating Learning for Students with Special Needs: A Review of Technology-Supported Special Education Studies, *J. Comput. Educ.*, 7, 131–153. https://link.springer.com/article/10.1007/s40692-019-00150-8. Accessed on 6 February 2023.
This article reviews technology support for pupils with special needs. The references provide links to articles dealing with specific technologies and specific special needs.
Florian, L. and Hegarty, J. (2004) *ICT and Special Educational Needs*, Maidenhead, Open University Press.
A key text on SEND and ICT including staff development, virtual learning environments, computer-based assessment, historical information, management of special education and whole school approaches.
Hodkinson, A. and Vickerman, P. (2009) *Key issues in Special Educational Needs and Inclusion*, London, SAGE.
For further discussion about definitions, see Chapter 5. This book provides a solid foundation on SEND and numerous case study examples.
Loreman, T., Deppeler, J. and Harvey, D. (2010) *Inclusive Education: Supporting Diversity in the Classroom*, Oxon, Routledge.
This book provides research-based practical methods to support mainstream inclusive practice and provides an overview of creating enabling environments.

Websites

https://www.jisc.ac.uk/. Accessed on 6 February 2023.
The UK advisory service on technology and special education. This site provides current research initiatives in SEND and ICT and links to online courses, events and news.
http://www.ed.gov/. Accessed on 6 February 2023.
The U.S Department of Education website provides a starting place for further information on best practices in teaching, current news and government guidelines.
https://archive.futurelab.org.uk/publications/FUTL20/FUTL20.pdf. Accessed on 6 February 2023.
Futurelab is an independent not for profit organisation that supports innovative approaches to education with technology. The site has a wide range of resources to support classroom practices through the use of technology.
https://www.gov.uk/government/organisations/department-for-education. Accessed on 6 February 2023.
The department for education is responsible for education and pupils' services in England. Resources on current research, polices, and statutory guidance is available.
https://www.gov.uk/government/publications/assistive-technology-research-and-development-work-2021-to-2022. Accessed on 6 February 2023.
This site provides general information on assistive technologies and has an in-depth section on creating accessible documents.
MyChoicePad. http://www.mychoicepad.com/. Accessed on 23 November 2023.
This website provides information on the MyChoicePad app and can direct potential users to the correct app they need for them.
Proloquo2Go (2012). https://www.assistiveware.com/products/proloquo2go. Accessed on 9 January 2023.

This website allows Proloquo2Go users to navigate the app, gain online support and access online training for the app.

https://www.inclusive.com/uk/. Accessed on 6 February 2023.

This site provides technology devices and aids to support learners with additional needs when using ICT.

https://www.2simple.com/. Accessed on 6 February 2023.

This site hosts the software for Purple Mash.

https://www.gov.uk/government/publications/keeping-children-safe-in-education--2. Accessed on 6 February 2023.

Statutory guidance for schools and colleges on safeguarding children and safer recruitment.

References

Anderson, S. (2011) The Twitter Toolbox for Educators, *Teacher Librarian*, 39(1), 27–30.

Barnes, C., Oliver, M. and Barton, L. (2002) *Disability Studies Today*, Cambridge, Polity Press.

BECTA (2003) *What the Research Says About ICT Supporting Special Educational Needs and Inclusion*, Coventry, BECTA. http://www.mmiweb.org.uk/publications/ict/Research_Barriers_TandL.pdf. Accessed on 6 February 2023.

BECTA (2009) *Harnessing Technology Schools Survey: Analysis Report*, Coventry, BECTA. https://dera.ioe.ac.uk/1546/1/becta_2009_htssreport_report.pdf. Accessed on 4 February 2023.

Blackstone, S., Williams, M. and Wilkins, D. (2007) Key Principles Underlying Research and Practice in AAC, *AAC: Augmentative and Alternative Communication*, 23, 191–203.

Bower, M., Hedberg, J. and Kuswara, A. (2010) Framework for Web 2.0 Learning Design, *Educational Media International*, 47(3), 177–198.

Cross, E., Richardson, B., Douglas, T. and Vonkaenel-Flatt, J. (2009) *Virtual Violence: Protecting Children from Bullying*, London, Beatbullying.

DES (1978) *Special Educational Needs: Report of the Committee of Enquiry in the Education of Handicapped Children and Young People (The Warnock Report)*, London, HMSO.

DES (2001) *Special Education Needs: Code of Practice*, London, HMSO, updated to become DfE (2015).

DfE KCSIE (2022) *Keeping Children Safe in Education*. https://www.gov.uk/government/publications/keeping-children-safe-in-education--2. Accessed on 8 December 2022.

DfE (2015) *Special Education Needs: Code of Practice*, London, HMSO. https://assets.publishing.service.gov.uk/government/uploads/system/uploads/attachment_data/file/398815/SEND_Code_of_Practice_January_2015.pdf. Accessed on 29 January 2023.

Florian, L. and Hegarty, J. (2004) *ICT and Special Educational Needs*, Maidenhead, Open University Press.

Frederickson, N. and Cline, T. (2009) *Special Educational Needs, Inclusion and Diversity*, Maidenhead, Open University Press.

Friedman, M. and Bryen, D. (2007) Web Accessibility Design Recommendations for People with Cognitive Disabilities, *Technology and Disability*, 19, 205–212.

Glazzard, J. (2011) Perceptions of the Barriers to Effective Inclusion in One Primary School: Voices of Teachers and Teaching Assistants, *Support for Learning*, 26(2), 56–63.

Hodge, S. (2007) Why Is the Potential of Augmentative and Alternative Communication Not Being Realized? Exploring the Experiences of People Who Use Communication Aids, *Disability and Society*, 22, 457–471.

Hodkinson, A. and Vickerman, P. (2009) *Key Issues in Special Educational Needs and Inclusion*, London, SAGE.

Johnstone, D. (2001) *An Introduction to Disability Studies*, London, David Fulton.

Joseph, L. and Konrad, M. (2009) Help Students Self-Manage Their Academic Performance, *Intervention in School and Clinic*, 44(4), 246–249.

Jutai, J.W., Strong, J.G. and Russell-Minda, E. (2009) Effectiveness of Assistive Technologies for Low Vision Rehabilitation: A Systematic Review, *Journal of Visual Impairment and Blindness*, 103(4), 210–222.

Kuegel, C. (2013) Special Educational Needs and Technology. In Leask, M. and Pachler, N. (eds.), *Learning to Teach using ICT in the Secondary School*, Abingdon, Taylor/Francis, 173–181.

Oliver, M. (2004) The Social Model in Action: If I Had a Hammer. In Barnes, C. and Mercer, G. (eds.), *Implementing the Social Model of Disability: Theory and Research*, Leeds, The Disability Press, 18–31.

Slobodzian, J. (2009) The Devil Is in the Details: Issues of Exclusion in an Inclusive Educational Environment, *Ethnography and Education*, 4, 181–195, 10.1080/17457820902972804.

Sugai, G. and Horner, R. (2002) The Evolution of Discipline Practices: School-Wide Positive Behavior Supports, *Child and Family Behavior Therapy*, 24(1/2), 23–50.

Sze, S. (Fall 2009) A Literature Review: Pre-Service Teachers' Attitudes Toward Students with Disabilities, *Education*, 130(1), 53–56.

UK Government (2014) *Children and Families Act 2014*, London, HMSO. https://www.legislation.gov.uk/ukpga/2014/6/part/3/crossheading/special-educational-needs-etc/enacted?view=plain. Accessed on 14 February 2023.

UPIAS (1976) *Fundamental Principles of Disability*, London, Union of the Physically Impaired Against Segregation.

Web Accessibility Initiative (WAI) (2011) *Making the Web Accessible*. http://www.w3.org/WAI/. Accessed on 6 February 2012.

Yuen, S., Yaoyuneyong, G. and Johnson, E. (2011) Augmented Reality: An Overview and Five Directions for AR in Education, *Journal of Educational Technology Development and Exchange*, 4(1), 119–140.

5 Digital technologies and assessment

Gary Beauchamp, Paul Brooks and Josephine Farag

Introduction

Assessment is an integral part of the everyday life of teachers. Indeed, the main challenge facing us in this chapter is to reconsider how familiar assessment practices can be adapted, radically changed, enhanced or even replaced with the use of increasingly sophisticated and pervasive digital technologies. An added complication is the constant and fast-moving development of technologies, allied to the fact that many pupils begin primary school as highly skilled and experienced users of technology. We need to consider how best to use these skills and experiences to allow pupils not only in their own learning but also in the assessment of themselves and others. In the past, assessment was often something which was done *to* pupils. Although elements of this remain in some types of summative assessments, increasingly pupils are seen as active partners in their learning, and assessment is something which is done *with* them and *for* them. Indeed, it may be argued that assessment is also done for the parents of these pupils, and we need to consider how to involve them in the process and share relevant information using a variety of media to help them gain a better understanding of how their child is achieving. In this chapter, we will explore how all members of the school community can benefit from using digital technologies in assessment.

Objectives

At the end of this chapter you should be able to:

- recognise the potential of digital technologies for assessment
- identify the affordances of digital technologies in supporting assessment for learning
- perceive the potential of digital technologies to instigate, implement, share and give feedback on assessments to learners and the wider school community.

In the past, most primary school assessments were paper-based or involved verbal questioning. What is new, for instance in written tests, is how digital technologies can facilitate a wide variety of means of undertaking and recording written tasks to suit all learners, being able to build them collaboratively (such as blogs and wikis), to transform the sharing of assessments (for instance by scanning and emailing, or putting on a website) or distribute them to a potentially worldwide audience. The use of sound recordings can also now be enhanced by high-quality video (in 2D and 3D), and all recordings can be easily undertaken, edited and distributed, often from one device by pupils or teachers. Indeed, the advent of more immersive technologies, such as virtual (VR) and extended reality (ER)

DOI: 10.4324/9781003408925-5

and artificial intelligence (AI), can provide completely new ways of assessing pupils which we will discuss below. In addition, it is important that assessment with technology is built into classroom activities across the curriculum. When discussing the assessment of dance in the primary school in Australia, Torzillo and Sorin (2016: 33) assert that

> when assessment is part of the ebb and flow of teaching and learning, it takes advantage of the processes in the arts classroom, such as the integration of creating, responding, and presenting, which are part of the creative process.

Although discussing dance, in particular, this argument also extends to assessing different phases of the many creative activities primary pupils do in areas such as art, music, drama, PE and so on. Hence, as a teacher, the lens you adopt to look at assessment *with* digital technologies must take account of, and exploit, the many advances both in technology and pupils' ability to use it.

Assessment with digital technologies: why bother?

In this chapter, assessment with, or mediated by, digital technologies allows teachers and pupils to use any digital tool or resource to make a judgement about progress in a range of subjects or areas of learning. In the past, much of this work was covered by the term ICT, but across the United Kingdom (UK), this is being replaced by digital technologies, or variations of this (e.g. Digital Competence in Wales). In this chapter we will use digital technologies to cover all types of technology (both hardware and software) that may be found in the primary school now, or in the near future. We suggest that using digital technologies can help assessment in many ways, including making it more 'efficient, transparent and accessible' (Webb, 2010: 616).

Types of assessment

For the purposes of this chapter, we will divide assessment into two types: formative and summative. The distinction between formative assessment (explores understanding and identifies next steps) and summative assessment (a more formalised summing up) is well documented. Mansell *et al.* (2009: 9) highlight the fact that these terms should not be used as labels for different types of assessment, but rather describe how these types of assessments are used. They provide a useful list, Table 5.1, of the characteristic differences between them, which will help us to consider the use of digital technologies in assessment in this chapter.

Table 5.1 Characteristic differences between formative and summative assessment

Formative assessment	Summative assessment
part of the learning process	comes at the end
attempts to develop learning	assesses learning at a chosen point in time – normally by the teacher or examining board
on-going and dynamic, between both pupil and teacher	static and one-way, normally done by a teacher or examiner to a pupil
'follows the flow of spontaneous dialogue and interaction, where one action builds on (is contingent upon) an earlier one'	'follows a set of pre-defined questions.' (Mansell *et al.*, 2009: 9)

Additionally, Black and Wiliam (2009: 8) assert that formative assessment consists of five key strategies:

1. Clarifying and sharing learning intentions and criteria for success
2. Engineering effective classroom discussions and other learning tasks that elicit evidence of pupil understanding
3. Providing feedback that moves learners forward
4. Activating pupils as instructional resources for one another
5. Activating pupils as the owners of their own learning.

Please undertake Task 5.1 to consider these strategies in relation to the use of digital resources.

Task 5.1: Formative assessment with digital technologies

On your own, or in discussion with others, consider each of these five key strategies in turn and identify how particular digital resources you have used or are familiar with, can be used in each.

The role of digital technologies in formative assessment could perhaps better be labelled as formative e-assessment:

> to support the iterative process of gathering and analysing information about pupil learning by teachers as well as learners and of evaluating it in relation to prior achievement and attainment of intended, as well as unintended learning outcomes, in a way that allows the teacher or pupil to adjust the learning trajectory.
>
> (Pachler *et al.*, 2009: 1)

This definition establishes that pupils are equally important in assessment as the teacher and that this process is continual, and not a one-off event. In addition, it is vital to remember that 'no assessment technology is in itself formative, but almost any technology can be used in a formative way – if the right conditions are set in place' (Pachler *et al.*, 2009: 2).

In order to make a decision about whether you should use digital technologies to undertake an assessment, you need to consider the unique features they possess that can be used. In doing this, you should recognise that assessment can take many forms, or modes, such as visual, sound and text, and that digital technologies have the capability to work with all of these. In addition, we should also remember that many existing assessments which do not use digital technologies remain valid. In making a decision to use digital technologies in assessment, we need to consider what digital technologies are good at and reflect on whether we should use them or not.

The affordances of digital technologies for formative and summative assessment – what are they good at?

The first step in this process is to consider the affordances digital technologies offer. An affordance 'refers to the perceived and actual properties of a thing, primarily those functional properties that determine just how the thing could possibly be used' (Pea, 1997: 51). While the actual properties of a piece of technology, such as the pen for an interactive whiteboard, can be obvious, some are less so, but 'the affordance is there, it has always been there, but it needs to be perceived to be realised … The world is full of potential, not of things' (Hammond, 2010: 206). It is important to note that the affordances for assessment may be different than the affordances for teaching with the same device, and that they can be recognised at any time. For example, if you discover a new feature in a piece of hardware or software you didn't know about, it may trigger an assessment strategy you hadn't thought of before. Or you see potential in a completely new piece of technology. For example, using 360° headsets to put a pupil in a Welsh village to learn and assess Welsh language use, or putting them in a rainforest and asking questions afterwards.

Therefore, to help recognise the affordances of digital technologies for assessment we need to consider what they are actually good at. When discussing the unique features of technologies, Beauchamp (2017: 18–19) suggests the key features include:

- **speed**: *making things happen more quickly than by other methods, both for the individual on a device or for the whole class*
- **automation**: *making difficult processes happen automatically e.g. filming and editing video on an iPad*
- **capacity**: *the storage and retrieval of large amounts of material, including online and outside of the classroom*
- **range**: *access to materials in different forms and from a wider range of sources than otherwise possible, including outside of the classroom*
- **interactivity**: *in this definition, the ability to respond to user input repeatedly – without getting bored like a person! – and provide (pre-programmed) feedback based on the input by the user.*

Pachler *et al.* (2009) also add

- **communication**: *the rapid sharing of ideas to a variety of audiences by one person, a class or whole class or school in a way that can be captured (for instance in a podcast).*

It is these features, and others, which provide the affordances of assessment with digital technologies, and we should note that these features apply to all forms of technologies, ranging from

> touch screens with drag and drop and multi-touch features, augmented reality (AR), virtual reality (VR), mixed reality (MR), robots, and behavioral monitoring (e.g., voice recognition, eye gaze, face recognition, touchless user interface). It is at this nexus where innovative education theory, psychology, computer science, and engineering can combine to optimize classroom assessment practices and provide clear links between assessment, teaching, and learning.
>
> (Neumann *et al.*, 2019: 1)

We will now discuss how the features that technologies offer can be applied to support assessment – but this is only the beginning, we are sure you can think of more.

Speed

Before we consider the potential benefits of the speed of digital technologies, we need to remember that although they allow things to happen quickly, 'the teacher remains central to the *control* of this speed, guided by the needs of the learners' (Beauchamp, 2012: 4). Nevertheless, if a pupil has produced a piece of work or a performance in drama, music or PE, the ability to take a digital photograph, sound recording or movie in an instant can be vital to making a record of something which would otherwise be ephemeral, and mobile devices play an important role here. Examples of this could be the recording of the spontaneous composition of a piece of music or a very young pupil (who may not be able to write fluently yet) explaining how they completed a task. Having completed an assessment quickly, however, it is also important to be able to store this with the same speed somewhere that is safe and easily accessible. In this instance, the use of mobile devices linked to cloud storage solutions, or a school network, are very important. Again, the ability to do this quickly saves you time. This can also be important if, for instance, pupils have recorded their own sequences in a PE lesson and want to review them immediately on a large screen back in the classroom. Another use of speed, which has come with advances in internet access, is the ability to share evidence assessment (see also the 'Communication' section) with a range of stakeholders almost immediately.

Automation

When using mobile devices, such as an iPad or other tablet, the fact that the device can make an automatic backup of all images if connected to a wireless network, is a good example of the benefits of automation in assessment activities and record keeping. Other examples of automation might include saving a mind mapping exercise to summarise learning undertaken by groups or the whole class on an interactive whiteboard / touchscreen display – which can then quickly be shared with others or emailed to yourself to help in future planning and assessment.

Another potential benefit of automation in assessment is the ability to search for electronic examples of a pupil's work much more quickly than if it was in a folder, in a box in a cupboard somewhere in the school. This does assume that there is an agreed policy for the format of naming electronic files (such as Y4_class 3_group 3_reversible changes) and this is something that you should consider carefully when saving assessments – a basic minimum perhaps being the pupil's name and the date of the assessment, including the year.

Automation is perhaps particularly useful for summative assessments, particularly if completed using technology where the process of collecting, storing and backing up data (e.g. a pupil completing an online test) is automated in a searchable format. It may also become more relevant as advances are made in Artificial intelligence (AI). Cui and Zhang (2021: 412) define AI as:

> …the simulation of the human mind in computer systems that are programmed to think like humans and mimic their actions such as learning and problem-solving. AI should be able to perform tasks that normally require human intelligence, such as visual perception, decision-making, and communication.

For instance, in the case of automation, pupils who struggle with writing or have limited mobility can use the technology to transcribe words using speech recognition software in assessments.

Please read and consider Task 5.2 to reflect on one possible use of AI in the primary classroom.

Task 5.2: AI as support for learning

Another example of AI is a Smart Assistant, like Siri and Alexa, which is able to search and read aloud information from a range of sources. Such devices can act as a source of information to answer other bigger questions. Cook (2021: 9) suggested that they could act as 'as a knowledgeable computer system that someone desiring of knowledge can interact with to aid their development'. While this reflects elements of Vygotsky's (1978) concept of a more knowledgeable other, who is able to support learners in a zone of proximal development, it also acknowledges the limitations to the technology, in that it cannot go beyond responding to the questions asked.

Nevertheless, on your own, or with others, consider what opportunities (if any) can you see for using a Smart Assessment (such as Siri or Alexa) as part of an assessment task, where gaining information the learners may not know could be helpful in answering another bigger question, that is not simply factual?

Capacity

We have already briefly discussed the potential benefits of storing assessments, but the ability to retrieve them (quickly) from different places and different devices can be just as important. This can apply to both teachers and pupils, and indeed parents. In the past, much of the evidence of assessment took up a lot of much-needed space and was potentially hard to access. With the use of Cloud storage, school networks, Virtual Learning Environments (VLEs), websites, blogs and so on, we are only limited by our imagination and the amount of storage that the school makes available. This does not mean that we need to neglect storing and moving records of work via older media, such as USB pen drives or similar, but it does mean that the range of options available is now much wider, potentially more secure and accessible to more people (including inspectors) from more places.

Range

As technology advances, there is an ever-increasing range of devices and affordances available to teachers to access assessments in different forms. While this is important for all pupils, it can be particularly beneficial in providing a medium to interact *with* and *through* for those with particular needs, or for very young children who are not yet ready to undertake assessments that involve the ability to interpret text or respond in writing.

In recent times, developments in immersive technologies provide a unique range of ways of engaging with and assessing new experiences, which can promote deep learning and motivate pupils. For instance, Virtual Reality (VR) is an emerging educational technology, widely used in gaming, offering unique affordances for assessment. VR 'is a technology integrating computer graphics and human–computer interfaces to create an immersive 3D virtual world where the user can feel as if situated in the real world' (Ou *et al.*, 2021: 2). Pellas *et al.*, (2021: 835) suggest that 'each user has the illusion of "being there" (sense of presence) surrounded by a three-dimensional (3D) … 360-degree (360°) environment'. The environment can be explored freely and it is also possible to interact with visual objects, such as using handsets to click on questions embedded in the video. (Also see the chapter on digital storytelling for more information on using VR in the classroom.)

Many pupils, and indeed teachers, may be aware of this through using computer games, but it also has great potential for assessment. This type of learning and assessing allows pupils to circumvent the barriers of time and space, for instance, strolling through the city in the Roman empire (Taranilla *et al.*, 2022) and then answering questions posed by the teacher. VR offers a sense of presence and allows the user to explore the environment freely. This illusion of 'being there' affords the participant a hands-on experimental experience in which they can interact with visual objects (e.g. 3D games, simulations or virtual worlds). In addition, such technologies create an immersive environment without damaging actual environments or causing danger to the individual. The possibilities of immersing pupils in an environment that would otherwise be impractical, or impossible to undertake in the real world, and then assessing their understanding, begins to open up novel types of assessment.

Please read and reflect on Case Study 5.1 which outlines a possible use from Wales of 360° in the primary teaching.

Case Study 5.1: 360° technology in action

In Wales, since 2021 the Welsh Government has funded the *Wales Collaborative for Learning Design* (WCLD) to explore the use of interactive technologies in learning design. This includes working with teachers to create 360° videos that can be used in teaching and assessment. The project provides teachers with a 360° camera and other equipment and technical support to make and edit videos based on their own locality or topic. For instance, a primary teacher was doing a topic with her class (aged 5–6) on 'Bright lights of the city'. Due to their age, it was difficult to take them into the city at night, but with a small 360° camera a recording was made of a walk through the city in day time, and then the same walk at night time – with the added bonus that the Christmas lights were on at the time. The class was able to view the edited video individually through cheap 360° goggles (e.g. Google Cardboard) to gain the full immersive experience or on the class screen where the teacher could manipulate the video to show different angles using the mouse or trackpad on the computer. The assessment involved discussing the differences with individuals or the whole class. This meant using the technology as the stimulus for assessment by doing something it was good at and could not be done any other way, but then moving to use the teacher's skills of questioning for assessment.

Using video in assessment does not, however, have to use high-tech solutions. Pupil-generated video creation is an innovative and emerging form of assessment. This assessment method has several benefits, notably in supporting the development of digital and communication skills relevant to today's world and in enhancing learning – indeed the act of creating them is a form of assessment of their technology skills. For instance, collaborative video creation projects promote an open dialogue to explore deeply the topic in question. Two contemporary approaches to pupil-generated videos are vlogs and vodcasts. Vlogging is short for 'video blog', and blog is short for 'weblog'. In essence, a vlog is an online diary in video form. The term 'vodcasting' is used to specify content composed by video, and not merely by audio. The prefix 'vod' comes from the expression 'video on demand'.

In parallel to this, the pupil creators can be challenged (assessed) to defend their perspectives, think critically about their views, and discuss the process they went through to create the vlog/vodcast. The latter promotes metacognitive processes, as the pupil must reflect upon how they have learned what they know and examine their thought processes. Assessment choices such as these communicate a strong message to pupils as to the skills and qualities that are valued in education.

Please undertake Task 5.3 to reflect upon using a vlog as an alternative means of assessment.

Task 5.3: Using a digital vlog for formative assessment

A teacher has a class of Year 5 pupils, and the topic for the lesson is deforestation. The teacher wants to encourage the pupils to summarise the key points from the session and provide their opinions. Rather than adopting a traditional formative assessment method e.g. Q&A, the teacher decides to ask the pupils, in groups, to record their responses in the form of a digital vlog. As the pupils were confident users of technology, they were asked to make a short video of themselves talking about what they had learned in the lesson on deforestation.

On your own, or with others, consider:

- How could this method be used to support peer collaboration and peer assessment?
- How can this assessment method promote engagement in metacognitive processes?
- What are the benefits and limitations of this vlog approach?

Using digital technologies to access, present and record assessments (as in making a record of something, not just sound or video recording) in different forms can also be beneficial for those with additional learning needs. It forms part of what Abbott (2007: 6) calls 'e-inclusion', which is the use of digital technologies 'to enable inclusive learning practices for people with learning difficulties'. For instance, pupils who have difficulty with writing can now make a video or audio recording of their thoughts, which is just as valid an assessment as a written task or picture. In addition, the use of voice recognition software can help pupils with visual impairments or other needs that make it hard to type. In one study of using assistive technology in a primary school, one pupil reported that 'Technology acts as my eyes' (Abbinett, 2017). Furthermore, pupils whose handwriting may be hard to understand can produce legible records of their work through the use of keyboards (both real and virtual) and voice recognition software.

Another advantage of assessments with digital technologies is that they can be presented in a wide range of formats, many of which can be less intimidating than some more traditional forms of assessment. For instance, assessment can be presented through games. This is sometimes called gamification, which is 'the use of game design elements (e.g., points, leaderboards, and badges) in non-game contexts to promote user engagement' (Attali and Arieli-Attali, 2015: 57). This can provide a variety of assessment activities that learners may consider less challenging, more engaging and motivating as well as potentially more fun – both those produced by commercial organisations and, increasingly, assessments developed by teachers themselves. The latter has the advantage of allowing the teacher to personalise the assessment to their class and make it more engaging by using settings familiar to the children, such as their classroom or school.

Interactivity

The use of games-based assessments is a good example of the use of interactivity as an affordance of interactive technologies. Although there are many different definitions of interactivity with technology, in this context, it applies to its ability to respond to user input repeatedly, without getting bored. Kennewell and Beauchamp (2007: 231) defined this type of interactivity as *feedback*, which is 'the provision of a response by the tool which is contingent on action by the user'. The response can take many forms ranging from sound effects (for right or wrong answers) to spoken feedback (but only pre-programmed responses). Hence digital technologies can be very effective in summative assessments which only require the collection of scores (for example in a maths test, where results can be easily collated and shared for later use), the completion of multiple-choice type questions, or other assessments that do not require formative feedback. We need to remember that interactive technologies allow pupils 'to make the same mistake every time as, unless it is programmed to do so, ICT resources are not really able to give a response which allows for personalised formative feedback' (Beauchamp, 2012: 7). This means we need to consider carefully how to use interactivity and assessment with digital technologies.

Communication

Although communication has been central to teaching with technology, recent advances in the availability of portable devices and increased accessibility and speed of internet connections means it now occupies an even more central role – particularly since the forced use of technology during the COVID pandemic (see Leask and Younie, 2022). These communications, including assessments, can involve the use of many forms of media and modes of communication, can take place in real-time (synchronous) and will be recorded and accessed later (asynchronous). These communications can be saved to ensure that they provide a record of achievement (assessment) but can also be used as a potential teaching tool for future years. For example, if a group of pupils make a podcast that shows what they have learned, this not only provides a record of their achievement which can be shared with a global audience if required, but can also be used by the teacher as an example of what a podcast actually is with a future class. There are, of course, potential e-safety issues that need to be considered, but this should not prevent primary teachers from making full use of the ability to communicate, and indeed celebrate, the achievements of their pupils.

Please complete Task 5.4 to consider the role of digital technologies in communicating with different audiences for assessed work.

Task 5.4: Using technologies to communicate with audiences for assessed work

Consider Figure 5.1 which shows some of the potential audiences for pupils' assessments. In discussion with others, or on your own, decide:

1. Is this list complete? If not, who needs to be added?
2. How could you share assessments using digital technologies (for example, through the school website?) Who would you share them with? What form may this take?
3. How can you ensure that the assessments are only seen by their intended audience?

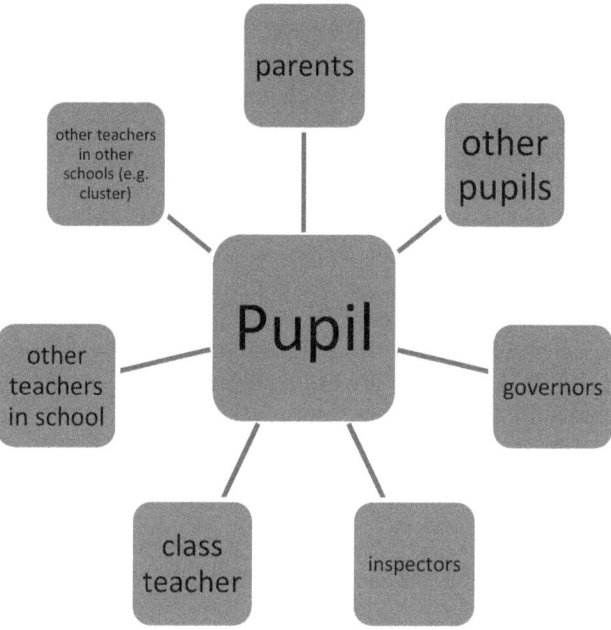

Figure 5.1 Audiences for assessed work

Having briefly examined the features of interactive technologies that can be used effectively in assessment, we will now turn to consider how these can be used to instigate, implement and provide feedback on assessments for whole classes, groups and individuals.

Mobility

Perhaps the most significant advance in recent years is in the availability, affordability and sophistication of mobile technologies. In the case of assessment, this opens up many opportunities to set up, mark, provide feedback and share these assessments in a wide range of settings, both inside and especially outside of the classroom – see Chapter 19 on Outdoor

Learning and Technology. This does not mean just taking traditional assessments outside but re-imagining how technologies can enable new forms of authentic assessment.

While primary teachers have long had the opportunity to use digital cameras (both still and moving images), sound recorders, as well as laptops and fixed PCs, these were often separate devices. In addition, material from these devices needed to be transferred to a laptop or PC to be shared. Now, not only are all of these facilities available in one mobile device, but results can easily be shared instantly both within the classroom and beyond. The ability to mirror these devices on other classroom technologies, such as the interactive displays, opens up opportunities for peer assessment, as well as discussion of ideas.

Summary and key points

In this chapter, we have:

- Explored the potential of digital technologies for assessment.
- Examined how the features of interactive technologies and the emergence of other technologies, such as VR and AI, offer a range of affordances for assessment in all areas of learning, at all ages and of all abilities.
- Seen that it is essential for both pupils and teachers to recognise these affordances and that this enables assessments to be shared with a wide range of stakeholders, both within the school community and beyond. In primary school, pupils' achievements can often be spontaneous and transitory, and it is only through the use of technology that some of these can be captured and shared.
- Recognised the potential of digital technologies in assessment as a means of recording, celebrating and sharing the achievements of pupils in many forms, from annotated explanations to musical performances to creative writing, blogs and vod/podcasts.

Further resources

Oldfield, A., Broadfoot, P., Sutherland, R. and Timmis, S. (undated) *Assessment in a digital age: A research review.* Available at https://www.bristol.ac.uk/media-library/sites/education/documents/researchreview.pdf.

This report provides some research background (which you can update with other reading) by a university-based team and introduces key ideas and concepts. It aims to 'progress the debate on the role and utility of digital technologies within assessment as a catalyst in shifting the paradigms and improving the practices of assessment to ultimately benefit student learning'. You can ask yourself, with all recent advances in technologies, has enough changed since this was published around ten years ago? Have paradigms shifted?

Education Endowment Fund (2019) *Using digital technology to improve learning: Guidance report.* Available at https://educationendowmentfoundation.org.uk/education-evidence/guidance-reports/digital.

Although the primary focus of this report is using technology in learning, it also considers how technology has a role in improving assessment and feedback.

References

Abbinett, E. (2017) *"Technology acts as my eyes": The use of assistive technology to support the academic needs of primary school pupils with a visual impairment.* Unpublished PhD thesis. Cardiff Metropolitan University.

Abbott, C. (2007) *E-inclusion: learning difficulties and digital technologies*. London: Futurelab.

Attali, Y. and Arieli-Attali, M. (2015) 'Gamification in assessment: Do points affect test performance?', *Computers and Education*, 83: 57–63.

Beauchamp, G. (2012) *ICT in the primary school: From pedagogy to practice*. London: Pearson.

Beauchamp, G. (2017) *Computing and ICT in the primary school: From pedagogy to practice*. 2nd ed. London: David Fulton/Routledge.

Black, P. and Wiliam, D. (2009) 'Developing the theory of formative assessment', *Educational Assessment, Evaluation and Accountability*, 21(1): 5–31.

Cook, R. (2021) *Connecting the echo dots: An exploratory ethnographic study of 'Alexa' in the classroom*. Unpublished PhD thesis. Available at https://eprints.glos.ac.uk/10707/1/10707%20Richard%20Cook%20%282021%29%20Connecting%20the%20Echo%20Dots%20An%20Exploratory%20Ethnographic%20Study%20of%20'Alexa'%20in%20the%20Classroom.%20PhD%20thesis.pdf (accessed 12 December 2022).

Cui, M. and Zhang, D.Y. (2021) 'Artificial intelligence and computational pathology', *Laboratory Investigation*, 101(4): 412–422.

Hammond, M. (2010) 'What is an affordance and can it help us understand the use of ICT in education?', *Education and Information Technology*, 15(3): 205–217.

Kennewell, S. and Beauchamp, G. (2007) 'The features of interactive whiteboards and their influence on learning', *Learning, Media and Technology*, 32(3): 227–241.

Leask, M. and Younie, S. (2022) *Education for all in times of crisis: Lessons from Covid-19*. Abingdon: Routledge.

Mansell, W., James, M. and the Assessment Reform Group. (2009) *Assessment in schools. Fit for purpose? A commentary by the Teaching and Learning Research Programme*. London: Economic and Social Research Council, Teaching and Learning Research Programme.

Ou, K.-L., Chu, S.-T. and Tarng, W. (2021) 'Development of a virtual wetland ecological system using VR 360° panoramic technology for environmental education', *Land (Basel)*, 10(8): 829.

Pachler, N., Mellar, H., Daly, C. Mor, Y. and Wiliam, D. (2009) *Scoping a vision for formative e-assessment: A project report for JISC version 2.0*. London: Institute of Education.

Pea, R.D. (1997) 'Distributed intelligence and designs for education', in Salomon, G. (ed.) *Distributed cognitions: Psychological and educational considerations*. Cambridge: Cambridge University Press, 47–87.

Pellas, N. Mystakidis, S. and Kazanidis, I. (2021) 'Immersive virtual reality in K-12 and higher education: A systematic review of the last decade scientific literature', *Virtual Reality*, 25, 835–861.

Taranilla, R., Cózar-Gutiérrez, R., González-Calero, J. and Cirugeda, I. (2022) 'Strolling through a city of the Roman Empire: An analysis of the potential of virtual reality to teach history in Primary Education', *Interactive Learning Environments*, 30(4): 608–618.

Torzillo, M. and Sorin, R. (2016) 'Showing what we can do: Assessment of primary school dance', *The International Journal of Assessment and Evaluation*, 23(4): 29–42.

Vygotsky, L.S. (1978) *Mind in society: The development of higher psychological processes*. 1st ed. London: Harvard University Press.

Webb, M. (2010) 'Beginning teacher education and collaborative formative e-assessment', *Assessment and Evaluation in Higher Education*, 35(5): 597–618.

6 Digital dilemmas in the early years

*Graham Bell, Susan Borland, Rachael Summerscales
and Philippa Thompson*

Introduction

Technology as part of early years practice has been the subject of considerable research over the past thirty years. In the late 1980s, computers were introduced to nursery and reception classes on a trolley often in the corner of the room, and for most children this was the only access to digital technology. At this time television for children was developing and was seen as a threat to children's learning in a similar way to how mobile phones and social media are perceived today (Rubinstein, 1978; Richards, Caldwell and Go, 2015).

This chapter explores interactions that children have both at home and in early years settings and how technology is part of young children's lives even before they are born e.g., antenatal scans. Mobile phones, tablets, laptops and gaming consoles are all part of everyday lives for many. The chapter also explores the concept of a digital divide and an understanding of how poverty impacts access to technology, alongside the challenge of the age of agency in young children, which provides challenges for practitioners.

Changes to policy, practice and pedagogy are explored alongside an exploration of children's agency leading to learner empowerment. A consideration of how Initial Teacher Education (ITE) can support practitioners' skills to develop confidence and bring this knowledge and expertise into early years settings provides the final part of this chapter.

Objectives

At the end of this chapter you should be able to:

- reflect on your own experiences of technology and consider how you could develop or support others to use technology in early years settings
- understand how technology practice and pedagogy have developed over time in the early years setting
- develop an understanding of how technology can support young children's agency in their learning.

Young children and technology

Technology is not new to us and as it has developed throughout the previous decades, it has inflected the way that we live, work and play. The relatively recent advent of digital technology, which now permeates all areas of our lives, is embedded in the way that we live, assisting and documenting our lives: in some cases, before children are even born, for

DOI: 10.4324/9781003408925-6

example, through the sharing of antenatal photographs on social media. In addition to this, there is awareness of increasingly younger children's interactions with digital technology at home (Ofcom, 2022) that necessitates early support for young children to learn about digital technology effectively and safely.

Young children can also learn *through* digital technology, using its affordances to reinforce other areas of their curriculum learning. For example, digital tools such as virtual assistant technology can be used to develop 'Communication and Language'; supporting the wider, multimodal understanding of literacy and its role in communication (Kress, 2003; Evans, 2004; Marsh, 2019). In fact, learning about technology links with all areas of learning in the Early Years Foundation Stage [EYFS], although the only explicit reference to technology in the EYFS framework is in 'Understanding the World' (Department for Education [DFE], 2021).

By embracing the ubiquitous nature of technology and the opportunities presented by the play-based nature of learning in EYFS, practitioners can also lay the foundations for computational thinking, which is essentially an approach to problem-solving (Wing, 2006) and aligns with the characteristics of effective learning (DFE, 2021). Computational thinking supports children's learning in all areas of EYFS and fosters criticality (also see Chapter 16). However, despite the opportunities to enhance young children's learning about digital technology, there appears to be a lack of curriculum guidance to support parents and practitioners (Flewitt, Messer and Kucirkova, 2015).

Policy, practice and curriculum

The early years of education are critical to children's development and have a proven long-term impact on their future success, academically and socially (Tickell, 2011). It is surprising then to consider that the EYFS is a relatively modern introduction to the school system, only becoming statutory in 2008 (DCSF, 2008). This EYFS document heralded the expectation that children should start to have an understanding of everyday technology. The EYFS framework structures learning around children, developing learners to become resilient, capable, confident and self-assured, through positive relationships with adults and enabling environments (DfE, 2021). It is a flexible curriculum that bases learning around children's interests and allows teachers to embed technology throughout.

The latest revision of the EYFS framework removed all mention of the term technology from the Early Learning Goals (ELGs). This should not be a surprise, as our relationship with technology has changed so much since the framework's introduction. Technology has become such an embedded part of children's lives that it perhaps does not warrant an explicit assessment statement. This is highlighted by Ofcom (2022) who report that children's screen time is increasing rapidly and point out that 78% of 3–4-year-olds have access to a tablet and that 89% of them use video-sharing platforms.

Concerns have been raised that embedding technology into practice will result in more screen time, encouraging children to become passive and isolated. However, screen time is not inherently bad, as discussed by Stiglic and Viner (2019). The important factor is how children engage with screens. If children are passively consuming content for long spells, this could impact on social and physical development. The role of a skilled practitioner is to ensure that technology is used actively to create opportunities to communicate, collaborate, explore and create content.

The following task supports reflection and understanding of your own practice.

Task 6.1: Developing your practice

- How would you support children to use a tablet to create their own films to tell small-world stories?
- How would you ensure that this still allows for open-ended exploration and play with a real-life outcome?

Even though the term technology is no longer explicitly mentioned in the curriculum it does not remove it from practice. A settings-based curriculum goes beyond the statutory documents and encompasses the totality of all experiences that they offer to children. It should be open ended and flexible and developed to support and engage the children. Quality early years practice should be built from children's interests and designed to encourage children to explore and make sense of the world around them. Technology is such a significant part of that world; we therefore must embed it into practice and provision.

OFSTED (2022) suggests that children need to explore and practice skills that are developed alongside practitioners to fully embed them. This is particularly important when introducing new pieces of technology, for example, letting children explore the natural environment with electronic microscopes such as Easi scopes. Easy, handheld devices that connect to screens to allow children to explore textures and surfaces while creating a sense of awe and wonder, still require knowledgeable adults to support and scaffold deeper thinking.

Children are growing up in a visual world and many are used to taking and editing images from an early age. This allows them to see themselves in the world and to capture emotions or ideas; skills that children acquire long before reading and writing. This visual literacy is an important aspect of a child's development and can be harnessed throughout the curriculum in many ways such as the use of visual timetables or to document their own learning through photographs. It should always be remembered that not all children have a wide access to technology or the latest devices. Early years practitioners continue to use the essential early years skills of interaction and relationship building to understand what children already know and understand when using technology.

Digital divides: classroom and home

The lack of curriculum guidance around the teaching of technology presents a potential barrier to practitioners trying to identify best practice or looking to justify its inclusion. The lack of guidance also suggests that it is a low priority for curriculum-makers, whose apparent preference for traditional forms of literacy (i.e., the written or printed word and books) still dominate. Alternatively, it could be demonstrative of a reluctance to specify the way that children should learn about technology, perhaps because of its evolving nature and the assumption that it is already taught across the curriculum, as suggested by the Secretary of State for Digital, Culture, Media and Sport (HM Government, 2020). This raises the question of whether children are assumed to be 'digital natives' who develop a natural understanding of the digital technology that has surrounded them since birth (Prensky, 2001). However, there is a danger in this assumption (Dooly and Darvin, 2022), as it risks moving the responsibility for critical reflection of technology use onto younger users.

Other concerns about the extent to which digital technology is integrated into young children's learning may be linked to the amount of time young children spend with digital technology away from school. Prior to the Covid-19 lockdown, the UK government identified excessive screen time as a growing concern in their Online Harms White Paper (HM Government, 2019) and the World Health Organisation (2019) recommended that children under two years of age should not have any screen time at all. However, current research shows that concerns from parents are varied and linked to the type of online activity. For example, Ofcom (2022, p.14), reports that more parents of 3–4-year-olds agree that the benefits of playing online games outweighs the risks. Research by Marsh *et al.* (2018) supports the ability of digital technologies, in particular apps, to stimulate creativity and imaginative play in pre-school children. However, there is also acknowledgement that the rule-bound nature of some apps can inhibit very young children's free-play, choice and agency. It is important therefore that when technology is used to develop children's learning across the curriculum, its impact is assessed to determine whether it is providing an educational advantage to the non-digital alternative, as well as considering cost (Education Endowment Foundation [EEF], 2021).

To promote digital inclusion, it is important for teachers to understand the role that they can play in ensuring greater equality of access to digital technology and address the 'digital divide' (Jenkins, 2009; Lythreatis, Singh and El-Kassar, 2021) that has become more apparent to practitioners post-Covid-19 (Ofqual, 2021). Schools are well-placed to address digital exclusion, which research by Holmes and Burgess (2021) suggests is more likely amongst lower-income households (Office of National Statistics [ONS], 2019), by enabling young children's access to a range of digital technologies. This is especially important in the light of correlated links between digital capability and academic achievement, with Hu *et al.* (2018) citing evidence from the Programme for International Student Assessments (PISA) data from the Organization for Economic Co-operation and Development (OECD) in 2015. Now please look at Task 6.2.

Task 6.2: Perceptions of home use of technology

- Thinking about developing positive relationships with parents, how could early years practitioners develop a true understanding of children's use of technology in the home?
- Reflect on your own unconscious bias of children's use of mobile phones in the home. Are you allowing this bias to influence your use of technology in the classroom?
- How could you support parents who are concerned about their young child's technology usage?

Recent changes in practice and pedagogy

Fostering digital literacy in early years provides one way in which to make learning with technology culturally relevant (Plowman and Stephen, 2007; Parette, Quesenberry and Blum, 2010). The use of technology is changing the way that young children participate in social play (Arnott, 2016) and make meaning of cultural life (Edwards, 2013). It is increasingly allowing young children to experience and display their skills and characteristics beyond the traditional methods such as books, pencils and paper (Levy, 2009; O'Mara and Laidlaw, 2011). However, for some early years practitioners, the move to digitise children's learning in the classroom may seem quite unsettling without specific guidance (Palaiologou, 2014). Ingleby (2016) suggests that with the increase in children's agency, it is important to remember that for individual practitioners this can provide a challenge to their own self confidence with technology.

The growing concern amongst early years practitioners lies within visualising how technology integrates into the existing curriculum to support aspects of children's development, such as literacy and mathematics (Aubrey and Dahl, 2008). If we take this curriculum change and layer it with the existing uncertainty of adopting a digital pedagogy, such revision may take practitioners down a path that either seeks the best ways in which technology can support early learning and development and integrate this in playful ways (Bird and Edwards, 2014) or exclude digital technologies from the classroom on the grounds of statutory omission.

Around a similar time to the release of the revised statutory framework for the early years foundation stage, the education system experienced an unexpected digital catapult in 2020; the coronavirus pandemic changed the way practitioners practised and engaged with their children for a sustained time (Leask and Younie, 2022). With limited access to resources, a staple part of early years pedagogy, practitioners had to adapt to teaching digitally. Fortunately, the accessibility and affordability of education-based digital tools and software in recent years had already enabled practitioners to embrace smarter ways to evidence children's learning using digital software and platforms to store such achievements and share this with parents (Laxton, Cooper and Younie, 2021). So, for some practitioners, this plunge into teaching digitally further developed their confidence and technological repertoire, whereas for others no doubt it awoke the need to invest in their digital expertise.

The rise of social media and digital networking has been popularised since the pandemic; an aspect of professional learning that seems to be here to stay post-pandemic. This bitesize, learn-on-the-go knowledge exchange serves early years professionals well as it generally provides snapshots and digestible visions of how technologies can be integrated and interacted with by young children. For example, young children can use video editing software to create their own movies using construction materials and small-world resources to 'act out' their stories. Presenting digital software alongside familiar resourcing eases and opens the conversation about digital pedagogy.

There are many broad and nuanced factors for practitioners to consider, past that of personal experience and confidence, when we discuss systemic change to practice and pedagogy. What remains clear however is that practitioners should be encouraged to reflect on their own digital literacy as they would do with any other aspect of their pedagogy as part of their continual professional development. Practitioners' pedagogical beliefs about technology therefore influence how it is embedded in practice and it can be concluded that broader professional opportunities are needed to enhance teacher knowledge of children's use of technology if changes to pedagogy and practice are to modernise (Vidal-Hall, Flewitt and Wyse, 2020).

Young children's agency

Children are natural innovators and creators and developing their digital expertise is the modern way of complimenting their cognitive characteristics of what they see, hear, interpret and express with efficiency, productivity and creative flair. Children's understanding of technology supports their ability to solve problems, display their threads of thinking and showcase their knowledge in a variety of contexts (Moyle, 2010).

Using digital technologies can promote play and creativity across cultural, social, physical and cognitive domains and offer multimodal ways to engage children who otherwise may struggle with traditional practices, such as writing with a pencil and paper. Touch screens in particular ensure that children without good reading and writing skills are able to interact effectively with multimodal text on electronic devices. It can support children's difficulties with word reading and spelling as they can respond to aural instructions by dragging and dropping instead of having to type words, and immersive readers can enable them to hear aloud the written text. Touch screens can also support children's physical impairments, for example, they can do number exercises even if they cannot write numbers very well. They can match and organise shapes without the need for good motor skills. The formation of a number becomes much more understandable on a screen when colour and animation and a spoken instruction are available to help. Assistive technology is therefore a digital intervention that can support children to apply their knowledge.

It is useful, however, to hold in mind the words of Cingel (2021, p.298) who argues 'there is not a one-size-fits-all approach to technology use within the classroom'. Instead, when considering how we empower young children we should firstly reflect on what behaviours we are normalising. In the classroom for example, how often do teachers type their thoughts on a note or document, communicate with others via email or video conferencing, and record audio to capture the present moment. Although some adult-centred applications and software may present challenging interfaces for young children, there are attempts to merge thinking past that of seeing children as 'not ready' and more towards 'inexperienced'.

We can see this pedagogical shift happening more prominently in schools where young children are given the opportunities to exercise their digital literacy and creativity like adults do. Traditionally, for example, teachers display children's work to highlight their achievements; modernising such practice allows digital recordings of the work to be viewed by scanning or viewing the work through a digital device camera lens, offering explanations of written text or images. What was once a passive observation therefore has the potential to become an interactive experience. The same thinking applies to how children re-work their creations, adding digital depth to their 2D drawings by using applications that provide the addition of moving parts and speech in 3D. The advancement of digital skills and technologies means that experiences for our youngest children are becoming much deeper than simply searching for information on the internet instead of in a book.

Case Study 6.1: Exploring the MakEY project

Integrating digital technology into the classroom can also function as a supplement to traditional practices. The 'Makerspaces in the early years: enhancing digital literacy and creativity' (MakEY), an EU research-funded project that ran from 2017–2019, turned much-needed attention towards young children's (ages 3–8 years) engagement in digital and non-digital technologies and their development of digital skills for the 21st century (Marsh, 2020). Early years practitioners enrolled on the project were invited to use a range of traditional and contemporary books as a stimulus for which technological activities were centred around; MakEY boxes became the digital representation of the story sack concept.

Activities in the MakEY boxes are themed, such as light or nature, and offer digital experiences, such as coding and 3D creative design, alongside enhancing non-digital play like dough with circuits and LEDs and making box models move or vibrate. The project invited practitioners to see past the dominant rhetoric surrounding young children's entertainment with screen-based devices and opened up the space to triangulate children's characteristics of effective learning (children's learning dispositions and habits of mind) with their natural interest in science, maths and engineering, supporting the increased policy drivers around STEM (science, technology, engineering and maths) to foster future computer programmers and engineers.

Young children recorded their thoughts in many ways including visually and using sound. They were still articulate through mediums that differed from traditional reading and writing activities. The children in the project had opportunities to express their creativity using digital technologies which, it could be suggested, served them better in demonstrating their knowledge, understanding and skills associated with a particular interest.

Supporting ITE students

Initial teacher education (ITE) is continually evolving with each ITE provider, using their own approaches and strategies to draw out what they see as important knowledge and skills for their trainee teachers. No one method is correct, but all have the same goal, to produce Early Career Teachers that have a passion for education, a desire to make a difference and start them on a journey of continued professional development that will see them grow in knowledge and skills throughout their career. To ensure consistency, depth of knowledge and a sound understanding of the complexities of teaching, the DfE have recently launched a common curriculum framework for providers called the Core Content Framework (DfE, 2019). This provides clear guidance on what to cover in training establishments as well as with expert colleagues in school.

ITE is an intense experience with training modules in complex areas including learning theory, safeguarding and inclusion as well as developing beginning teachers' core teaching skills e.g., how to sequence and plan for effective learning. ITE provides a foundation for beginning teachers to develop into reflective practitioners, equipping them with skills to evaluate and review their own practice and identify areas for future learning. Beginning teachers who embrace this reflective practice will become highly effective, organised and proficient in many areas including the use of technology. Reflective practice also requires analysis of new and potentially engaging methods of teaching and learning in a digital world.

A consequence of the global Covid-19 pandemic was the arrival of Virtual Learning Environments (VLEs) as a quick solution to teaching face-to-face in a virtual world. VLEs are platforms that have been around for over two decades but provided new pedagogical challenges for beginning teachers, practitioners and lecturers. During this period, online teaching and learning became the norm, causing a cultural shift in education (Velle *et al.*, 2020). ITE providers have modelled online teaching and hybrid approaches to learning as teaching in Higher Education has shifted in pedagogical approaches. Distance learning technology, once feared by beginning and qualified teachers, became standard practice almost overnight in order to solve the problem of potentially missed education (Eksail and Afari, 2020).

ITE aims to provide safe spaces for beginning teachers to practice their pedagogical approaches and try new ideas with the support of school mentors. The experience they gain from using everyday teacher technology is vital, from tracking systems for attendance and attainment to target setting and writing reports, technology is embedded in everything teachers do. Planning and assessment on virtual networks. creating resources and presentations on PowerPoint or Activlearn, searching sites like Twinkl or NCETM to find relevant resources, communicating with parents through messaging apps, sharing progress and children's work through software like Learning Ladders, encouraging reading at home with apps like Fonetti. The list of software is endless, touching every aspect of school life.

One of the biggest barriers to teachers' extending their use of technology is the fear of using it. As Hatzigianni and Kalaitzidis (2018) suggest the profession is not yet ready to embrace the social inevitability of the proliferation of technology in EYFS. Yet the beginning teachers coming through ITE are already on this journey, these digital natives (Prensky, 2001) are the most competent technology users ever. ITE provision therefore is designed to ensure that these skills are honed for the classroom. Through assignments, beginning teachers practice the skills they will need to be effective, creating presentations, lesson plans and multi-sensory resources. They will also need to consider how to incorporate technology effectively into all aspects of learning and most importantly ensure they have the confidence and understanding to determine which tools to use for most impact. Technology has become part of the fabric of society, but as Bhatt and MacKenzie (2019) point out, without strong digital literacy skills our beginning teachers will struggle to determine what is useful.

Interactive whiteboards changed the way classrooms worked at the start of the 21st century. We moved from a transmission model of teaching to a more responsive approach with technology at the centre. Technology allows beginning teachers to transport children into other worlds through interactive boards; the internet opens the wonders of the world by putting virtual visits to museums and galleries in every classroom. It allows children to link with other schools across the world and share their stories through email and online conferencing platforms like Zoom and Pictures.

Summary and key points

It is clear that technology is here to stay, and all children need to learn about *how* it operates in our increasingly digital world.

- This chapter exemplifies the ways in which we can create opportunities for children to actively learn *with* and *about* technology, to foster the digital and computational skills that they need now and in the future.
- The chapter provides a consideration of the impact of learning *through* technology and whether this is greater than non-digital alternatives?
- Awareness of the digital divides caused by poverty and age is essential as is understanding ways that this may be alleviated at school level.
- The role of ITE then is not to teach trainee teachers how to use specific pieces of software or hardware although it undoubtedly will form part of their learning, but it

is to open their eyes to how they could incorporate what they already know and use to inspire learning.

- Programmes and software will change rapidly but the attitudes and approaches will remain.
- The perception of trainees' own technology skills is important as this has a direct impact on them moving forward as effective teachers (Sansone *et al.*, 2019).

Further resources

Computing at School website https://www.computingatschool.org.uk/.
   This website provides a wealth of information for those starting out as well as those leading on computing in the EYFS.
Arnott, L. (ed.) (2017). *Digital technologies and learning in the early years*. London: SAGE Publications Ltd.
   This book is a great resource for those who would like to understand how children may experience technology. It also offers case studies from a global perspective.
Hello Ruby books https://www.helloruby.com/books.
   Hello Ruby has a series of books and also a website to support young children to learn about computing and technology.

References

Arnott, L. (2016). An ecological exploration of young children's digital play: framing children's social experiences with technologies in early childhood. *Early Years*, 36(3), 271–288. DOI: 10.1080/09575146.2016.1181049.
Aubrey, C. and Dahl, S. (2008). *A review of the evidence on the use of ICT in the Early Years Foundation Stage*. University of Warwick, Becta.
Bhatt, and MacKenzie, A. (2019). Just Google it! Digital literacy and the epistemology of ignorance. *Teaching in Higher Education*, 24(3), 302–317.
Bird, J. and Edwards, S. (2014). Children learning to use technologies through play: A digital play framework. *British Journal of Educational Technology*, 46(6), 1149–1160.
Cingel, D.P. (2021). Exploring key issues in early childhood and technology. *Journal of Children and Media*, 15(2), 297–299. DOI: 10.1080/17482798.2021.1896201.
Department for Children, Schools and Families (DCSF) (2008). *The Early Years Foundation Stage: Setting the standards for learning, development and care for children from birth to five*. London: DCSF.
Department for Education (DfE) (2019). *Initial teacher training (ITT): Core content framework*. https://www.gov.uk/government/publications/initial-teacher-training-itt-core-content-framework.
Department for Education (DfE) (2021). *Early years foundation stage (EYFS) statutory framework*. https://www.gov.uk/government/publications/early-years-foundation-stage-framework--2.
Dooly, M. and Darvin, R. (2022). Intercultural communicative competence in the digital age: Critical digital literacy and inquiry-based pedagogy. *Language and Intercultural Communication*, 22(3), 354–366.
Education Endowment Foundation (2021). *Using digital technology to improve learning*. https://educationendowmentfoundation.org.uk/education-evidence/guidance-reports/digital.
Edwards, S. (2013). Digital play in the early years: A contextual response to the problem of integrating technologies and play-based pedagogies in the early childhood curriculum. *European Early Childhood Research Journal*, 21(2), 1752–1807. DOI: 10.1080/13502936.2013.789190.
Eksail, F.A.A. and Afari, E. (2020). Factors affecting trainee teachers' intention to use technology: A structural equation modeling approach. *Education and Information Technologies*, 25(4), 2681–2697.

Evans, J. (2004). *Literacy moves on: Using popular culture, new technologies and critical literacy in the primary classroom*. David Fulton Publishers. https://doi.org/10.4324/9780203963272.

Flewitt, R., Messer, D. and Kucirkova, N. (2015). New directions for early literacy in a digital age: The iPad. *Journal of Early Childhood Literacy*, 15(3), 289–310.

Hatzigianni, M. and Kalaitzidis, I. (2018). Early childhood educators' attitudes and beliefs around the use of touchscreen technologies by children under three years of age. *British Journal of Education Technology*, 49, 883–895.

Holmes, H. and Burgess, B. (2021). *New horizons: Digital exclusion and the importance of getting online*. Cambridge Centre for Housing and Planning Research. University of Cambridge. https://www.cchpr.landecon.cam.ac.uk/files/media/new_horizons_digital_exclusion_report_final.pdf.

HM Government. (2019). *Online harms white paper*. https://assets.publishing.service.gov.uk/government/uploads/system/uploads/attachment_data/file/973939/Online_Harms_White_Paper_V2.pdf.

HM Government. (2020). *Government response to the digital, culture, media and sport select committee report on immersive and addictive technologies*. https://assets.publishing.service.gov.uk/media/5ede300cd3bf7f2c9f49a1fd/CCS207_CCS0520664408-001_Gov_Resp_DCMS_Committee_Report_CP_241_Web_Accessible__1___1_.pdf.

Hu, X., Gong, Y., Lai, C. and Leung, F. (2018). The relationship between ICT and student literacy in mathematics, reading, and science across 44 countries: A multilevel analysis. *Computers & Education*, 125, 1–13. https://doi.org/10.1016/j.compedu.2018.05.021.

Ingleby. E. (2016). 'We don't just do what we're told to do!' Exploring pedagogical technology development needs. *International Journal of Early Years Education*, 24(1), 36–48.

Jenkins, H. (2009). *Confronting the challenges of participatory culture: Media education for the 21st century*. The MIT Press.

Kress, G. (2003). *Literacy in the new media age*. Abingdon: Routledge.

Laxton, D., Cooper, L. and Younie, S. (2021). Translational research in action: The use of technology to disseminate information to parents during the COVID-19 pandemic. *British Journal of Educational Technology*, 52(4), 1538–1553. https://doi.org/10.1111/bjet.13100.

Leask, M. and Younie, S. (2022). *Education for all in times of crisis: Lessons from Covid-19*. Abingdon: Routledge.

Levy, R. (2009). 'You have to understand words...but not read them': Young children becoming readers in a digital age. *Journal of Research in Reading*, 32, 75–91.

Lythreatis, S., Singh, S. and El-Kassar, A. (2021). The digital divide: A review and future research agenda. *Technological Forecasting and Social Change*, 175, 1–11.

Marsh, J., Plowman, L., Yamada-Rice, D., Bishop, J., Lahmar, J. and Scott, F. (2018). Play and creativity in young children's use of apps. *British Journal of Educational Technology*, 49(5), 870–882. https://doi.org/10.1111/bjet.12622.

Marsh, J. (2019). Researching the digital literacy and multimodal practices of young children: A European agenda for change. In O. Erstad, R. Flewitt, B. Kümmerling-Meibauer, and Í. S. P. Pereira (eds.), *The Routledge handbook of digital literacies in early childhood* (pp. 19–30). Abingdon: Routledge.

Marsh, J. (2020). Makerspaces in the early years: Enhancing digital literacy and creativity. In C. Donohue (ed.), *Key issues in technology and early childhood*. Abingdon: Routledge.

Moyle, K. (2010). *Building innovation: Learning with technologies*. Australian Council for Educational Research.

Ofcom. (2022). *Children and parents: Media use and attitudes report 2022*. https://www.ofcom.org.uk/__data/assets/pdf_file/0024/234609/childrens-media-use-and-attitudes-report-2022.pdf.

Office for National Statistics. (2019). *Exploring the UK's digital divide. London: Office for National Statistics*. https://www.ons.gov.uk/peoplepopulationandcommunity/householdcharacteristics/homeinternetandsocialmediausage/articles/exploringtheuksdigitaldivide/2019-03-04.

Ofqual. (2021). *Learning during the pandemic: Review of research from England.* https://www.gov.uk/government/publications/learning-during-the-pandemic/learning-during-the-pandemic-review-of-research-from-england.

OFSTED (2022). *Education inspection framework.* https://www.gov.uk/government/publications/education-inspection-framework.

O'Mara, J. and Laidlaw, L. (2011). Living in the iworld: Two literacy researchers reflect on the changing texts and literacy practices of childhood. *English Teaching: Practice and Critique*, 10, 149–159.

Palaiologou, I. (2014). Children under five and digital technologies: Implications for early years pedagogy. *European Early Childhood Education Research Journal*, 24, 1–20.

Parette, H., Quesenberry, A. and Blum, C. (2010). Missing the boat with technology usage in early childhood settings: A 21st century view of developmentally appropriate practice. *Early Childhood Education Journal*, 37, 335–343.

Plowman, L. and Stephen, C. (2007). Guided interaction in preschool settings. *Journal of Computer Assisted Learning*, 23, 14–21.

Prensky, M. (2001). Digital natives, digital immigrants Part 1. *On the Horizon*, 9(5), 1–6.

Richards, D., Caldwell, P. H. and Go, H. (2015). Social media and the health of young people. *Journal of Paediatrics and Child Health*, 51, 1152–1157.

Rubinstein, E. A. (1978). Television and the young viewer: The pervasive social influence of television on children is being increasingly documented, but has yet to be translated into a continuing and effective social policy. *American Scientist*, 66(6), 685–693.

Sansone, A., Cesareni, D. Bortolotti, I. and Buglass, S. (2019). Teaching technology-mediated collaborative learning for trainee teachers. *Technology, Pedagogy and Education*, 28(3), 381–394.

Stiglic, N. and Viner, R. M. (2019). Effects of screentime on the health and well-being of children and adolescents: A systematic review of reviews. *BMJ Open*, 9(1), e023191.

Tickell, C. (2011). *The early years: Foundations for life, health, and learning – An independent report on the Early Years Foundation Stage to Her Majesty's Government, Department for Education.* https://assets.publishing.service.gov.uk/media/5a7ac0ec40f0b66a2fc02915/DFE-00177-2011.pdf.

Velle, L., Newman, S. Montgomery C. and Hyatt, D. (2020). Initial teacher education in England and the Covid-19 pandemic: Challenges and opportunities. *Journal of Education for Teaching*, 46(4), 596–608.

Vidal-Hall, C., Flewitt, R. and Wyse, D. (2020). Early childhood practitioner beliefs about digital media: Integrating technology into a child-centered classroom environment. *European Early Childhood Education Research Journal*, 28(2), 167–181. DOI: 10.1080/13502936.2020.1735727.

Vygotsky, L. S. (2004). Imagination and creativity in childhood [M.E. Sharpe, Inc. (Trans.)]. *Journal of Russian and East European Psychology*, 42, 7–97. (Original work written 1930).

Wing, J. M. (2006). Computational thinking. *Communications of the ACM*, 49(3), 33–35. https://doi.org/10.1145/1118178.1118215.

World Health Organisation. (2019). *Guidelines on physical activity, sedentary behaviour and sleep for children under 5 years of age.* https://apps.who.int/iris/bitstream/handle/10665/325147/WHO-NMH-PND-2019.4-eng.pdf?sequence=1&isAllowed=y.

7   Digital technology and art

Jean Edwards

Introduction

Before discussing the merits of how digital technologies can support the teaching of art, it is necessary to begin by reminding ourselves of the key components to any art curriculum in primary schools. These include:

- using a range of practical materials, techniques and processes such as drawing, painting, collage, printmaking, textiles, sculpture and other three-dimensional techniques and increasingly, digital technologies to make art
- learning about the visual elements of line, tone, colour, texture, pattern, shape, space and form in the art we make and the art made by others
- responding to art made by a diverse range of artists, craftspeople and designers from different times, cultures and locations.

Digital technology can and should contribute to and be a part of all of these components and has some unique qualities of its own to enhance and transform the art curriculum. We might consider how the digital tools, apps and sites available can, first, support the making and viewing of art and, second, can be a process and technique of their own, standing alongside drawing, painting, collage, sculpture and textiles. Going further, Hickman and Heaton (2016:19) note the potential for digital technologies to harness creativity, collaboration within and beyond the classroom and further cross-cultural understanding. The OECD (2019:8–10) identifies the key role that music and arts play in developing cognitive and metacognitive skills along with the need for pupils' digital skills to evolve alongside technological developments.

In any primary art curriculum, the components noted above are likely to be found, perhaps expressed in different ways, different combinations and with different levels of detail. The current national curriculum framework for England in its relative brevity allows teachers and schools to interpret and make choices as they seek to 'engage, inspire and challenge pupils, equipping them with the knowledge and skills to experiment, invent and create their own works of art, craft and design (Department for Education, 2014:225).

This chapter will provide you with an introduction and some practical guidance to incorporate digital technologies into your art curriculum both in making and responding to art.

DOI: 10.4324/9781003408925-7

Objectives

At the end of this chapter you should be able to:

- understand how digital technologies can be integrated into the art curriculum to support and enhance learning
- understand how digital technologies can be used to transform some art making into a more wholly digital form
- explore some digital sites, tools and apps that are useful in the primary art curriculum
- explore some art made by artists who use digital technologies in their artmaking.

Digital technology and the art curriculum

The existing art curriculum in your school will have techniques and artists mapped out across half terms, years and key stages in themes or units of work. These might be underpinned by a published scheme, by units devised by the school or a mixture of both. Many published schemes are increasingly including optional digital approaches in their materials: these include Access Art, Kapow and the Oak National Academy resources. There is potential for you to critically evaluate your current art curriculum and start to integrate digital technologies into your existing art curriculum.

You might consider this evaluation and change in relation to enhancement and transformation outlined in the Substitution, Augmentation, Modification and Re-definition (SAMR) model (Puentedura, 2015), see Table 7.1. When evaluating the use of digital technologies in the art curriculum you could consider:

- Enhancement: where digital technologies can support and be a part of a unit that is based around a technique or process, such as using the photocopier to enlarge drawings; using a painting app to explore tones of a colour or exploring the work of an artist in an online gallery. Here digital technologies are used as a tool to support aspects of the learning but where the outcome will be non-digital.
- Transformation: where digital technologies can be the process itself or a key part of it leading to an outcome which is digital in nature and does not exist outside the digital world, such as making a digital animation to play on a screen or taking and manipulating photos to create a new image or video clip. Here digital technologies are a tool to transform learning.

In Table 7.1 some examples in the context of the art curriculum are included to start your thinking about your own art planning and teaching.

Table 7.1 The SAMR model in the context of art

Re-definition	Transformation	Making a piece of art that is made using digital
Technology allows for the creation of new tasks, previously inconceivable		tools and can be seen and experienced only in the digital world, for example, making and placing objects in augmented reality.

(Continued)

Table 7.1 (Continued)

Modification Technology allows for significant task redesign		Making a piece of art that is made with both physical materials and digital tools, for example, where pupils make a mini-sculpture and use digital tools to change its scale and insert it into real world locations.
Augmentation Technology acts as a direct tool substitute with functional improvement	Enhancement	An app or tool is used that works in a similar way to a physical tool with some additional and different features, for example, a drawing / painting app is used to make marks and explore colour on the screen with quick and easy colour choice and change of width and opacity of marks.
Substitution Technology acts as a direct tool substitute, with no functional change		An app or tool is available as a substitute or short cut, for example, looking at a reproduction of a piece of art in a book or on the screen of a laptop.

Adapted from Puentedura's (2015) SAMR model.

In the art curriculum we would not be seeking to replace all art learning with digital approaches but rather to provide pupils with opportunities to use digital devices and tools as part of their repertoire so that they can make purposeful choices and extend their creativity. As Hickman and Eglinton (2014:156) state 'we need to ensure that the activities done by students in 'art' lessons are meaningful and worthwhile for the digital age, while valuing traditional practice that values craft and skill in meaning-making'.

The art curriculum and long-term plan, scheme or units of work that support teachers in their planning and teaching will likely be well-established around the traditional and longstanding techniques and processes such as drawing, painting, printmaking etc. As a teacher you might wish to consider how to integrate digital technologies into your art curriculum and develop them more fully. A first step on this pathway is to identify the digital devices, tools, apps and sites that are currently available in school and those which you might want to plan to budget for in the future.

Identifying the digital technologies available

One of the barriers to integrating digital technologies into the art curriculum can be the concern that specific, different and expensive equipment is necessary. A starting point is to review the devices and the apps, tools and sites that are readily available to you and use these to build from. The software already installed on the devices used in classrooms has the potential to be used in art making and viewing.

It is possible to use the drawing tools available within Microsoft, Apple and Google software if there isn't a specific art tool or app available. It is also possible to work in stop motion, digital animation and green screen in this software too. There may be software that is used in other curriculum areas that can also be used in art: whatever coding tool you use in computing will likely have the possibility of making art; you can attach a pencil or pen to the programmable robots you use and a digital magnifier or microscope can enhance observational drawing. Using the internet to access collections of art and artists' work on screen and through augmented and virtual reality is also possible.

As with any art making it will be necessary to buy some tools just as the school would buy drawing pencils, brushes and print rollers. If you have identified what is already available and planned to use it as effectively as possible you can then make some informed decisions about which apps and tools it is necessary to budget for and purchase over time as you develop your art curriculum with more digital approaches becoming built in.

Task 7.1 can help you to gather the information you need.

Task 7.1: Identifying the digital technologies you can access and use

Task 7.1	Possibilities	In your setting
Digital devices	PCs Laptops Tablets Other mobile devices Photocopiers / scanners Cameras Stands / tripods for tablets or cameras Visualiser Projector / mobile projector VR headsets / handsets	
Art-specific devices	Styluses to use on tablets or screens Lightbox	
General software, apps, tools, sites	Microsoft (Word, Powerpoint, Excel) Apple (Notes, Pages, Keynote, Numbers) Google (Docs, Slides, Sheets) Safe internet search tools	
Art specific software, apps, tools, sites	Photo collage maker Photo / video editing tool Art making apps (open) Art making apps (closed) Green screen Stop motion Digital animation AR and VR apps	
Apps, tools and sites used in other subjects but also useful in art	Coding apps, tools, sites such as Scratch Programmable robots Digital microscopes / magnification apps	

In completing Task 7.1 you will have a clearer view of what is available and can plan to work from the existing devices, sites, apps and tools available to you and plan ahead to budget for some art-specific digital resources.

Using digital technology to enhance practical art making

There are many tools available to use through digital technology that pupils can use in art making to enhance their learning. In some instances these can make learning more engaging or inclusive for pupils. These include using the scanner / photocopier to make copies, enlarge and reduce; exploring composition using the shapes available in slide making tools alongside exploring still life; using a digital magnifier or microscope to zoom in and draw from observation and using the remove background / green screen tool to combine images and backgrounds and change their scale. In this section you will explore one approach where using digital tools can combine with and complement working with real materials.

Drawing and painting on screen

Creating marks and images on the screen of digital devices using a mouse, finger or stylus is an aspect of digital art making that can complement drawing with pencils and painting with brushes on surfaces. There are simple and more complex sites, apps and tools that can be used in the classroom to explore this with children. In Task 7.2 you will be guided to explore the tools within a digital painting and drawing app. This will help you get to know it and consider how to use it with your pupils.

Task 7.2: Exploring digital tools to paint and draw

When teaching art it is always important to try out tools, materials and processes for yourself. This gives you an understanding of how they work and how they can best be used in your classroom.

Explore a drawing or painting tool already available to you or from the list below. Have a go with:

- the mark making tools (Which tools are available? What sort of marks do they make? How can they be changed? (width / opacity)
- the colour changing tools (How are the colours presented? (grid, spectrum, sliders)
- any other options (shapes, shape fill, shape outline, eraser)
- how the image can be saved and if it can be edited later

Evaluate how the site, app or tool works and consider the benefits and challenges in relation to your pupils' age and experience with the devices and software. Think about how it could be used to support exploration of colour, line and shape in combination with using physical art materials such as pencils, felt pens and paint.

You could try one or two of:

Drawing tools in slide making software eg Keynote on an iPad or Powerpoint on a laptop
Site: PaintZ https://paintz.app/
Site: Tate Paint https://www.tate.org.uk/kids/games-quizzes/tate-paint
App: if your school already has any art specific apps such as Draw and Tell, Brushes, ArtSet, Tayasui Sketches, ProCreate, you could try one of those here.

While there are some features in common with using 'real' drawing and painting tools on surfaces, the differences are why you might build in these digital opportunities to your drawing and painting units in the art curriculum. Borg (2019:17) notes the way that digital painting tools are 'reminiscent of, but still not the same as, analogue painting'. Matthews and Seow (2007:258) suggest that the way the tones and hues of colours can be selected from a logical visual presentation allows pupils to select, use and mix many colours that they would find challenging to mix using pigment. This could support pupils' learning about colour, using it in their own art making across a range of processes and responding to it in the art made by others. Price *et al.* (2015:139) note the potential of digital painting on iPads for including some pupils who dislike the sensation of using practical materials or find the management of them physically problematic.

Building in opportunities to use digital apps, tools and sites within units that are primarily focused upon practical art making can widen the possibilities and provide new ways in that enhance the art learning through use of the technology.

Using digital technology to transform practical art making

Establishing some units of work in the art curriculum that are mainly or wholly digital in nature may inspire you to use existing technologies in a more creative way or introduce some new technologies for the art curriculum. In this section some possibilities will be explored including making digitally animated gifs; working in augmented reality and connecting art making with computing.

Making animated gifs

The slide making tools built into the devices that are often used in schools can be used in art to design and create images with moving elements that can be captured and shared as gifs, existing only in the digital world. A gif, short for graphics interchange format, is a visual artefact that although saved and shared as an image contains movement. Working in this way can involve pupils composing images using shape, colour, line, pattern and digital effects in combination and thinking through a series of actions in order to add movement by causing elements to appear, move and disappear. The limited time available can focus their thinking: gifs are short, up to 15 seconds in length and often shorter than this. The use of a list of steps in order can be linked to their learning about and making their own algorithms in the computing curriculum. In the example screenshot in Figure 7.1 you can see use of shapes and drawn lines as well as the animation steps list, which can be reordered to change the way the gif plays. Although pupils' gifs will only be visible digitally, they are easy to play on school screens; embed into school websites and use on social media. If they are added to a Padlet they will all play continuously and each one can be attached to a QR code which can be stuck into each pupil's sketchbook as their finished outcome.

Working in augmented reality

Pupils are aware of and are likely to be active users of augmented, mixed and virtual realities in their play at home and outside in the world as many locations now use these approaches in play and leisure. Dede *et al.* (2017:8) suggest that the immersive nature of this

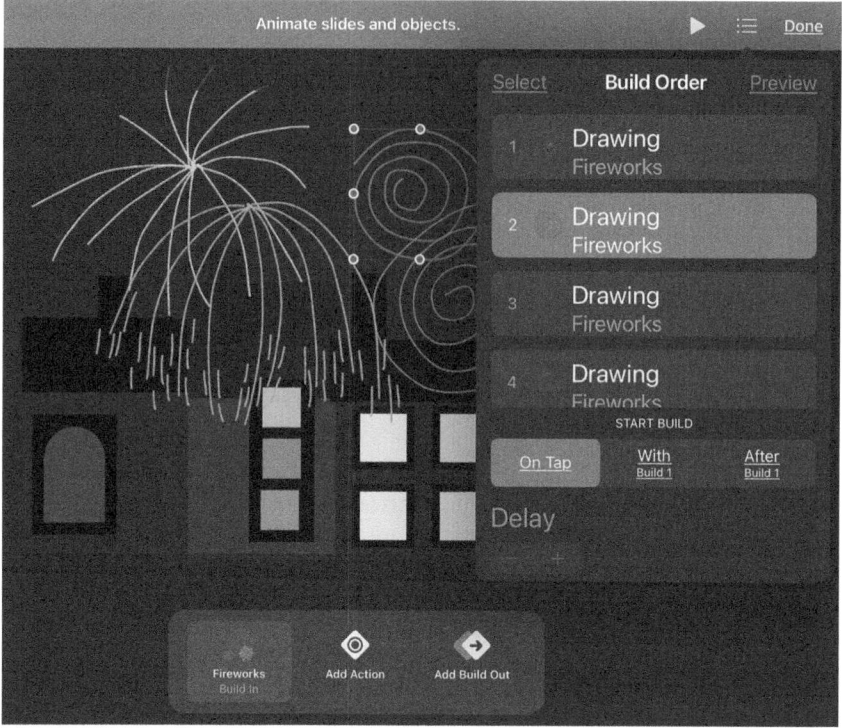

Figure 7.1 Animated gif (order of animation steps)

kind of activity when used in learning allows those using the tools to create within their own immersive environments in a constructionist approach 'based on the assumption that knowledge occurs best through building artefacts (physical or digital) that can be experienced or shared (Papert, 1991)'. Since this is a relatively new area it is useful to explore some definitions so that we can use the vocabulary accurately with pupils.

Some definitions of key terms

Virtual reality (VR): sensory immersion using a helmet and hand controls to create the illusion of being in a simulated setting and interacting with it.

Augmented or mixed reality (AR): a combination of physical and digital, such as being able to see and 'capture' Pokemon outdoors using a mobile device.

Multi-user virtual environment (MUVE): using a digital avatar to be immersed in a digital world on screen, as in Minecraft.

(Adapted from Dede *et al.*, 2017:3–4)

Virtual reality is increasingly used in schools to provide pupils with experiences that they could not readily have in real life in subjects across the curriculum: going on virtual field trips to significant locations in geography and history, for example. In these experiences they might view and interact but if we can use these tools in the art curriculum pupils can be the creators of what they see in the VR and AR environments, an infinitely more powerful experience. It is possible for pupils to use the devices we have in classrooms to create in augmented reality.

Two ways in are to create surface patterns, by using either physical art materials or art making apps and 'wrap' these around 3d objects in the free IOS app ARMakr, or to make digital objects in any painting app or tool that has the feature to save on a transparent background (Keynote, Powerpoint, Sketches) and then imported into ARMakr. In both these instances pupils can then use the features available in ARMakr to position their art in augmented reality and add movement to it, screen recording it to capture it as a complete piece of video art that can be replayed to viewers. Working collaboratively to make and combine individual digital pieces into a combined piece of AR art can be an inspiring next step.

In Table 7.2 there are three apps that can be used in the primary classroom to make and place art in AR and VR, which are explained as a way of introducing them to you.

Table 7.2 Apps to make and place art in AR and VR

Apps	Information	Notes and examples
ARMakr	For Apple devices Free https://www.armakr.app/	ARMakr is a free app that allows users to import their own creations, place them in augmented reality, add movement to them and record them. You can explore a how to digital book exploring an AR project here: https://read.bookcreator.com/tg913HXhY6gHEVix2Qnd01mxJ8h1/uun1sp7eQRWYOpxTH2mdJw.
CoSpaces Edu	For Apple devices and available via a website https://cospaces.io/edu/ Free and pro versions	CoSpaces is a site and app that allows objects and spaces to be made in virtual reality and shared with viewers as a VR experience. You can explore an example of a collaborative art gallery made by pupils in the UK and Denmark: https://edu.cospaces.io/QFG-WVY.
ScavangarEDU	For Apple devices Free https://www.scavangar.world/about	ScavangarEDU is an app that allows you to import digital objects into a real-world space, place them and then challenge others to find them using mobile devices. Pupils can navigate their way around looking for art that their friends have made and collect it as they follow a route. You can explore experiences others have made in the app to see what is possible.

When we think about art created by digital technologies in augmented and virtual reality alongside the drawings, paintings, prints and sculptures that we have always explored in schools it is interesting that research by Flint *et al.* (2018:205) noted that in their collaborative creation of a sculpture park in Minecraft children 'frequently respond[ed], react[ed], and engage[d] the same across both the real and virtual representations'.

Art and computing

There can be positive and valuable connections between pupils' learning in computing and their making in the art curriculum. Many pupils are first introduced to coding through using 'Scratch', a free tool available online here: https://scratch.mit.edu/. (See Chapters 17 on programming in primary schools and 24 on coding.) Scratch can be used to create art on the screen by choosing the Pen extension tools which allow pupils to use the sprite as a pen and pick up and put down the pen, change the size of the line, set and change colours of the line and erase.

In addition to this there are apps and online tools that allow pupils to explore generative art: art made using algorithms. In the free app 'Endless Art' pupils can experiment with changing parameters of shape, colour, position, size and rotation to see how their changes affect the art generated on the screen. This can inspire their own abstract painting or collage or be a piece of video art in itself.

Digital technology and viewing and responding to art

As well as making art, a key part of the art curriculum is that pupils will learn about artists, craft makers and designers and respond to their art as viewers, evaluating and analysing it (Department for Education, 2014:225). Some additional detail is provided as pupils progress through key stages but the very lack of specificity and detail enables schools and teachers to make their own choices about the art their pupils engage with and personalise the curriculum to their school and locality. Digital technologies provide a wealth of resources to support this and ensure that teachers have access to a diverse range of artists from times, places and cultures around the world to use as inspiration and role models in their curriculum. The National Society of Education in Art and Design (NSEAD) is a vital resource here and provides an Anti-Racist Art Education Checklist to support teachers in making thoughtful choices of artists, works of art and consider how they are used appropriately. The checklist is available here: https://scratch.mit.edu/.

Selecting and viewing art

In practical terms digital technology is vital to teachers and pupils in their access to artists and works of art through using what is available through artists' own websites and through local, regional, national and international art galleries and their collections. This might be through looking at art on the large screen in the classroom, exploring collections on laptops and tablets or using AR and VR gallery tours. Google Arts and Culture allows you to find art galleries, artists and art chosen around themes as well as access resources to support creating art. Art UK is a site that is an online collection of art in the UK from public collections along with learning resources and the opportunity to make 'curations' so that you can collect groups of art works to use with pupils or allow them to make their own collections.

In Task 7.3 you can explore two key websites that support selecting, viewing and interacting with a wide range of art that can support your own subject knowledge and your teaching.

Task 7.3: Websites for selecting, viewing and interacting with art

Explore UK Arts (https://artuk.org/). If you create an account you can curate collections of the art available on the site. This is useful for using in the classroom. You might make collections based on artists (Rachel Whiteread), techniques (collage), types of art (landscape) or subjects (animals).

Explore Google Arts and Culture (https://artsandculture.google.com/). This tool offers a wide range of ways in to art collections around the world including virtual walk throughs in galleries, exploring categories of art (times, themes, collections, places, mediums, art movements and more) and suggested activities to explore art further.

As well as these national and international digital resources it is also useful for you to find and bookmark the websites for the galleries near to you.

Taken together these digital resources can help you bring a wide and diverse range of art into the art curriculum.

It has become so easy to 'collect' works of art digitally this aspect of the art curriculum is a useful context in which to reinforce the need for pupils to recognise and respect intellectual property, give credit to the artists and makers for their work and avoid taking and using copyrighted work, so that pupils 'use technology safely, respectfully and responsibly' (Department for Education, 2014:231).

Artists who work digitally

As well as incorporating digital technologies as tools for making art, it is important to widen the range of art and artists we introduce pupils to so that we include artists using digital technologies as part of or as their main media for creating art. In Task 7.4 you are introduced to some artists whose work using digital technologies you can explore as a starting point. You can also find examples of contemporary artists and their work shared on various social media channels so it's a good idea to save links to those that interest you in terms of the art curriculum in your school on a Padlet or on Pinterest so you can return to them later.

Now undertake Task 7.4 exploring artists who work digitally.

Task 7.4: Exploring artists who work digitally

Explore the art made by the artists suggested below and consider how they and their approaches could enrich your art curriculum either by being part of the artists pupils look at and respond to, and / or suggest ideas for making their own art taking inspiration from what they do.

Olafur Eliasson is an Icelandic artist whose art is often collaborative in nature and inspired by the effects of climate change. He uses digital technologies as part of creating his art and sometimes the end piece of art exists digitally only. You can explore his art here: https://olafureliasson.net/. Have a look at the piece called Earthspeakr and consider how it uses art and technology to connect children and read what the artists says about it as a piece of art.

Clare Willberg is a contemporary artist printmaker working in London. Alongside her printmaking she makes stop motion animations and films using elements of her printmaking practice. You can explore her art here: http://www.clairewillberg.com/. It is interesting to see her using both traditional materials and processes combined with digital technologies to create her digital work.

Harold Cohen was one of the early pioneers of computer-generated art. He created AARON, a computer program designed to make art and predicted the role that technologies would have in the arts. You can explore his art here: https://aaronshome.com/aaron/index.html. There are some useful resources related to Cohen's art available on the Computers at School site in 'resources' if you search for 'art'. You can join this organisation and it is a great source of support for computing and digital technologies.

Yayoi Kusama is a Japanese artist whose art is made using drawing, painting, sculpture, film, and installations. Her 'infinite mirror rooms' installations are immersive environments using light projections and mirrors that the viewer can walk through. You can explore her art here: https://www.tate.org.uk/kids/explore/who-is/who-yayoi-kusama and access a digital book about using her mirror rooms with pupils here: https://read.bookcreator.com/tg913HXhY6gHEVix2Qnd01mxJ8h1/mO64JKKnQVqrpbqBxBeuBw.

Digital technology and sharing art

Traditionally what pupils make in art lessons has been visible in classrooms and around the school on display. The additional use of digital technologies in helping to capture and record physical and digital art can lead to a wider audience for pupils' art, helping them gain a sense of motivation and appreciation from people beyond their immediate classroom. Capturing the process and finished pieces of art through video and photography is an effective way of saving and sharing outcomes especially where they are digital, collaborative or challenging to keep and store in real life. Art that pupils have made that is digital in outcome will need to be saved and shared in different ways. These could include using a class or individual digital sketchbook; attaching digital products to QR codes stuck into pupils' sketchbooks and adding links to video and images to a Padlet.

Digital tools can also be used to share pupils' work in digital galleries giving them the experience of being an artist whose art is seen by others on completion. Using tools such as Padlet, Google Slides and BookCreator to create digital galleries is straightforward. Going further, there are several digital tools available that support digital gallery making, including: ArtSteps (app and website), D EmptySpace (app and site) and various Art on the wall apps that present the art in augmented and / or virtual reality. Digital outcomes and galleries of these can be shared on school websites and through school social media, further valuing pupils' art.

Summary and key points

Digital technologies become available to use in primary classrooms with increasing rapidity and it is our responsibility as teachers to remain alert to the potential of these devices and tools to enhance and transform our teaching and the curriculum. Pupils are surrounded by visual culture and immersed in multimedia environments as users. Art can give them the opportunity to become creators and take active roles in making and sharing as well as enabling them to think critically about what they see on screens and in the digital world. Pavlou (2019:209) suggests that 'an art perspective that is technologically enhanced can transform the way knowledge is understood and competencies developed'.

Key points:

- Digital technologies can be used to support the making of art in other media.
- Digital technologies can be a main media in which to create art that exists and is viewed digitally.
- The visual elements of line, tone, colour, texture, pattern, shape, space and form can be explored through viewing and making with digital technologies.
- Digital technologies can provide us with access to a diverse range of artists, craftspeople and designers from different times, cultures and locations.
- We can explore art made using digital technologies and existing digitally.

Further resources

Access Art: https://www.accessart.org.uk/
  Access Art is a visual arts charity which supports learning and teaching of the visual arts in primary schools. You can browse the free resources available or subscribe as a school to access the full range of resources.
Computing at School: https://www.computingatschool.org.uk/
  Computing at School (CAS) is a community for teachers of computing. You can join CAS and have access to supporting resources, training opportunities and a network of supportive people.
Edwards, J., Caldwell, H. and Heaton, R. (2021) *Art in the primary school. Creating art in the real and digital world.* 2nd ed. Abingdon: Routledge.
  This is a handbook for beginner teachers of art with a focus on including digital technologies in the art curriculum.
Fermynwoods: https://fermynwoods.org/education/
  Fermynwoods is an educational charity based in Northamptonshire and online. It works with digital art and artists and pupils in a range of educational settings and there are many inspirational ideas and approaches outlined on its website.
Gomersal School Art site and blog: https://www.gomersalfirst.org.uk/our-classes/art-mrs-barrett
  This is an example of a school with a lively and contemporary art curriculum including use of digital technologies. You can explore examples of art projects here: http://gomersalprimaryschoolart.blogspot.com/
National Society for Education in Art and Design (NSEAD): https://www.nsead.org/
  NSEAD is the UK's art and design educators' professional body. It supports art and design education at all levels and has a wide range of supporting resources through its website and social media. Of particular interest is its Facebook support group for primary art educators Primary Art: Ask NSEAD https://www.facebook.com/groups/172951536063143 which is supported by a group of experienced art educators who answer questions daily.
Starter Padlet: https://uon1.padlet.org/jean_edwards/artappstools
  This is the padlet I use to help pupils and teachers get started with integrating digital technology into their art curriculum.

References

Borg, M. (2019) 'It's not for real': the tablet as palette in early childhood education. *International Journal of Education and the Arts.* 20 (14), pp.1–20.

Dede, C., Jacobson, J. and Richards, J. (2017) Introduction: virtual, augmented and mixed realities in education. In: Liu, D., Dede, C., Huang, R. and Richards, J. (eds.) *Virtual, augmented, and mixed realities in education*, pp.1–16. Singapore: Springer Singapore.

Department for Education. (2014) The national curriculum in England. Framework document. *GOV.UK.* [online] Available from: https://assets.publishing.service.gov.uk/government/uploads/system/uploads/attachment_data/file/381344/Master_final_national_curriculum_28_Nov.pdf [Accessed: 03/01/2023].

Flint, T., Hall, L., Stewart, F. and Hagan, D. (2018) Virtualizing the real: a virtual reality contemporary sculpture park for children. *Digital Creativity.* 29 (2), pp.191–207.

Hickman, R. and Eglinton, K. A. (2014) Visual art in the curriculum. In: Fleming, M., Bresler, L. and O'Toole. (eds.) *The Routledge international handbook of the arts and education*, pp.145–158. Abingdon: Routledge.

Hickman, R. and Heaton, R. (2016) Visual art. In: Wyse, D., Hayward, L. and Pandya, J. (eds.) *The SAGE handbook of curriculum, pedagogy and assessment*, pp.343–358. London: Sage.

Matthews, J. and Seow, P. (2007) Electronic paint: understanding children's representation through their interaction with digital paint. *The International Journal of Art and Design Education.* 26 (3), pp.251–263.

OECD (2019) Skills for 2030 concept note. *OECD.org* [online] Available from: https://www.oecd.org/education/2030-project/teaching-and-learning/learning/skills/Skills_for_2030_concept_note.pdf [Accessed 03/01/2023].

Papert, S. (1991). Situating constructionism. In: Harel, I. and Papert S. (eds.) *Constructionism: Research reports and essays, 1985–1990*, pp.1–11. Norwood, NJ: Ablex.

Pavlou, V. (2019) Art technology integration: digital storytelling as a transformative pedagogy in primary education. *iJADE.* 39 (1), pp.195–210.

Price, S., Jewitt, C. and Crescenzi, L. (2015) The role of iPads in pre-school children's mark making development. *Computers and Education.* 87, pp.131–141.

Puentedura, R. R. (2015) SAMR: a brief introduction. *Hippasus.com* [online] Available from: http://hippasus.com/blog/archives/227 [Accessed: 02/01/2023].

8 Technology and dialogue in the primary classroom

Gary Beauchamp, Nick Young and Louis Major

Introduction: the importance of dialogue in teaching and learning

Language is a teacher's main pedagogical tool. 'Classroom dialogue' can be thought of as a specific use of language, that involves using talk as a cultural and psychological tool in a way that is productive for learning (Major *et al.*, 2022). Dialogic teaching approaches emphasise dialogue through which pupils learn to discuss, reason, argue and explain to develop their higher-order thinking and oracy skills (Jay *et al.*, 2017). Through a process of thinking with others, dialogue can support teachers and learners to creatively build knowledge together (Wegerif, 2005). In this way, talk is not only used to interact, it is also used to 'interthink' (Littleton and Mercer, 2013).

Research suggests that learners' academic performance is influenced by the quality of educational dialogue in both small-group and whole-class situations (Cook *et al.*, 2018; Howe and Abedin, 2013). Evidence demonstrating the role of dialogue in improving learning continues to grow, including in primary school contexts. A 'dialogic teaching' intervention involving 5000 primary school children in England (aged 9–10) indicates a positive effect on attainment: pupils who experienced only 20 weeks of dialogic teaching made, on average, two months' additional progress on standardised tests relative to their peers (Alexander, 2018). Consistent positive effects in English, science and mathematics were found for all children. The result was similar when looking only at children eligible for free school meals.

Other large-scale research in UK primary schools demonstrates how, when pupil participation was high, high levels of elaboration and challenging of ideas were positively associated with national SATs test scores (Howe *et al.*, 2019). These findings are corroborated by a meta-analysis – examining 71 studies – that found peer interaction to be more effective in promoting learning in comparison with other types of learning conditions across gender and age groups (Tenenbaum *et al.*, 2019). Such outcomes are also consistent with other research on classroom dialogue, for instance demonstrating more positive attitudes to schooling (Resnick *et al.*, 2015) and the beneficial impact of dialogue on pupils' reasoning and problem-solving (T'Sas, 2018).

Wider work concerning the forms of classroom dialogue that are productive for learning indicates how these centre around exchanging, evaluating and ultimately reconciling contrasting perspectives (e.g. Michaels and O'Connor, 2012; Howe and Abedin, 2013). Dialogue is thus distinguished from 'just talking', with a dialogic pedagogy requiring teachers and learners to actively comment and build on each other's ideas and construct shared interpretations and 'common knowledge' (Edwards and Mercer, 1987). Further, dialogic

DOI: 10.4324/9781003408925-8

pedagogy has a participatory imperative that seeks to legitimise and develop contributions from all parties in classroom interactions (Nystrand *et al.*, 2003). A central intention then is 'to foster learner agency, whereby pupils collaborate with others in seeking understanding, building from their own ideas and allowing other ideas and opinions to mediate and modify their thinking' (Flitton and Warwick, 2012:3).

This does not, however, mean that all lessons will be entirely 'dialogic'. Shifts between authoritative and dialogic discourse continue to play an important part in teaching. For example, teacher-led authoritative passages of interaction can often act as a seed, prompt or stimulus for dialogue in the classroom and vice versa (Scott *et al.*, 2006). In this chapter we explore how technologies can be used to initiate, promote and sustain a balanced use of dialogue between pupils in different settings and how technologies can play their part. The result should be 'learning as conversational", consisting of a series of iterative cycles of interaction between teacher/learner/peers in a variety of combinations which may make use of technologies to greater or lesser degrees' (Pachler *et al.*, 2010:716).

In this chapter, we consider how technologies can be used in this way to develop dialogue *within* classrooms in one setting and *between* classrooms in different locations.

Objectives

At the end of this chapter you should be able to:

- recognise that language is a teacher's main pedagogical tool and that you can use technology effectively to support this in the primary classroom
- feel better prepared to realise the potential of a balanced use of technologies to initiate and sustain dialogue *within* and *between* classrooms, both local and international
- recognise the affordances of technologies on their own, or in combination, that can be used to encourage dialogue to support learning in the primary classroom.

The interaction between dialogue and digital technology within the classroom

We begin by looking at how technologies can be used *within* a primary classroom to stimulate meaningful dialogue. In recent years, much attention has been paid to the interaction between dialogic pedagogy and digital technology. How to effectively integrate the two continues to be a cutting-edge topic and an area of interest for both researchers and practitioners (Hao *et al.*, 2020). Aligned with an appropriate pedagogy, dialogue and digital technology can interact to enhance learning in various ways (Major *et al.*, 2018). For instance, within a classroom, by combining spoken and written interaction, learner knowledge can be externalised (made visible) as 'digital artefacts' (Hennessy, 2011). For example, the interactive whiteboard (IWB) (and potentially other large interactive digital displays) can be used to support classroom dialogue by enabling teachers and learners to together create – and manipulate – digital knowledge artefacts that constitute interim records of collective activity (Mercer *et al.*, 2019). These might include, for example, using screens that link text, pictures, video materials, sound files, links to online materials and so on, to display a representation of key ideas and the ways in which relationships between them are understood. Digital artefacts produced on interactive displays may thus offer an externalised representation of the dialogic activity that is taking, and has taken, place (Hennessy, 2011). Interaction with digital artefacts can also make new conceptual perspectives available to learners by making them open to collective scrutiny as a whole class, as learners may interactively build on, organize, modify or revisit their own and others' digital artefacts in some way (Chen *et al.*, 2018). This can have a positive impact on learning, for instance, by enabling differences between perspectives to be highlighted and making reasoning more explicit (Stahl, 2004).

In addition to representing visible, dynamic and constantly evolving resources constituting interim records of activity (Warwick *et al.*, 2010), digital artefacts can help to extend the idea of 'interthinking' (Littleton and Mercer, 2013) and open up a 'dialogic space' (Wegerif and Major, 2018). In this context, 'Technologically mediated forms of discourse and interaction (can also) provide new forms of discussion' (Stahl *et al.*, 2014:118). This includes enabling dialogic interactions that are not face-to-face, or are asynchronous (e.g. Pifarré and Staarman, 2011). As a result, the alignment of classroom-based digital technologies with a dialogic pedagogy seems to suggest the possibility of 'transformative' learning.

Having considered above how technologies may support dialogue *within* a classroom, we will now unpack these ideas further focusing on two case studies, which exploited the unique affordances of technology to enable dialogues *between* classrooms in a way that could not have happened any other way – in itself perhaps the best justification of using technology!

Now undertake Task 8.1.

Task 8.1: Facilitating shared discussion and shared understanding with technology

On your own, or with others, consider your own experience (as learner and teacher) of how classroom-based digital technologies have allowed (made visible) shared discussion and building shared understanding. Consider:

- what made it effective (or not);
- how this was planned and built into the lesson;
- what records (e.g. saved file from annotated interactive screen) were kept and why – evidence and/or assessment;
- how often, and in what areas of learning, should this activity take place;
- what was the role of the teacher (e.g. prompting, questioning and annotating)?

Affordances, talk and technologies

In a technology-supported learning environment, affordances are provided by the interaction between the hardware and the software, resources and pupils (Webb, 2005), as part of a learner-centric ecology of resources (Luckin, 2008). As such, technology can be used to provide a range of multimodal resources to promote dialogue, both within the classroom and beyond. This dialogue can take many forms, both synchronous and asynchronous, and exploit different media (such as tablet or laptop) and modes (such as writing or video), on their own or in combination. This allows pupils to engage in dialogue that, if necessary, can be edited and shared quickly as an individual or as part of a group (Beauchamp, 2017), unlike traditional classroom resources such as pen and paper. Another unique affordance of technology may be the ability to communicate and work collaboratively with others anywhere in the world, as we will see in the case studies below. Aligned with an appropriate pedagogy, technology may also enable the active involvement of all pupils working as a group to contribute to collaborative dialogue. This active involvement of learners (at physical and cognitive levels) is necessary in a socio-constructivist conception of interactivity, where children construct new knowledge within the social context of the classroom (Jones and Tanner, 2002). In this context, technologies can stimulate, facilitate and record learners bringing something of themselves to interactions through dialogue, as they contribute in different ways and at different times to collective understanding in the classroom.

Indeed, the affordances of modern technology can enable dialogue and collaboration that was not possible just a few years ago. For example, advances in the mobility of technology and the ability to connect distant partners have created new collaborative opportunities. For instance, recent advancements in video conferencing software allow pupils based in different geographical school locations to be connected in seconds and able to interact on a shared problem by using wi-fi mobile devices (as noted in the case study below). Developments in remote technology and wi-fi-connected tablet technology have thus enabled groups to co-construct a range of materials and collaborate in real time combining talk and technology to create meaning (Beauchamp *et al.*, 2019). During the lifetime of this book no doubt teachers will find many more ways to use technologies to deepen and extend the learning of pupils.

It is important, however, to acknowledge that introducing technology into a collaborative activity does not, in itself, result in successful collaboration or effective dialogue. It needs an understanding of the principles of collaborative learning, as learners establish shared goals, engage in sharing knowledge and monitor each other's progress (Jeong and Hmelo-Silver, 2016). Your role and skills as a teacher are central to making this work, if you are prepared to give it a try.

Having looked at how technologies can help dialogue *within* the classroom, we will now move to look at how they can be used *between* classrooms with two case studies using different technologies.

Case Study 8.1: Dialogue through video stimulated by multi-touch technology

Introduction

The first case study illustrates an iterative process of research, which explored talk, technology and collaboration in three phases, each building on what had preceded. It began in phase one with primary pupils in one room in a university, like a laboratory environment, using custom-built, large multi-touch, networked tables with pupils talking to each other face-to-face. This case study outlines how this was developed and taken into different primary classrooms in phases two and three, in different locations, using smaller mobile, wi-fi-connected devices with pupils communicating through video technology.

Multi-touch technology enables several people to control and interact with the information on the same screen, simultaneously (Shen *et al.*, 2009). Interest in multi-touch surfaces has grown within classrooms as educators seek to employ tools that could enhance the potential for learning. The pedagogical possibilities of multi-touch technology have been investigated due to their potential to increase learning, especially through collaborative learning (Higgins *et al.*, 2011; Reiser and Tabak, 2014; Mercier *et al.*, 2017). Multi-touch technology also provides opportunities to explore *how* learners collaborate during educational tasks in a digital environment and to investigate how children use interactions such as dialogic or technical interactivity to build collective meaning together (Higgins *et al.*, 2011).

Phase 1: Large networked multitouch tables in a 'laboratory' setting in the same location

The *SynergyNet* project began at Durham University with a collective of researchers from different academic disciplines working together to explore the use of multi-touch tables in the primary classroom. This work was premised on the idea that the opportunity for joint control, rather than the single point of control provided by a mouse or single touch screen, was suited to collaborative activity around the table surface (Higgins *et al.*, 2011). Introductory *SynergyNet* studies were university-based, using large multi-touch tables connected by fixed, wired networks with pupils working together in the same location (Hatch *et al.*, 2009; Higgins *et al.*, 2011; Mercier and Higgins, 2013; Joyce-Gibbons, 2016). Children's dialogic and technical interaction was captured during joint problem-solving tasks by multiple cameras and these interactions were analysed by the research team. Figure 8.1 shows three pupils using one of the large table-top mounted multi-touch tables within the *SynergyNet* lab-based classroom.

Figure 8.1 Children working in small groups around the multi-touch table based in the lab-based classroom

The shared problem-solving history task

One of the tasks was a history task, based on an incident in a coal mine in 18th-century Northeast England. At the start of the task, the teacher read aloud a statement about the accident, in which a 10-year-old boy, Robert Dixon, lost his leg. The children then received 16 clues to help them determine what happened to Robert Dixon and who was responsible for the accident – see Figure 8.2. This task was designed to encourage divergent argumentation, with multiple possible answers.

 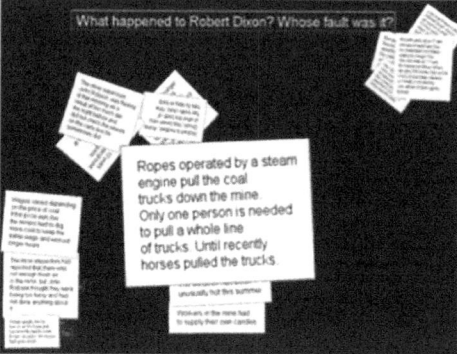

Figure 8.2 The shared problem-solving history task in the multi-touch format at the start and during the activity

One feature of the multi-touch table was that the clues could not be picked up the way that pieces of paper can. However, the facility to manually move and resize the clues was quickly adopted by most groups, and pupils enlarged the information to make reading easier, both as individuals, but then for other members of the group to follow along as one of them read aloud.

Through dialogue, pupils used the table space available to them to organise their clues, including resizing the clues to signify importance. The learners responded to and built on each other's ideas in an exploratory way by discussing and debating the contributions of different group members.

Phase 2: National dialogue – multi-touch technology in primary classrooms in different geographic locations (North-East England and South Wales)

Due to evolving technology, subsequent iterations of the study moved out of the 'laboratory' and into real primary schools and explored pupil behaviour in a more authentic classroom context (McNaughton *et al.*, 2017; Beauchamp *et al.*, 2019). Additional technological advances enabled children not only to work within their own classroom but also to be able to collaborate with children who were not physically in the same location. Using wireless networks, the multi-touch tables enabled groups in different geographic locations to work together on the same shared problem hosted on the tables. The pupils were able to see, and most importantly, talk to each other through Skype on a laptop. Figure 8.3 demonstrates how the technology

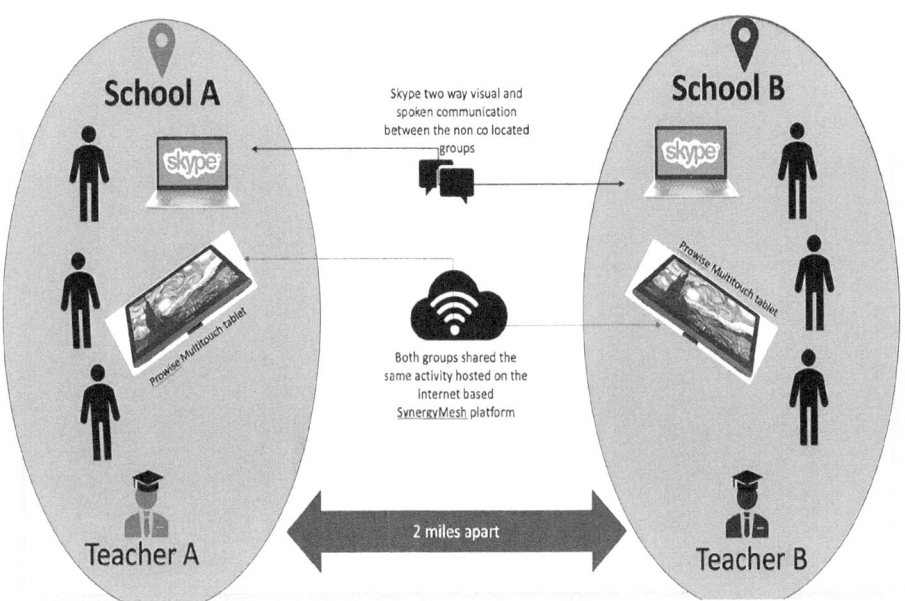

Figure 8.3 Overview of the study which enabled x3 pupils to work x3 pupils in a different location

allowed small pupil groups from one school (school A) to work with another small pupil group (school B) to collaborate on a shared history problem, similar to the study mentioned above.

A new 'flick' gesture (McNaughton *et al.*, 2017) was added to the shared problem-solving task platform which enabled information to be transferred from a screen in one location to a screen in another location by 'flicking' the information towards the top of the screen. As one pupil stated: 'It was really cool how they got the information that we had on our screen'. It is important to note, however, that the flicking was not random (even though the pupils regarded it as 'fun'), but the result of dialogue within and between the groups in different locations. As one pupil explained:

> we had to listen to each other, so you could know what the information they got, and what information we got. And we just basically worked together to see what information needs to go to [name of] school.

This study found that multi-touch surfaces could support synchronous, collaborative dialogue between groups in different classroom locations, which proved to be memorable and engaging for the participants. The immediacy of the flick gesture and the resultant dialogue initiated by sharing clues built a memorable and motivating link which inspired meaningful collaborative interactions between remote groups. As one pupil stated: 'We got to speak to people far away where I have never been … we learnt from different people and got to use a piece of technology for the first time ever. I loved it'.

Even technical problems with connections did not put the pupils off. Indeed, they became the subject of further dialogue and humour!

Figure 8.4 sums up the findings of this part of the project.

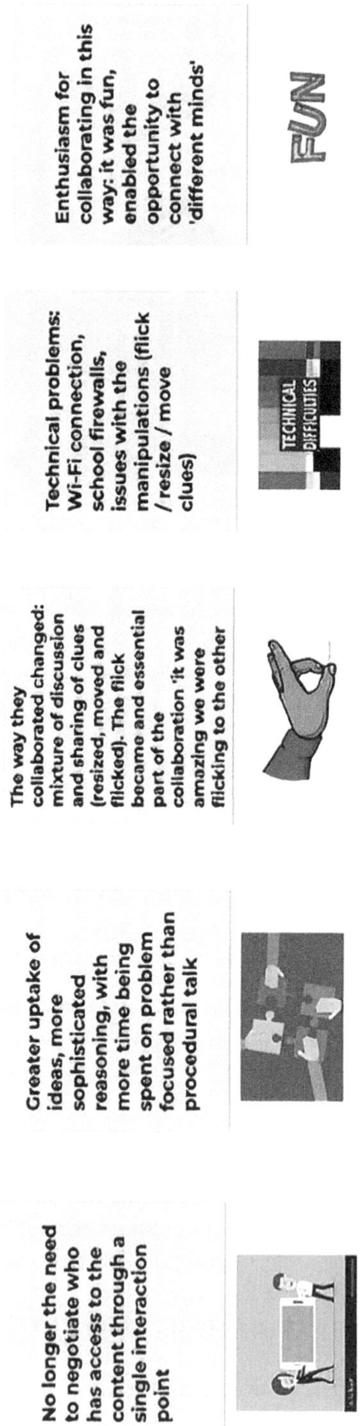
No longer the need to negotiate who has access to the content through a single interaction point
Greater uptake of ideas, more sophisticated reasoning, with more time being spent on problem focused rather than procedural talk
The way they collaborated changed: mixture of discussion and sharing of clues (resized, moved and flicked). The flick became and essential part of the collaboration 'it was amazing we were flicking to the other
Technical problems: Wi-Fi connection, school firewalls, issues with the manipulations (flick / resize / move clues)
TECHNICAL DIFFICULTIES
Enthusiasm for collaborating in this way: it was fun, enabled the opportunity to connect with 'different minds'
FUN

Figure 8.4 Summary of benefits and challenge of collaborative problem-solving in phase 2

Phase 3: National dialogue: remote collaboration using smaller mobile multi-touch technology in primary classrooms

Recent technological advances enabled the use of even smaller, mobile, multi-touch devices connected by wi-fi in primary classrooms. This study, like previous iterations, set out to explore the synchronous collaboration between pupils situated in two physically distant schools but also to explore how mobile multi-touch tablets and video conferencing software contributed to the collaboration. Figure 8.5 shows the small pupil groups situated in different schools (the pupils on the left from school A and the pupils on the right were situated in school B) working synchronously via the technology to solve a shared problem-solving activity. Pupils' verbal and technical interactions were video recorded and analysed.

Figure 8.5 Six pupils (three from school A, three from school B) working collaboratively from separate locations to solve a joint problem-solving activity

This study found that mobile multi-touch tablets could support effective collaborative dialogue between small pupil groups situated in different school locations. The multi-touch technology facilitated a wide range of meaningful digital and verbal interactions. The dialogue facilitated by the remote technology provided the opportunity for pupils to be exposed to alternative perspectives of other pupils they did not know at the start of the project. The flick gesture, and resultant discussion, again encouraged and supported collaboration as distant pupils could share information quickly. This led to dialogue and in some cases more dialogic talk.

Case Study 8.2: International dialogue through video conferencing between countries: primary pupil teachers in south Wales, primary school pupils in south Wales and primary school pupils in Rwanda

The first case study used technology to move from dialogue with no technology within one classroom, to dialogue through technology between different schools on a national level. The second case study outlines how technology can enable international dialogue, in this case, a three-way discussion between student teachers and primary school pupils in two different countries.

Parties involved the project

Primary Education Studies Level 5 (year 2) university student teachers based in a Welsh University
   Year 5 class based in a Welsh primary school
   Year 5 class based in a Rwandan primary school – see Figure 8.6.

Figure 8.6 Year 6 pupils from the Rwandan class we worked with during our international dialogue exchange project

Technology used to stimulate dialogue

Spoken dialogue: Video conferencing platform Facetime
   Written dialogue: Google docs
   Developing a global perspective is an important curriculum outcome, but is one of the more challenging priorities to achieve. Today modern school leavers and graduates need to operate within global markets, to develop empathy and the ability to communicate in a global context is a core competency. To achieve these lofty goals, we have had to open the walls of our classrooms to collaborate with others on an international scale. As part of a university student teacher education course, a project was developed with a primary school based in Rusizi district in Rwanda over seven years and embedded work

with their school into university modules, also working with a Welsh Primary school for the previous four years. As part of the project, participants learned through spoken and written dialogue facilitated by technology, including setting up the project.

Finding an international partner was easy through the British Council 'Connecting Classrooms' online portal. After registering and noting which region we wanted to work with, a list of potential partners was displayed. We contacted the head teacher from one of the Rwandan schools from the list and began to exchange emails in which we shared information about the schools and university involved in the project. After a few test calls, a sharing event was hosted through video conferencing in which pupils and student teachers from Wales communicated and shared their culture with Rwandan pupils and teachers. Prior to the video call, all participants in the project researched their international partners and began to craft questions that could be asked during the sharing event and, importantly, to stimulate dialogue. Led by the lecturers and teachers in each location, pupils and student teachers were encouraged to share through song (national anthems were sung from both locations), and basic Welsh and Ikinyarwanda phrases were taught to each other. In addition, school / university routines were also shared, as well as tasting traditional meals from each region. All parties were enthused by the call and wanted to learn more about the location and culture of their international partners. A communal online Google document was shared with the schools and universities involved in the project to provide a platform to enable communication to continue after the call – see Figure 8.7.

Figure 8.7 Pupils and student teachers produced written dialogue as they communicated using the shared online Google Document

Interestingly, and unexpectedly, the shared document evoked more further dialogue than the original video call. The majority of students and pupils contributed to the document and posed questions, included information about themselves and responded to comments and questions. Pupils and students also recorded short video tours of their schools/university, took pictures and shared these on the Google document. The communication in written form became more dialogic as ideas were built upon and an understanding was constructed together. Pupils and students discussed their differing daily routines and common film interests. When asked why the pupils and university students had been more engaged in dialogue with this document than the call, a university student noted that 'it was a bit daunting speaking on a screen to someone we had never met, I loved the call but with the shared document I felt more comfortable sharing information about myself, learning about our international partners and asking them questions directly'. The technology used in this project afforded immediate communication, so pupils and university students could create meaning by sharing their own ideas (in various multi-modal forms) while allowing others to mediate and modify their understanding of each other's settings. The process is summarised in Figure 8.8.

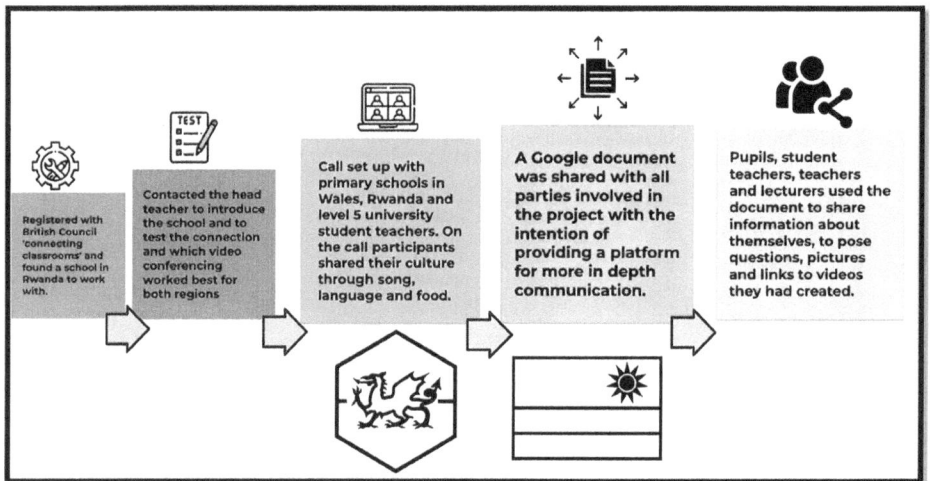

Figure 8.8 The logistical process of the project

Tip: It is important to arrange a test call with your international partner before your arranged call with pupils. As we learned the wi-fi connection was stronger in Rwanda in the morning, we arranged for a call during this period. The test call provides an opportunity to investigate the most appropriate video conferencing platform for both regions. The video conferencing platforms 'Teams' and 'Zoom' didn't work on our project, so we had to use 'FaceTime' which provided a clear sound and video in both locations. Also, it is important to consider the time zones of the region you are working with and to establish the most appropriate time that works for both parties. Now undertake Task 8.2.

Task 8.2: What are the benefits of international partnerships?

On your own, or with others, discuss how and why you might set up an international partnership with another primary school, what country would you like to link with (and why) and what area of learning you might focus on?

Summary and key points

In this chapter we have begun to explore the potential of using technologies to support dialogue within, and between, schools. We have seen that:

- Technology can initiate, support and enhance dialogue within and between primary classrooms, including in different locations.
- Technology can support collaborative problem solving and encourage dialogue between pupils in different locations.
- Technology can help develop international dialogue between primary pupils around the world to develop an international dimension to their work.
- Technology can be effective in developing dialogue in learning, but should be part of a balanced approach to dialogic teaching with and without technology.

Further resources

Classroom Dialogue and Learning https://www.meshguides.org/guides/node/1148. Accessed on 6 February 2023.
> Although not focusing specifically on dialogue and technology, this MESH guide was developed by colleagues at the University of Cambridge who belong to the Cambridge Educational Dialogue Research Group (CEDiR). Drawing on research over a number of years, it provides an introduction to the concept of Classroom Dialogue. It also highlights a number of practical resources and strategies to support teachers in developing a dialogic pedagogy.

SynergyNet software: http://synergy-dev.red-robot-dev.co.uk/. Accessed on 6 February 2023.
> *SynergyMesh* is software that houses several activities to promote collaborative activity in the classroom. The open source *SynergyMesh* link is mentioned in the case study above and is free for all educators to use.

Major, L., Warwick, P., Rasmussen, I., Ludvigsen, S., and Cook, V. (2018) Classroom dialogue and digital technologies: A scoping review. *International Journal of Educational Research*, 23, pp.1995–2028. https://doi.org/10.1007/s10639-018-9701-y. Accessed on 6 February 2023.
> This article presents a systematic scoping review of the literature focusing on interactions between classroom dialogue and digital technology. It is the first review of its type in this area. It reviews 72 studies and both maps extant research and investigates the role of technology in supporting classroom dialogue.

References

Alexander, R. (2018) Developing dialogic teaching: genesis, process, trial, *Research Papers in Education*, 33(5), 561–598.

Beauchamp, G. (2017) *Computing and ICT in the primary school: from pedagogy to practice*, 2nd Edition, London, David Fulton/Routledge.

Beauchamp, G., Joyce-Gibbons, A., McNaughton, J., Young, N., and Crick, T. (2019) Exploring synchronous, remote collaborative interaction between learners using multi-touch tables and video conferencing in UK primary schools, *British Journal of Educational Technology*, 50(6), 3214–3232.

Chen, J., Wang, M., Kirschner, P. A., and Tsai, C. C. (2018) The role of collaboration, computer use, learning environments, and supporting strategies in CSCL: a meta-analysis, *Review of Educational Research*, 88(6), 799–843.

Cook, V., Major, L., Hennessy, S., Ahmed, F., and Calcagni, E. (2018) *Classroom dialogue and learning*, MESHGuides. https://meshguides.org/guides/node/1148. Accessed on 6 February 2023.

Edwards, D., and Mercer, N. (1987) *Common knowledge: the development of understanding in the classroom*, London, Methuen.

Flitton, L., and Warwick, P. (2012) From classroom analysis to whole-school professional development: Promoting talk as a tool for learning across school departments, *Professional Development in Education*, 39(1), 99–121.

Hao, T., Chen, X., and Song, Y. (2020) A topic-based bibliometric analysis of two decades of research on the application of technology in classroom dialogue, *Journal of Educational Computing Research*, 58(7), 1311–1341.

Hatch, A., Higgins, S., and Mercier, E. (2009) SynergyNet: Supporting collaborative learning in an immersive environment STELLAR alpine rendez-vous workshop, *Tabletops for Education and Training*, 2–3 December, Garmisch–Partenkirchen.

Hennessy, S. (2011) The role of digital artefacts on the interactive whiteboard in supporting classroom dialogue: dialogue and IWB artefacts, *Journal of Computer-Assisted Learning*, 27(6), 463–489.

Higgins, S., Mercier, E., Burd, E., and Hatch, A. (2011) Multi-touch tables and the relationship with collaborative classroom pedagogies: a synthetic review, *International Journal of Computer-Supported Collaborative Learning*, 6(4), 515–538.

Howe, C., and Abedin, M. (2013) Classroom dialogue: a systematic review across four decades of research, *Cambridge Journal of Education*, 43(3), 325–356.

Howe, C., Hennessy, S., Mercer, N., Vrikki, M., and Wheatley, L. (2019) Teacher–student dialogue during classroom teaching: does it really impact on student outcomes?, *Journal of the Learning Sciences*, 28(4–5), 462–512.

Jay, T., Willis, B., Thomas, P., Taylor, R., Moore, N., Burnett, C., and Stevens, A. (2017) *Dialogic teaching: evaluation report and executive summary*, UK, Education Endowment Foundation. https://files.eric.ed.gov/fulltext/ED581114.pdf. Accessed on 6 February 2023.

Jeong, H., and Hmelo-Silver, C. E. (2016) Seven affordances of computer-supported collaborative learning: how to support collaborative learning? How can technologies help?, *Educational Psychologist*, 51(2), 247–265.

Jones, S., and Tanner, H. (2002) Teachers' interpretations of effective whole-class interactive teaching in secondary mathematics classrooms, *Educational Studies*, 28(1), 265–274.

Joyce-Gibbons, A. (2016) Observe, interact and act: teachers' initiation of mini-plenaries to scaffold small-group collaboration, *Pedagogy and Education: Technology*, 26(1), 1–18.

Littleton, K., and Mercer, N. (2013) *Interthinking: Putting talk to work*, Abingdon, Routledge.

Luckin, R. (2008) The learner centric ecology of resources: a framework for using technology to scaffold learning, *Computers and Education*, 50(2), 449–462.

McNaughton, J., Crick, T., Joyce-Gibbons, A., Beauchamp, B., Young, N., and Tan, E. (2017) Facilitating collaborative learning between two primary schools using large multi-touch devices, *Journal of Computers in Education*, 4(3), 307–320.

Major, L., Warwick, P., Rasmussen, I., Ludvigsen, S., and Cook, V. (2018) Classroom dialogue and digital technologies: a scoping review, *Education and Information Technologies*, 23(5), 1995–2028, https://doi.org/10.1007/s10639-018-9701-y.

Major, L., Smørdal, O., Warwick, P., Rasmussen, I., Cook, V., and Vrikki, M. (2022) Investigating digital technology's role in supporting classroom dialogue: integrating 'enacted affordance' into analysis across a complex dataset, *International Journal of Research and Method in Education*. https://doi.org/10.1080/1743727X.2022.2032632.

Mercer, N., Hennessy, S., and Warwick, P. (2019) Dialogue, thinking together and digital technology in the classroom: some educational implications of a continuing line of inquiry, *International Journal of Educational Research*, 97, 187–199.

Mercier, E., and Higgins, S. (2013) Collaborative learning with multi-touch technology: developing adaptive expertise, *Learning and Instruction*, 25(3), 13–23.

Mercier, E., Vourloumi, G., and Higgins, S. (2017) Student interactions and the development of ideas in multi-touch and paper-based collaborative mathematical problem solving, *British Journal of Educational Technology*, 48(1), 162–175.

Michaels, S., and O'Connor, C. (2012) *Talk science primer*, Cambridge, MA, TERC.

Nystrand, M., Wu, L. L., Gamoran, A., Zeiser, S., and Long, D. A. (2003) Questions in time: investigating the structure and dynamics of unfolding classroom discourse, *Discourse Processes*, 35(2), 135–198.

Pachler, N., Daly, C., Mor, Y., and Mellar, H. (2010). Formative e-assessment: Practitioner cases, *Computers and Education*, 54(3), 715–721.

Pifarré, M., and Kleine Staarman, J. (2011) Wiki-supported collaborative learning in primary education: how a dialogic space is created for thinking together, *International Journal of Computer-Supported Collaborative Learning*, 6(2), 187–205.

Reiser, B., and Tabak, I. (2014) Scaffolding, in R. K. Sawyer (ed.) *The Cambridge handbook of learning sciences*, Cambridge University Press, New York.

Resnick, L., Asterhan, C., and Clarke, S. (2015) *Socializing intelligence through academic talk and dialogue*, American Educational Research Association. DOI: 10.3102/978-0-935302-43-1_1.

Scott, P. H., Mortimer, E. F., and Aguiar, O. G. (2006) The tension between authoritative and dialogic discourse: a fundamental characteristic of meaning making interactions in high school science lessons. *Science Education*, 90(4), 605–631.

Shen, E., Tsai, S., Chu, H., Hsu, J., and Chen, C. (2009) Double-side multi-touch input for mobile devices, *The conference on Human Factors in Computing Systems*, April, 4339–4344.

Stahl, G. (2004) Building collaborative knowing. Elements of a social theory of CSCL, in J. Strijbos, P. Kirschner, R. Martens, and P Dillenbourg (eds.) *What we know about CSCL and implementing it in higher education*, Norwell, MA, Kluwer Academic Publishers, 53–85.

Stahl, G., Cress, U., Ludvigsen, S., and Law, N. (2014) Dialogic foundations of CSC, *International Journal of Computer-Supported Collaborative Learning*, 9(2), 117–125.

T'Sas, J. (2018) *Learning outcomes of exploratory talk in collaborative activities*, PhD Thesis, University of Antwerp, https://doi.org/10.13140/rg.2.2.10883.81449.

Tenenbaum, H. R., Winstone, N. E., Leman, P. J., and Avery, R. E. (2019) How effective is peer interaction in facilitating learning? A meta-analysis, *Journal of Educational Psychology*, https://doi.org/10.1037/edu0000436.

Warwick, P., Mercer, N., Kershner, R., and Staarman, J. K. (2010) In the mind and in the technology: the vicarious presence of the teacher in pupil's learning of science in collaborative group activity at the interactive whiteboard, *Computers and Education*, 55(1), 350–362.

Webb, M. (2005) Affordances of ICT in science learning: implications for an integrated pedagogy, *International Journal of Science Education*, 27(6), 705–735.

Wegerif, R. (2005) Reason and creativity in classroom dialogues, *Language and Education*, 19(3), 223–237.

Wegerif, R., and Major, L. (2019) Buber, educational technology, and the expansion of dialogic space, *AI and Society*, 34(1), 109–119, https://doi.org/10.1007/s00146-018-0828-6.

9 Digital storytelling

Helen Caldwell and Emma Whewell

Introduction

Storytelling is an important aspect of our lives; historically it has been a tool for sharing knowledge and values, for transmitting history and heritage, and for coming together to celebrate. Stories can bring a sense of coherence to our experiences, whether informally amongst family and friends or more formally within our school curriculum and working lives. The digital context adds an extra dimension to how narratives are communicated and shared, expanding ways in which children's creativity can be developed through a range of media. Rodríguez *et al.* (2021, p.21) identify digital storytelling as a means by which both language and digital literacy can be improved. They highlight that digital storytelling allows children to become protagonists in their own learning, empowering their voices and engaging them in their learning journeys (Rodríguez *et al.*, 2021).

Nair *et al.* (2021) further propose that digital storytelling can provide children with the opportunity to develop 21st-century skills to be lifelong learners, suggesting that well-constructed creative opportunities support children to develop problem solving, negotiation and decision-making, and to work as part of a team or independently. In addition to this, digital storytelling can foster an appreciation of the world around us and provide opportunities related to the green curriculum, sustainability and the Sustainable Development Goals (SDGs) set by the United Nations in 2015 (see Case Study 9.1).

This chapter focuses on digital storytelling through the lens of empowering children to develop cultural and digital capital. It uses a series of case study vignettes to exemplify tools and pedagogical approaches that will help you embed digital storytelling in your primary classroom. Five key themes are introduced through case studies from practice:

- Working with digital media
- Supporting language development
- Using shared online spaces
- Extended reality environments
- Drama and game-based learning.

We also suggest a number of tasks to help you plan to use digital storytelling in your pedagogic practice.

DOI: 10.4324/9781003408925-9

Objectives

At the end of this chapter, you will be able to:

- understand and define what digital storytelling means in the primary classroom
- plan for digital storytelling in your classroom drawing on appropriate pedagogy
- consider how you might assess and share digital storytelling
- explore a range of technologies associated with digital storytelling.

Defining digital storytelling in the primary classroom

Storytelling is a helpful educational tool, whether it be for reading or creating stories. It can support the development of literacy skills, including reading, writing and speaking. Narratives can contextualise learning and enable children to visualise, imagine and empathise with characters and contexts. Immersion in stories provokes emotion and connection, helping children to see the world from different perspectives.

Digital storytelling adds another dimension by providing an environment for capturing and sharing stories in a variety of media. Wu and Chen (2020) suggest that the production of a short digital story in an educational setting typically contains some mixture of images, text, narration or music and film. The process of applying cognitive and practical skills in this way can build what is often termed digital literacy. A digitally literate person, Prensky suggests, will be able to: 'bend digital technology to one's needs, purposes … just as in the present we bend words and images.' (Prensky, 2008, p.1). If they are to become digitally literate, children need to learn to manipulate the material they find or generate using technology, whether it is computer code, words, numbers, images, sound or video, and to remix and recombine it in meaningful ways. A goal is to be able to do this across a range of devices and tools, so that they are equally familiar with making an eBook on a tablet as they are collaborating remotely to program an animation on a laptop. Making digital stories provides learners with the chance to be creative and productive with technologies, to make decisions on how best to use them and to make connections between them. Through the process they gain what Prensky terms 'digital wisdom' (Prensky, 2012).

Smeda *et al.* (2014, p.2) also draw attention to the advantages of the digital environment by defining digital storytelling as an 'effective pedagogical tool that enhances learners' motivation and provides learners with an environment conducive for story construction through collaboration, reflection and interpersonal communication'. Niemi and Multisilta (2016, p.586) propose that when children are creating their own stories they are 'not passive receivers yet active creators in the learning environment'. Furthermore, Nair *et al.* (2021) suggest that digital storytelling improves children's speaking skills by offering increased agency and independence in retelling their own stories. Digital storytelling can thus be a multimodal way of developing reading, writing and speaking skills alongside technical capabilities through the use of media. As Smeda *et al.* note, it can be 'a vehicle for combining digital media with innovative teaching and learning practices' (2014, p.6). Digital storytelling therefore enables children to develop a higher order and creative thinking, and to experience tangible connections between their own experiences and the real world. The emphasis is on active engagement in digital storymaking, developing solution-focused thinking skills and understanding the real-world relevance of their digital skills.

Digital storytelling and digital literacy

Digital storytelling aligns with a social constructivist approach to learning by providing a context for co-constructing knowledge. This approach values the pedagogical approaches of collaborative learning, experiential learning, reflective thinking and child centredness. It suggests an environment that is rich in interaction, where children learn with and from each other through an active learning process that emphasises conversation and reflection.

These ideas also sit well with Luckin *et al.*'s (2010) learner-centric framework of Learner Generated Contexts, which sees learners gaining control through interacting around a common learning goal. This model highlights that technology changes the boundaries 'between learners and teachers, formal and informal education and the producers and consumers of knowledge' (Luckin *et al.*, 2010, p.72). Seen in this way, the learning context is less a physical location and more the combination of interactions a learner experiences across multiple physical and digital spaces and times. Luckin *et al.* (2010, p.74) describe the learning context as 'a constant, dynamic interaction between internal and external sources'. They suggest that technologies can provide a platform for an 'architecture of participation' (Luckin *et al.*, 2010, p.80). An aim of combining digital technology with storytelling might therefore be to create more open, creative and participatory learning experiences.

Taking these ideas into account, a digitally literate storyteller will need a stock of skills to draw upon that includes competence with a range of digital tools, but also comprises familiarity with strategies for learning in today's socio-technical learning landscape. This includes the ability to navigate a shifting network of resources, social connections and learning habitats across times and spaces. In this context, it is important to understand how interaction between people, digital and physical spaces and technologies can influence the creative process.

Planning to put digital storytelling into practice

The emphasis on learner-generated content and self-directed learning may call for a change in the role of the teacher (Bates, 2015), and you will need to give careful thought as to how to create the conditions for your pupils to collaborate to generate digital stories.

When planning a digital storytelling project, then, consider your pupils and how they learn. They may benefit from training in collaborative learning and teamwork skills, or opportunities to exercise agency in choosing themes and tools, as suggested by Wu and Chen (2020). Think about how you organise your classroom space, groups and children, as well as the technologies you choose to use. Digital stories can be made in groups or individually. Working as a group can enhance pupils' experience of creative writing and can help to develop literacy skills and digital skills to a higher level. This aligns with the constructivist pedagogical approach by enabling children to learn with and from each other.

A constructivist learning approach uses prior knowledge as building blocks for developing new knowledge. You will need to set clear goals and identify the learning outcomes for your project that include the elements of literacy that you plan to develop alongside the development of digital skills. It may be useful to link aims to timings to ensure the project has an appropriate scale. Also think about linking outcomes with assessment criteria and remember to build in formative assessment. If this is going to be a project over several lessons, it may be useful to devise a checklist to help your pupils see how they are moving forward and ensure deadlines are met.

Consider the variety of ways you might introduce digital storytelling into the classroom and the types of stories you plan to create. In their systematic review of digital storytelling,

Wu and Chen (2020) highlight various educational uses of stories, such as to develop understanding or reconstruct meanings of concepts, to develop autonomy by choosing themes of interest, to reflect on new learning experiences, or to create identity stories that develop pupils' understanding of themselves and their relationships with others. How you create your context for digital storytelling will depend on how much storytelling your class has undertaken, the learning themes they are currently exploring and their ability to use the digital tools you have access to.

Digital stories are usually 3–10 minutes in length (Nair *et al.*, 2021) and typically draw from a range of multimedia components including images, audio and text. Storyboards can be a useful supportive tool for children to plan their work. A storyboard might consist of a piece of paper or a digital document split into boxes. Pupils organise ideas into a coherent story by drawing or writing into each box to show the structure of the story. With digital storytelling you might also ask pupils to include information on which technologies or media they will be using. You may need to explain how to use relevant digital tools, although most pupils will already have developed knowledge of a range of these. As your pupils create their digital story, they will need to solve many problems including those experienced when using technologies. This will develop your pupils' computational thinking and digital literacy.

Regardless of what digital tool you choose to use, it is important that you check that it is working and plan for charging your devices. Remember to build in sufficient time for the end phase of the digital story creation; adding titles, music and transitions develops creativity in the classroom but needs careful time-management and scaffolding. In line with the constructivist teaching approach, you also need to allow time for reflection and discussion.

Table 9.1 summarises some of the pedagogical considerations when designing the learning process and choosing digital tools.

Table 9.1 Pedagogical considerations in planning for digital storytelling

Pedagogical approach	*Considerations*	*Recommendations*
Experiential learning (Learning by doing)	Does the tool offer a range of ways that children can engage with their story and make choices about how it is represented?	Multimodal representations that include media, film, image, text and the spoken word.
Metacognition (Talking / thinking about the process and decisions made)	Does the tool allow children to verbalise and reflect on their own learning and be independent in decision making?	Tools that allow children to make edits, remake, duplicate and reorder.
Collaborative learning (Working together to achieve a common goal)	Does the tool allow children to collaborate synchronously or asynchronously?	Tools that can be used on multiple platforms with multiple users.
Learner autonomy (Taking charge of your own learning)	Does the tool allow the children to be able to modify, edit, manipulate and reorder content?	Tools that allow children to make editing decisions, create nonlinear stories and choose how they display their story.

Now turn to Task 9.1, where you will be asked to think about how you might go about introducing digital storytelling to your curriculum and class, this task will help you consider the needs of your context.

Task 9.1: Introducing digital storytelling

Having had an introduction to digital storytelling, list the things you would need to do to plan a digital storytelling project for your class.

Identify a space in your curriculum for digital storytelling, giving consideration to children's prior learning in terms of literacy and language as well as experience of technologies.

Consider your access to technologies. Are there technologies your class know how to use or could learn to use through their digital stories?

An authentic audience is an important motivation for storytelling. Think about how you will share children's work.

Plan any changes you need to make to the arrangement of your classroom and take health and safety into account.

Keep your plan in front of you while you read the rest of this chapter and add your reflections as you develop your knowledge of how you could use digital storytelling.

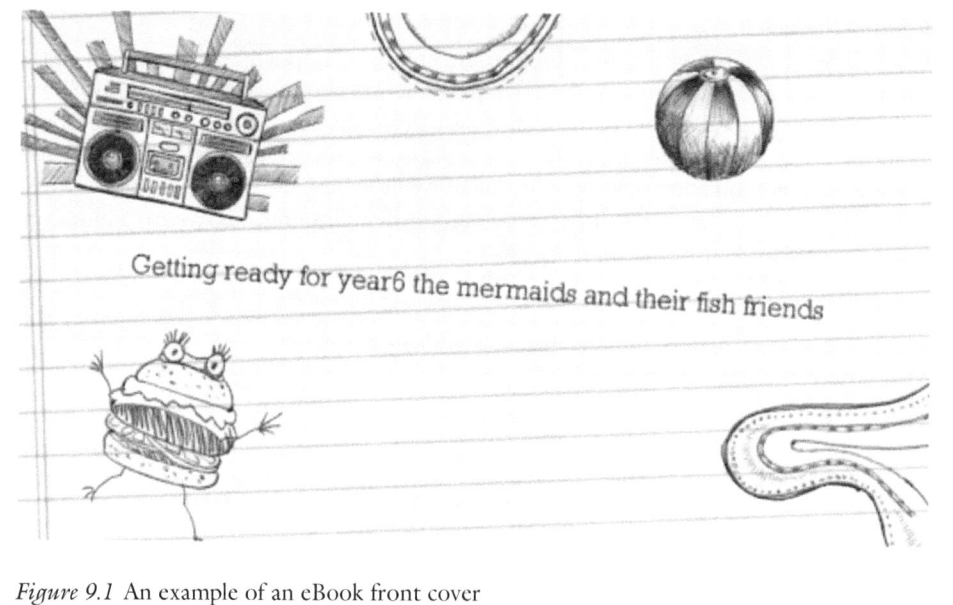

Figure 9.1 An example of an eBook front cover

Additional planning considerations for digital storytelling

At this point review your plans and think about what additional preparation is needed such as storing data and ensuring internet connections and licences. Evaluate the range of technologies your pupils have access to; they may need help sheets or video clips on how to use them. Plan to create or source media assets for your pupils to use in their digital stories. These might be images, sounds or videos that they create themselves, perhaps as part of drama or outdoor activities, or as part of a curriculum activity such as a science experiment.

You should also consider online safety in your planning (see Chapter 23 for further information). The Department for Education (2019, p.3) suggest that rather than focusing upon trying to keep up to date with the latest app or platform, teachers should convey the 'underpinning knowledge and behaviours that can help pupils to navigate the online world safely and confidently regardless of the device, platform or app'. This should be embedded as a wider school approach wherein online safety is everybody's responsibility. Take some time to familiarise yourself with your school's approach and decide the prior learning necessary for children to safely access the planned digital tools. Find out whether you will need to communicate your sharing intentions to parents, and if so, how early you will need to do this in relation to the start of the digital storytelling activity.

Assessing and sharing digital storytelling

A further aspect of the preparation needs to focus on how pupils will demonstrate their knowledge and understanding. As with any task that is going to be assessed you need to have criteria to share with your pupils. You may want to assess a range of aspects, such as elements of literacy skills, their planning, the artefacts created such as the storyboard, uses of technology, and the overall presentation of content. Literacy skills may include written, oral, cultural, information and visual. You will also want to make clear links to the school curriculum plans and identify which aspects will be assessed. If the story has been developed by a group, you may choose to assess how each pupil worked within their team. There is an opportunity to build in some peer and self-assessment formative feedback, in line with the constructivist approach to learning and the value of metacognition. This will help individuals or groups to assess their progress at planned times during the project, such as during the development of the storyboard.

Table 9.2 summarises some of the outcomes you may choose to measure. They are drawn from Wu and Chen's systematic review of digital storytelling (2020, p.6) and exemplify assessment opportunities that may be appropriate to your learners.

Table 9.2 Outcomes of digital storytelling

Type of outcome	Description	What to look for
Affective Learning	Attitudes and emotional engagement	Positive attitudes, empathy, motivation, sense of accomplishment
Cognitive Learning	Critical and creative thinking	Interpreting and evaluating arguments, sequencing, prediction and concluding
Conceptual Understanding	Understanding of concepts and reconceptualization	Identifying themes, characters, roles, motives and mission
Academic Skills	Research, enquiry and academic performance	Self-directed learning, positive choices and application of research
Technological Skills	Use of media, platforms and tools	Skills such as editing, uploading, cropping, recording and sharing
Language Skills	Reading, writing, expression and genre	Multimodal means of expression, use of sequencing and story structure
Social Skills	Collaboration, teamwork and communication	Working well with others, helping others, explaining and communicating their ideas, negotiation and consideration
Ontological Learning	Self-awareness and awareness of others	Understanding of others, their situation, their needs and their role

Finally, consider how pupils will share their completed digital stories and with whom. Sharing stories and gaining feedback from a wider audience will provide a sense of achievement and celebration. Using online platforms allows the children's work to be shared with parents, carers and other children in the school. They also facilitate sharing more widely via the school website or through sites such as eTwinning which enables classes to connect across countries. The Case Study 9.1 illustrates the process of collaborating and sharing.

Case Study 9.1: Connecting classrooms and sharing learning

Digital Learning Across Boundaries (DLAB) project

DLAB was an international partnership across classrooms in five European countries. Each classroom was paired with a class in another country. Pairs of classes collaborated closely around designated international days to create shareable digital artefacts that had built-in interdependence. Collaboration was intrinsic to these outcomes so that there was a planned flow of ideas as each country worked with another to make the digital product that represented their work. Scrolling Twitter walls and Skype sessions were built into the international collaboration days so that there was continuous interaction and a sense of purpose as each class could see images of the progress being made elsewhere. The posted images made the Twitter wall a powerful window into the other classrooms during the international days.

There was a strong emphasis on pursuing STEM themes through storytelling to develop a shared understanding of concepts across the paired classrooms. To give some examples:

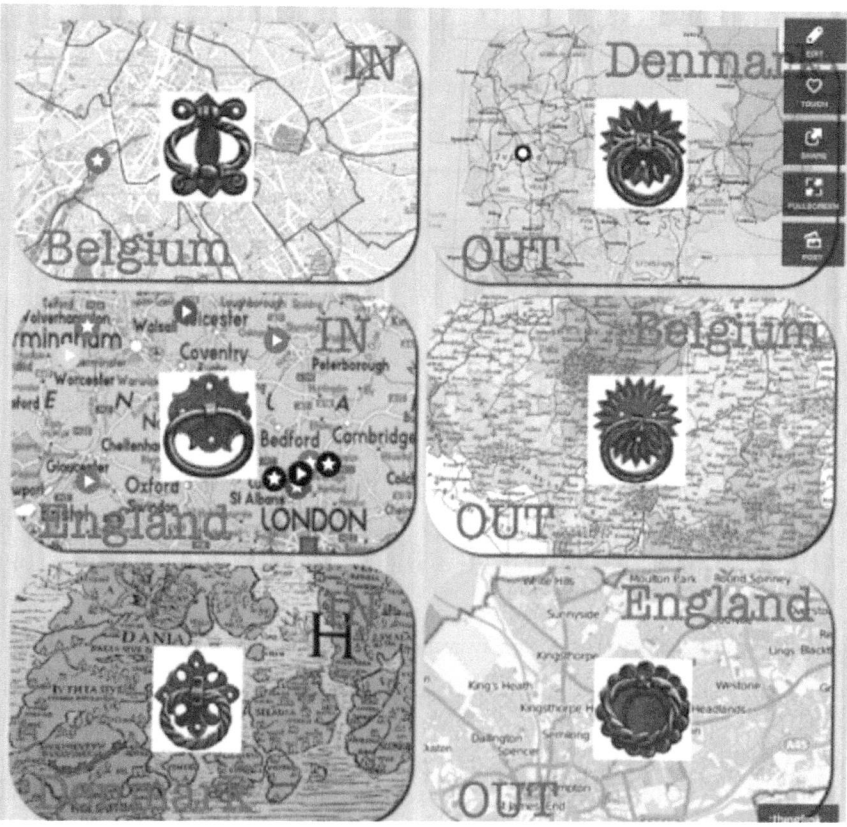

Figure 9.2 Thinglink 'in' and 'out' drawers used to support Wild Writing

- Inspired by the trigger question 'what if our senses changed?', four classes worked on different aspects of the theme of the super senses of the animal world, swapping their research on mammals, fish, birds and reptiles, and creating a combined media presentation.
- Exploring the theme of Wild Writing, classes used an interactive image of a set of 'in' and 'out' drawers using the tool Thinglink to post media inspirations and responses for each other, as we see in Figure 9.2.
- Investigating environmental issues in their countries through 'Science Outdoors', the partner classes used infographic tools to post information and then swapped them to suggest solutions for each other, combining their results into an eBook. Thinking about the theme of 'Art in the Environment', virtual sculptures were exchanged and green screened into each other's environments. The results of the exchanges were captured as tags on a digital art map and used to inspire writing.

Figure 9.3 Virtual sculptures on the fourth plinth in Trafalgar Square

These examples highlight ways in which technology can impact language and literacy practices, and the rich choice of authoring technologies children can now choose from in their production of multimodal texts. In this way of working, physical and digital ways of exploring and representing experience seem inseparable, as is the use of technology for collaboration and connectivity. One digital artefact inspires the creation of another, and through swapping and responding to artefacts, learners are corresponding through visual media as well as words.

This process can be likened to multimodal literacy approaches that recognise how shared meanings can develop across time, space and modalities. A key idea is that the multimodality of the exchanges facilitated joint meaning making for connected classrooms across geographical divides. In the context of the DLAB international project work, digital storytelling using a range of media acted as a communication tool that bypassed language barriers and built intercultural understandings.

Exploring a range of technologies

The following sections of this chapter exemplify a range of tools that you can use to implement digital storytelling into your classroom. It is helpful to become familiar with a handful of open-ended digital tools that you can return to. These might include a tool for creating flip books such as BookCreator, an online whiteboard such as Padlet or Jamboard, a film editing tool such as iMovie, a collaborative writing environment such as Google Docs or Microsoft 365, and an augmented/virtual reality environment such as CoSpaces.

Our examples from practice explore five key themes and each is illustrated by a case study.

1. *Working with digital media*

Digital storytelling allows children to build narratives that include music, sounds, film and images. Multimedia tools can stimulate children's imagination and increase their interaction and engagement with the story. A constructivist pedagogy encourages scaffolding, therefore children will benefit from modelled examples and stimuli. Next see Case Study 9.2.

Case Study 9.2: Using iMovie to retell stories

The use of apps within teaching and learning can enhance experiences, increase engagement and offer new ways to learn (Gómez and Garganté, 2016). Many apps can be used in a cross-curricular manner for numerous purposes, including retelling stories digitally. One such app is iMovie, a video editing software tool. iMovie allows users to create short videos by inserting different media, including images, video and audio files, into free projects or pre-created trailer templates. Recent studies have shown iMovie to be in the top 10 apps used within Primary settings (Hepburn, 2021).

The example shown in Figure 9.4 is taken from a module on a BA Primary Education course where university students explored how digital technologies, including robots, apps as well as Virtual Reality (VR) and Augmented Reality (AR), can enhance teaching and learning within the primary classroom environment. This example shows how two students, Bella and Sophie, used iMovie to re-tell the fable The Tortoise and the Hare.

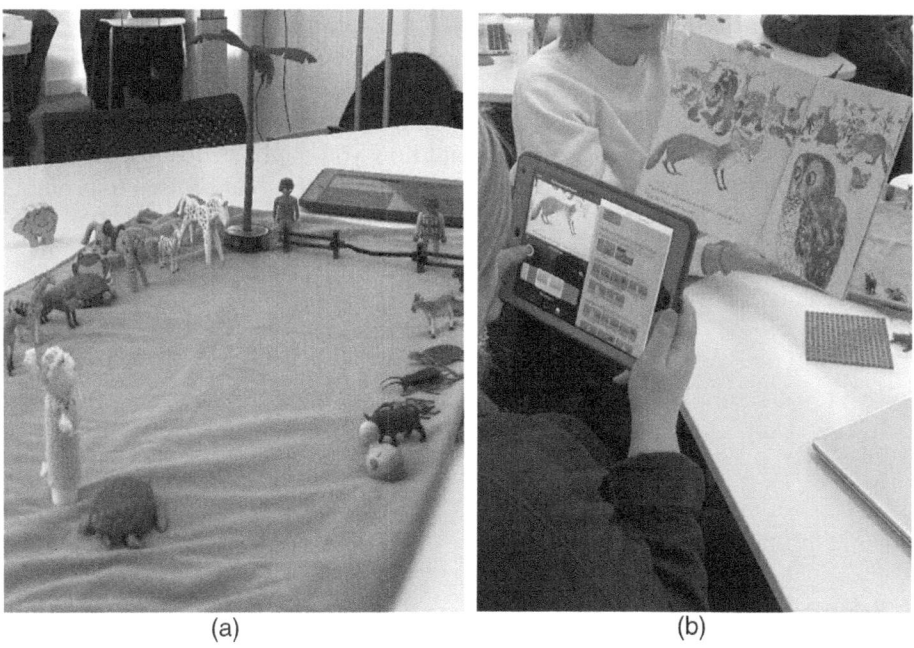

(a)   (b)

Figure 9.4 Using green screen technology to retell The Tortoise and the Hare

To create the files they required to retell the story, Bella and Sophie recreated the location from the fable using miniature animal figures and then took photos and recorded small videos of different stages of the story using the iPad camera. Whilst doing so, the university students noted how they could have enhanced the quality of their videos further by combining this with a green screen app we had previously explored. Additionally, Bella and Sophie used a physical copy of the book to directly link back to the story itself. Then the students chose a pre-created trailer template and were able to drop in each of the media files they had created to sequence their retelling of the story. They were then able to edit any accompanying text to videos and images. In total, their iMovie clip took around 45 minutes to create before these were shared with colleagues whose stories included Dear Zoo, The Gruffalo and The Great Fire of London.

Follow-up discussion focused on how digital storytelling could be used in a number of ways, including as a stimulus or hook for a new class story, to allow children to sequence a story in the correct order or to encourage them to communicate their understanding of a story in another format. This supports the view of Smeda *et al.* (2014) that digital storytelling can enhance engagement, foster collaboration, personalise learning and develop digital literacy.

Now turn to Task 9.2 which asks you to look at your current curriculum and identify opportunities where you could integrate digital storytelling, digital storytelling can sit in multiple subject areas and have much to offer in enhancing the wider curriculum.

Task 9.2: Identifying prompts

Review your class curriculum and identify a story book, project, event or opportunity where you could use digital storytelling. Decide which prompt you might use, the technology tools you have available and how you might structure your activity over a set of lessons, for example the image in Figure 9.5 could be used to prompt a discussion on how water consumption could be reduced.

Figure 9.5 An example of an eBook cover created on the theme of 'wasting water'

2. Supporting language development

As a collaborative activity, digital storytelling can provide a context for engaging with others through creating and editing media content. This process can benefit language learners and support aspects of language development, including reading, writing and speaking (Yilmaz and Goktas, 2017). The potential to orchestrate meaning through a balance of media aligns well with Universal Design for Learning (UDL) principles that seek to establish inclusive learning environments by offering multiple means of representation, of engagement, and of action and expression (see: https://udlguidelines.cast.org) (CAST, 2018). A digital storytelling approach that enables learners to have choices in how they express their ideas through various media advocates for a diversity of learners, some of whom might be more comfortable with the spoken word and others with the use of images. The end products can be equally powerful. A choice of visual and auditory modes of access and expression alongside text can enrich learning and help to meet learner needs, making the storytelling experience personally meaningful and inclusive (Rose and Meyer, 2002). Next, see Case Study 9.3.

Case Study 9.3: Digital storytelling supporting language development

I explored the impact reading for pleasure has on reading attitudes, attainment and practices for pupils using English as an Additional Language (EAL) in a Southeast London primary school. During this research, digital texts played a significant role in increasing pupils' engagement in reading for pleasure, supporting their English language proficiency and developing an active reading community. The research project consisted of five reading sessions where pupils using EAL were invited to participate with their parents/carers and siblings to gain a holistic view of the pupils' reading identities and experiences. Below are two examples of the applications used.

BookCreator

BookCreator is a popular application amongst schools and contains interactive elements that support teachers and pupils in creating their own digital stories (for example, the ability to upload photos and videos, insert text and record audio clips). I used BookCreator in the research project to record the progress of the reading sessions as the features of the app helped to overcome the language barrier. The participants were able to upload emojis and record their voices to share their opinions in the eBook we created.

Furthermore, BookCreator provided an accessible medium for participants to share their experiences of reading for pleasure and their reading identities in their own voice. Some chose to create their own versions of wordless picture books using photos whilst others recorded audio as narration in their home language. Being able to upload the finished digital books as a video file to the school system meant that others could also access the books and share the experience, resulting in a growing, multilingual reading-for-pleasure community. Figure 9.6 shows an example of one of the digital stories that was made using BookCreator.

Figure 9.6 Digital storytelling with pupils using EAL

eBooks

eBooks are an increasingly popular medium of storytelling for pupils. Many schools turned to eBooks available online as a source of reading materials during the Covid-19 pandemic because schools and libraries were closed. For EAL students, this had a particularly damaging impact as they did not have access to quality examples of written English. They could not practice their language skills with their peers and many also did not use English at home due to the proficiency of their family members. The features of eBooks and their availability provided the participants of the research project opportunities to be more independent in reading outside of the classroom.

Oxford Owl and Bug Club were two examples of eBook websites used with the participants. Both contained useful features. These included read-aloud options that supported phonics and pronunciation and interactive games that supported comprehension and understanding. Moreover, the participants were able to increase their English vocabulary because they could easily translate words or phrases using platforms such as Google Translate and Say Hi. The results from the research project indicated a positive correlation between the frequency of pupils engaging in reading for pleasure at home independently and with other family members, and their engagement with eBooks as a reading medium.

Figure 9.7 The Oxford Owl home page (https://home.oxfordowl.co.uk/)

The school library in both its physical and online formats is a powerful resource for supporting your learning and teaching. Turn to Task 9.3 which will challenge you to think about your school's current provision.

Task 9.3: Using eBooks

Meet with your school librarian or English coordinator to discuss what eBooks are available for the children to access. Think about which of these might appeal to your children. Identify the needs of any children who are reluctant readers, need further support or who are learning English. Plan where in your curriculum you could use eBooks to support learning and achievement.

Figure 9.8 Children accessing eBooks on a tablet

3. Using shared online spaces

Shared online spaces allow children to work synchronously and asynchronously across different timelines and in different spaces. Children can collaborate on their story building and co-creating the content, timeline, media and images. Tools such as Google Docs, BookCreator, Padlet, Miro and Office 365 offer online spaces in which children can work together to create stories that include a range of media. They support a social constructivist pedagogy by promoting teamwork, negotiation, sharing, reflection and discussion. Next, see Case Study 9.4.

Case Study 9.4: Using shared online spaces for co-creation

The example, shown in Figure 9.9, comes from a university student undertaking her Foundation Degree in Learning and Teaching.

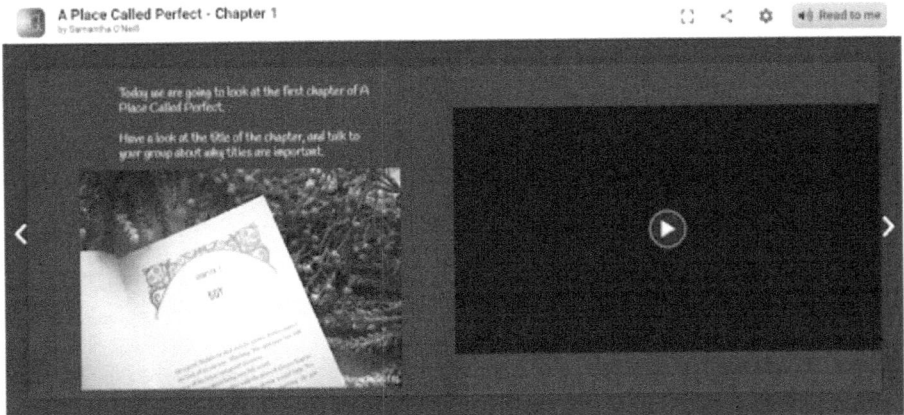

Figure 9.9 Sam's BookCreator eBook based upon the story 'A Place Called Perfect'

Sam has used a book that she created as a stimulus for teaching her students in a Primary School in the East of England. She has included a video of herself explaining the task, as well as asking some additional questions addressed to her class to extend their learning. This is considerate of a constructivist teaching approach where modelling good practice or offering stimuli can inspire and support children. Sam was able to explore the story *A Place Called Perfect*, by including sounds and images to exemplify what the story was about, creating stimulating discussions with children regarding metaphors and their place in fictional stories. Multimodal expression of content allows the book to appeal to a range of learners and offers them a range of suggestions for how they might construct their own stories.

Sam shared her eBook with her colleagues so that they could use it within their teaching. She could 'publish' her book, meaning it will be added to a library of books that can be adopted by anyone with a BookCreator account. Children subsequently published their own books using a QR code in their school newsletter that allowed parents and carers to access their work and share in assembly with the school community.

Celebrating children's work and achievements is important to demonstrate the value your school puts on their learning and achievement. Task 9.4 guides you to identify ways in which you can share children's work, their learning and the skills they have developed.

Task 9.4: Identifying opportunities

Work with your teaching team to identify opportunities in the school year, such as World Book Day, where you can share stories with other classes, schools and audiences. Investigate the potential to use Twitter accounts or eTwinning to collaborate with other classes.

Figure 9.10 A 'Save Our Planet' poster used by children to collaborate on environmental issues

4. Extended reality environments

Extended reality is an umbrella term for immersive computer-generated environments such as augmented and virtual reality. These can provide rich interactive environments for storytelling (Miller, 2019). Augmented Reality (AR) allows interactions between digital and physical spaces by displaying virtual information in real-world environments. Yilmaz and Goktas (2017, p.76) suggest that AR 'transforms empty spaces into rich learning environments' and can be highly motivating, offering different ways of interacting with characters, events and 'a sense of magic'. Virtual Reality (VR), on the other hand, offers a fully immersive experience via a headset and has the potential to transport the user to an entirely different world. In the context of storytelling, users can experience fictional environments set in different dimensions of time or space.

Both AR and VR put the user in control of exploring and interacting with the environment, increasing the feeling of being immersed in a story. There is also the potential for pupils to use a 360-degree camera to create story worlds for others to experience, either as 3D images or as VR films. Consider the multiple ways you could enhance descriptive language to represent a 'giant green tree' or a 'sly old fox' through music, sound effects, images or 3D augmentation. Next, see Case Study 9.5.

Case study 9.5: Extended reality environments

BA Primary Education students explored how VR and AR can enhance storytelling through immersion. The benefits of using VR and AR in teaching and learning are widespread including greater recall, promotion of active learning and increased motivation (Timovski *et al.*, 2020).

Figure 9.11 is a VR retelling of Jack and the Beanstalk taken from Seymour and Lehrn online resources (https://www.seymourlerhn.com/). Within this re-telling, children can immerse themselves and explore the setting of the story whilst listening to an audio overlay of the story. This can be conducted by dragging the video itself using fingers or a mouse or by placing a tablet into a VR headset. The university students explored a range of VR experiences using the YouTube VR Channel and the YouTube Channel for Seymour and Lehrn which has VR resources for a range of cross-curricular topics taught in Primary schools including The Egyptians, The Victorians and Dinosaurs.

Figure 9.11 A VR retelling of Jack and the Beanstalk from Seymour and Lehrn

Figure 9.12 is an example of how AR apps are developing within storytelling. Here, Tabitha, another student on the course, has used the My Caterpillar app

Figure 9.12 Using the My Caterpillar app to retell the story of 'The Very Hungry Caterpillar'

which allows children to explore and retell the story of The Very Hungry Caterpillar in their own environment. By scanning a clear space, using the camera, the caterpillar and the food it eats in the story appear in the room. By tapping the screen, the caterpillar moves to each new piece of fruit in the same order as it does in the story. This allows children to explore the story, make predictions about which fruit is next and sequence the story more clearly.

5. Drama and games-based learning

Creativity is characterised by problem solving, original thinking and creating new connections. In digital storytelling creativity takes place through the story content and its production. Many digital stories involve game-like elements (Miller, 2019) and these can facilitate problem solving, deduction and prediction. The role of a protagonist can develop, through embedding game-based decisions. Non-linear stories, where the reader makes choices about the direction of the story, are popular in gaming, and digital tools can allow for game-like elements such as multiple endings, missions and jeopardy.

Drama has the potential to offer a physical experience of acting out real and imagined events. It allows children to contemplate the feelings and thoughts of others, developing social and emotional understanding and empathy, as well as providing the opportunity to develop their own confidence and self-awareness. Use of freeze frames supports the building of storyboards and can help children to identify key moments in their narratives. Digital tools such as iMovie trailers can capture drama, role-play or dance scenes and turn them into shareable artefacts. This can enable a class to revisit their theme at the beginning of each lesson and build upon their drama ideas over a series of sessions.

It is also worth considering the use of a green screen to provide imaginative backdrops for filming drama or puppetry. In a similar way to extended reality, this can increase the sense of being immersed in a story. Experiment with homemade green screens: try using display board paper, green material or even a green PowerPoint slide. Being able to film and share stories can be a powerful incentive to write, and group media projects such as these provide opportunities for children to take a variety of roles.

There is potential to adopt different methods of story making: maybe the soundtrack or a set of images is the starting point rather than a written script, and choice is a feature of the process, increasing learner autonomy (Wu and Chen, 2020). Next, see Case Study 9.6.

Case Study 9.6: Creating multi-sensory spaces for storytelling

An example of combining drama and technology is the creation of immersive multi-sensory spaces. Such spaces can combine tangible and digital objects by using devices such as projected images, sensory apps, torches in dark dens, robots, green screening or virtual reality combined with tangible materials. They particularly lend themselves to Early Years or SEND teaching. Building on the work of Preece (2015), students at the University of Northampton developed this idea as part of an assistive technology module and created sensory spaces for local children with special needs to explore the story 'We're Going on a Bear Hunt' by Michael Rosen. One child described their immersive sensory story experience, 'We're not just reading it, we're in it!'.

(a)   (b)

Figure 9.13 A sensory space for children to experience the story of 'We're Going on a Bear Hunt'

This chapter has guided you through a number of ways you can embed digital storytelling into your curriculum, each context is different, your learners, your resources and your school's vision all impact upon the way in which you can develop your digital storytelling. Our final task, 9.5, encourages you to consider your next steps in moving forwards.

Task 9.5: Key takeaways

As a final task for this chapter, sum up your three key takeaways for implementing digital storytelling in your classroom. Think about the benefits and challenges. Refine your ideas for implementing a project.

Figure 9.14 A child's drawing as part of a storyboarding exercise to plan their digital story

Summary and key points

In this chapter we have explored what digital storytelling means in the primary classroom and how you might use this in your professional practice. We have considered the ways in which you might approach digital storytelling, in terms of the tools you might use and the pedagogical approaches you might take within the themes of media, language development, online spaces, extended reality, drama and games-based learning. Similarly, we have exemplified through our case studies how a range of curriculum content can be taught and have illustrated the potential to use digital storytelling to teach children about SDG goals.

Key points:

- The potential to support a diverse range of learners to develop a love for language and literacy can be enhanced by the use of digital tools.
- Digital storytelling can offer learners a range of ways to demonstrate their learning and understanding, to access stories and to share their work with an authentic audience.

- Children can demonstrate a wide range of skills and learning, spanning their personal and social development, their technological skills and their reading, writing and speaking skills.
- The digital aspect of storytelling will change as different technologies are introduced.
- The storytelling environment can be the main element through which you introduce your class to technologies, creative writing and literacy elements of the National Curriculum.

However you decide to teach digital storytelling, remember to plan it carefully, consider the pedagogy, the development of creative and technological expertise, and then think about which tools will be the most appropriate, thus developing pupils' digital capital. Aim to embrace the approach as a way to engage pupils in sharing their lived experiences and to connect them with wider contemporary issues and potential global audiences.

Further resources

MESHGuide on Reluctant Writers. https://www.meshguides.org/guides/node/38/.
This is a useful online resource. A reluctant writer is one who experiences one or more barriers to the writing process on a regular basis. Barriers may be exhibited during the process of writing as well as, or instead of, the start of the process. In addition, a reluctant writer may be defined as one whose writing is habitually superficial, either because ideas are not expanded or because the writing is executed in haste. The evidence presented here is from a three-year research project funded by the Bedford Charity (Harpur Trust) in the UK (2007–2010).

Into Film. https://www.intofilm.org/about/.
Into Film supports teachers to use film and cinema to inspire children and connect with cinema. Their resources include the Into Film+ film streaming platform, a network of extra-curricular Into Film clubs, resources for use in clubs or the classroom, face-to-face and online training opportunities, an annual cinema-based film festival and the prestigious Into Film Awards.

Research.com: Digital storytelling. https://research.com/education/digital-storytelling/.
A useful guide to digital storytelling in education.

Seymour & Lerhn. https://www.seymourlerhn.com/
An educational virtual reality platform designed to work with a range of technologies.

Acknowledgements

Thank you to the following contributors for the vignettes and illustrations from practice: Adam Chapman, Olivia Carpenter, Simon Chapman, Jean Edwards and the Digital Learning Across Boundaries project.

References

Abderrahim, L. and Gutiérrez-Colón Plana, M. (2021). A theoretical journey from social constructivism to digital storytelling. *The EUROCALL Review* [Online], 29(1), 38–49. https://files.eric.ed.gov/fulltext/EJ1305303.pdf.

Bates, A.T. (2015). *Teaching in a digital age* [Online]. *BC Open Textbook Collection*. Available from: https://open.bccampus.ca/find-open-textbooks/?uuid=da50f5f1-bbc6-481e-a359-e73007c66932&contributor=&keyword=&subject [Accessed 30 December 2022].

CAST. (2018). *Universal design for learning guidelines version 2.2*. Retrieved from http://udlguidelines.cast.org [Accessed 27 November 2023].

Department for Education (2019). Teaching online safety in schools. Guidance supporting schools to teach their pupils how to stay safe online, within new and existing school subjects. https://www.gov.uk/government/publications/teaching-online-safety-in-schools.

Gómez, D.M. and Garganté, A.B. (2016). Exploring the use of educational technology in primary education: Teachers' perception of mobile technology learning impacts and applications' use in the classroom. *Computers in Human Behaviour*, 56, 21–28.

Hepburn, H. (2021). Are these the 9 most popular apps in primary schools? *TES Magazine* [Online]. Available from: https://www.tes.com/magazine/news/primary/are-these-9-most-popular-apps-primary-schools.

Luckin, R., Clark, W., Garnett, F., Whitworth, A., Akass, J., Cook, J. and Robertson, J. (2010). Learner-generated contexts: A framework to support the effective use of technology for learning. In: M. Lee and C. McLoughlin, eds. *Web 2.0-based e-learning: Applying social informatics for tertiary teaching*, 70–84. Pennsylvania: IGI Global.

Miller, C. (2019). Digital storytelling: A creator's guide to interactive entertainment (Fourth edition.). CRC Press.

Nair, V. and Yunus, M.M. (2021). A systematic review of digital storytelling in improving speaking skills. *Sustainability*, 13(17), 1–15.

Niemi, H. and Multisilta, J. (2016). Digital storytelling promoting twenty-first century skills and student engagement. *Technology, Pedagogy and Education*, 25(4), 451–468.

Okumus, A. (2020). The perceptions and preferences of 8th grade students in digital storytelling in English. *International Online Journal of Education and Teaching*, 7(2), 585–604.

Preece, D. and Zhao, Y. (2015). Multi-sensory storytelling: A tool for teaching or an intervention technique? *British Journal of Special Education*, 42(4), 429–443.

Prensky, M.R. (2008). *Programming is the new literacy* [Online]. George Lucas Educational Foundation: edutopia. Available from: http://lablearning.eu/documents/doc_inspiration/prensky/programming_is_the_new_literacy.pdf [Accessed 1 January 2023].

Prensky, M.R. (2012). From digital natives to digital wisdom: Hopeful essays for 21st century learning. Corwin Press.

Rodríguez, C.L., García-Jiménez, M., Massó-Guijarro, B. and Cruz-González, C. (2021). Digital storytelling in education: A systematic review of the literature. *Review of European Studies*, 13, 13–25.

Rose, D.H. and Meyer, A. (2002). *Teaching every student in the digital age: Universal design for learning*. Alexandria: Association for Supervision and Curriculum Development.

Scott, R. (2021). Language and learning loss: The evidence on children who use English as an Additional Language. *The Bell Foundation* [Online]. Available from: https://www.bell-foundation.org.uk/app/uploads/2021/06/Language-learning-loss.pdf [Accessed 19 May 2022].

Smeda, N., Dakich, E. and Sharda, N. (2014). The effectiveness of digital storytelling in the classrooms: A comprehensive study. *Smart Learning Environments*, 1(1), 6. https://doi.org/10.1186/s40561-014-0006-3.

Timovski, R., Koceska, N. and Koceski, S. (2020). *Review: The use of augmented and virtual reality in education*. International Conference on Information Technology and Development of Education. ITRO. October 2020. Zrenjanin, Republic of Serbia.

Wales, and Mohamed, M. (n.d.). *Digital storytelling and drama in the English language classroom*. In Lee Yong Tay and Cher Ping Lim, eds. *Creating holistic technology-enhanced learning experiences*, 59–73. SensePublishers. https://doi.org/10.1007/978-94-6209-086-6_4.

Wu, J. and Chen, D.-T.V. (2020). A systematic review of educational digital storytelling. *Computers and Education*, 147. https://doi.org/10.1016/j.compedu.2019.103786.

Yilmaz, R.M. and Goktas, Y. (2017). Using augmented reality technology in storytelling activities: Examining elementary students' narrative skill and creativity. *Virtual Reality: The Journal of the Virtual Reality Society* [Online], 21(2), 75–89.

10 Using short film to develop children's moving image literacy

Marian Henry

Introduction

In this chapter you will learn how to teach the pupils in your class to "read" and "write" using the media of moving image and sound. By viewing, analysing and discussing short films with the children in your class, you can help them to develop a broad range of literacy skills. By giving the children opportunities to create their own short films, you can reinforce this learning and enable them to explore and value their own creative expression. The chapter is based on successful approaches in my own school.

When we think about fostering children's literacy in the 21st century, we need to continue to develop their print literacy, but we also need to broaden the scope to encompass moving images and sounds. The media environment that the children engage regularly with may contain videos, text and sound and so giving children the skills necessary to critically engage with this is the focus of this chapter.

The premise is that the development of children's literacy in relation to film is beneficial in two key ways. The first is using short films is an engaging way of meeting the targets set out in literacy curricula. Comprehension skills such as inferring, predicting, summarising can be effectively nurtured using film just as easily as using a book. The second is that literacy learning in this area is relevant to the communications environment that the children live and learn in both in school and outside of school.

Objectives

By the end of this chapter, you should be able to:

- critically understand change and continuity in literacy
- have ideas and strategies to promote the "reading" of moving images in the classroom
- have ideas and strategies for how to facilitate children to create or "write" their own short films
- understand about the benefits and challenges in working with film with children.

Change and continuity in children's literacy

What does it mean to be literate in the 21st century? Literacy is defined as the ability to read and write (Oxford English Dictionary, 2002: 828). However, in the 21st century, as we reflect on our reading and writing practices, we see that being literate is not limited to words on pages. The technologies of reading and writing have evolved over the past

DOI: 10.4324/9781003408925-10

millennia, from scratches on cave walls to hieroglyphics to the invention of the alphabet, the printing press, radio, video and the internet. Literacy at any point in time is closely related to the technologies of communication of that time. As technologies evolve, so too must our understanding of what it means to be literate. In Ireland, The Literacy and Numeracy for Learning and Life Strategy states that:

> Traditionally we have thought about literacy as the skills of reading and writing; but today our understanding of literacy encompasses much more than that. **Literacy includes the capacity to read, understand and critically appreciate various forms of communication including spoken language, printed text, broadcast media, and digital media**.
> (Department of Education and Skills 2011: 8 [bold in original])

This statement represents a broader conception of literacy. We must now foster literacy across a wide range of modes of communication from spoken language to digital media. When digital media are discussed in relation to education, there can be a focus on the technology and on helping children develop skills. In contrast, the approach in this chapter is to focus on the child and their developing literacy. Technical skills to use the technology are important, but one also requires literacy. Livingstone (2003: 15) argues that when children engage with digital technologies:

> evidently there is not only skill involved but also an interpretive relationship with a complex, symbolically encoded text as mediated by a particular technology. It is this engagement with text that distinguishes information and communication technologies from other technologies – which is why we call a competent user of the washing machine or car "skilled" but not "literate."

The focus on developing literacy rather than skills is not simply semantics. It shifts our focus away from the technology and more onto the learner. It allows us to put the child at the heart of the learning experience. Instead of thinking of great ways to use various technologies or apps, the question is: how will each child's literacy develop because of these lessons?

In this chapter, it is not possible to cover all areas of literacy in the 21st century. The focus is on film. Film is a moving image literacy. It shares commonality with print literacy in terms of storyline and characters, but it also adds new lessons in relation to moving images, sounds, and camera shots, for example. Fostering children's literacy in relation to moving images is useful in relation to films, but also television, and online videos. These are core elements of many children's media experiences.

Case Study 10.1: The film club

What follows is an account of workshops that I ran in my own primary school over many years. As di Bari (2019) has noted it can be quite challenging for a teacher to develop good reflective media education lessons as one class teacher with a large group of children. To fully explore and experiment with the format and content, I chose to create an afterschool club called The Film Club. I facilitated 90-minute workshops, once a week for six weeks with approximately 25 children. Each workshop involved an element of "reading" and "writing" short films. Each week, we watched, discussed, and analysed a short film and then the children worked in groups to create their own short films. While structured, the atmosphere in the club was more relaxed than the classroom with more freedom and emphasis on collaboration, creativity and exploring ideas. It can be tricky when organising these kinds of experiences to find the balance between leaving space to be creative and have fun while also maintaining an environment where the children are reflecting and developing their understanding of the medium of film.

Though every effort was made to ensure a broad experience of film for the children, there are limits to what can be done in any situation. Therefore, the examples I give are ideas for you to use as jumping-off points, rather than an exhaustive or complete programme of work. You may use some of the ideas or they may be the inspiration for you to develop your own original lessons. The focus is on the learning outcomes for the children. How are they developing in their critical and creative skills? How are they playing, engaging, creating, and reflecting on their work? How are they bringing their own ideas, concepts, and skills together and moving forward in their learning? Finally, how are they finding their own voices and supporting the voices of their classmates?

Children reading short films

In each workshop, we spent some time "reading" a short film. Shorts that are three- to six-minutes long work well for several reasons (See the resources mentioned in the Further Reading and Websites at the end of the chapter.) Firstly, children are less likely to have seen the shorts before so there is no familiarity or situation where some children know what will happen and some do not. Secondly, short films allow for multiple viewings of the text. This is not a new concept for you most likely, as when you work on reading comprehension with your pupils, you encourage them to read the piece more than once. With each short film viewing, you can draw the children's attention to a different concept or element. Asking some questions before the viewing is an effective way of focusing the children's attention while they are watching so that they watch the shorts in an analytical and active way. Stopping the film during the viewing to ask questions is a good way of checking for understanding or highlighting an element. Similarly, the questions you ask after a viewing helps to explore children's comprehension of the story, their new learning, and their individual responses to the film. While children have many opportunities to watch film and television in their day-to-day lives, the experience in Film Club is different due to the focused questions and discussion. As Domke, Weippert and Apol (2018: 51) write, film-viewing experiences "often hold untapped potential for literacy learning". By analysing films as texts in the classroom children build their critical visual and media literacy skills.

To structure the "reading" of these film texts, I used the recommendations from the *Starting Stories* pack that was produced by the British Film Institute in 2003. This is no longer available for purchase but their approach to reading films that I outline here provides guidance for you in structuring your lessons. While you will be able to make connections with your traditional print literacy lessons, it is also important to note that "film has its own rules and language used to describe and discuss its form, content, and concepts" (British Film Institute 2003: 14). These concepts are not necessarily difficult for children to grasp. As Bazalgette (2010) writes, when children come to school, very often they already possess these skills to a more sophisticated level than in traditional print literacy. By teaching in a more explicit way the language and grammar of film we can enhance the children's experience, and understanding, of moving image media. The authors of *Starting Stories* summarise the main elements that together "make a film work". These elements are:

- story,
- setting,
- sound,
- colour,
- character, and
- camera.

Focusing on discussion in each of these elements allows you to help children explore film as a text in detail.

Story

By the time children enter school they are normally familiar with following a story in books, cartoons, television programs, films and videos. They are familiar with plot and storyline, characters, and visual clues. Through analysis and discussion of the story in short films, children can further develop their skills of sequencing, ordering, reporting, recounting, predicting and extrapolating characters' feelings and motivations in different scenarios. As you would if you were working with a book, you can use questions to enhance children's engagement with the story. Some general questions you can use to focus on this element are:

- What happens at the beginning, middle and end of the story?
- What are the most important events in the story?
- Who or what is the story about? How can you tell?
- What do you think happened before the story began?
- What might happen next, after the end of the story?
- Does this remind you of other stories? How?

There are many short films suitable for children that have no dialogue. Therefore, when the children retell and talk about the story, they use their own words to describe the setting, the characters, the plot and so on. This is a rich experience in terms of oral language development. One aspect of the story that you can focus on with the children is how in telling a story the creator decides what information the audience has at each point in the story. For example, we may initially believe a character to be "bad" because of how they look, something they do or the soundtrack but as the story unfolds, it turns out that this character is the hero. The power of the storyteller is that they make decisions about how much or what information the reader or audience has. This is a rich area of discussion and learning. The children enjoy figuring out how the filmmaker communicates the story and how this contributes to the experience of the viewer. This insight is also beneficial for them in thinking of how to tell their own stories when they create films.

Setting

The setting is where the film takes place. In film, the setting is visual and it can play a role in identifying the mood or situation quickly and it can help the audience to understand the actions or feelings of the characters. Films often contain more than one setting. When we engage children in conversations about the setting of the story, we can encourage them to consider what is shown and not shown. Some general questions you can ask are:

- Where does this story happen? How do you know?
- Why does it take place here?
- Is there more than one setting?
- Could the same story have happened in a different place?
- Would a different setting change the story?
- Were there important places you didn't see in the story?

When you look at the setting with children they have to use a lot of descriptive language to talk about where the film takes place. Higher order thinking questions, such as if the story would change if the setting changed, yield lots of ideas and adaptations of the storyline. We see this often in contemporary culture where a story can be retold in a different time in history, for example. Encouraging children to pay attention to the details in the setting, how it is communicated to the audience and how it shapes the storytelling is foundational for their understanding when they are creating and developing their own stories.

Sound

The soundtrack for films plays a significant role in how we experience the story. It is easy for children to recognise and recall the dialogue. What they may be less cognisant of is the soundtrack that may contain a theme for a character or musical background. Additional sounds play a significant role in creating the mood or feel for the audience. One of the clearest examples of this is the soundtrack for Jaws and the simple "duh-duh" sound that creates an atmosphere of foreboding. Here are some general questions for you to ask:

- What sounds did you hear in this film?
- Does the music change throughout the film? What effect does this have?
- Do any of the characters speak? What do you think they might say?

This is an area that the children enjoy thinking and talking about. Sometimes while watching a film, you can pause it and ask, "how are you feeling now?". They children may answer "nervous" or "scared" and then you can explore how the film has conjured this feeling. The soundtrack plays a significant role in creating the feeling that something bad is about to happen, or that all is better now. The children enjoy figuring this out and noticing it in other films. The soundtrack is an important way of bringing the children's attention to the mood of the film and the feelings it creates in them as the audience. It is one of the less visible aspects of film but drawing attention to it, allowing them to explore and become cognisant of it, is empowering for them.

Colour

How a film looks is influenced by colour. Bright, vibrant colours will have a different impact than more muted colours. There could also be visual contrast between a colourful character against a dull backdrop. Colour may help in showing how time is passing from night to day or over the longer term. Some general questions you can ask are:

- What colours did you see in this film?
- In general, are the colours in this film bright or dark?
- How do the colours relate to the story?
- Did they change over the course of the film? How? Can you think of why?
- What would the film have been like in black and white?

The children readily discuss colour in films. They are already familiar with the use of black and white to make something appear as if it was long ago or jumping back in time. What is interesting to explore is the use of weather in the plot. The presentation of weather links with discussions of the setting, soundtrack and colours. For example, setting part of a story in a storm at sea would represent a period of challenge for the characters. The colour palette grows darker, the images of large waves and a boat being thrown around are frightening, while the soundtrack may be full of loud, foreboding sounds and music. The use of colour to help set the mood and tell the story was a new way of talking about film for the children but it was not too complex for them and led to enthusiastic discussions.

Character

Children will be familiar with characters from books, movies, TV shows and digital games. In literacy lessons and stories, we talk about characters in meaningful ways. When looking at the characters in short films, you can encourage the children to look at what a character does, how they are feeling and why they behave in a particular way. Some general questions in relation to character are:

- Who are the characters in this film?
- What do they do?
- How are they related to each other?

- Do any of the characters have particular music or sounds?
- Which character interests you most? Which character would you like to know more about?
- Do any of the characters remind you of others in another story or film? Who? Why?

Pausing the film during the viewing to check in with how a character is feeling is effective in helping children to understand the role of characters in storytelling. It is important to get the children to think about the motivations of the characters. It is also an enriching exercise in critical literacy to explore how the story could be told from the point of view of another character and how their perspective on the events of the story may be different.

Camera

Learning to think about the camera may be a new venture for the children. This is an element they may not be used to discussing but it is central to understanding choices about how a story is told. The camera is like a narrator showing sequences of shots leading us through the story. The audience only sees what the camera shows. Close-up shots can be used to focus on detail or emotion, while longer shots convey setting and establish a broader context. The angles and movements of the camera are tools for generating moods and feelings in the audience. Here are some general questions for you to ask:

- What shots are used in this film? Close-up, medium, and long shot?
- When do you see a long shot or a close-up shot?
- What is the long shot used for?
- What do the first shots tell us about the story, the setting, character and so on?
- What would your last shot in the film show?

The novelty of recognising shots such as close-ups is enjoyable for children. Pausing the film and naming the types of shot used and the effect it has on the storytelling is an engaging activity. You can also explore how when we see a close-up of a character's face and then it cuts to another shot, it has the effect of showing us what that character sees. This is a core lesson in understanding whose perspective is being shared. As I was working with 7–8 year olds, we did some critical thinking in this area but it would be even more suitable with older children.

Children creating films

Each week in The Film Club we practised both reading and writing films. The reason for this is that they are closely related to each other. As children critically engage with reading films, they learn about some of the strategies of good storytelling. These lessons can inform their own choices when making their own short films and also be beneficial for their print literacy.

Giving children some level of direction for when they are making films is important. It helps when they have a focus. It works well where there is a link between the short film you watch with the children and the theme for their own creations. Ideally, what they learn from reading films informs how they approach making their films. Children will most likely be familiar with lots of live action and animation films and TV series. They enjoy learning more about the processes of how these are created.

Live action short movies

The first opportunity that children had to make their own films was making a live action movie. The group of children would come up with their storyline and act it out in front of the camera. For these lessons, it was helpful to ask the children to pitch their idea to the rest of the group and to give them a few questions they needed to answer:

- Who is in the story?
- Where does the story take place?
- What happens in the story?

We talked about the story having a problem or conflict that could then be resolved. The children loved making these live action films and sometimes the idea developed over the weeks.

The children also had the experience of controlling the video camera and directing the films; saying "cut" if someone was not in the shot or the camera needed to be moved for a new setting. Some children preferred to work behind the camera rather than in front of it. I was accepting of this. There are many people who work in film and television who are never in front of the camera.

Puppets telling jokes

For one of the workshops, the children worked in pairs and used puppets to tell jokes. The benefit of this was for the children to only focus on projecting their voice and speaking clearly and slowly so the camera could pick it up. I had several jokes suitable for the age group but if they had their own joke, they could use that too. A key lesson for the children in The Film Club was to move from enjoying themselves telling jokes or acting something out to thinking about how an audience would experience their work. This is a major shift in perspective for children. This simple task took the emphasis off props and storylines so that the children could focus on communicating the joke to a prospective audience. While they enjoyed working with the puppets and making each other laugh, the lesson of communicating the joke clearly to the audience and camera was a fundamental skill to develop for their subsequent filmmaking.

Stop motion animation

Animation is a format that children are familiar with. However, if you try to explain the concept of how animation works to them, it seems somehow unreal. Animation is essentially an optical illusion where we see many pictures that are almost the same but with small changes. When we see these pictures in very quick succession, such as 24 images per second, they appear to be moving. The images have become animated.

To begin to teach about animation with the children we made simple flip books. I gave each child a small book of post-it notes. I showed them how we could animate a small dot; that is to make it look like its moving as we flip the pages of the post-it notes. We started with drawing on the last page and with each page moved the dot further across with each post-it. When we flipped the post-it notes from back to front it gave the illusion that the dot was moving across the page. The children were delighted by this activity. Some children tried to do more complicated drawings, but they realised that the picture on every page needs to be almost identical to the one before and so the workload is intense. If you have older children or more time, you could progress to a ball going into a goal or a basketball net. Making flip books was enjoyable for the children and gave them an appreciation for how much painstaking and careful work is involved in animation.

Following this lesson, we would do another one on stop motion animation using a computer programme called Monkeyjam. Using a desktop computer and a webcam, Monkeyjam allows the user to take multiple photos and then it shows the photographs in quick succession so that they appear animated. In The Film Club, we did stop motion films with play-doh characters moving around, and with Lego structures being built one piece at a time. Sometimes, the children used their own small toys or Lego and set up scenes where the pieces were moving around to tell a story. We also did a chocolate Santa or Easter bunny, slowly being unwrapped and then being eaten. In stop motion animation attention to detail is paramount. Any larger movement between two photographs makes the film feel jumpy. Ensuring the camera is fixed and doesn't move is also important. The children learned that when we work carefully and methodically the result can be something to be proud of.

With their knowledge and experience of stop motion animation, we would then watch a Wallace and Gromit episode. The children could understand and appreciate in a whole new way the incredible creativity and work involved. Often, they would comment on how the characters were made or the props in the set. Far from destroying the illusion of animation, it was empowering for the children to watch the film with their new understanding of the incredible work of the animators.

Green Screen

Working with Green Screen technology was such a great experience in The Film Club. Children frequently watch movies, television and video where this technology is used. Working with Green Screen was not too much of a challenge. I used the large rolls of classroom backing paper in vivid green and covered a large area of the wall. This does take time and needs to be done carefully for the films to look well at the end. I then used an iPad app called Green Screen by Do Ink to record the movies. In this app I chose to work with a photograph as a backdrop. I looked for photographs that are free to use of various landmarks such as the Eiffel Tower or the Statue of Liberty. I also had a weather forecast chart, a moonscape, under the sea, and pictures of jungles and dinosaurs. The children could work in small groups, choose a picture as the setting for their short film and then come up with their script. We recorded their shorts on the iPad and the other children were fascinated when they looked at the iPad at how the green wall became the background. This was exciting technology to use with the children and they were very engaged by it.

Teaching moving image literacy: benefits and challenges

Benefits

Teaching about film can create opportunities for many areas of literacy development from communication and language development to exploring personal, social and emotional development. There are common areas between what we emphasise when developing children's print literacy and how we can develop moving image literacy. Analysing films and allowing children to make their own films are creative processes where the children are actively engaged in a process that has meaning for them. "Some children who are struggling with reading and writing may be able to succeed at interpreting, analysing, and even making image texts" (Bazalgette 2010: 44). In my own experience, some children who have difficulty with reading print can be articulate and active in discussions based on short films. Similarly, children who appear inattentive or unengaged in other school subjects can be totally absorbed in the process of telling their story through making a short film.

Giving children the space to make their own films is an opportunity for them to work creatively. In The Film Club, children could express what they were interested in telling stories about. They made films about ninjas, playing video games, getting lost in the supermarket, getting kidnapped and someone saving them, being approached on the internet and how to deal with that safely, TV talent shows, animal documentaries and so much more. They had ownership over their creativity and were actively engaged in the learning process.

Working with film is different from doing a school performance. The first take doesn't have to be perfect. The children could change aspects of their story or how they were telling it as they made the films. In this way the learning process is play-based learning. The meaningful discussions that children had with each other were rich in terms of oral language development. Just like adults, children can be more comfortable working in different areas: fact, fiction, being in front of the camera, or behind the camera, coming up with ideas or acting out the ideas. There was a space for children to reflect on what aspect of film they were most drawn to.

Teaching about film is a chance for you as a teacher to develop your creativity. Teaching through The Film Club changed how I watched and understood films. When I reflected on how to support the children in their films, I learned more about how to give structure to tasks so that the children could focus on one or two goals and create films they were happy with. I edited all the children's films together so that we could screen them both for the children in The Film Club and have a special screening for their parents. For me, this was a creative process where I made choices about how to present the films, and which sounds, music and captions to use.

Challenges

Teaching children about reading film can be challenging in terms of taking time to choose suitable texts to watch and analyse with the children. Becoming familiar with the elements of film that may be new to you such as camera or sound also may require some time and effort. Working on how you question and facilitate discussions where the children feel comfortable offering their opinions is important. You want to avoid giving the impression that you have a "correct answer" in your head. You need to engender an open and curious approach to the children's discussions. This is important both for the child answering a question, but also as a model for the other children of how we respect and respond to each other during a discussion.

Facilitating the children to work collaboratively is a challenge for lots of group work activities in our classrooms, not just in making short films. Working in a way that is respectful and productive is something that develops over the weeks. There can be children who struggle to be a part of a group, to have their ideas heard, or to be willing to work on someone else's idea. You may have to have many discussions about listening to others, taking turns and taking on board other people's suggestions.

In my experience, the children had a familiarity with the area of film and so in their own films they often wanted to recreate what they enjoyed watching. At the beginning, there were lots of action films with no plot. Sometimes, there wasn't even a dialogue between the characters. The children were enjoying role play where they were heroes and action characters. They may have had a plot in mind, but it was difficult for the audience to grasp it. With experience, I realised that I needed to give the children some guidance to focus them on their creative work. The questions about the characters, setting and plot mentioned above gave them a checklist that helped shape their story. Finally, I always stayed open to their ideas, asking questions to prompt them to improve their film rather than imposing my own ideas.

What is challenging for children is to think in terms of how others will understand their story. They must step into the mind of the prospective audience and think about how to bring them on this film journey. Simple things such as speaking clearly, not walking and talking at the same time and keeping their face visible to the camera are fundamental in getting the story recorded on the camera in a way the audience can receive it. The children need to think about how they can signal to the audience who each character is by saying "Good morning *mom*" at the beginning of the scene instead of just "Good morning". Keeping their ideas simple can also be a challenge. The collaborative nature of The Film Club allowed for discussions to help with this. The children were each other's audience for the filmmaking process providing positive feedback, sharing ideas and learning from each other.

Summary and key points

In this chapter you have considered how literacy in the 21st century is closely linked to the tools of communication we use. Children are growing up in a media environment that is more than printed words on pages. The purpose of this chapter is to help you to broaden the scope of how you approach children's developing literacy by incorporating lessons in moving image literacy. Using film is an engaging way of meeting some of the targets set out in literacy curricula and moving image literacy is necessary in the communications environment that the children live in every day.

The case study of The Film Club shares direct experience of how to do this work with primary school children and is the culmination of many years of practice. The chapter gives you practical advice on

- Questions to ask to enable children to critically analyse moving images in the elements of story, setting, sound, character, colour and camera.
- Ideas for how to support children in creating their own films across a range of genres and technologies, such as live action films, green screen and stop motion animation.

- The importance of nurturing a culture that is supportive of questioning, collaboration and creativity.
- How to be aware of some of the challenges and benefits of doing work in this area.

Working with children in developing their moving image literacy is engaging and exciting work. The classroom can be alive and brimming with creativity. It is important to remember that creativity involves taking risks. Sometimes it's great and other times it is less so. This can be the case for the children and for you as the teacher. However, the process will always yield lessons for you and the children to use in the future.

Further resources

The Literacy Shed has lots of short films that deal with many themes and are suitable for use with children. You could use these to discuss the six elements of film literacy mentioned in this chapter. https://www.literacyshed.com/, Accessed on 4 February 2023.

Here is a link to a list of short films for use in the primary classroom. https://www.intofilm.org/films/filmlist/38, Accessed on 4 February 2023.

The British Film Institute created this wonderful resource that is available to download from their website. It will give you lots of additional and supplementary ideas for how you can use moving images in your classroom. https://www.bfi.org.uk/find-resources-events-teachers/resources-teachers/moving-images-classroom, Accessed on 4 February 2023.

The Irish Film Institute created study guides for use with particular films. They have a set specifically for primary school level. https://ifi.ie/studyguides, Accessed on 4 February 2023.

References

Bazalgette, C. (Ed.) (2010) *Teaching Media in Primary Schools*. London: Sage.

British Film Institute (2003) *Starting Stories: A Film and Literacy Resource for Three- to Seven-Year Olds*. https://www.bfi.org.uk/find-resources-events-teachers/resources-teachers/moving-images-classroom, Accessed on 4 February 2023.

Department of Education and Skills (2011) *Literacy and Numeracy for Learning and Life*. Dublin: Stationery Office.

di Bari, C. (2019) 'Digital Technologies in the 0-6 Years Educational Services: A Media Education Experience in Nursery School and Preschool'. *Studi sulla Formazione*, 22, 177–186.

Domke, L.M., Weippert, T.L., and Apol, L. (2018) 'Beyond School Breaks: Reinterpreting the Uses of Film in Classrooms'. *The Reading Teacher*, 72(1), 51–59.

Livingtone, S. (2003) *The Changing Nature and Uses of Media Literacy*. Media@LSE Electronic Working Papers, http://eprints.lse.ac.uk/13476/1/The_changing_nature_and_uses_of_media_literacy.pdf, Accessed on 4 February 2023.

11 Using technology creatively in English and mathematics

David Morris, Gurmit Uppal and Daniel Ayres

Introduction

Your ability to be creative with technology comes down to your confidence and capacity to use these devices and applications, and your understanding of their pedagogical value in the learning environment. This chapter draws upon empirical evidence from the primary classroom which explores the ways in which technology-based practices can enhance the teaching and learning of English and mathematics. Examples of leading-edge practice in primary classrooms are presented and a range of tools are considered, including mobile devices, video collaboration and web-based technologies, as well as Quick Response [QR] codes. This chapter will provide you with practical guidance on planning and organising technologies to support teaching and learning in English and mathematics. The coronavirus (Covid-19) pandemic changed the ways in which teachers delivered lessons, and how pupils engaged with their learning. This chapter reflects that shift in the educational landscape and how this can continue to play a role in the transformative nature of EdTech in schools.

Objectives

By the end of this chapter you should be able to:

- use a range of online resources and tools to enhance your teaching of English and mathematics
- incorporate technologies into your lessons, to support creativity
- apply approaches (including those learned during the pandemic) to enrich classroom-based environments using a range of technologies.

Background

The potential of technology to revolutionise education, raise attainment and establish new pedagogical approaches has long been recognised (Laurillard, 2008). This vision has also been supported by successive government strategies, curricula, and initiatives (DCSF, 2008; DfE, 2013; DfE, 2020). Over recent years, technology has been increasingly adopted by schools as an approach to drive efficiency, tackle workload, improve inclusion, pupil outcomes, and provide an ever-expanding range of teaching and learning tools (DfE, 2018; DfE, 2019c).

The spotlight on technology was further enhanced more recently during lockdowns imposed during COVID-19, where schools were required to move much of their learning

DOI: 10.4324/9781003408925-11

provision online (Leask and Younie, 2021). For many schools this was not a barrier because the digital infrastructure which they already had in place allowed for a smooth transition to online learning. However, there were schools which needed assistance and this came in the form of the government-funded EdTech demonstrator programme – a network of leading-edge schools which was tasked with supporting other schools in their implementation of technologies and tools to address areas of need (DfE, 2020). During this time, many teachers reported gains in terms of their technology-based professional development, including the acquisition of new skills and the use of new tools (NAACE, 2020). Whilst debates have already begun over whether any long-term changes to pedagogy and education systems will be seen as a result of online learning provision (Selwyn, 2022), the access and breadth of creative digital tools available to teachers and learners continue to flourish.

Improvements in the development of educational technology, coupled with encouraging government efforts in this area, mean that teachers and pupils can now access and use technology across many areas of school life. Since 2013, the National Curriculum (DfE, 2013) in England is no longer explicit in how technology should be used within specific subjects, although it does recognise the importance of technology and its links with mathematics. Similarly, in England, the removal of the technology strand from the Early Years statutory requirements signals that children's interactions with technology for learning and play are now commonplace; therefore, the minimum entitlement outlined in statutory guidance affords flexibility to settings in their approach to technology (DfE, 2021; Caldwell and Goto, 2019). Despite recognition that the technological landscape in schools and wider society has changed over the years, teachers acknowledge that pupils' proficiency in terms of technology should not be presumed (Curtis, 2021). As teachers, it is essential that developing pupil skills such as navigating systems, keyboard/touchpad shortcuts, saving and sharing files are also considered in the design and delivery of lessons.

Classrooms today provide access to a range of hardware, software, tools, and applications for teaching and learning use, yet we must consider how well such resources are being utilised and how teachers' perspectives of technology shape its use (Dunn and Sweeney, 2018). Research looking at teachers' perspectives on the use of technology in literacy found that many teachers believed that technology had the potential to engage pupils, and could have a positive impact on reluctant readers and writers (Picton, 2019). Pupils' spelling skills and phonics-based literacy skills, such as decoding words for reading, are areas in which research documents positive impact (Vincent, 2020).

Where positive impact on attainment and engagement is observed, it is attributed to multisensory features, attractive graphics, interactivity, ease of navigation, opportunities to earn rewards, and the immediacy of feedback for the learner (Vincent, 2020). These features serve to provide pupils with independent experiences in fun, personalised digital environments in which barriers to learning are reduced. The range of applications available offers novelty and opportunities for exploration. But this has implications for teachers who need to familiarise themselves and build confidence with programs (Picton, 2019).

Regardless of the quality of EdTech, the impact of technology on core subjects depends on teachers' perceptions and utilisation of it. Where it is monitored and supported, teachers' confidence is enhanced (Picton, 2019). The level of usage correlates with teachers' perceptions, with a fifth of teachers both citing that they rarely or never use it, thus questioning its impact (Picton, 2019). The documented impact on attainment varies with teachers' perceptions, the availability of technology, teacher training or time to practise, and a school's expectations of hand-written outcomes (Dunn and Sweeney, 2018).

Technology in itself has no magical powers to engage or improve outcomes, instead we must consider how the technology is used. Interactions with technology must be tailored to the specific needs of learners (Picton, 2019). Its use must also be meaningful, collaborative, and creative if teachers are to move beyond the use of digital resources which only serve as substitutions for other non-digital approaches (Puentedura, 2013). One such example of task redesign, can be seen in a three-month Scottish research study where upper primary pupils used mobile tablet devices during maths activities which resulted in increased performance outcomes (Fabian, Topping, and Barron, 2018). The design of learning activities for this project provided creative experiences for pupils which involved digital photography, Quick Response (QR codes), scavenger hunts, augmented reality geometry, and collaborative data gathering. With careful planning and resource evaluation, it is these types of activities, and those which follow that have the potential to transform teaching and learning experiences.

Creativity

Any attempt to define creativity often leads to the conclusion that it involves not just originality but also effectiveness which in turn implies other positive attributes such as being imaginative or inquisitive (Runco and Jaeger, 2012). However, it can be difficult to exemplify or illustrate these characteristics in the context of technology use in the classroom. Therefore, the notion of defining creativity in terms of what actually may be uncreative practice can be a useful one (Simonton, 2016). In terms of how you consider being creative in your use of EdTech it is worth referring to Task 11.3 which encourages you to explore the SAMR (substitution, augmentation, modification, redefinition) model of adopting technology in teaching (Puentedura, 2013). In order to plan for the creative use of technology you should avoid the simplistic substitution of tech tools and aim to integrate and use the tools to 'redefine' your teaching and pupil learning in innovative and imaginative ways which go beyond routine delivery.

Although using 'drill and kill' software may improve test scores in standards-based education environments, it does not enable teachers to deliver content in novel or creative ways which respond to the interests and needs of individual learners (Henriksen, Mishra and Fisser, 2016). There is, therefore, a need for teachers to develop creative thinking skills and in turn model the innovative use of technology to their pupils with an emphasis on the ease, immediacy and versatile ways that content can be discovered and shared (Henriksen and Hoelting, 2016). This leads to considering three dimensions which are often overlooked: Persistence – or perseverance in terms of computational thinking – is desirable, as is the capacity to work collaboratively given the social aspects of working with technology, and being disciplined whilst doing so (Lucas, 2016).

Finally, it's worth noting that teachers who are receptive to using technology are more likely to be more successful in applying EdTech tools creatively as they are more confident in willing to try new and/or novel approaches (Mehta, Henriksen and Rosenberg 2019). Designing a creative curriculum which employs EdTech effectively may be achieved through your own technological knowledge and preferences, and aligned to your approaches to teaching. Technologies provide an ideal vehicle for the promotion of creativity when deployed effectively, providing flexibility and exploration, and presenting risk-taking opportunities.

Collaboration can be developed through the use of online, real-time writing tools such as Popplet or Padlet in English, whilst learning platforms, such as Mathletics, can be employed to encourage healthy challenges through personalised learning. Web-based resources (listed below) provide real-time collaborative writing and planning spaces which can be accessed by fellow contributors through sharing the content of the original page.

In this way, such tools are flexible in supporting collaborative work, as they can be utilised to facilitate interaction, develop critical thinking, and enhance and refine the effectiveness of pupils' communication. As in physical collaboration, when working online collaboratively, pupils need the chance to come together in groups, to have meaningful discussions, contribute towards shared goals, solve problems, or to work on projects.

Research indicates that online collaborative learning environments are both perceived positively by learners and that their writing benefits from such opportunities. In some cases, that novelty alone will support learner engagement and outcomes. However, the freedom and flexibility, the instantaneousness of peer and teacher-feedback, and opportunity to learn from other pupils (particularly those with a good level of competence in written English) also emphasises the need for drafting and editing work (Yee and Yunus, 2021).

Now undertake Task 11.1.

Task 11.1: Exploring online tools which promote creativity and collaboration

For Task 11.1, plan a lesson exploring the following online tools and identify how you and your pupils could use the resource to promote creativity and collaboration in the core subjects. Possible ideas may include using the tool for writing a collaborative poem; planning for a group or class project; posing a discussion question at the start of a lesson or an assessment question at the end.

Padlet: https://en-gb.padlet.com/
Popplet: https://www.popplet.com/
Google Docs: https://www.google.com/docs/about/

When planning the lesson, and evaluating its impact, think about the following questions:

- How will the use of EdTech enhance teaching and learning?
- How will technology support the development and retention of subject knowledge?
- Which ground rules will you need to set for your pupils, for the use of collaborative technology?
- What are the potential barriers or issues, and how might they be overcome?
- How can the use of EdTech be employed through a sequence of lessons?

The use of collaborative writing can feed into meaningful production of pupils' own texts. The sourcing or creation of images and illustrations plays an important role in the creative process. Here are some additional activities to allow pupils to create a finished product:

- Get pupils to design and create an interactive story book together, which can be shared with an online audience through Storybird: https://storybird.com/

start-with-art/picture-book or Culture Street: https://www.culturestreet.org. uk/activities/picturebookmaker/ or a tablet app such as BookCreator: https:// bookcreator.com/.

- Create a Portable Document Format (PDF) file using Word or Adobe software, and share it via a school website, Dropbox, or Google Play Books.

Collaborative quiz tools for retrieval practice

The science around how children learn has been brought to the fore of teacher education programmes in recent years (DfE, 2019a; DfE, 2019b). With this, there has been increased focus on approaches which support the all-important transfer of information between the working memory (where information is processed) and long-term memory (where information is stored) (Deans for Impact, 2015). In addition, pupils' ability to retrieve previously learnt knowledge from their long-term memory is also important to ensure that regular retrieval helps consolidation of learning over time. Agarwal *et al.* (2020, p.2) define retrieval as an active learning strategy, 'in which calling information to mind subsequently enhances and boosts learning.' Whilst the ability to retain information is often a requirement for assessments, the practice of retrieval focuses on developing learners' ability to comprehend and retain learning.

The use of technology-based maths quizzes and games is not new. For example, the use of drill-and-practice software tools, where users complete questions to revisit and remember learnt content, have been used since the 1980s. Such tools may often be in game format which aims for accuracy or speed, with immediate feedback to players. The repetitive nature of drill-and-practice tools aligns them to behaviourist approaches to teaching, whereas newer tools promote a more collaborative, social, and gamified approach to learning. Gamification, a term coined by Nick Pelling back in 2002 (Pelling, 2011), is used to describe a tactical design where features such as badges, rewards, points tables, and avatars, are used to engage users with activities which may not usually be games-based, such as knowledge retention. Learning through play and games is not something which is new to educational contexts, but the use of gamified systems has certainly grown in schools recently, with tools such as 'Class Dojo' (2022), 'Mathletics' (3P learning, 2022), 'Times Tables Rockstars' (Maths Circle Ltd., 2022) and 'Kahoot!' (2022) widely used in primary schools. With increased device access both at home and in schools, the use of collaborative quiz tools has provided renewed methods to engage and motivate pupils with knowledge retrieval and retention, as can be seen in Case Study 11.1.

Case Study 11.1: Collaborative quizzes – 'Kahoot!'

In Year 6, the class teacher first became aware of 'Kahoot!' during remote learning when looking for ways to develop interactivity during online lessons. Her pupils had always enjoyed playing starter games during maths lessons and enjoyed the competitive element. As a school, teachers participated in a trial which allowed full access to features, although a free version of the tool also provides sufficient access for many activities. Having created a login, the teacher was able to access an impressive library of user-generated quizzes across a wide range of subjects as well as a question bank which teachers can use or duplicate and modify for their own classes.

The teacher recognised that knowledge retention was a significant area of development for many pupils; therefore, she wanted to create an engaging way for them to retrieve and revisit specific areas of learning identified as gaps through assessment. 'Kahoot!' provided a platform where she created learning content which was specific to the needs of her pupils, rather than otherwise readily made material. She also interleaved (added) content which supported pupils' ability to make connections between topics. The 'Kahoot!' user interface was similar to a slide deck, which meant that quiz design was straightforward with options to set time limits for questions, and add visual image/ video prompts to support questions and answers. Accessibility features also allowed adaptations to be made to text size and compatibility with one child's screen reader.

Once the quiz was created, the teacher shared the game with players via a join code which was displayed on the teacher's screen. During live online lessons, all pupils were able to access the game via their devices to play synchronously, with instant feedback to individuals after each question and a changing leader board providing competition. Occasionally, the teacher also used the 'assign' option which allowed an asynchronous self-paced learning activity for pupils. During the game, the teacher was able to monitor those who had joined and was able to have an overview of pupils' responses. Post-game, she was then able to access analytics which allowed her to gauge how individuals had performed, as well as areas for development on a whole-class level.

Since schools have returned to in-person teaching, 'Kahoot!' has become one of the Covid-19 keepers and remains a popular teaching tool. Where device availability doesn't allow for one-to-one access, teachers use the 'Kahoot!' team-play option which allows a group of players to share the same device. A few lessons regarding digital classroom management have also been learnt along the way, such as switching on the friendly nick-name generator to avoid inappropriate names being used in the game and using the option to randomise the order of questions and answers to keep pupils guessing!

Now undertake Task 11.2.

Task 11.2: Exploring collaborative quiz game tools

Collaborative and interactive quiz games can provide engaging opportunities for pupils across a wide range of subjects and topics. When planning to use digital teaching or learning resources, it is important that teachers take time to explore the features of the tool when creating their own content. Take time to learn more about the two tools outlined below:

'Kahoot!'

Kahoot! is a learning platform which can be used by teachers to create, share, and deliver quiz games with groups of pupils. Learn more about 'Kahoot!' here: https:// Kahoot!.com/student-centered-learning/.

'Lumio by SMART'

'Lumio' (SMART Technologies, 2022) is a platform which allows teachers to create interactive and collaborative learning activities for pupils to complete on their own or in groups. Learn more about 'Lumio' here: https://www.smarttech.com/en/lumio.

Having learned a little about both tools, choose one which you would like to explore in more detail. Select an area of mathematical learning for which you would like to create a retrieval activity. This may be a topic which you want pupils to revisit to support retention or an area where the retrieval practice will support new learning. Once you have selected a topic, create an account for your chosen tool and further explore the platform to create an interactive quiz or game which your pupils can use during an upcoming lesson. Remember to consider the device requirements for the activity in advance, and check the activity works on school devices for both teachers and for pupils.

Interactive fiction is the term used to describe stories where the reader is able to take an active role in making choices in how the story moves forward. Interactive fiction can be in the form of 'choose your own adventure' story books (Chooseco, n.d.) or in the form of software-based games such as the classic 'Colossal Cave' text-based adventure game created by William Crowther in 1976. Case Study 11.2 focuses on a group of Year 5 pupils who helped keep the tradition of interactive fiction alive through creating their own adventure game stories using presentation software.

Case Study 11.2: Creating 'choose your own adventure' stories using 'Google Slides'

One two-form entry school in an inner-city primary school, uses the 'Switched on Computing' scheme of work for computing provision across the school (Rising Stars, 2022). This scheme was chosen by the school for broad and balanced coverage of all strands of the National Curriculum for computing (DfE, 2013), as well as its range of cross-curricular units to support the application of knowledge and skills. One of the six units completed in Year 5 is an information technology project titled, 'We are adventure gamers' where pupils learn to create an interactive adventure story using presentation software. As a Google Workspace for Education school (Google for Education, 2022), the school used 'Google Slides' for this unit of work; however, it should be noted that the same project could also be completed using other presentation software.

Whilst the unit came from a computing scheme of work, the teacher recognised the strong links to story planning and writing which this topic presented. This was beneficial in providing opportunities to develop pupils' writing skills across different subjects which was a school-wide priority. The unit started with pupils exploring examples of interactive fiction, both in book form and through text-based online adventure games. This allowed pupils to develop a secure understanding of how the different pathways which readers could choose were mapped against the usual story mountain pattern of an opening, build-up, dilemmas/climax, resolution, and closure of the story. Pupils then mapped the possible pathways for their story on a planning slide, as can be seen in the example below:

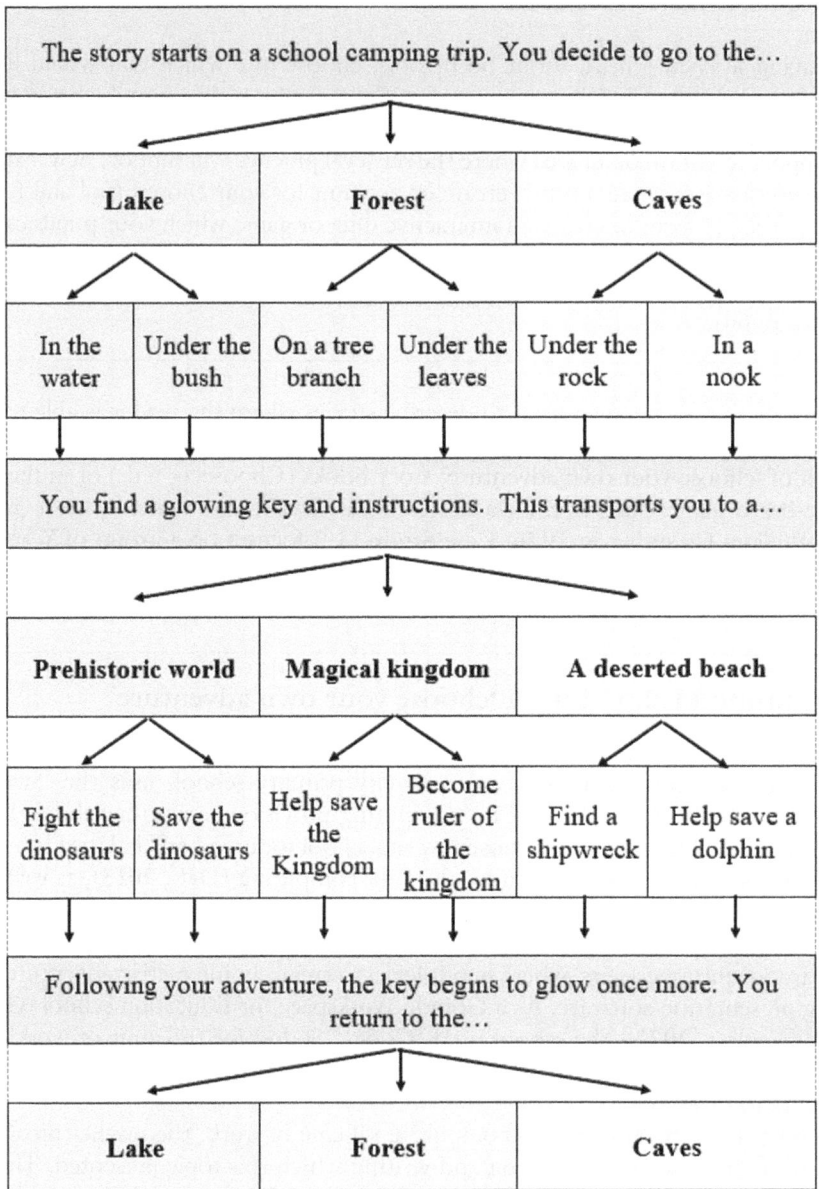

Figure 11.1 Using an online planning tool to plot story development

Having created a plan for their stories, pupils then moved onto creating the structure of their story using 'Google Slides'. Pupils were already familiar with presentation software, through teacher-use during lessons and through presentations which they had previously created. However, during this topic, they learned that presentations can be non-linear and were taught to add hyperlinks between slides to allow their readers to choose their own pathway through the story. As pupils' stories developed, they also added copyright-free images, backgrounds, and audio to their slides to create more of an immersive experience for readers. The teacher encouraged pupils to use the 'share' option within 'Google Slides' to allow peer review and feedback on a weekly basis. At the end of the unit, the teacher felt it was important that parents and pupils within the school community could also enjoy the interactive stories which had been created, and shareable links to projects were added to the school website for others to enjoy.

Now undertake Task 11.3 to reflect on how technology can be used to enhance or transform learning.

Task 11.3: Reflection on technology use to enhance or transform learning

The SAMR (substitution, augmentation, modification and redefinition) model (Puentedura, 2013) provides a framework by which educators can analyse and evaluate their use of technology to ascertain whether tools are simply used as a substitution resource, or to which degree the technology is enhancing or transforming learning. See Table 11.1 for the SAMR model and the four categories.

Table 11.1 The SAMR (substitution, augmentation, modification and redefinition) model (Puentedura, 2013)

Category	Description	Example
Substitution	Technology acts as a direct tool substitute, with no functional change.	Using plain text word-processing software to type a story rather than handwriting.
Augmentation	Technology acts as a direct tool substitute, with function improvement.	Using word-processing software which provides spell-check, a thesaurus, voice typing, formatting options, and so on.
Modification	Technology allows for significant task redesign.	Using the 'share' feature of word-processing tools to allow for feedback and collaborative editing.
Redefinition	Technology allows for the creation of new tasks which were previously inconceivable.	Using technology to create a multimedia story, for example, an audiobook or video film where collaboration with others could even be worldwide.

(Adapted from Puentedura, 2013)

Over the course of time, note the different ways in which technology is used in your classroom or school. For example, specific technologies may be used for the following purposes:

- Support resources for reading or writing.
- Intervention applications or software.
- Tools for pupils to create content.
- Devices for capturing audio, photos, or video.
- Online tools used for retrieval, knowledge retention, or assessment.
- Online forms or surveys used to collect information or for quizzes.
- Games used to support teaching and learning.
- Presentation tools used by teachers or pupils.

Next, reflect on how each of the tools identified links to the SAMR model categories by considering the following questions:

- Which SAMR category does this tool best align to?
- What benefits does use of the tool offer to learning?
- Which approach would be used if the tool or other technology was not available?
- Are pupils able to access and use the tool independently?
- Does the tool have a positive impact on pupils' learning?
- Could the tool be used more effectively to enhance or transform learning?

Quick response [QR] codes

Those schools who use EdTech innovatively and creatively will almost certainly place value on the motivational impact of mobile technologies on supporting and enhancing teaching and learning. Typically, they will utilise an assortment of devices which may include tablets, phones, BYOD (bring your own device), and games consoles. In many schools, the lead person for EdTech is supported by a team of digital leaders – often pupils whose responsibilities include testing and evaluating apps, as well as supporting peers and staff with their use of technology (EdFutures, 2020; Morris, 2019). Evidence of one school's integrated approach to the use of new technologies can be found in corridors as well as classrooms where QR codes bring displays to life and provide additional avenues for pupil interaction. In your daily life, you may well have come across, or even scanned and used, QR codes which frequently appear in the media and which look like this:

Figure 11.2 A QR code linking to plain text (created using a free QR code generator)

Figure 11.3 A QR code linking to a QR code generator website (created using a free QR code generator)

QR codes are two-dimensional barcodes which can be read using the camera function on smartphones and tablets to provide links to websites, text, videos, and other forms of content. QR codes are commonly used in print marketing and their ease of use makes QR codes an ideal resource for teachers and pupils to use.

More recently, QR codes have become increasingly visible, for example, their regular appearance on food menus (Covid-19) and on Covid-19 test kits. Not only do they act as a bridge between digital and print media, but they can be accessed via camera on most smartphones, without the additional installation of an app being required.

Getting started with QR codes is simple, there are many websites which can be used to generate and print QR codes, such as QRStuff: http://www.qrstuff.com/. Once a QR code has been created, anyone wishing to read and follow the code will require a QR code reader application on a smartphone, handheld device, or tablet, alternatively, a webcam can be used to read the code, in which case additional software will be required. Examples of QR code readers include Qrafter, Qmark, QRReader, and QR Droid.

In schools, QR codes are used on displays to provide additional information and questions about what the pupils have been studying. The QR codes can be used by pupils in the form of a learning trail, whilst parents and visitors are able to discover more about the processes behind the work on display. The educational uses for QR codes across the curriculum are broad in their scope, and their use in the core subjects of English and mathematics could include:

- teachers generating and placing question-based QR codes inside reading books, linking to comprehension questions about the text;
- pupils placing QR codes inside books, linking to audio clips of book reviews they have created;
- placing QR codes on homework sheets, providing a link to online support materials or video clips which explain strategies concerned with teaching and learning;
- using QR codes for self-assessment and checking of calculations in mathematics;
- pupils could create a mathematical treasure hunt for one another using QR codes linked to mathematical word problems;
- using QR codes in the classroom shop role-play area, allowing pupils to scan grocery items for product information and pricing.

Some initial pointers to working with QR codes and enhancing their use in the classroom, which may be useful, can be found here: https://www.qr-code-generator.com/blog/qr-codes-in-the-classroom/.

QR codes can also be versatile when used as an assessment tool, for example, the Plickers tool uses QR codes allowing pupils to participate in quizzes. These can be handy where access to tablet devices may be limited because only the teacher needs a device.

Now undertake Task 11.4 to create a mathematics based treasure hunt.

Task 11.4: Using QR codes to create a mathematics based treasure hunt

QR codes can be used in innovative ways to support and motivate pupil learning. A QR code treasure hunt can provide an engaging approach to learning where pupils can work together to follow a trail of QR code questions or clues to accomplish given tasks. Follow the steps outlined below to create your own QR code treasure hunt, alternatively pupils can create treasure hunts for each other.

1. Start by creating a list of questions which relate to your class's current mathematics topic, between five to ten questions is sufficient. Although any topic can lend itself to this task, practical mathematics topics such as those of measures and geometry will provide an ideal opportunity to take learning outside the classroom.
2. Use a QR code generator website such as QR Code Generator (https://www.qr-code-generator.com/) to create a QR code for each question. It is advisable that QR codes are printed at a size which is easy to capture, especially by young pupils. You may also wish to add additional start and finish QR codes which contain instructions or prompts. For example, how would you like pupils to record their answers? Many handheld devices and tablets have a camera function which could be used to record answers.
3. Print the QR codes and display them around the classroom or the school. Colour coding or numbering the QR codes allows for the task to be differentiated through directing your pupils to specific codes.
4. In groups, pupils complete the treasure hunt by using a QR code reader application on a handheld device or tablet to access each question, before collaboratively solving the problem and recording or photographing the evidence.
5. At the end of the treasure hunt teams can peer assess their results or present evidence to the teacher before winners are announced.

The task above could be adapted by substituting the QR codes, which link to questions, with links to multiple choice answers, or to clues which provide further guidance where needed.

Video collaboration

The Covid-19 pandemic, necessitating a national shift to online learning, normalised the use of video for teaching and learning. The pre-existence of digital cameras on devices such as smartphones and tablets meant that for many pupils having to isolate, a level of interaction continued, including live and pre-recorded teaching, learning, and even parents' evening via video.

Video communication technologies can be used to open up global learning opportunities for young learners. Using video conferencing equipment as part of a topic opens up the world and, with relatively little preparation, discussions can be held with subject experts in distant locations, saving time, money, and resources. Opportunities for pupils to create videos in English and mathematics in cross-curricular ways could include:

- Small groups of pupils could record a synopsis of the beginning, middle, and end of their story. Then other pupils could peer-assess, and the video can form a resource to support the drafting process.
- Recording interviews with pupils acting as, for example, Mary Seacole, Michael Morpurgo, and The Gruffalo. (Dressing-up is optional, but encouraged!)
- Pupils could present a worded maths problem and demonstrate how they achieved the answer by illustrating or describing the steps.

If you do employ the use of video when teaching, it's important to ensure that the pupils are shown how to use the cameras themselves, as their own ability to capture footage allows them to gain greater self-awareness and confidence. The task below outlines examples of how digital video can be used by pupils to record and evaluate their work. The use of digital video can also be used to document the process behind the completion of pieces of work, enabling an audience to gain an insight into the skills which pupils have used.

Also, see Chapter 20 on video conferencing. Now undertake Task 11.5.

Task 11.5: Using digital video

Using either digital stills or video, either:

- Get pupils to take photos of their work in progress, before compiling them (using YouTube Photo Slideshow, Animoto or Windows Movie Maker or, the iMovie app on iPad) to document the process behind completed work. PowerPoint could also be used and allows for screencast recording where pupils can talk over their work, or
- Produce a video as the outcome of a piece of work, instead of writing in exercise books. For example, pupils could record a video explaining how to use and apply the 'chunking method' in numeracy.

Summary and key points

Once you have read this chapter, and carried out the tasks, you should be able to use technology creatively to support teaching and learning, with an emphasis on the teaching of English and mathematics. You will also know how to use EdTech to motivate and engage pupils in order to enhance their literacy and numeracy skills as well as understand how technology can provide opportunities to be creative in the classroom.

- Good practice depends on motivating and engaging pupils in meaningful, creative learning activities. Technology and EdTech tools can help you to achieve this, as a lesson outcome or as part of a learning journey, by facilitating independent or collaborative practices, exploration, and problem-solving requiring higher-order thinking.
- You should not have to depend on high levels of investment in technology, as free and easily available tools can facilitate instant access.

Finally, you should consider this chapter as a starting point and it should enable you to realise the pedagogical value of using technology. If you are a beginning teacher, check which requirements for your course you have addressed through this chapter.

Further resources

Hart-Davis, G. (2017) Deploying iPads in the classroom: Planning, installing, and managing iPads in schools and colleges, Durham: Apress.
  This text provides extensive coverage including trouble shooting issues with iPads, as well as sections on planning and managing the use of iPads in the classroom. Consideration is given to comparisons with other tablets and technologies.
Atherton, P. (2018) 50 ways to use technology enhanced learning in the classroom: Practical strategies for teaching, London: Learning Matters.
  This is a highly accessible guide to using EdTech in the classroom and includes sections on video and audio tools, collaborative working, and games, polls, and student response systems. The pedagogical aspects of using EdTech are considered throughout.
Wishart, J. (2017) Mobile learning in schools: Key issues, opportunities and ideas for practice, Abingdon: Routledge.
  This book explores the potential for using mobile technologies in and outside of the classroom. Each chapter includes questions for reflection and further discussion.
Rising Stars (2022) Digital Resources, Rising Stars UK.
  This online platform is linked to Rising Stars schemes of work and offers free access to a range of digital resources. Rising Stars provides EYFS and Primary teachers with cross-curricular tools to help support creative EdTech projects: https://www.risingstars-uk.com/subjects/digital.

References

3P learning (2022) *The world's leading maths program*, viewed 25 November 2022 from: https://www.mathletics.com/uk/.
Agarwal, P., Roediger, H., McDaniel, M. and McDermott, K. (2020) *How to use retrieval practice to improve learning*, Washington: Retrieval Practice, viewed 25 November 2022 from: http://pdf.retrievalpractice.org/RetrievalPracticeGuide.pdf.
Chooseco (n.d.) *Choose your own adventure*, CYOA, viewed 25 November 2022 from: https://www.cyoa.com/pages/about-us.
Class Dojo (2022) *Class Dojo*, viewed 25 November 2022 from: https://www.classdojo.com/en-gb/.
Curtis, A. (2021) *What have we learned about moving education online?*, viewed 25 November 2022 from: https://schoolsweek.co.uk/what-have-we-learned-about-moving-education-online/.
DCSF (Department for Children, Schools and Families) (2008) *Harnessing Technology: Next Generation Learning*, Coventry: Becta, viewed 25 November 2022 from: https://dera.ioe.ac.uk/8287/2/A9R3172_Redacted.pdf.
Deans for Impact (2015) *The science of learning*, Austin: Texas, viewed 25 November 2022 from: http://www.deansforimpact.org/wp-content/uploads/2016/12/The_Science_of_Learning.pdf.
DfE (Department for Education) (2013) *The national curriculum primary programmes of study and attainment targets for key stages 1 and 2*, London: DfE, viewed 25 November 2022 from: https://www.gov.uk/government/publications/national-curriculum-in-england-primary-curriculum.
DfE (Department for Education) (2018) *School workload reduction toolkit*, London: DfE, viewed 25 November 2022 from: https://www.gov.uk/guidance/school-workload-reduction-toolkit.
DfE (Department for Education) (2019a) *Early career framework*, London: DfE, viewed 25 November 2022 from: https://assets.publishing.service.gov.uk/government/uploads/system/uploads/attachment_data/file/978358/Early-Career_Framework_April_2021.pdf.

DfE (Department for Education) (2019b) *Initial teacher training (ITT): Core content framework*, London: DfE, viewed 25 November 2022 from: https://www.gov.uk/government/publications/initial-teacher-training-itt-core-content-framework.

DfE (Department for Education) (2019c) *Realising the potential of technology in education: A strategy for education providers and the technology industry*, London: HMSO.

DfE (Department for Education) (2020) *Get help with technology for remote education*, London: DfE, viewed 25 November 2022 from: https://www.gov.uk/government/collections/get-help-with-technology-for-remote-education.

Dunn, J. and Sweeney, T. (2018) 'Writing and iPads in the early years: Perspectives from within the classroom', *British Journal of Educational Technology*, 49 (5), 859–869.

EdFutures (2020) *EdFutures*, viewed 25 November 2022 from: http://edfutures.net/.

Fabian, K., Topping, K. J. and Barron, I. G. (2018) 'Using mobile technologies for mathematics: Effects on student attitudes and achievement', *Education Technology Research and Development*, 66 (5), 1119–1139.

Google for Education (2022) *Google Workspace for Education*, viewed 25 November 2022 from: https://edu.google.com/intl/en_uk/workspace-for-education/editions/education-fundamentals/.

Henriksen, D., Hoelting, M. and the Deep-Play Research Group (2016) 'Rethinking creativity and technology in the 21st century: Creativity in a YouTube World', *TechTrends*, 2 (60), 102–106.

Henriksen, D., Mishra, P. and Fisser, P. (2016) 'Infusing Creativity and Technology in 21st Century Education: A Systemic View for Change', *Educational Technology and Society*, 19 (3), 27–37.

Hodder Education (2022) *Switched on computing*, viewed 25 November 2022 from: https://www.risingstars-uk.com/series/switched-on-computing.

Kahoot! (2022) *Kahoot!*, viewed 25 November 2022 from: https://kahoot.com/.

Laurillard, D. (2008) *Digital technologies and their role in achieving our ambitions for education*, London: Institute of Education.

Leask, M. and Younie, S. (2021) *Ensuring schooling for all in times of crisis - Lessons from Covid-19*, Routledge Taylor Francis.

Lucas, B. (2016) 'A five-dimensional model of creativity and its assessment in schools', *Applied Measurement in Education*, (29) 4, 278–290.

Maths Circle Ltd. (2022) *Times Tables Rockstars*, viewed 25 November 2022 from: https://ttrockstars.com/.

Mehta, R., Henriksen, D. and Rosenberg, J. M. (2019) 'It's not about the tools', *Educational Leadership*, 76 (5), 64–69.

Morris, D. (2019) *Student voice and teacher professional development: Knowledge exchange and transformational learning*, London: Palgrave Macmillan.

National Association of Education Technology (NAACE) (2020) *COVID-19 Education Impact Report*, Nottingham: NAACE.

Pelling, N. (2011) *The (short) prehistory of "gamificatio"*, Funding startups (and other impossibilities), viewed 25 November 2022 from: https://nanodome.wordpress.com/2011/08/09/the-short-prehistory-of-gamification/.

Picton, I. (2019) *Teachers' use of technology to support literacy in 2018*, London: National Literacy Trust.

Puentedura, R. R. (2013) *SAMR: Moving from enhancement to transformation*, Ruben R. Puentedura's Weblog - Ongoing thoughts on education and technology, viewed 25 November 2022 from: http://www.hippasus.com/rrpweblog/archives/000095.html.

Rising Stars (2022) *Switched on Computing*, viewed 25 November 2022 from: https://www.risingstars-uk.com/series/switched-on-computing/products/switched-on-computing-5-third-edition.

Runco, M. and Jaeger, G. J. (2012) 'The standard definition of creativity', *Creativity Research Journal*, 21, 92–96.

Selwyn, N. (2022) *Education and technology - Key issues and debates*, London: Bloomsbury Academic.

Simonton, D. K. (2016) 'Defining creativity: Don't we also need to define what is not creative?', *The Journal of Creative Behavior*, 52 (1), 80–90.

SMART Technologies. (2022) *Smart Tech Lumio*, viewed 25 November 2022 from: https://www.smarttech.com/en/lumio.

Vincent, K. (2020) 'Closing the gap: supporting literacy through a computer-assisted-reading-intervention', *Support for Learning*, 35 (1), 68–82.

Yee, L. Y. and Yunus, M. M. (2021) *Collaborative tools in enhancing ESL writing during Covid 19: A systematic review*, International Conference on Business Studies and Education (ICBE), viewed 25 November 2022 from: https://www.icbe.my/wp-content/uploads/2021/07/Lo-Yuok-Yee.pdf.

12 Using technology in primary science

Paul Hopkins

Introduction

Since the last edition of this book in 2015 there has been a major event in UK education, the pandemic, and the response to this in schools. Technology, especially online video conferencing and remote access technology suddenly became centre stage (Leask and Younie, 2022). Whilst there had always been online support materials from excellent organisations such as the Primary Science Support Trust (PSST) and others there was a plethora of other online support aligned to a particular pedagogic approach.

Science and technology are natural bedfellows and a good place to start is by defining what we mean by technology. The young pupils in today's primary classrooms will have grown up in a world where technology will have meant the laptop, the notebook and the interactive whiteboard more than the desktop and they are truly 'digital natives' (Prensky, 2001) or 'HomoZappiens' (Veen, 2004) happy and familiar with technology as an integral part of their and their parents' lives. Much of this technology will be mobile and portable and as more and more primary schools around the world are introducing tablet computers (see studies such as Burden *et al.*, 2012; Webb, 2012) this chapter considers how the mobile computer will lie at the heart of technology usage to support science in the primary classroom of the near and continuing future and the affordances that such mobile devices give over the fixed computer (Traxler, 2007). Whilst we recognise that not all schools will have yet invested in these mobile technologies, others have written about the use of existing technology, and in the space available, this chapter will focus on the use of mobile technologies. Think back to your own time in the primary classroom. What technology did you use in your primary classroom? Digital cameras? Dataloggers? Video? Computers? The rate of change over the last few years has been fast and incredible and it is for this reason that this chapter focuses on the more recent technology; that of the mobile learning devices and the affordances that such devices offer. In this chapter we explore some core pedagogic ideas for using the technology of the near future in the primary classroom. We also recognise that the changes in curriculum, if you are in the UK, since the first edition (DfE, 2013) and the fiscal constraints in schools may restrict the available opportunities.

Many schools will ban or deter pupils from bringing their own technology into the classroom but the Ofcom *Children and Parents: Media use and attitudes report* (2022: 11) indicates that 91% of children aged 11 had their own smartphone which offers a significant opportunity for technology use.

DOI: 10.4324/9781003408925-12

Objectives

At the end of this chapter you should be able to:

- understand how mobile technology can enhance and/or transform the learning and teaching of science in the primary classroom
- explore some key activities and ideas for using mobile technology in the classroom to teach science
- feel confident to introduce the available technology into your teaching of science and consider the introduction of mobile technologies.

Good practice in teaching science in the primary classroom

Before looking at the technology we need to consider what is good science in the primary classroom. I argue three core principles for the science that takes place in the primary classroom, these are similar to those argued by Harlen (2010) and supported by the key issues found in primary science teaching (Bianchi *et al.*, 2021).

(a) *It is real science*: The science that takes place in the primary classroom has at its heart the same scientific method used by all scientists. It may not be new to the world, but it is likely to be new, creative and original to the pupils and thus has real value (NAACE, 1999). It is "science that builds on the children's natural curiosity, inventiveness and wonder" (Rose, 2008: 8), and as Harlen and Qualter (2018) argue, all science curriculum activities should deepen understanding of scientific ideas.

(b) *It is rooted in investigative work*: Whilst there is an important place for learning information and facts about science the best science in the primary classroom is the hands-on, investigative work, "primary schools should ensure that pupils are engaged in scientific enquiry, including practical work," (Ofsted, 2011: 8) where children are exploring questions that have relevance and meaning to them: "children need time to pursue their own ideas in science" (Harlen and Qualter, 2018: 49). The teacher plays a pivotal role in the teaching of scientific enquiry in teaching the skills involved as well as the scientific concepts (McCrory, 2017).

(c) *It develops models and criticality*: concepts that can be built upon and developed rather than teaching immutable facts about science that might have to be "unlearned" later in their science learning life, "Children must be given the opportunity to challenge their existing ideas" (SCORE, 2013: 7).

So, we need to consider how technology use by the teacher and by the pupils can enhance and support these core ideas. BECTA (2009) suggested nine main applications for ICT (technology) in science:

1. providing information
2. supporting fieldwork
3. assisting observation
4. recording and measuring
5. sharing data with others

6. facilitating interpretation
7. simulating experiments
8. providing models or demonstrations
9. enhancing publishing and presentation

(BECTA, 2009: 2)

Considering these three core principles and the nine areas we can consider the use of technology in three key areas:

1. by pupils as a tool for data capture, analysis and evaluation including video, audio, data logging and presentation and for the development and expansion of their own subject knowledge,
2. by teachers as a tool for information presentation, modelling and demonstration, simulations and virtual experiments and developing resources,
3. as a tool for knowledge enhancement, planning and assessment.

There are a number of frameworks that consider the interface between technology and pedagogy including the Technology, Pedagogy and Content Knowledge (TPACK) model (Mishra and Koehler, 2009), the Enhancement, Efficiency and Transformation (EET) model (McCormick and Scrimshaw, 2001) and the Substitution, Augmentation, Modification and Redefinition (SAMR) model (Puentedura, 2011). The use of technology should never be just for the sake of using the technology: there should always be a pedagogic driver – a reason why the use of the technology improves the teaching or the learning or both. We can think of these drivers in two ways:

1. technology that *enhances* the experiences in the classroom
2. technology that *transforms* the learning in the classroom.

In Table 12.1, I have combined the EET and the SAMR models, whilst taking note of TPACK, to give us the key drivers of enhancement and transformation of learning.

Table 12.1 Frameworks for change (based on Burden *et al.*, 2012: 102)

	McCormick and Scrimshaw (2001)	*Puentedura model (2011) SAMR*
Enhancement	Technology used to do things more **efficiently** (productivity)	**Substitution** (technology acts as a direct tool substitute with no functional change or improvement)
		Augmentation (technology acts as a direct tool substitute with functional improvement)
Enhancement	Technology used to **extend** the reach of teaching and learning/the task (e.g. using the internet to work with experts or other pupils abroad)	**Modification** (technology allows for significant task redesign)
	Technology used as **transformational** device (e.g. allowing you to do things that were (to all intents) impossible or impractical before the technology)	**Replacement** (technology allows for creation of new tasks previously inconceivable)

Pupils' use of technology

In this section we explore a number of ways in which pupils can use mobile technologies to support their understanding and learning in science. However, before you start you should explore, through Task 12.1 how technology is being used in your classroom or the classroom you are in whilst on your teaching practice.

Task 12. 1: Where are we at?

Talk to the teacher and the pupils in a class you have access to about the technologies that they use in their science lessons. Especially ask them if they:

- use technology to record their investigation,
- use technology as data capture during investigations,
- use technology to develop their subject knowledge,
- use technology to analyse, evaluate and model data,
- use technology to show their findings when reporting back.

Consider how the technology is used in other parts of the curriculum. When you have had these conversations go back to your medium-term plans to consider what might need to be changed to encourage the use of technology or what skills you will need to teach the children – consider the questions around "fake news" and verification of information found online.

Using technology to record pupils' investigations

Pupils are naturally curious and enjoy conducting investigations. An essential part of this is for them to record carefully and accurately what is happening as they carry out their investigation and experiments. For the youngest pupils, having to record things in writing can be physically quite difficult. Whilst it is possible for one pupil to take on the role of the recorder while the other is the experimenter most pupils want to be involved in the hands-on activity. This is where video is an excellent tool. Many primary schools will already have small handheld video recorders such as Digital Blue (https://www.learningresources.co.uk/zoomy-2-0-blue) or FlipCams© but all modern mobile devices (smartphones or tablets) come with a good quality still camera and video camera and video editing software is available for very low cost. The only limitation of these devices is the quality of the audio recording, and the school policies on the use of devices.

The use of video to record has a number of advantages that can be seen in the case study, 12.1:

Case Study 12.1: A fruit Olympics

A reception teacher is exploring with a small group of pupils' ideas around floating and sinking and wants to challenge the pupils' ideas about what might float and what might sink. They begin with a class discussion about objects in their house that they think will float or sink. The teacher has developed a carousel of activities one of which is to explore the floating and sinking properties of common fruits and vegetables. She shows the pupils a selection of fruits and vegetables and asks them to discuss which of these they think will float and which of these they think will sink.

(a)   (b)

Figure 12.1 Children undertaking the 'fruit Olympics'

Each group is asked to discuss and then record a short piece of video where they explain (i) what they think will happen and (ii) why they think this will happen. Once they have recorded this video they are given their fruits and vegetables and they then carry out the investigation by carefully putting the fruit or vegetable into the tank of water and seeing if it floats or sinks. Each time they put one of the objects into the tank they video the process and their discussion.

When they have explored all their objects they can compare their initial predictions with their observed results and they are then asked to draw some conclusions from their results and again video this so that they can present this to the teacher and to the rest of the class when they feed back later in the sequence of lesson. This activity* is part of a carousel exploring floating and sinking and the teacher uses the video later in the sequence of lessons.

*This activity is based around the POE (predict, observe, evaluate) principle (Kearney, 2001).

Task 12.2: Using video to capture pupils' thinking

Consider this use of technology using the enhancement and transformation framework above. What are the advantages for the pupils in using video to record their thinking and planning as opposed to other methods? Are there any disadvantages? Explore the options you have in your school for recording video and plan to use these in a science session soon and evaluate, with the pupils, the impact that this makes.

As well as using video, which is a very powerful tool in the primary classroom, mobile devices have a range of other affordances, which will allow the pupils to spend more time on the investigation:

Stills Camera: Pupils use the camera to capture the stages of their investigation or key moments or events. These can then be annotated using an application such as *iAnnotate* or *Explain Everything*. As well as the built-in camera there are a number of adaptations that will allow you to use your camera to capture the big and the small and to make slideshows, animations and annotate stills.
Audio: Using the built-in recording device pupils can record their ideas and thoughts from their investigations. Again, though the built-in microphone has limited capacity there is a huge range of add-ons to enhance the capacity of the device.
Dictation: Free software will allow the pupil to dictate their observations, which will then be transcribed by the device. *Dragon Dictate©* offers free software for both iOS and Android platforms.
Apps: There are a range of excellent applications which can be used by pupils as part of their science knowledge learning – these range from quizzes to information apps, to virtual and simulated investigations.

Using technology to capture enquiry data

Another key element of investigative science is recording data, and this can be difficult and error-prone when being undertaken by pupils. Technology can play a vital part in this data capture and such use of technology is at the heart of every science lab in the world and should be present in the primary classroom (Davie *et al.*, 2012). There have been a number of attempts to get data logging or data capture technologies into primary classrooms; this has included initiatives such as giving a digital microscope, which could be hooked up to a computer, to all English primary schools but without providing support or professional development, not surprisingly many of these never made it out of the box.

The 2013 English National Curriculum guidance states that pupils should, "learn how to use new equipment, such as data loggers" (DfE, 2013: 16). Whilst some primary schools are using data logging equipment that can be connected to laptops or desktop computers this is rare as this equipment is expensive and fairly complex.

Mobile technologies come with a range of applications that can be used to capture data. Some of these will use the affordances of the device whilst others utilise a range of accessories. See Table 12.2 next.

Table 12.2 Data capture via applications

Area of the curriculum	Examples of data to be captured	Equipment needed
Biology	Pulse rate	Timer (built in) Pulse Monitor Heart Rate
	Plant recognition	Leafsnap Application TreeID Application
	Micro-organisms	Proscope© microscope for iPad
	Humidity	Humidity Probe
	Variation	Camera
Chemistry	Temperature / Heat flow	Celsius Temperature Probe
	Reflectivity	Light Sensor
Physics	Sound	Recording App on Device
	Light	Light Sensor (built in)
	Forces	Accelerometer (built in) Inclinomter
	Earth and Space	Camera (built in)
	Movement and Time	iLab Timer Accelerometer (built in) Stopwatch (built in)

There is also a growing range of sensor devices that will interface with a tablet device. Whilst these are not cheap they can offer an amazing range of opportunities for primary science giving children the opportunity to carry out more sophisticated scientific enquiries, such as measuring the humidity levels around their classroom to determine the best place to grow plants, exploring temperature change around the school to consider the heat absorptive properties of different materials or more accurately capture the speed of a car as it travels down an inclined plane in order to explore the relationship between gravity and acceleration.

Two to consider are Globisens Labdisc (www.globisens.net) which contains a range on internal sensors and PASCO SparkLinkAir (www.pasco.com) which allows you to connect a range of over 70 external sensors to your iPad. Both of these work via a Bluetooth connection.

Task 12.3: The affordances of the mobile device in the classroom

Explore the affordances of the mobile device to see what capabilities it has for the recording of data in your classroom. Explore also how these can be enhanced with inexpensive add-ons. If you already have mobile devices in your school, carry out an audit of the applications for science and explore what you could add for a relatively low cost.

Using technology to analyse and evaluate data

Capturing data is, of course, only the beginning of the process. Once you have captured data it can be very difficult for the primary pupil to analyse the data in order to make the link between their hypotheses and then to draw both specific and more general causal links between the independent (the variable that is to be changed) and dependent variables (the variable that is being tested). This is where having easy and immediate access to a range of technologies can bring great benefits.

There are a number of ways in which the pupils in your class can analyse and evaluate data using spreadsheets, graphing programs and databases. See Case Study 12.2 next.

Case Study 12.2: Using a spreadsheet when investigating friction

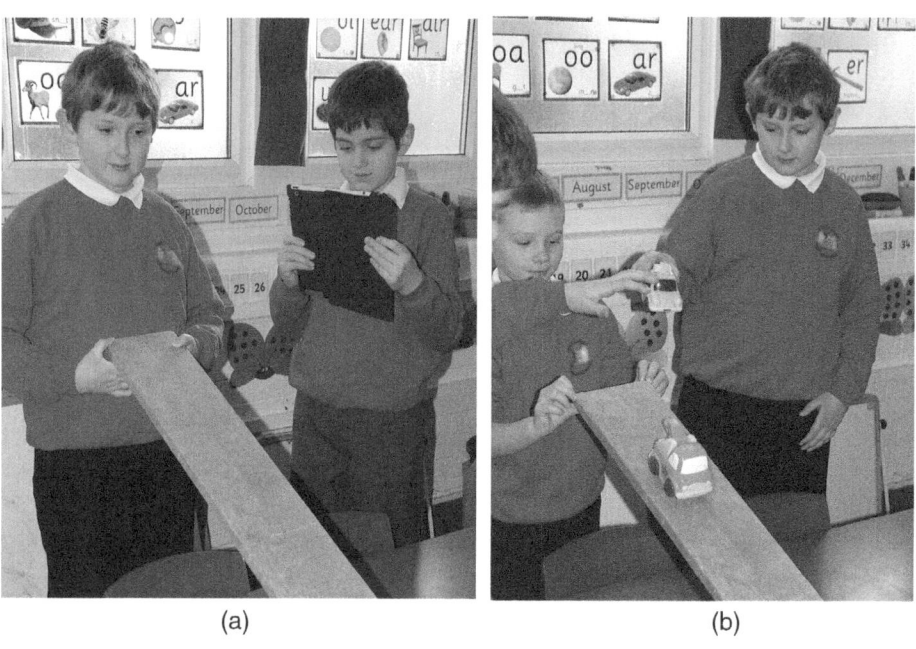

(a)   (b)

Figure 12.2 Investigating friction and analysing data with a spreadsheet

A Year 5 teacher is exploring the concept of friction as a force that opposes motion in moving objects. The pupils have devised their experiment using an inclined plane, a range of materials and some toy cars. They intend to time the cars going from a fixed point on the slope and then across a fixed amount of the material they will then calculate the speed of the cars. The teacher has also been talking to them about the importance of eliminating errors and how this can be helped by repeated measurements. In order to help them with their calculations they have programmed a spreadsheet to work on the speed of the vehicle and also to work out the mean of their measurements using the following calculations:

Speed = distance/timeMean = (Test 1 + Test 2 .... / Number of tests)

This allows the pupils to concentrate on the design of their investigation and once they have measured the time taken (using a stopwatch app on their device) they are able to enter this time into their spreadsheet, which quickly calculates the speed.

As they enter repeated measurements the spreadsheet calculates the mean time for their set of measurements thus improving the reliability of the investigation. The application is also able to present their data in a range of graphical formats allowing them to choose the best option in order to present their data.

The technology allows children to access more easily the analysis of the data – thus they can explore the accuracy of their hypotheses and in changing the values of variables, model different situations – this allows them to do science in ways that professional scientists do.

Now move on to Task 12.4.

Task 12.4: It's more than just recording the data

Consider this use of technology using the enhancement and transformation framework in Table 12.1. What are the advantages for the pupils in using the spreadsheet to analyse their data as opposed to other methods? Are there any disadvantages? Working with other teachers in your Key Stage, or with the IT co-ordinator explore what spreadsheets you could write, or adapt from ones found online, for your science curriculum.

Using technology to present and assess their findings

Having planned and carried out the investigation and analysed the data the final stage for the pupils is to be able to present their data, a requirement of the National Curriculum in England for Science, where pupils should be engaged in, "a range of activities including collecting, presenting and analysing data" (DfE 2013: 3). Traditionally this might have been an oral report to the class or as a piece of written work for marking by the class teacher.

The mobile device allows the pupil to present their investigation in a more creative and dynamic way. There is a large and growing range of inexpensive tools that can be used by the pupil to present the multi-modal data that they have collected in the planning, recording and data-gathering parts of their investigation (see website www.mmiweb. org.uk/hull/ipad/index_0.html for more details). These include video editing software, animation software, eBook creation software as well as presentation or desktop publishing software.

Once an artefact has been constructed there is also now a range of tools that will allow the teacher or other pupils to comment, critique and explore further developments for the work – drawing the pupil, the teacher and their peers into a collaborative learning cycle (Kolb, 1984). As well as developing the range of presentation styles giving pupils choice encourages them to think about audience and purpose, a beneficial learning outcome in itself.

Next, read Case Study 12.3.

Case Study 12.3: Making an eBook to showcase achievements

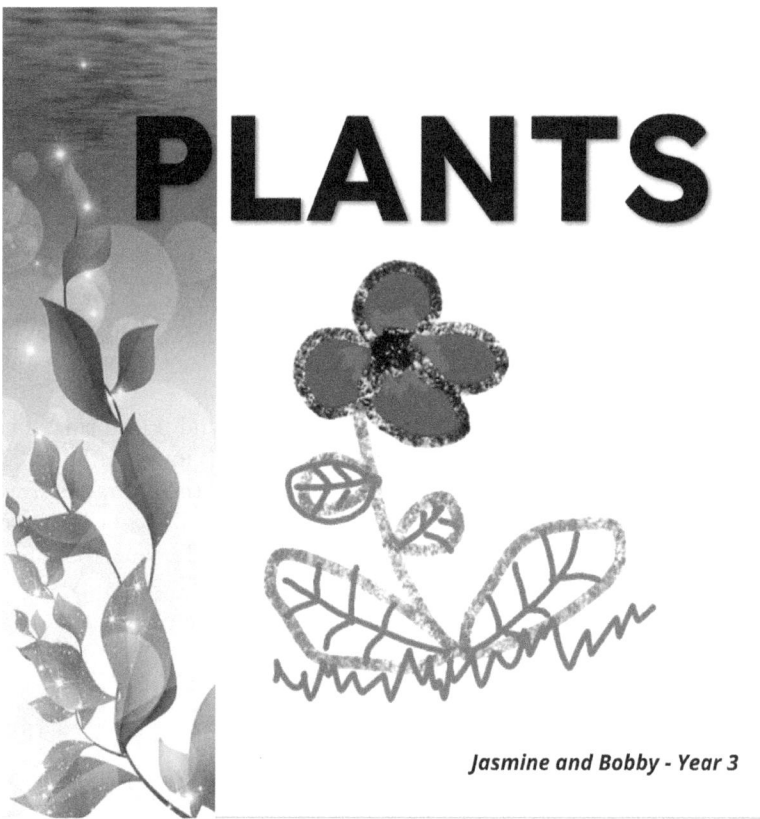

Figure 12.3 Developing an eBook for recording data and findings

A Year 3 teacher has been doing some work with the children on plants. The children have been identifying the functions of different parts of flowering plants and the requirements of plants for life and growth and the plant life cycle as a module of work over a six-week period. The children have gathered a range of data including photos, drawings, video and tabular data and they have been looking for a way to put this all together.

The teacher introduces them to BookCreator (https://bookcreator.com/) and the children are able to make a short eBook which tells the narrative of their work. They can edit and adapt as the module progresses and can add their images and videos as well as record their hypotheses, findings, analysis and conclusions as both written and audio commentary as well as having feedback from the teacher.

Once the books have been completed they can be shared with parents and careers and with other children using the online publishing option.

Using technology to develop and extend knowledge

Perhaps the most widely used affordance of technology is in individual learning and researching. Assuming that the school has a robust wi-fi network the mobile device becomes the "more knowledgeable other" (MKO) (Vygotsky, 1978) giving the pupil access to a wide range of support materials. These may be directly from the internet or more suitably from a range of support materials chosen by the teacher to which the pupil has access. There is a huge range of support materials, and the nature of this material is such that any list will soon be out of date. One of the roles and skills of the twenty-first century teacher is in being able to use appropriate web curation tools to curate resources for their pupils to use (see Barber and Cooper, 2012). This role of MKO is developing as the software becomes more sophisticated and more interactive teaching and learning interactions take place; this could be in the form of assessment activity that adjusts depending on the answers given, access via video sites to expertise (e.g. the Khan Academy model: http://www.khanacademy.org) or the developing use of interrogative algorithms that allow the user to interface with the software. This is being developed in tools such as Siri [The Mac iOS interface] and the Wolfram Alpha search engine [http://www.wolframalpha.com].

However, as well as access to the internet via a browser, or even to your school's Virtual Learning Environment there are a large and growing number of applications that help enhance subject knowledge. These include applications that will recognise the songs of different birds (Birdsong ID), allow you to explore the elements (Elements) or identify trees from their leaves (TreeID). There are also science dictionary, glossary and encyclopaedia apps (both general and specialist), most of which are multi-modal in format (e.g. Video Science) as well as apps, which will allow you to identify the stars and other heavenly bodies (GoSkyWatch).

There are also applications, which offer simulations to explore scientific ideas and models. Again, a growing range of these can be found (for examples see the Hull University website 'ipads for teacher education') which allow the pupils to change the parameters of an investigation and explore how this impacts on the process – this modelling is a core part of the science taking place in laboratories all over the world and brings real world context into the primary classroom.

Teachers' use of technology

In this section we are going to explore a number of ways in which you can use technology to extend and transform your teaching, and hence the learning, in your classroom. As you will have seen from the first part of this chapter the opportunities for pupils that mobile devices offer are huge and this should change the way that we as teachers will operate in the classroom. This should move us away from the need to give information and much more to situate and contextualise it and to make sure that the learning is individualised for the differing needs of the pupils. As the technology takes on some of the roles that we might have had as teachers (knowledge store, skills tutor) we become learning architects and personalised learning facilitators developing learning pathways for our pupils and situating and setting challenges so that the maximum learning can take place. Fullan and Langworthy (2014) explore these ideas in their report *A rich seam: how new pedagogies find deep learning*. See Figure 12.4.

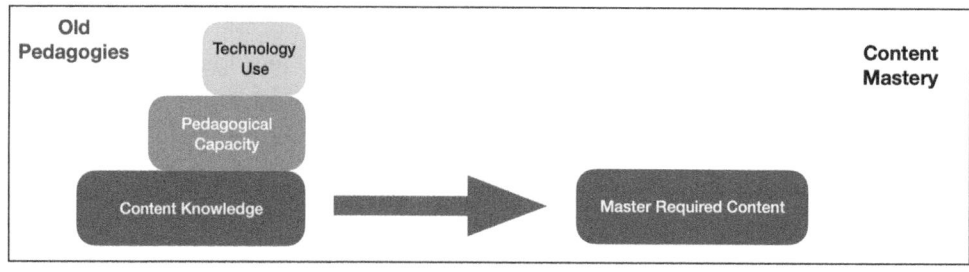

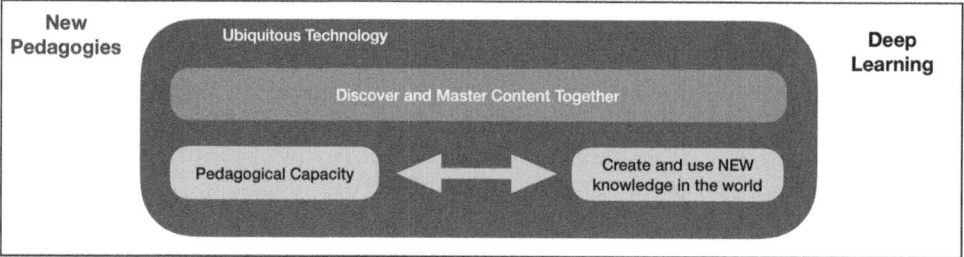

Figure 12.4 Deep learning adapted from Fullan and Langworthy (2014: 3)

Using technology to present and demonstrate

A core role of technology for the teacher is using it to present information to the pupils. The danger in presenting information disassociated from the investigation is that the information is de-contextualised and outside of the pupils' experiences (Eshach, 2006; Murphy and Beggs, 2003) and this can lead to boredom and disengagement.

So, information transfer should be kept to a minimum and driven by the needs of the pupils (Rosenshine, 2010). The use of mobile devices allows the information, curated by the teacher, to be available to the pupils when they demand it. This information can then be accessed by, and presented to the pupils, in a variety of creative ways (e.g. presentation, visualisers, video).

The lack of facilities in the primary classroom can make access difficult to some areas of the curriculum and again this is where the use of the mobile technologies can be of great use to the teacher with the added affordances of portability and touch-screen adding to the affordances of the desktop machine.

The 2020 Covid-19 pandemic and lockdown highlighted the opportunities and necessities for the use of online and virtual technologies for the delivery of learning. Whilst this was expedient it is important to reflect on when this might be useful and how teachers are using virtual environments to support pupils' learning.

Collaboration and virtual visits and visitors

'Beaming in' visitors via video conference software (e.g. Skype, Facetime) is relativity easy, and this can be to the whole class or to smaller groups or individuals. This can allow you to develop links to scientists working in local industry and allow them to give you virtual tours of their facilities where access would be difficult, time-consuming or too dangerous. It also allows your pupils to work in collaboration with pupils from other schools locally, nationally or even internationally. A number of projects have used this approach such as

"Toys in Space" – where the children go to explore how objects move in zero and micro-gravity environments, "Food for Thought" – where the children go to think about the requirements for food on a long space mission to Mars (both NASA), the "Osprey Flyaway project" where a bird migration expert was "brought into" the classroom (Leicester and Rutland Wildlife Trust] and the benefits of Euglena – an algae that is 0.5mm but contains most of the nutrition needed for humans to live (Japan).

A growing area of this, which is covered elsewhere in the book, is the use of Virtual Reality to explore places that would be otherwise impossible to reach – the ultimate virtual visit. Whilst the cost of the equipment can be high, by working in collaboration with other schools this can be affordable. Also, commercial organisations such as ClassVR (https://www.classvr.com/) offer opportunities to trail and explore this technology.

Simulations

The use of technology for simulations is an important area for the science teacher. Allowing the pupils to have some experiences that would otherwise be impossible (for example visiting the Sun!). There are a growing number of websites that have simulations on this but also a number of applications that allow the teacher to demonstrate, and then the pupils to explore these resources. An exciting one is Frog Dissection, which allows you to, as the name suggests, dissect a frog: a difficult thing to do in the primary classroom.

This ability of the technology to bring experiments into the classroom, which otherwise would not be possible due to time, health and safety or cost, allows an enrichment of curriculum and applications to offer low-cost solutions. For example, when looking at sound the application Sound Generator puts a signal generator in the hands of the teacher, or the pupils, for a few pence rather than a piece of equipment that would cost hundreds of pounds and might only be used once or twice a year.

Modelling change

In the case study above we saw how technology allowed the pupils to model ideas using a spreadsheet. The teacher could build on this by using the spreadsheet to model how changing the incline of the slope could impact both the speed of the vehicle and the resultant frictional forces using a model either they had developed or one that they had sourced online. The way in which the technology enables the "dull calculation" to happen in the background allows the pupils to explore the relationships between dependent and independent variables without the barrier of mathematical skills; it is not that these skills are not important but, as we have seen above, if the skills are a barrier to the investigative work the children are more likely to get bored.

Demonstration and sharing of practice

Most mobile devices are equipped with a camera and an ability to send images, via a wireless network, to the screen in the room. Thus, your mobile device with a simple stand (often constructed "Heath Robinson-like" from a couple of piles of books!) becomes a visualiser for teacher demonstrations and also a portable visualiser to allow pupils to see, and share, in the work of others in the classroom. The added affordance is that it is also easy to capture video of these occurrences providing differentiated support, opportunities for re-use and assessment possibilities.

Technology that supports professional practice

In this final section we explore a number of ways in which you can use technology to develop your own subject knowledge and to aid in planning and assessment as well as the development of Personal Learning Networks (PLNs).

Lack of teacher confidence and subject knowledge is identified as one of the major issues in the teaching of primary science (Murphy *et al.*, 2007). The technology can help with this as it allows the teacher access to resources as well as greater confidence to set research tasks for their pupils.

The technology also gives them access to a number of support networks both within the teaching and the scientific community. Easy access to social media makes the setting up of PLNs a reasonably simple task. Technologies such as Facebook or Twitter allow the less confident primary school teacher to develop networks with both greater confidence and/or experienced colleagues but also with the scientific community and, as we have seen above, the possibility to bring those resources into their classroom. The TES is one of the largest of these international communities (http://www.tes.co.uk/teaching-resources/] and some of the developing communities on Twitter include @theASE @tesScience and @ITEfaraday.

Assessment in science with mobile technologies

The mobile device gives great opportunities for the teacher to both gather evidence of achievement and provide feedback on this. The still camera, video and audio recording affordances allow the teacher to capture data as pupils undertake investigations, to record conversations with the pupils and to capture evidence from their written work – all of which can then be used for formative and summative feedback and assessment (see for example the app *ExplainEverything*).

During lessons data capture tools such as SurveyTools or NearPod allow more inter-activity allowing you to gather live data to use to inform and develop practice. Quizzing software such as Kahoot! allows quick knowledge checking and retrieval practice – though these do need devices for all pupils. An alternative is Plickers (https://get.plickers.com/) where printed cards offer the opportunity for formative assessment and data collection with a single smart device.

Additionally, it enables you to, discreetly, gather formative assessments on the pupils in real time making a demonstrable impact on the teaching and learning in the classroom. Gathering data in this way allows the teacher to target specific pupils, or specific groups of pupils based on real-time data for focused feedback and improvement – a key factor in individual pupil progress (Hattie, 2009). Access to the tablets also allows the teacher to direct the pupils to previously curated resources allowing for independent or peer learning.

Summary and key points

Whilst such a short chapter is limiting, I hope that the ideas explored above have opened your eyes, or perhaps only opened them wider, to the immense possibilities that the adoption of mobile technologies can offer to the primary science teacher. The use of the tablet device allows the teacher to get closer to my defined "core principles" for excellent primary science.

- It promotes the idea of children doing **real science** – tablet technologies are more and more prevalent in professional science labs and so children undertake science that is more like science outside the classroom.

- It encourages **practical, enquiry-based investigative** work as the transmission of information can be done via curated or specially written resources, which the children can access "just in time" rather than "just in case" given the teacher more time to work with the children on investigative science.
- It allows, using simulations and other tools, the children to explore a range of **models of science** and allows them to adapt and develop these models as their own understanding becomes more sophisticated.
- It may be that your school is still considering the introduction of tablet / mobile technologies, that you are thinking about the efficacy of BYOT (bring your own technology), that you have a small number of devices you can book out, or that you have larger scale plans in place [a growing number of schools are exploring how they can organise 1-1 ownership of devices that remain with the pupils (see Burden *et al.* (2013) for examples of these in Scotland). Wherever you are I hope that you are now more excited, and informed about how these devices can impact on learning and teaching in science.

Further resources

Meadows, J. (2004). *Science and ICT in the classroom*. London, Fulton.
  This book explores in more depth the uses of technology in the primary classroom using existing rather than tablet technologies – useful if you have not yet ventured into tablets.
Barber, D. and Cooper, L. (2012). *Using Web 2.0 tools in the primary classroom*. London, Routledge.
  This book explores the use of tools such as blogs, wikis and other social tools including some good ideas for the science teacher.
Fullan, M. and Langworthy, M. (2014). *A rich seam: how new pedagogies find deep learning*. Pearson (access via: http://www.michaelfullan.ca/wp-content/uploads/2014/01/3897.Rich_Seam_web.pdf).
  This publication explores why the technology is not enough but it should instigate both pedagogic and personal change.

References

ASE/BECTA. (2009). *Primary Science with ICT: Pupils' Entitlement to ICT in Primary Science*. Coventry: BECTA.
Barber, D., and Cooper, L. (2012). *Using New Web Tools in the Primary Classroom*. London: Routledge.
Bianchi, L., Whittaker, C., and Poole, A. (2021). *The 10 Key Issues with Children's Learning in Primary Science in England*. Manchester: The Ogden Trust.
Burden, K., Hopkins, P., Male, T., Martin, S., and Trala, C. (2012). *iPadScotland Evaluation Report*. Hull: The University of Hull. Retrieved from https://www.researchgate.net/publication/264464463_iPad_Scotland_Evaluation (Accessed November 23, 2023).
Byrne, J., and Sharp, J. (2002). *Using ICT in Primary Science Teaching*. London: Learning Matters.
Davies, D., Collier, C., and Howe, A. (2012). A Matter of Interpretation: Developing Primary Pupils' Enquiry Skills using Position-Linked Datalogging. *Research in Science and Technological Education*, 30(3), 311–325.
Dewey, J. (1916). *Democracy and Education*. New York: Free Press.
DfE (2013). *A Science National Curriculum for England*. London: HMSO.
Eschach, H. (2006) *Science Literacy in Primary Schools and Pre-Schools*. Springer, Dordrecht.
Fullan, M., and Langworthy, M. (2014). *A Rich Seam: How New Pedagogies Find Deep Learning*. Pearson. Retrieved from http://www.michaelfullan.ca/wp-content/uploads/2014/01/3897.Rich_Seam_web.pdf (Accessed January 15, 2023).

Harlen, W. (2010). *Principles and Big Ideas about Science*. Hatfield: ASE.

Harlen, W., and Qualter, A. (2018). *The Teaching of Science in Primary Schools*. 7th edn. Abingdon, Oxon: David Fulton.

Hattie, J. (2009). *Visible Learning: A Synthesis of over 200 Meta-Analyses Relating to Achievement*. London: Routledge.

Kearney, M., and Treagust, D. (2001). Constructivism as a Referent in the Design and Development of a Computer Program using Interactive Digital Video to Enhance Learning in Physics. *Australian Journal of Educational Technology*, 17(1), 64–79.

Kolb, D. A. (1984). *Experiential Learning Experience as a Source of Learning and Development*. New Jersey: Prentice Hall.

Laxton, D., Cooper, L., and Younie, S. (2021). Translational Research in Action: The Use of Technology to Disseminate Information to Parents during the COVID-19 Pandemic. *British Journal of Educational Technology*, 52(4), 1538–1553.

Leask, M., and Younie, S. (2022) *Education for All in Times of Crisis: Lessons from Covid-19*. Abingdon: Routledge.

McCormick, R., and Scrimshaw, P. (2001). Information and Communications Technology, Knowledge and Pedagogy. *Education, Communication and Information*, 1(1), 37–57.

McCrory, A. (2017). *Scientific Enquiry and Engaging Primary-Aged Children in Science Lessons Part 2: Why Teach Science via Enquiry?*, JES, 28–39.

Mishra, P., and Koehler, M. J. (2009). Technological Pedagogical Content Knowledge: A Framework for Teacher Knowledge. *Contemporary Issues in Technology and Teacher Education*, 91(6), 60–70.

Murphy, C. (2003). *Futurelab Report 5: Literature review in Primacy Science and ICT*. Bristol: Futurelab. Retrieved from https://www.nfer.ac.uk/publications/literature-review-in-primary-science-and-ict/ (Accessed November 23, 2023).

Murphy, C., and Beggs, J. (2003). Children's Perceptions of School Science. *School Science Review*, 84(308), 109–116.

Murphy, C., Neil, P., and Beggs, J. (2007). Primary Science Teacher Confidence Revisited: Ten Years On. *Educational Research*, 49(4), 415–430.

NAACE (1999). *All Our Futures: Creativity, Culture and Education*. Retrieved from http://sirkenrobinson.com/pdf/allourfutures.pdf (Accessed January 15, 2023).

Ofcom (2022). *Children and Parents: Media Use and Attitudes Report 2022*. Retrieved from https://www.ofcom.org.uk/__data/assets/pdf_file/0024/234609/childrens-media-use-and-attitudes-report-2022.pdf (Accessed January 15, 2023).

Ofsted (2011). *Successful Science: An Evaluation of Science Education in England 2007–2010*. London: Ofsted Publications. Retrieved from http://www.ofsted.gov.uk/resources/successful-science (Accessed January 15, 2023).

Osborne, J., and Hennessey, S. (2003). *Futurelab Report 6: Literature Review in Science Education and the Role of ICT: Promise, Problems and Future Directions*. Futurelab: Bristol.

Prensky, M. (2001). Digital Natives, Digital Immigrants. *On The Horizon*, 9(5) [online]. Retrieved from https://www.marcprensky.com/writing/Prensky%20-%20Digital%20Natives,%20Digital%20Immigrants%20-%20Part1.pdf (Accessed November 23, 2023).

Puentedura, R. (2011). *SAMR and TPCK in Action*. Retrieved from http://www.hippasus.com/rrpweblog/archives/2011/10/28/SAMR_TPCK_In_Action.pdf (Accessed January 15, 2023).

Rose, J. (2008). *Independent Review of the Primary Curriculum: Final Report*. London: HMSO. Retrieved from https://education-uk.org/documents/pdfs/2009-IRPC-final-report.pdf (Accessed November 23, 2023).

Rosenshine, B. (2010). *Principles of Instruction*. Educational Practices Series, Vol. 21. The International Academy of Education.

SCORE (2013). *Resourcing Practical Work in Primary Schools*. SCORE: London. Retrieved from https://www.stem.org.uk/resources/collection/3982/score-practical-work-school-science-reports (Accessed November 23, 2023).

Traxler, J. (2007). Defining, Discussing and Evaluating Mobile Education. *International Review of Research in Open and Distance Learning*, 8(2). Retrieved from http://www.irrodl.org/index. php/irrodl/article/view/346 (Accessed January 15, 2023).

Veen, W. (2004). *Homo Zappiens: Growing Up in a Digital Age*. New York: Network Continuum Education.

Vygotsky, L. S. (1978). *Mind in Society: The Development of Higher Psychological Processes*. Cambridge, MA: Harvard University Press.

Webb, J. (2021). *The iPad as Tool for Education – A Case Study*. NAACE. Retrieved from https:// www.maltonschool.org/wp-content/uploads/2021/07/The-iPad-as-a-Tool-for-Education-study-NAACE-9ine-Consulting.pdf (Accessed November 27, 2023).

13 Using mobile technology to raise STEM attainment and develop scientific thinking

Karen Blackmore

Introduction

This chapter explores the potential of using mobile learning (m-learning) in the form of handheld devices (m-devices) as a means of promoting collaborative interactions between primary age pupils. It draws on the seminal work of Burden and Kearney (2016, 2017) who demonstrated that m-learning had the potential to enhance collaboration, social interactivity, *in situ* learning, sharing and communication between peers, across all phases of education, including initial teacher education (ITE).

Since developing research literacy has been shown to be an important positive indicator of successful ITE and transition to the early career teaching phase (Boyd, Szplit and Zbróg, 2021), this chapter will be structured around three classroom-based research studies. These studies focus on facets of Science, Technology, Engineering and Mathematics (STEM) teaching to explore current best pedagogical practice. Whilst the research evidence presented is associated with STEM, many of the strategies used can be applied across the entire primary curriculum.

M-learning is particularly suitable for inquiry-based STEM, where experimental outcomes can be transient and need rapid recording *in situ*. Interpreting data from the first case study, which used data loggers in a whole school inquiry; it is argued that m-devices allow pupils to document and share all stages of inquiry. These stages include the initial experimental design, recording observations and findings, collation and analysis of the results and importantly the dissemination of findings to peers.

In the second case study, 13.2, which represents a summary of a three-year longitudinal classroom-based research project, the potential impact of the collaborative use of iPads on building scientific literacy and understanding is explored. It examines a specific example of how this child-led m-learning approach can be used to enhance multimedia experimental report writing.

The third case study 13.3 features the use of more sophisticated m-devices in the form of LEGO© Mindstorms robots and Raspberry Pi© microprocessors and sensors, and charters the progress of pupils from the same year group but from different schools, within a Multi Academy Trust (MAT). As such the research gives an insight into the potential of m-learning to forge new relationships between pupils with similar prior educational experiences.

Objectives

At the end of this chapter you should be able to:

- design collaborative learning opportunities using m-technology in primary schools

DOI: 10.4324/9781003408925-13

- reflect on potential m-learning strategies to support the formation and maintenance of social relationships in your classroom
- critique methods of child-led formative assessment to support learner collaboration and metacognition.

Case Study 13.1: Supporting collaborative scientific inquiry in the primary classroom

This study took part in a larger than average primary school with a high number of children on roll from challenging socio-economic backgrounds (pupil premium = 38%, national average = 25%) over a period of three months. Semi-structured observations, a short pupil questionnaire as well as paired conversations with pupils were used to ascertain their learning in science and attitudes to using m-technology. The research centred on a whole school problem-based inquiry to explore sound levels around the school. This followed observations by pupils that certain areas of the school were noisy. Children made predictions which areas would be the noisiest and quietest places in the school and how the noise levels varied in different places during the school day. Following this initial exploratory phase the eldest pupils in Year 6, were asked to design fair tests to determine the sound muffling capacity of different insulator materials, with a view to designing a sound proofing strategy for the school. The following key findings pertaining to social and learning relationships emerged from the study (for full details of the study see Blackmore, 2020).

Key findings of the study

1. Pupils like to work with their friends

    Observations and questionnaire responses provided evidence that the use of m-devices supported pupils to engage in collaborative learning experiences. Pupils were seen to be engaged in a range of exploratory talk including discussing the many different potential ways to carry out the investigation. A key feature of the dialogue observed was questioning in groups and turn-taking to demonstrate their key ideas. The pupils were observed asking many questions and seeking others' advice about their experimental approaches. In addition, they were often seen to ask each other to check they had used the data loggers correctly and measured the sound levels accurately.

    Following the science inquiry, pupils expressed their satisfaction at working in small groups and three quarters said they preferred working with their friends. They appreciated that there were social elements to interacting during the scientific investigation. When asked whether there was any effect on communication within a group if they knew each other well or were friends, one boy responded:

    > Well we are all in the same class, so we have obviously worked with them before so you really know what they are like to be with, you would know how to speak to them or how to treat them, and it's fun to work with your friends.

    (Craig, Year 6)

This key finding agrees with those found by Miell and MacDonald (2000) who identified that friends could positively influence outcomes of creative collaborative tasks during musical learning.

Pupils also felt that working with their friends resulted in effective learning, when asked if designing the investigation with peers worked well, one boy answered:

> *Yes, because* you *can share ideas and communicate better.*

(Jacob, Year 6)

Whilst this finding is supported by the research by Kutnick and Kington (2005), who found that pupils preferred working with their best friends, due to off-task behaviour (particularly with friends who were boys) this approach was not always associated with the highest degree of cognitive enhancement.

Several pupils mentioned that they felt they did not learn their best on occasion when working collaboratively using m-devices, especially if the group size was too large. The following two quotes from a pair of Year 6 boys in a larger than usual group, illustrates this perspective.

> *If you go with ten people, then all you are going to hear is like wittering ... and laughing.*

(Jacob, Year 6)

> *And it's more likely that you are going to have friends in your group, and that you are going to want to talk and not get anything done.*

(Brian, Year 6)

2. Pupils often like to work with their peers without teacher intervention

The study revealed that pupils expressed satisfaction at being given the opportunity to be self-sufficient within their group and not have to rely on input from their teacher, as illustrated from the following exchange with the researcher:

> *Do you think it helps having a group to work with in science?*

(Researcher)

> *I think it does because you can discuss it with each other and they can explain it if you don't understand, instead of you having to go to the teacher all the time*

(David, Year 6)

3. Pupils sometimes use m-learning in the classroom to deepen/forge friendships

During interviews several pupils described how working together during science inquiry strengthened and encouraged them to initiate new friendships. As described by a female pupil who worked in a mixed group and a boy who worked in an all-male group as follows:

> *A pupil that you are* friends *with, but you don't really spend time with them, then you will get on ... but at the same time making more of the friendship.*

(Tamara, Year 6)

We worked with two people who we don't usually work with, and we got on. Sometimes we try to play now.

(Stephen, Year 6)

Links to theory

These findings are supported in principle by MacDonald, Miell and Morgan (2000) who found more transactive discussion was observed between friends, who appeared to be able to anticipate each other's points of view. This led to a degree of enhanced communication which appeared to support creative problem solving as well as nurturing on-going friendships. These gains in terms of social and learning relationships can have a wide reach as illustrated by Bath (2009) who argued that learning can be enhanced if pupils feel a sense of belonging and social success and hence have a significant impact on the more holistic nature of education.

Building on Bath's (2009) work, Carter and Nutbrown (2016) termed the phrase *Pedagogy of Friendship* and highlighted the importance of teachers supporting children to make sense of their friendship experiences and in many cases use these developing relationships as a means to enhance future learning. They advocate teachers observing interactions between pupils during creative and problem-solving tasks, in order to inform planning and scaffold future learning experiences.

At this point in the chapter, teachers are encouraged to undertake Task 13.1, in order to reflect on their learning.

Task 13.1: Reflection on social learning opportunities

After reading Case Study 13.1, what do you as a teacher, consider the most important messages in terms of promoting opportunities for pupils to develop positive relationships with each other?

Have you been aware of any instances of pupils articulating their learning preferences during your classroom practice?

Were you surprised by any of the pupil responses in the study?

How could you use the insights from Case Study one to develop your on-going practice?

Case Study 13.2: Supporting subject-specific literacy through collaborative learning with iPads

This case study mobilises a portion of the findings of a three-year longitudinal classroom-based study focused on the deployment of m-technology in the form of tablet computers (iPads), during Inquiry Based Science Education (IBSE). The research took place in a larger than average primary school in the West Midlands, U.K. (>300 pupils on roll), with a strong commitment to m-TEL. iPads were used as an integral collaborative m-learning tool across the entire curriculum, with all pupils in years 5 and 6 having access to them throughout the school day. This study focuses on learning during bespoke Science-Weeks, consisting of intense periods of pupil-led science inquiry. During these weeks pupils were encouraged by their teachers to use the iPads as a source of reference materials using a range of science-specific apps and on-line science dictionaries. Pupils' learning behaviours and attitudes to m-learning were explored through observations by the research team consisting of beginning teachers, established teachers and teaching assistants. M-learning attainment was assessed through team scrutiny of samples of pupils' work (>60 per task), consisting of multi-media presentations and experimental reports across three years of Science-Weeks, (for full details of inquiries, see Appendix A). The scoring (see Appendix B [i–iii] for full details) was reviewed and rechecked on multiple occasions by an additional researcher to ensure the reliability of the method. The pupils' attainment was scored according to three main criteria:

- scientific vocabulary use
- scientific process recording
- understanding of the key scientific concepts.

Overall analysis of the pupil attainment

Please see Figure 13.1 which looks at the results of pupils' work assessment and shows a graph depicting the scorings of the science investigation reports produced by Year 5 pupils using iPads.

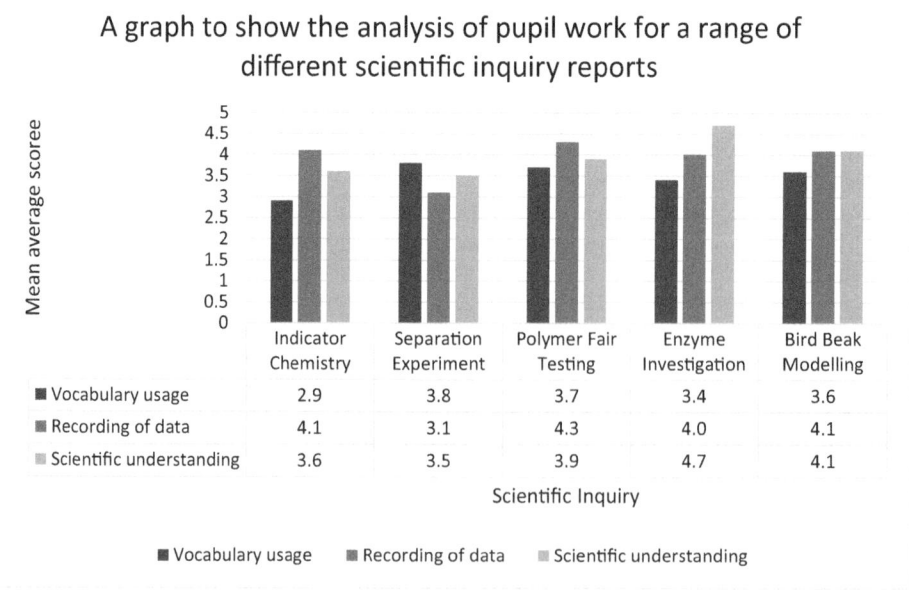

Figure 13.1 Results of pupils' work assessment

Key findings of the study

1. Pupils used iPads to effectively plan, record and present their science investigations.

    Analysis of pupil work consisting of multi-media investigation reports/presentations show good levels of attainment were apparent overall. In terms of vocabulary usage, a mean of 3.5 was achieved, corresponding to the appropriate use of five to seven science-specific keywords in each report. Pupil recording of investigation design was also strong with a slightly higher mean score of 3.9, corresponding to the vast majority of relevant experimental steps being recorded and the inclusion of suitable graphics. Scientific understanding was the highest scoring component (mean=4.0), corresponding to strong evidence of the understanding of the key concepts.

    Further qualitative evidence in the form of an eBook created by a pair of Year 5 pupils using the Apple app *Explain Everything* is presented in Figure 13.2.

The enzyme, fruit & jelly experiment
- Our prediction is that the enzymes will make the fruit sink to the bottom of the jelly.
- Equipment: jug, stirrer, ruler, pipette, plastic container and petri dish.

Setting up the experiment
- After putting the jelly crystals in the jug with some hot water, we mixed the solution.
- We poured part of the liquid into a container and mixed it with some cold water to cool it. We left it to set so it wouldn't be a liquid any more but a semi-solid.

Fair testing and results
- We put the pineapple (with enzymes) in one petri dish and in the other we put kiwi and on the last just jelly. We took photographs every hour to see what happened.
- The results of the experiment were that the fruit had sunk because the enzymes had turned half the jelly into a liquid.

Figure 13.2 An example of an *Explain Everything* eBook created by Year 5 pupils

2. Using the multi modal capability of iPads resulted in strong articulation of key science processes, including the use of key vocabulary.

    Examining the eBook created by two Year 5 pupils, it can be seen that the multi-modal nature of the eBook app was supportive in the expression of the key scientific ideas. For example, the stages of the investigation (including a scientific prediction) are clearly defined with suitable associated graphics. In terms of assessing the pupils' understanding of 'fair testing', the capability for pupils to use graphics was particularly helpful for teacher judgments. Specifically in this case (see eBook page as depicted in Figure 13.2), it can be seen that the fruits were tested separately, and a control sample was set up in the form of a petri dish containing only jelly.

It can also be seen that the eBook depicts many facets of the 'working scientifically' requirements of the National Curriculum for Primary Science (DfE, 2015). Appropriate technical terminology including the terms *enzymes, pipette, petri plate, semi-solid* and *solution* are used accurately. There is also evidence of the application of mathematical knowledge to the pupils' understanding of the science investigation; for example during the initial measuring of the depth of the jelly solution and the taking of photographs over a defined period of time. Monitoring the progress of the experiment was a key utility of the iPads; indeed in another case, two female pupils used the time lapse video capability to record the fruit sinking into the jelly as a result of the fruit enzyme activity.

Next, see Figure 13.3, which is a word cloud depicting key scientific vocabulary use in the 'Survival in a bottle' separation reports by pupils of years 5 and 6.

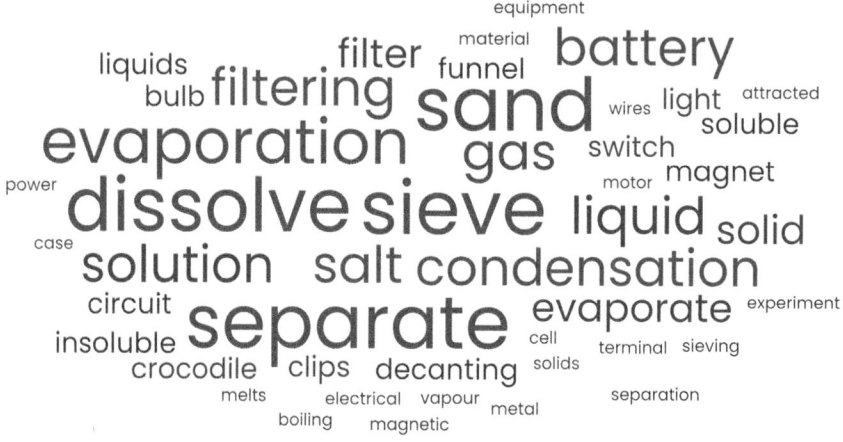

Figure 13.3 Word cloud depicting key scientific vocabulary

A word frequency analysis of 60 inquiry reports undertaken by four members of the research team indicated a wide range of scientific vocabulary being used by Year 5 pupils in their investigation reports. The range and relative frequencies are illustrated in Figure 13.3 which shows over 40 different keywords which were appropriately used in the reports. It is interesting to note that some conceptually challenging terms, for example *evaporation, condensation, dissolve* and *solution* were present in high frequencies which indicates a strong level of scientific literacy for Year 5 learners.

Links to theory

The results of the formative assessment of pupils' scientific literacy, in Case Study 13.2, support the findings of several longitudinal studies focusing on attainment (Grolig, 2020; Kidd, Donnelly and Christiansen, 2018). These studies demonstrate that early language acquisition is strongly related to children's language environments and opportunities to engage in preliminary dialogue. They also showed that multi-modal representation of language (as afforded by shared reading of children's picture books) can aid understanding of key vocabulary. These findings resonate with those of Shanahan and Shanahan (2008) whose study into adolescent language acquisition revealed that sharing and meaning making of key scientific terms using on-line dictionaries was facilitative for increasing specific terminology. In terms of challenging and shaping scientific beliefs, pupils need opportunities to engage in dialogic learning through dissemination and critique of their own and peers' scientific inquiry (Ford and Forman, 2006; Yacoubian and BouJaoude, 2010). This involves pupils using language in complex ways (Lee *et al.*, 2013) and acquiring scientific literacy skills.

At this point in the chapter, teachers are encouraged to undertake Task 13.2 to inform their formative assessment design.

Task 13.2: Reflection on pupil attainment during m-learning

After reading Case Study 13.2, what do you consider the most important messages in terms of designing formative assessment strategies during m-learning?

Is it important that pupils are offered opportunities to write collaboratively?

Drawing on your experience of pupil led inquiry, can this approach support the acquisition of key subject-specific vocabulary?

How could you use the insights in terms of multi-media formats, to develop your on-going practice?

Case Study 13.3: Forging positive learning relationships using problem-based m-learning

The third case study involves a three-month collaborative partnership between two schools within a MAT, working together to afford pupils an opportunity to engage with other Year 6 pupils, just prior to their transition to the same secondary school. With the aid of a specialist technology consultant, the pupils were able to design and construct a rover using Lego© Mindstorms components. The rover housed a Sense-HAT sensor capable of detecting and transmitting temperature, orientation and environmental information to a locally hosted website which gathered live data. The sensor was controlled by a small Raspberry Pi microprocessor. In this way the pupils could deploy their rover over varied terrain outside the ground control laboratory and gather real-time data as to its progress and environment. Pupil and staff attitudes and perceptions to this ambitious mode of teaching were obtained by undertaking semi-structured observations and interviews during and after the m-learning process.

Key findings of the study

1. Pupils from different schools valued working collaboratively with each other:
   Semi-structured observations revealed that there was an initial exploratory element of the collaborative working, where pupils played with the equipment first within their own small groups. This was followed by a construction phase, where pupils worked often in pairs or threes, to construct different parts of the rover vehicle. During the construction phase pupils from the two different schools were frequently observed to approach each other and share ideas and potential solutions to problems.

Pupils voiced that they enjoyed the experience of working together and they valued the views of their peers when problem solving as detailed by two Year 6 girls from different schools:

The problem was that the box was too heavy, so we have made it flexible so it can move with the weight. We worked together so I could hold the chassis and she changed the frame.

(Angela, Year 6, School A)

They also appeared to be able to use their shared knowledge of Scratch to overcome robot functionality issues pertaining to coding, as articulated by a Year 6 boy working with another male pupil.

The robot stopped working so we changed the variable, then tested to see whether it worked.

(Evan, Year 6, School B)

As the project progressed month by month, pupils from the two different schools frequently shared solutions with each other during construction sessions. Some of the solutions were complex multi-step processes, consistent with high attainment for this level of study, for example during the remote collection of environmental data when the rovers were outside on the test terrains. Much of the problem solving was collaborative between pupils from different schools as illustrated by the following observed exchange:

One Year 6 boy who was a talented mathematician initially commented:

I am making a graph to show what is going on outside. It is a live feed. I can get the orientation sensor to work but not the air temperature one.

(Sean, Year 6, School B)

Another boy who attended the Scratch coding club from the other school, followed this up:

I can help you with that, you can switch out to this sensor because my friend has given me the code.

(Callum, Year 6, School A)

2. Pupils liked to work in parallel on their own task, as part of an overall collaborative approach:

Observational data confirmed that pupils mostly adopted a trial-and-error approach to problem solving rather than a systematic step-by-step approach. The three teachers acted as facilitators rather than specifically directing the m-learning. Individual pupils were seen to work on different aspects of the task and appeared to be absolutely absorbed in problem solving for significant amounts of time. There was evidence of pupils co-constructing knowledge, by using prior experience as evidenced from the following exchange:

I am trying to work out how to attach the camera to the side of the rover. It's not working, and I don't know how to do it, can you help please?

(Anita, Year 6, School A)

> *Of course, I had that problem because the wires got in the way, I fixed it by putting these two pieces like this.*
>
> (Bethan, Year 6, School B)

Pupil interviews after the m-learning sessions confirmed observations that they often solved their problems by watching what others were doing. When asked how they progressed when they became stuck on an aspect of the rover's construction or programming, pupils often articulated how they walked around the classroom and watched other group's problem-solving activity. When struggling with an aspect of imbalance with the sensor housing component of the vehicle, one pupil commented:

> *I have seen the other group using a trailer so I'm building one to test it out.*
>
> (Rob, Year 6, School B)

Following a positive exchange with the group who had solved the sensor imbalance issue, the same pupil returned to seek their advice during a subsequent session. When asked about this by the researcher he explained:

> *They got their trailer to go backwards and that helped it also go forward, because it had greater momentum. I tried that with our trailer, and it worked, they really helped me.*
>
> (Rob, Year 6, School B)

3. Pupils thought about the possibilities of using this type of m-learning after their transition to the next phase of education:

   This was less prominent than the aforementioned themes, but it was commented on by a few pupils. This could be because the head of the MAT had specifically mentioned this aspect during the first few sessions, when they expressed the wish that the pupils from both schools would get to know each other, since they would probably be going to the same secondary school. Mostly the comments were made by female pupils as follows:

   > *I wonder if it will be like this when I go to high school? I hope we get to work together on big projects.*
   >
   > (Kristen, Year 6, School A)

   > *It has been nice to meet girls from the other school, I enjoyed working with them and would like to see them again.*
   >
   > (Rebecca, Year 6, School B)

These comments suggest that some of the pupils were encouraged to work collaboratively with their peers in the future, possibly as a result of forging positive learning relationships during the project.

Links to theory

As well as supporting understanding of the key principles within the primary Computing and Design Technology curriculum, school staff voiced the opinion that they felt similar mobile Technology Enhanced Learning (m-TEL) opportunities might facilitate social readiness prior to transition, in agreement with research in older pupils by Van Herpen *et al.* (2020). This perspective resonates with the research of Arif (2020) who undertook a small-scale empirical study with eight newly transitioned Year 7 pupils and six secondary teachers. Semi-structured interviews revealed that pupils highlighted feeling a *sense of belonging* was most important to them and that this was improved following meaningful social interactions with their peers. This viewpoint was echoed by teachers who advocated a range of collaborative problem-solving opportunities as positive facilitators for educational transition to secondary school provision.

At this point in the chapter, teachers are encouraged to undertake Task 13.3, to reflect on the importance of social learning opportunities.

Task 13.3: Reflection on social learning

How can you design learning opportunities within your classroom to support the forging and maintaining of children's friendships?

What can you do if a pupil struggles to make or maintain friendships? Or prefers to work alone?

Are there certain curriculum subjects which provide more opportunities for social learning?

When planning, would you consider friendships of pupils working in small groups?

Thinking about the wider picture in terms of transition to secondary school, is problem-based learning an area you would like to explore?

Summary and key points

The research presented in this chapter, explored through the lens of effective classroom pedagogy, builds on the aforementioned affordances of m-learning to support learning across STEM curriculum subjects. It provides evidence that:

- Pupils exhibit highly positive attitudes to working collaboratively with their peers using m-devices.
- Forging and maintaining positive social and learning relationships can be catalysed using m-learning approaches.
- m-TEL can contribute to a facilitative classroom environment.
- m-learning is a powerful tool for formative assessment especially with respect to pupils creating their own multi-modal reports and presentations to explain their understanding.

You as a teacher have been invited to:

- Explore ways in which you can develop your practice to deploy m-learning approaches.
- Consider how you might afford pupils opportunities to forge and maintain learning relationships.

- Challenge the early assumptions that m-device use leads exclusively to lone pupil-centric learning – often characterised by autonomous and non-social interactions.
- Develop and refine your m-TEL assessment strategies to capture and monitor pupil learning and progression.

In conclusion, throughout the chapter you have been guided to reflect upon research-based evidence, in order to develop your own range of collaborative m-TEL teaching approaches. Advocating the adoption of such an approach, the author has argued that m-technology can be used as an effective conduit within collaborative peer learning. As an added advantage, this allows pupils to deepen their social exchanges and in doing so forge positive learning relationships with each other. In turn, this supports the maintenance of a positive learning environment for both pupils and their teachers resulting in enhanced understanding and progression.

Further resources

MESHGuide to Assessment in Primary Science by Alan Howe. Available at http://www.mesh-guides.org/guides/node/186?n=203.
This is an excellent resource for informing the formulation of assessment strategy in primary science at individual pupil, class, year group and whole school levels. It contains details of the seminal Teacher Assessment in Primary Science (TAPS) research project, undertaken by the Centre for Research in Early Scientific Learning (CRESL) at Bath Spa University. In addition, it acts as a repository for a range of accessible research articles exploring best primary science classroom practice.

Best practice in teaching Primary Science, by Jane Turner. Available at https://www.youtube.com/watch?v=23jPyUhKMsk.
This eight-minute videoclip by Jane Turner who is the Director of the Primary Science Quality Mark (PSQM) and all-round primary science expert, talks about the key features of designing and delivering outstanding science lessons.

Integrating Technology into a Preschool Classroom, by Boise State University. Available at https://www.youtube.com/watch?v=uYoCfBA9Xpc.
This six minute videoclip by Boise State University (BSU) College of Education and the BSU Children's Center explores and advances our understanding of Early STEM Education using handheld m-devices.

Geer, R. (2017-03). Emerging pedagogies for the use of iPads in schools. *British Journal of Educational Technology*, 48(2), 490–498.
This article provides an excellent illustration of iPad use in primary classrooms across the curriculum. It focuses on the potential changes in pedagogy associated with m-learning and implications for teacher professional development.

Lewis-Neill, S. (2020). Making the most of technology to explore nature. *Primary Science*, 161, 24–26.
This short accessible article in the Association for Science Education (ASE) Journal - Primary Science provides a detailed practice-based account of how m-technology can be used as a conduit for primary pupils into the natural world. Steven Lewis-Neill has extensive experience in primary education as teacher, science lead, mentor and trainer and has provided hands-on workshops for schools through his *WildWorkshops* company.

References

Arif, M. (2020). 'The role of social and emotional learning during the transition to secondary school: an exploratory study', *Pastoral Care in Education*, 38(1), 23–41.

Bath, C. (2009). *Learning to belong: Exploring young children's participation at the start of school.* London: Routledge.

Blackmore, K. (2020). 'Enabling primary science inquiry: The role of Mobile Technologies to support peer learning'. In A. Kington and K. Blackmore (eds.), *Social and learning relationships in the primary schools.* Bloomsbury Academic, 47–70.

Boyd, P. (2021). 'Teachers' research literacy as research-informed professional judgment'. In P. Boyd, A. Szplit and Z. Zbróg (eds.), *Developing teachers' research literacy: International perspectives.* Kraków: Wydawnictwo Libron, 17–44. Viewed 12 October 2022 from https://insight. cumbria.ac.uk/id/eprint/6366/.

Burden, K. and Kearney, M. (2016). 'Future scenarios for mobile science learning', *Research in Science Education*, 46(2), 287–308.

Burden, K. and Kearney, M. (2017). 'Investigating and critiquing teacher educators' mobile learning practices', *Interactive Technology and Smart Education*, 14(2), 110–125.

Carter, C. and Nutbrown, C. (2016). 'A Pedagogy of Friendship: Young children's friendships and how schools can support them', *International Journal of Early Years Education*, 24(4), 395–413.

Department for Education [DfE] (2015). *Statutory guidance: National curriculum in England: Science programmes of study.* Viewed 20 November 2022 from https://www.gov.uk/government/publications/national-curriculum-in-england-science-programmes-of-study/national-curriculum-in-england-science-programmes-of-study#upper-key-stage-2--years-5-and-6.

Ford, M. and Forman, E. A. (2006). 'Refining disciplinary learning in classroom contexts', Review of *Research in Education*, 30, 1–33.

Grolig, L. (2020). 'Shared storybook reading and oral language development: A bioecological perspective', *Frontiers in Psychology*, 11. https://www.frontiersin.org/articles/10.3389/fpsyg.2020.01818/full.

Hargreaves, E., Buchanan, D. and Quick, L. (2022). '"Look at them! They all have friends and not me": The role of peer relationships in schooling from the perspective of primary children designated as "lower-attaining"', *Educational Review*, 74(7), 1224–1242.

Kidd E., Donnelly S. and Christiansen M. (2018). 'Individual differences in language acquisition and processing', *Trends in Cognitive Science*, 22, 154–169.

Kutnick, P. and Kington, A. (2005). 'Children's friendships and learning in school: Cognitive enhancement through social interaction?', *British Journal of Educational Psychology*, 75(4), 521–538.

Lee, O., Quinn, H. and Valdes, G. (2013). 'Science and language for English language learners in relation to next generation science standards and with implications for common core state standards for English language arts and mathematics', *Educational Researcher*. Available at https://ul.stanford.edu/sites/default/files/resource/2021-05/3_EdResearcher%2011%20April%202013%20Lee_Quinn_Valdes%20copy.pdf.

Macdonald, R., Miell, D. and Morgan, L. (2000). 'Social processes and creative collaboration in children', *European Journal of Psychology of Education*, 15(4), 405–415.

Miell, D. and MacDonald, R. (2000). 'Children's creative collaborations: The importance of friendship when working together on a musical composition', *Social Development*, 9, 348–369.

Shanahan, T. and Shanahan, C. (2008). 'Teaching disciplinary literacy to adolescents: Rethinking content-area literacy', *Harvard Educational Review*, 78(1), 40–61.

Van Herpen, S., Meeuwisse, M., Hofman, A. and Severiens, S. (2020). 'A head start in higher education: the effect of a transition intervention on interaction, sense of belonging, and academic performance', *Studies in Higher Education*, 45(4), 862–877.

Yacoubian, H. and BouJaoude, S. (2010). 'The effect of reflective discussions following inquiry-based laboratory activities on students' views of nature of science', *Journal of Research in Science Teaching*, 47(10), 1229–1252.

Appendix A – STEM: sample of the scientific inquiries

Details of a sample of the scientific inquiries taking place during Science Weeks.

Name of Scientific Inquiry	Details of the Scientific Inquiry
Indicator Chemistry	Red cabbage leaves were ground with sand in a bowl and then treated with hot water to extract the pigment. The sand was removed by two rounds of filtration. The resultant extract was then painted onto blotting paper to produce indicator strips. These were used to test everyday solutions to determine acids and alkalis/bases. All stages of the investigation were captured using the iPad camera.
Separation Experiment	Survival in a bottle separation investigation. This was a problem-solving experiment where a two-litre plastic bottle was filled with a range of soluble, insoluble, metal and plastic materials. The children used their own methods to separate each substance and obtain pure water. They also built a functioning electrical circuit with key components. All stages of the investigation were recorded using the iPad camera.
Polymer Fair Testing	"Flubber" production: a semi-solid polymer from PVA glue and Borax solutions, using a chemical change. The investigation involves mixing the two liquids in various proportions to obtain an array of polymers with different physical properties, which were then tested. Measurements of physical properties e.g. maximum bounce height (including a scale) were undertaken using the iPad video recording capability.
Enzyme Investigation	This inquiry arose as a result of children's questions surrounding the digestion of food molecules. The action of the plant enzyme Bromelain in the form of pineapple slices was investigated using gelatine as a substrate. The children set up the experiment including corresponding control samples and monitored the digestion over several hours. Measurements were taken to determine the rate of digestion using the time-lapse video utility on the iPads.
Bird Beak Modelling	A pupil-led inquiry in response to pupil's research into variation in bird beak anatomy and function. Different household implements e.g. tweezers and plastic straws were used to mimic bird beaks which gathered suitable foods. All stages of the inquiry (including initial online research) were undertaken using the iPads.

Appendix B – Scoring for assessment of pupil work

Details of scoring for assessment of pupil work:

(i)   Scientific vocabulary usage: All terminology use in the reports was recorded and an overall score out of five was assigned according to the following descriptors:

1 = very few (0–2) science specific key words
2 = a few (3–4) science specific key words
3 = a satisfactory number (5–7) of science specific key words
4 = frequent (8–10), appropriate science specific key words
5 = extensive (>10), array of science-specific key words correctly used;

(ii) Recording scientific process: The use of both relevant graphics (photographs/video clips) and associated narratives to record key steps was assessed. An overall score was assigned as follows:

1 = few relevant steps recorded, associated with poorly chosen graphics
2 = some relevant steps recorded, associated with appropriately chosen graphics
3 = most relevant steps recorded, associated with most suitable graphics
4 = good record of steps, associated with well-informed graphics
5 = all relevant steps very well recorded, associated with excellent graphics;

(iii) Understanding of key scientific concepts. The reports/presentations were analysed to determine the degree of scientific understanding according to the following system:

1 = largely descriptive with little evidence of understanding of key concepts
2 = some evidence of understanding key concepts
3 = evidence of a satisfactory level of understanding of the key concepts
4 = good evidence of the understanding of the key concepts
5 = very good evidence of the understanding of the key concepts.

14 Foreign language teaching using digital tools

Marnie Seymour and Monika Pazio

With an additional case study from Patrick Carroll

Introduction

As a famous Chinese proverb says: "Do not confine your pupils to your own learning, for they were born in another time.' Pupils today are born into a digitalised world, grow up with it and learn through it: pupils with digital tools can access the Google translate tool both for initial translations of their own texts and for reading texts in another language. The app DuoLingo provides online personalised language tuition accessible to young pupils and there are many other digital tools which can support your pupils in their language learning.

The aim of this chapter is to present creative and innovative ways in which technology can be used in the classroom in individual, group and whole class activities. It is based on research by Pazio (2015) undertaken at a time when developing new modern foreign language (FL) pedagogy was a priority in the English system. The term 'Foreign Language (FL) is now being used to include all languages. The chapter starts with the discussion of pedagogical and theoretical principles and looks at different projects or activities that, to a large extent, incorporate those principles. Since digital technology resources vary depending on available equipment, the examples and case studies presented are suitable for some contexts but inappropriate for others. However, the examples are meant to serve as an inspiration and illustration of what teachers do and how they adapt technology to benefit language learners. See also the eTwinning examples in Chapter 22 which provide advice for connecting your pupils to pupils in other countries to undertake shared projects, which can be undertaken in the language of choice of the teachers involved.

Objectives

By the end of this chapter you should be able to:

- identify digital technologies which support FL teaching
- understand where you can integrate digital technologies into your teaching
- describe examples of innovative practice
- determine when it is appropriate to use digital tools to enhance FL learning.

Digital tools for FL

Many benefits of using educational technologies are common to all subjects and relate to motivation and engagement through the introduction of an element of fun and play. However, educational technology has much more to offer language learners and teachers

DOI: 10.4324/9781003408925-14

(Farr and Murphy, 2016; Chapelle and Sauro, 2017). As it is pointed out in Dearing's report (DES, 2007), technologies provide access to authentic and current target language materials and culture that make technologies such a valuable tool:

> Young people's familiarity with ICT (information and communication technologies) offers a great opportunity to language teachers. It seems to us that a determined commitment to use this world, which is so familiar to young people, is a key to increasing the engagement of young people of all ages with languages. New technologies can facilitate real contacts with schools and young people in other countries. They can also provide stimulus for creative and interactive work.
>
> (DES, 2007)

Despite this, however, OFSTED's (2021a) recent high profile Curriculum Research Review for Languages (OCRR) is devoid of any mention of the potential benefits of technology to support or enhance language learning in our schools. This is argued by Woore *et al.* (2022) to be a significant oversight, particularly in relation to the wealth of resources available online to support the development of children's intercultural understanding as well as affording opportunities for 'genuine communicative interaction' (p.148).

The use of technology to teach languages is not new. Technology integration in FL education dates back to the 1960s and has been traditionally referred to as Computer Assisted Language Learning (CALL). The term initially referred to the use of PCs, however usage evolved along with the new technology that was introduced to education. The use of the term has been challenged and alternative acronyms have been proposed including Blended Learning, Technology Enhanced Language Learning and recently Mobile Assisted Language Use (MALU) (Jarvis and Achilleos, 2013). Nevertheless, CALL remains to be the most popular acronym and nowadays serves as an umbrella term that incorporates a variety of digital tools.

Where is computer assisted language learning (CALL) going?

The evolution of CALL is clearly documented in the literature. Warschauer and Healy (1998), Warschauer and Meskill (2000) and Bax (2003), for example, offer a typology of CALL stages. These typologies give us insight into the history of technology integration in FL education and additionally an indication of where we should be going, namely normalisation (Bax, 2003). In Bax's words normalisation is achieved:

> when computers (or other technological equipment) are used every day by language students and teachers as an integral part of every lesson, like a pen or book, without fear or inhibition, and equally without an exaggerated respect for what they can do. They will not be the centre of any lesson, but they will play a part in almost all. They will be completely integrated into all other aspects of classroom life, alongside course books, teachers and notepads. They will go almost unnoticed.
>
> (Bax, 2003, p.23)

Accomplishing that stage demands fulfilling certain conditions related to attitudes, logistical solutions, training (Bax and Chambers, 2006) and as a result, changes in pedagogy. Those changes lead to effective, normalised teaching which maximises learning.

Effective teaching with technology

The discussion of normalisation and what it entails leads us to the question what is meant by effective language teaching with Technology. Just like technology integration in other subjects, technology integration for FL education has been technologically rather than pedagogically driven. Thornbury (2011) best describes this situation as the 'technological tail wagging a pedagogical dog.' This creates obstacles to effective teaching where technology is used without clear pedagogical purposes. In order to answer the question about what is meant by effective FL teaching, we need to consider two aspects; namely what effective integration entails and what effective early language learning is. Now undertake Task 14.1.

Task 14.1: Reflecting upon effective FL teaching

Think about your own practice and beliefs about teaching languages to young learners, or primary teaching in general if you are a generalist. Create a table with two columns. In one column write down what makes effective FL teaching in the primary classroom. In the second column think about how digital technologies can enhance that. Discuss your ideas with others; think of examples of activities that you use in class. Reviewing materials on some of the websites listed at the end of the book might give you ideas.

When discussing effective teaching with digital technologies it is important to consider when to use digital tools. Generally, if the same outcome can be achieved without the technology, then there is no need to, or indeed merit of, forcing it into the lesson. Technology should be able to transform learning and the teacher's skills, knowledge and attitudes and their planning are the main agents in executing that change. The SAMR model (Substitution, Augmentation, Modification, Redefinition) included as Figure 14.1 offers an

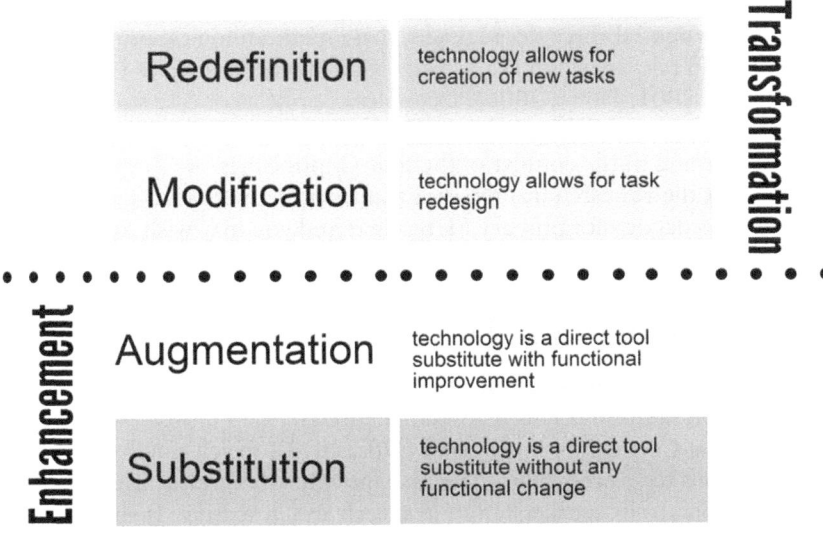

Figure 14.1 Adapted from the SAMR model (Puentedura, 2009)

examination of levels of integration and guidance as to what integrated technology should be able to help the teacher achieve.

The SAMR model shows technology integration as a series of steps, starting at a mere substitution, for example replacing flashcards with PowerPoint and then augmentation and moving towards modification and finally redefinition. The SAMR model serves as guidance for effective digital technologies integration in general. The goal is to aim for task redefinition at which stage technology offers a completely different learning experience which otherwise could not be possible.

Now undertake Task 14.2.

Task 14.2: Understanding the SAMR model

Study Figure 14.1 and research The SAMR model (use Google Scholar to type in SAMR Puntedura). Think about an activity that you do with your pupils that involves digital technologies integration. Where would you place your activity at the SAMR scale? How would you amend the activity at each level of the model? Discuss your ideas with colleagues.

When considering how digital technologies can support language teaching, we need to consider what is essential for successful primary FL in general. Sharpe (1992, 2001) proposes four key principles, known as the four Cs, which, he suggests, underpin successful primary FL teaching:

- communication
- culture
- context
- confidence

Despite being proposed three decades ago, these methodological principles have maintained currency and relevance and are broadly aligned with principles identified by other sources (Cameron, 2001; Pinter, 2006). Examples of projects or case studies are examined below as a means of exemplifying how technology can be used to support and enhance early language learning in the context of the four Cs principles.

The website for the Research in Primary Languages Network (RIPL) also provides extensive advice on pedagogy for primary FL teachers and you may wish to spend some time reviewing their examples.

Communicative Language Teaching (CLT)

In Communicative Language Teaching (CLT), the emphasis is placed first and foremost on the ability to communicate. This is also emphasised in the Purpose of Study in the KS2 Languages National Curriculum in England (DfE, 2013), which states that 'the teaching should enable pupils to express their ideas and thoughts in another language and to understand and respond to its speakers, both in speech and in writing. It should also provide opportunities for them to communicate for practical purposes.'

Now undertake Task 14.3.

> **Task 14.3: Reinforcing communication and developing speaking skills**
>
> Think about how you reinforce communication in your classroom / how you support the development of speaking skills. Write down some examples of task design to support this. Do your examples involve technology? Now think about your use of technology and whether and how it promotes communication and interaction in both written and spoken form.

The most popular projects that involve and focus on communication are eTwinning projects and these will be discussed in the culture section below. The examples chosen here to illustrate how technology can be used to reinforce and teach written and spoken communication are less obvious and more innovative in nature.

IPads/tablets are now a common feature in today's classrooms. There are numerous apps available on iPads which will support children's oracy skills, such as Puppet Pals and Green Screen (see 'Further Resources' section). These are worth exploring as a means of engaging and motivating young learners and can be used in a variety of contexts and topic areas e.g. sport and hobbies, ordering food in a café, describing their family, and so on.

One example of an innovative way of introducing communication in the classroom with iPads is using the Comic Life app (Dempster, 2012). Teachers use dialogue as a form of practising speaking with a very common warm-up activity at the beginning of the lesson, i.e. a 'talk partner' activity. Linaker Primary School took on board this simple tested pedagogic approach and turned it into a paired written activity reinforcing written communication in the classroom.

Comic life app

The activity was used with Y6 pupils learning Spanish. The teacher asked the pupils to create comic strips of their conversation using the Comic Life app on iPads. Some pupils used pictures of themselves they took with iPad cameras, others searched for photos on the internet or used images from their photo libraries to create a conversation.

This activity is an interesting way of reinforcing literacy skills in a foreign language, is suitable for children with limited language and can be treated as a follow-up to the spoken task.

Another example from Linaker Primary is the Mi Familia project (Dempster, 2012). The final result of the project was an oral description. This meets the English National Curriculum attainment target to 'present ideas and information orally to a range of audiences' (DfE, 2013).

Mi Familia project

For this project you need an augmented reality app – see Donnelly (2022) for free AR apps. These allow the user to blend real-world images with interactive content such as videos and other animations referred to as auras.

> Lesson Objective – to reinforce the use of vocabulary and structures for talking about 'my family' both in speaking and in writing.

The pupils were discussing the topic of My Family in Spanish. In the first stage of the project the pupils focused on vocabulary that would be useful in the further part of the project – describing their families. The app should give an opportunity to deliver key vocabulary in a more creative way e.g. first create a vocabulary page with covered vocabulary which you then transform with the app into a piece of augmented reality.

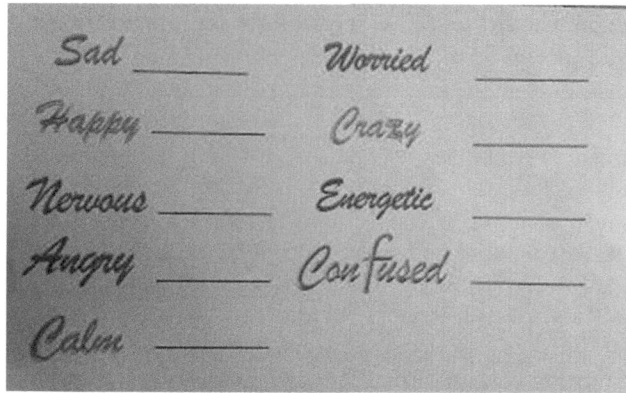

Figure 14.2 Augmented reality vocabulary activity (adapted from Dempster, 2012)

The first stage of the project used the blank worksheet as a trigger image with the keywords typed in as an overlay. After discussing the relevant vocabulary the next step was writing a paragraph in Spanish about their families. Each child emailed a photo of their families to the teacher for printing and was recorded speaking about their families. The printed photo was set as a trigger and the video of them talking about their families served as an overlay (aura). Just as in the first stage the trigger was again a sheet/image but when the device was held over the trigger, a video was shown instead.

The activities involving the use of the app evoked enthusiasm in the pupils and encouraged them to be creative. The pupils were motivated to complete the task and had greater opportunities to practice pronunciation and develop both writing and speaking skills.

Both projects/activities described above presented an original application of new technology to reinforce written and spoken communication. In both cases the use of technology reinforced communication rather than created obstacles to it. This can be done with any technology but teacher planning and task design is crucial in achieving the lesson objective.

The following is an example of the use of an augmented reality (AR) app.

Using augmented reality apps

With thanks to Patrick Carroll

Shaw Wood Academy in Armthorpe Doncaster is a large primary school in a former mining village. The Year 6 pupils had been experimenting with an augmented reality app within writing so they wanted to see whether or not it could be used to support other subjects.

In class we were creating role play situations in French about activities that we did at home. For example, looking after our pets, or mentioning some of the different sporting activities that we took part in outside of school. Many of the pupils were wanting to improve their sentences by listing all of the activities that they completed at home but were not able to remember all the vocabulary they needed.

To support the pupils to recall the words and phrases that they were wanting to use I put up a display with the names of the activities that we had talked about such as swimming or playing football as well as the names of the different pets that they were wanting to mention, such as taking the dog for a walk or feeding the rabbits. Next, I linked up some of the free animations from the app to each picture through the iPad (each word had been written in a distinctive font so that the app would differentiate between fonts so that it would play the correct animation with the matching word).

Consequently, when the pupils were in groups putting together sentences for their role play if they were stuck on a word they could check what the word was in French by holding up an iPad to the words on the display to see the animation. The technology had an impact because after a few views of the animations many of the pupils did not have to check the display as they were able to link the word to the animation instinctively. Therefore, instead of me having to repeat the words many times the pupils would automatically remember the word. The pupils were then eager to use the app to record their group work. So, on their sheet, they placed a picture of an animal or activity that they had mentioned alongside their sentences that were in English. They then recorded themselves on the iPad, linked the picture on their sheet to the app so that if anyone wanted to listen to them translating the English text into French they could by simply using an iPad.

Now undertake Task 14.4 to test out augmented reality apps.

Task 14.4: Developing your skills in using augmented reality software

Find a photograph of yourself. Then record a description of yourself in another language using a mobile device that has an AR app. (See Donnelly (2022) for free Apps replacing the popular Aurasma software.) Using the app, link the video to the photograph so that when you hold up your mobile device to the picture it changes from a picture of you to your video description.

Embedding culture in your teaching

The Purpose of Study in the National Curriculum for Languages in England (DfE, 2013) begins with the following statement:

> Learning a foreign language is a liberation from insularity and provides an opening to other cultures. A high-quality languages education should foster pupils' curiosity and deepen their understanding of the world.

This is also emphasised by the more recent OFSTED (2021a) report, although cultural awareness is conspicuously absent from the three 'Pillars of Progression' the report promotes as being essential to ensuring a high-quality languages education. This lack of explicit focus on intercultural awareness, among other things, is posited by Porter *et al.* (2022) to narrow and constrain language learning opportunities resulting in 'less focus on interaction and communication for a range of purposes, and a restriction on the use of authentic materials and culturally rich content' (p.2). They contend that 'the teaching and learning of cultural awareness and intercultural understanding … whilst acknowledged for the development of metacognitive skills, are also likely to contribute to language learning motivation' (p.1) and should therefore sit alongside linguistic progression as a key facet of a high-quality languages curriculum.

To this end, technology offers teachers wide-ranging and high-quality opportunities for promoting intercultural understanding in our classrooms. There are, for example, numerous websites to support teachers to explore different cultures and lifestyles in other countries and festivals e.g. Euroclub schools, the BBC, and others (see 'Further Resources' section).

The two projects described below also use different technologies in order to deepen pupils' understanding of different cultures.

Case Study 14.1: eTwinning citizenship and FL project

The two partner schools exchanged mascots – a Scottish teddy and a French cockerel. The mascots' experience of life in the other country was recorded by pupils through the use of digital camera/blog/e-mail. Both sets of pupils made puzzles in their own language for others to solve. Both groups made storybooks on local history/geography.

A novel was written between the schools with one chapter in French and one in English alternately, along with illustrations. It tackled comparisons between school lunches, playground games and cultures.

The pupils were inspired and motivated. They had a great deal of fun working collaboratively on the many different projects. More importantly, they gained increased confidence in speaking a foreign language.

See Chapter 22 for further ongoing eTwinning projects.

The second project also aims at cultural understanding through exchanges, however it is more creative when it comes to technology use. QR codes have been in use for quite a long time mostly for marketing but also have been adopted to use for educational purposes. The most common uses involve creating QR treasure hunts or QR posters. The codes are extremely easy to create and read. To create them you just need to copy and paste the link to the video or document that you want to link the code to into a QR generator like for example KAYWA and to read them download a reader app like i-nigma.

Case study 14.2: eTwinning project culture outside the box – an example of the use of QR codes

The British Council described the project as follows: the aim of the project was to raise cultural awareness and teach pupils greater appreciation of their own region and understand how technology can reinforce that. The project involved sending to each partner school things that represent their cities, details about the regions or states and finally objects that represent our countries. Each object was given a QR code so that pupils in the partner school can scan them to find out more information. After receiving a description or item the pupils blog about what they have got and share what they have learnt through discussion and photos. As a result the students gain greater cultural understanding of each other and greater understanding of how technology can support achieving that understanding.

The aim of both eTwinning projects was raising cultural awareness and cultural understanding and, through this, instilling positive attitudes in the learners, along with language learning.

Language in context through digital storytelling

The use of a meaningful context plays an important role in early language learning. Indeed, in their systematic review of the literature, Murphy *et al.* (2020) draw the conclusion that 'teaching approaches that are largely meaning-oriented, providing rich, authentic, and stimulating FL input for students' (p.4–5) play an important role in children's learning of another language. Listening to and reading stories and texts in another language can provide such a context for learning. Not only can stories support the teaching of phonics and reading skills but Woore *et al.* (2022) argue that they can also provide young learners with the strategies and resilience necessary to tackle unknown language and are therefore judged to be 'valuable learning opportunities and sources of motivation' (p.150).

The findings from Murphy *et al.*'s (2020) review also point to the key role technology can play in providing opportunities for digital story telling. The internet provides teachers with a wealth of stories and literature to explore with young learners as well as websites and apps where they are able to create their own such as Story Jumper and Story Bird (see Further Resources section below).

Digital stories

Pazio (2015) found Northwood primary used 'Scruffy Kitty' to explore different languages. The language is presented in context and offers opportunities to refer to the language structures and analyse them. Additionally the sentences are read aloud so the pronunciation is modelled for the pupils. The pupils are encouraged to try to translate the sentence using the pictures and words they have already encountered so they build on their own understanding. The pupils are then allowed to explore the stories in small groups on iPads and further analyse the language and practice repeating single words or full sentences.

Building confidence: yours and your pupils

Teacher competence in the foreign language is deemed to be one of the main prerequisites for high-quality teaching and learning of foreign languages in the primary school. The importance of teachers possessing sound levels of subject knowledge is highlighted in studies which sought to specifically evaluate primary foreign languages provision in England (Cable *et al.*, 2010; Martin, 2012; Tinsley and Board, 2017). Despite the perceived importance of teacher subject knowledge, a number of studies have highlighted the insufficient language skills of teachers as one of the greatest barriers to the successful implementation of FLs in the primary sector (Woolhouse *et al.*, 2013; Legg, 2013; Woodgate-Jones,

2015). This is particularly significant as the programme of study for languages as set out in the National Curriculum (DfE, 2013) has placed higher expectations on reading and writing in the FL which inevitably demands the explanation and application of a grammar system for which many teachers have only limited understanding (Seymour, 2018).

Teachers' formal subject knowledge and foreign language proficiency are judged to impact not only on the quality of the FL lessons they teach, but also on the extent to which they wish to teach the subject in the first place. The studies cited above, for example, found a clear association between limited knowledge of the foreign language and diminished teacher confidence (Seymour, 2018).

Those fears were expressed by a teacher contributing to the research underpinning this chapter who admitted he found it very difficult to teach pronunciation since it was new to him as well. Technology can, however, arguably go some way to supporting teachers with their subject knowledge. Availability of a resource like digital stories read by native speakers, for example, can provide good models of pronunciation, and websites can provide more accurate representations and information about aspects of the country's culture which may not be known to the teacher (see section above on 'Embedding Culture in Your Teaching').

In order to support the linguistic and communicative competence of young language learners, the teacher assumes a central role in ensuring that learners are provided with the tools necessary for communication, and lessons need to be carefully structured and scaffolded so that learners are able to apply their learning to communicate. Of equal importance is also the ability of the teacher to create a safe and engaging learning environment in which pupils are actively encouraged to take risks and where 'making mistakes becomes part of the learning experience' (Macaro, 2014, p.113).

An example of an engaging and linguistically beneficial project, which adopted a cross-curricular approach, was Nine Acres Primary school podcasting day. The project helped pupils to develop their confidence to speak and at the same time gave them an opportunity to publish their work.

Nine Acres primary school podcasting day

Led by teacher Joe Dale (2007), Year 3 pupils worked on a podcast which was later placed on a website to show to a wider audience. The idea of the project was to build imaginatively on what they had been learning in class and featured the pupils speaking, singing and rapping in French. The project was a collaboration between music coordinators and language teachers. The recording took three hours to complete from start to finish and about the same time to edit in Audacity (a free audio editing and recording programme). The pupils took the lead in the project creating the music and choosing the language.

The project delivered the learning objectives and pupils improved their pronunciation and confidence in the process. The pupils enjoyed speaking French and learning new words in a fun, motivating environment. As one of the coordinating teachers reported:

> Today we have achieved in three and quarter hours what I think to be a very splendid project which the pupils have really enjoyed to no end. We started from a plan which the adults put together but then we discussed it with the pupils. We used their ideas and their creativity.

We were impressed especially with their pronunciation which in the short space of time has improved greatly, not only for the pupils but also for us teachers as well. Working not only with the music but also with French we created a wonderful collaborative project which has stimulated the pupils to learn more French through music and dialogue.

The project was also well received by the families who were proud to hear their pupils speaking French and commented on the podcasts placed on the school's website (Nine Acres, 2007).

Speaking is the skill with which language learners need a lot of encouragement and need to feel comfortable to undertake. To help pupils break the barrier of public speaking and boost their confidence the teachers quite often use such apps as Morfo or Tellagami. Morfo and Tellagami are also quite often a perfect solution for including in projects those pupils who are not allowed to be filmed.

Using Morfo and Tellagami

Both are free apps that enable less confident pupils to record themselves speaking in the target language. The outcomes are then displayed as animation without the need for video recording. Tellagami additionally gives a possibility of inputting the text which is then read aloud for pupils who are extremely shy.

All the examples presented above aimed at developing learners' confidence to speak in a foreign language through creating engaging tasks. The aim isn't to wow the pupils with technology but rather use the technology in an engaging way to support and deepen learning. The same applies to all the examples described in this chapter. The technologies should transform the task and enhance learning as opposed to being a substitute for something already in use.

Summary and key points

- The examples in the chapter included different types of technologies for different pedagogical purposes – some just introduced to education and others that have been present for longer.
- No matter what equipment or software is used we need to remember that effective teaching incorporates both pedagogical principles about teaching young learners and knowledge of how technology should be integrated.
- The focus should be on the target language and learning and the use of technologies in the FL lesson should support planned learning goals.

Further resources

Audacity https://www.audacityteam.org, a free audio editing and recording programme. Accessed on 4 February 2023.
BBC https://www.bbc.co.uk/programmes/p0115gyf.
Euroclub Schools https://www.euroclub-schools.org/.
Green Screen https://apps.apple.com/gb/app/green-screen-by-do-ink/id730091131.
Kaywa https://qrcode.kaywa.com, a free tool for creating QR codes. Accessed on 4 February 2023.
Morfo http://www.appsinclass.com/morfo.html, an app morphing faces into other images. Accessed on 4 February 2023.

Puppet Pals http://literacyapps.literacytrust.org.uk/puppet-pals/.

Scruffy Kitty https://www.commonsensemedia.org/app-reviews/scruffy-kitty. Accessed on 4 February 2023.

Story Bird https://storybird.com/.

Story Jumper https://www.storyjumper.com/.

Teaching Schools Council (2016). Modern Foreign Languages Pedagogy Review. https://ncelp. org/wp-content/uploads/2020/02/MFL_Pedagogy_Review_Report_TSC_PUBLISHED_ VERSION_Nov_2016_1_.pdf. This document provides advice on FL pedagogy. Accessed on 4 February 2023.

Tellagami https://apps.apple.com/gb/app/tellagami/id572737805, an app which allows the quick creation of videos. Accessed on 4 February 2023.

Research in Primary Languages Network https://ripl.uk/research/. RIPL provides extensive advice for primary NFL teachers based on research and the outcomes of discussions in the network. Accessed on 4 February 2023.

References

Bax, S. (2003) CALL - past, present and future. *System*, 31(1), 13–28.

Bax, S. and Chambers, A. (2006) Making CALL work: Towards normalization. *System*, 34(4), 465–479.

British Council (2023) *E-twinning*. Available at: http://www.etwinning.net/tr/pub/connect/ browse_people_schools_and_pro/profile.cfm?f=2&l=en&n=81097#process. Accessed on 4 February 2023.

Cable, C., Driscoll, P., Mitchell, R., Sing, S., Cremin, T., Earl, J., Eyres, I., Holmes, B., Martin, C. and Heins, B. (2010) *Languages learning at key stage 2. A longitudinal study final report*. DCSF. https://dera.ioe.ac.uk/id/eprint/790/1/DCSF-RR198.pdf. Accessed on 24 November 2023.

Cameron, L. (2001) *Teaching languages to young learners*. Cambridge Language Teaching Library. Cambridge: Cambridge University Press.

Chapelle, C. and Sauro, S (eds) (2017) *The handbook of technology and second language teaching and learning*. Oxford: Wiley Blackwell.

Dale, J. (2007, March 14) *Nine Acres Primary podcasting day* (Online). Available at http:// joedale.typepad.com/integrating_ict_into_the_/2007/03/nine_acres_prim.html. Accessed on 4 February 2023.

Dempster, N. (2012) *Other iPad apps to use in MFL lessons*. Linaker Primary School. See Pazio (2015) for more details.

DES (2007) *Dearing Report: The languages review*. Available at: https://webarchive.nationalarchives. gov.uk/ukgwa/20070108161825/http://www.teachernet.gov.uk/teachingandlearning/ subjects/languages/languagesreview/. Accessed on 4 February 2023.

DfE (2013) *The National Curriculum in England: Framework document*. Available at: https://www.gov.uk/government/collections/national-curriculum, Accessed on 24 February 2023.

Donnelly, J. (2022) *Create AR using these 5 Apps. International Society for Technology in Education (ISTE)*. Available at: https://www.iste.org/explore/tools-devices-and-apps/create-ar-using-these-5-apps. Accessed on 4 February 2023.

Farr, F. and Murray, L. (eds) (2016) *The Routledge handbook of language learning and technology*. Oxon: Routledge.

Jarvis, H. and Achilleos, M. (2013) From computer assisted language learning (CALL) to mobile assisted language use. *TESL-EJ*, 16(4), 1–18. Available at: https://tesl-ej.org/wordpress/issues/ volume16/ej64/ej64a2/.

Legg, K. (2013) An investigation into teachers' attitudes towards the teaching of modern foreign languages in the primary school. *Education 3–13*, 41(1), 55–62.

Macaro, E. (2014) Grammar. The never-ending debate. In P. Driscoll, E. Macaro and A. Swarbrick (eds) *Debates in Modern Languages Education*. London: Routledge, 108–120.

Martin, C. (2012) Pupils' perceptions of foreign language learning in the primary school–findings from the Key Stage 2 Language Learning Pathfinder evaluation. *Education 3–13*, 40(4), 343–362.

Murphy, V.A., Arndt, H., Briggs Baffoe-Djan, J., Chalmers, H., Macaro, E., Rose, H., Vanderplank, R. and Woore, R. (2020) *Foreign language learning and its impact on wider academic outcomes: A rapid evidence assessment*. Education Endowment Foundation. Available at: https://files.eric.ed.gov/fulltext/ED612981.pdf. Accessed on 14 November 2023.

Nine Acres (2007) *Primary Podcasting Day: French Podcast* [Online]. Available at: http://nodehillfrench.typepad.com/two_stars_and_a_wish/2007/03/nine_acres_prim.html. Accessed on 4 February 2023.

OFSTED (2013) *Supplementary subject specific guidance for MFL.* http://www.ofsted.gov.uk/resources/generic-grade-descriptors-and-supplementary-subject-specific-guidance-for-inspectors-making-judgement. Accessed on March 2013 but no longer available online.

OFSTED (2021a) *Research review: Languages.* https://www.gov.uk/government/publications/curriculum-research-review-series-languages/curriculum-research-review-series-languages. Accessed on 4 February 2023.

OFSTED (2021b) *Languages in outstanding primary schools.* https://educationinspection.blog.gov.uk/2021/05/04/languages-in-outstanding-primary-schools/. Accessed on 4 February 2023.

Pazio, M. (2015) *Normalising computer assisted language learning in the context of primary education in England*. University of Bedfordshire. Available at: https://uobrep.openrepository.com/handle/10547/603542. Accessed on 4 February 2023.

Pinter, A. (2006) *Teaching young language learners*. Oxford: Oxford University Press.

Porter, A., Graham, S., Myles, F. and Holmes, B. (2022) Creativity, challenge and culture in the languages classroom: A response to the Ofsted Curriculum Research Review. *The Language Learning Journal*, 50(2), 208–217. Available at: https://doi.org/10.1080/09571736.2022.2046358. Accessed on 14 November 2023.

Puentedura, R. (2009) As we may teach: Educational technology, from theory into practice [Online]. Available at: http://www.hippasus.com/rrpweblog/archives/000025.html. Accessed on 4 February 2023.

Seymour, M. (2018) *Primary foreign languages: Beginning teachers' narratives of beliefs and practices*. University of Winchester, PhD Thesis. https://cris.winchester.ac.uk/ws/portalfiles/portal/2540717/Seymour_Marnie_PhD.pdf. Accessed on 24 November 2023.

Sharpe, K. (1992) Communication, culture, context and confidence, the four Cs in primary modern language teaching. *The Language Learning Journal*, 12, 40–42.

Sharpe, K. (2001) *Modern foreign languages in the primary school. The what, why and how of early language teaching*, London: Kogan Page.

Thornbury, S. (2011) *T is for technology* [Online]. Available at: https://scottthornbury.wordpress.com/2011/05/01/t-is-for-technology. Accessed on 24 November 2023.

Tinsley, T. and Board, K. (2017) *Language trends 2016/17. Language teaching in primary and secondary schools in England*. Survey Report. British Council. https://www.britishcouncil.org/sites/default/files/language_trends_survey_2017_0.pdf. Accessed on 24 November 2023.

Warschauer M. and Healey D. (1998) Computers and language learning: An overview. *Language Teaching*, 31, 57–71.

Warschauer, M. and Meskill, C. (2000) Technology and second language learning. In J. Rosenthal (ed) *Handbook of undergraduate second language education*. New Jersey: Lawrence Erlbaum, 303–318.

Woodgate-Jones, A. (2015) *Primary teachers in times of change: engaging with the primary modern foreign language initiative in England.* University of Southampton, Southampton Education School, PhD Thesis.

Woolhouse, C., Bartle, P., Hunt, E. and Balmer, D. (2013) Language learning, cultural capital and teacher identity: Teachers negotiating the introduction of French into the primary curriculum. *The Language Learning Journal*, 41(1), 55–67.

Woore, R., Molway, L. and Macaro, E. (2022) Keeping sight of the big picture: A critical response to Ofsted's 2021 Curriculum Research Review for languages. *The Language Learning Journal*, 50(2), 146–155.

15 Enhancing primary music with technology

Jon Audain, Helen Mead and Sarah Lloyd

What is shown in this chapter is that there are many ways that technology can be used in the primary classroom, and how that technology can support teaching and enhance the musical learning of the children. This chapter enables the reader to develop a working knowledge of ways technology can enhance their teaching and to understand the difference between musical activity and musical learning with technology. The chapter also enables the reader to challenge their thinking about ways children can use technology to be creative, which will enhance their musical learning.

Introduction

Music is intrinsically linked to technology. Most of the children we teach will be using devices to play, recreate and compose music from performing on Guitar Hero, to composing and sharing their own dance tracks in Garageband. The music children listen to is predominantly created using technology; it is a sound world they are immersed in and is relevant to them. For some, music technology could become their career pathway so therefore it is vital that we, as educators, equip them with the skills and musical knowledge they may need. Music technology allows children to create music akin to the music they know, therefore can reduce their frustration and barriers and make them motivated in the music classroom.

What we will show in this chapter is that there are many ways that technology can be used in the primary classroom, and how that technology can support teaching and enhance the musical learning of the children. Daubney (2017) reminds us that, 'Technology is not a bolt-on but is integral to supporting, enhancing and even being the vehicle for musical learning and has immense potential for inspiring use right across the curriculum.' We would also add that it is important to use technology within music not so that a music technology box can be ticked but *because there is musical learning* integrated as an outcome.

Objectives

By the end of this chapter you should:

- have a working knowledge of ways technology can enhance your teaching
- understand the difference between musical activity and musical learning with technology
- have challenged your thinking about ways children can use technology to be creative and technology which will enhance their musical learning.

DOI: 10.4324/9781003408925-15

How might technology enhance your music teaching?

We are going to begin this chapter in a different way from the standard chapter you might explore in an academic book. As Higgins *et al.* (2012: 3) explain, 'It is not whether technology is used (or not) which makes the difference, but how well the technology is used to support teaching and learning.' First, we want you to try an activity (Task 15.1) before we begin thinking about technology and how it can be used to enhance either the children's learning or your own teaching.

Task 15.1: Think, try, do and reflect

Explore one of these sites:

- Blob Opera: https://artsandculture.google.com/experiment/blob-opera/AAHWrq360NcGbw?hl=en
- Isle of Tune: https://www.isleoftune.com/

   Whilst writing this chapter, we, as authors had great fun exploring these sites, and we were absorbed by exploring these activities, but the question we asked ourselves was to what extent did the activities help me to learn musically?

The use of technology should enhance the music-making process. Not all activities can be considered as music. Making a musical instrument is not music, though playing it may be (Mills, 2009: 2). Just because something has music in the title, doesn't always mean that *musical learning* is happening.

Table 15.1 provides examples of where the use of technology might fit into the musical journey of the children.

The musical journey of the child

Table 15.1 Where might the use of technology fit into the musical journey of the children?

Age range	What should I see around me?	An illustration of practice using technologies
Younger children (3–5)	*Musical play, exploring, discovering and changing sounds.*	Exploring how a voice changer can make their voice sound like a robot and exploring elements of pitch to make the high and low sounds.
Lower Primary (5–7)	*Turning musical play into playing musically.*	Using software to place two sounds together to create the sound of Christmas.
Upper Primary (7–11)	*Playing musically with increasing confidence and control enhanced with the use of software or hardware.*	Compose a space soundscape in Garageband, using combinations of sounds and samples.

Technology for teaching

Using technology in your music teaching is a journey. Some teachers will be confident in exploring apps and platforms and in experimenting with using these in the classroom. Other teachers may be overwhelmed by technology and feel cautious about introducing technology to their class. It is important to identify where you are on your journey with music technology and recognise what you may need in terms of CPD, knowledge and experience.

There are many pathways in music technology that schools may decide to take. As with all things this can be a decision made on financial considerations or dependent on the technologies and tools the school has decided to use e.g., Chromebooks, iPads, Android tablets, and so on. Specialised music hardware and software can be expensive but there are many pathways to allow children to experience creative musical opportunities using technology that are cheap, or even free. Leicestershire Music Hub has an extensive list of browser-based free software (https://leicestershiremusichub.org/ks2-music-tech) and your local music hub may be able to guide you towards resources available in your area.

There is a wealth of resources which will support your teaching in music. In particular there are websites which will engage your children and present high-quality resources to support your children playing together, reading musical notation and musical learning in a range of ways. It is important to think how and when you will use these and how they will support your teaching.

The online offer is forever changing and evolving but Table 15.2 gives a small idea of the possibilities that are available to you to support your teaching.

Table 15.2 Online software

Title	Link	Classroom Application
Rhythm Grids	www.rhythmrandomizer.com	Quick recall of reading rhythmic notation.
Chrome Music Lab	https://musiclab.chromeexperiments.com/Experiments	Many ideas for using this can be found on the internet.
Online xylophone	https://playxylo.com/	Modelling changes in pitch, instrument layout, notes in scales, as an instrument to play on ipads/interactive whiteboard.
Instruments of the orchestra	https://www.classicsforkids.com/?s=orchestra+instruments	Explore the instruments and families of instruments in a European orchestra.

YouTube is a rich resource for music online. You can find many recordings and films of performances. A recording of an orchestral performance can bring a listening activity to life. For example, 'Chineke!' was Europe's first majority black and ethnically diverse orchestra and Florence Price was the first African-American woman to be recognised as a symphonic composer. The experience of watching the Chineke! Orchestra performing her first Symphony in E minor (1st movement) will help to align the perceived prejudice some children may have that orchestral music is predominantly white and male.

Many YouTube channels have created interactive videos to support learning and musical activity. Some key sites are listed in Table 15.3.

Table 15.3 Interactive videos to support learning and musical activity

Chanel	YouTube handle	Content
Musication	@musication	Play along films, body percussion, classroom percussion, Boomwhackers
Ukulalians	@Ukulaliens	Play along films for ukulele
Mr F	@mrf1362	Playalong films, rhythm and pitched instruments
Drummerwise/ Rhythm Rex	@drummerwise9611	Reading staff notation rhythms with less thinking time as children progress through levels
Rhythm Recess	@RhythmRecess	Playalong films for rhythms, ukulele and Boomwhackers

Remember with these videos that the playback speed of a YouTube video can be slowed down for the purposes of rehearsal by clicking the cog icon and reducing the playback speed.

Now we ask you to undertake associated Task 15.2.

Task 15.2: Stop and Think!

Choose some film to support your teaching.

Always watch a film the whole way through and consider if it is appropriate and the right resource for using with your class? Sometimes listening without visuals is the best option.

How and when would you use these films in your music lesson? Do they enhance or support learning or are they an 'added extra'? Always ask – what do I want the children to learn?

- Would you use them as a quick warm up?
- Would they be used to introduce a new concept?
- Could you use them as a performance piece at the end of a learning journey?

Technology in the early years (EYFS)

In the early years it is important to allow children to explore, record and manipulate sound through technology. Below are some suggestions that could be used in an EYFS setting:

- Voice Recorders – children can record their own voices or sounds and listen back immediately. Some microphones can adapt the recorded sound changing its timbre. This activity would allow discussion around the sounds.
- Listening – allowing children the opportunity to make independent choices when selecting and responding to music can be supported by technology. Sound buttons, sound pegs, and so on, can record musical extracts that children can playback easily. Generating QR codes that children can scan using a tablet can be a powerful way of offering a range of listening opportunities.
- Interactive Whiteboard/Panel applications – displaying music apps on the large whiteboard can allow children to make music alongside peers and to manipulate sound using gross motor skills. Applications that could be used in this way could be the Kandinsky app on chrome music lab (https://musiclab.chromeexperiments.com/kandinsky/),

Starry Night app (http://artof01.com/starryNight.html or Singing Fingers https://apps.apple.com/us/app/singing-fingers/id381015280.

Using technology to support children's access to music

It would be remiss during this chapter on technology and music to not also raise the consideration of the use of technology within lessons to support the music making process. Technology, or adaptations to the task using technology to facilitate the learning, can support access to music for children who may face barriers. For example, a child with physical issues who is trying to learn the guitar may find using a virtual instrument such as Garageband live instruments more accessible when playing chords on a guitar. This connects to the wider considerations within the inclusive agenda. Examples presented by Kinsella *et al.* (2018) and organisations such as Drake Music (https://www.drakemusic.org) provide a useful starting point.

Using technology to support assessment in music

Musical learning is best captured and reflected in film given the practical nature and importance of sound in the subject. Recording the outcomes of units along the way is vital for reflection and evaluation in the short and long term. Try to capture moments of musical learning by filming the class for a short 30-second activity; this could be during a warm-up activity, during group compositions. This will then inform your assessment and create a bank of musical evidence.

Filming for you as the teacher: filming and reviewing

Capturing musical moments is one of the most powerful tools you, as the teacher, have for reviewing and evaluating progress and musical outcomes. As well as final outcomes, take time to plan in points when you will film during the pupils' musical journeys. As the teacher, it is important to find and make time to reflect as you watch these films. Watching again means you will 'see' and hear some learning for the first time, it will allow you to notice children who are being successful and notice those who may need more support in your next session. Filming final outcomes allows you to truly reflect and evaluate the learning that has taken place, celebrate successes and notice children who are demonstrating progression in different skills.

Table 15.4 provides a reflective framework for you to use during the assessment process.

Table 15.4 Questions prompts to use when reflecting

Use the prompts in this table when watching an assessment video you have created, to support your analysis.

- Look at the key musical skills that the lesson is focusing on; can you see progress in these skills?
- Have the children achieved your planned final outcomes? What was most successful? What might need further teaching in order to refine and develop?
- Which children demonstrate secure knowledge and understanding of the skills?
- Were your adaptations in learning successful in ensuring all children made progress?
- Did any children 'surprise' you in the films? Consider why this might be and how you might need to plan for them in their next lessons.

Filming for the children: sharing and evaluating

Allowing children independent access to technology for recording during composition is an incredible tool as it allows them to actually 'hear' what their musical compositions and performances really sound like. By using these recordings on the journey, they will be able to listen back, make changes and improvements to their pieces. In addition to this, using the recordings at the end of the unit and giving time for sharing and evaluating in groups is very powerful. Major and Cottle's (2010) five phases of questioning and Lloyd, Mead and Audain's (2023) question starters (Table 15.5) could help you support children's self-reflection at these points of the lesson.

Table 15.5 Question starters for musical work (Lloyd, Mead and Audain, 2023)

What is happening...? (descriptive, affective, opinions)	*How will you...?* (reflective, opinion)	*How might it have...?* (reflective, opinion)	*How could you do this differently?* (opinion, reflective)	*How do you feel about...?* (affective, opinion, reflective)
What do you think...? (opinion, evaluation)	*Why did you do that or use that sound?* (exploration, description, opinion, affective)	*What do you think the problem is?* (opinion, descriptive, evaluation)	*What could you do to solve this problem?* (opinion, exploration, descriptive)	*Tell me about...*

Being creative with technology to enhance the children's learning

If music is one of the highest forms of creativity (DfE, 2013) then the use of digital technologies brings a different perspective to the process of making music. Technology allows the users to express themselves, to see, to hear and manipulate music differently. Whilst some pieces of musical software, through their design, might encourage a drag and drop approach to music making, it is essential that children use the technology to create a meaningful musical output rather than randomly stitching sounds together. Emphasis should be placed on musical skill development in order for pupils to demonstrate their musical learning rather than them just being busy in an activity.

Ian McMilan's fascinating audio documentary entitled 'The School Is Full of Noises' (https://www.bbc.co.uk/programmes/b066vyy7) explores this purposeful mix of technology and physical sound inspired through the work of John Paynter.

Technology provides a creative duality, as both the analogue and digital experiences combine into the music-making process. However, it is also important to consider the role an educator can have in the process. Anna Craft (2000, 2001, 2002) wrote about an approach entitled 'possibility thinking.' The teacher introduces different creative ideas to assist, or deliberately widen, the ideas children may develop within their compositions.

McMilian's documentary reflected that sense of creative exploration. However it is important to accept that in the process of using technology, it may not necessarily always result in a polished outcome, but there should be recognition that deeper musical learning has occurred. Children will still need scaffolds and models to make sense of this playful exploration. By keeping the musical skill that the children need to develop at the forefront of the learning, it allows for a quality musical output.

To conclude the chapter, we provide two teacher case studies where they explain how they have integrated technology into their music teaching.

Case Study 15.1: 'The Sound Collector'

Roger McGough, Y3 teacher

Context of learning: English poetry
Technology explored: Audacity or SampleBot

Musical Learning Journey

1. The musical learning journey began by sharing 'The Sound Collector' poem with children and having a discussion around the onomatopoeic words. In groups children considered a selection of words and how these could be performed vocally thinking about pitch, tempo, dynamics, timbre, duration.
2. Following this the children were challenged to create each sound vocally without saying the word but by creating the sounds of each object. These discussions were again rooted in the inter-related dimensions.
3. As a class we then created a performance of the poem, identifying parts to say at different tempo and dynamics and how to use the silent pause towards the end for effect whilst adding in contrasts on the onomatopoeic words and adding vocal sounds for effect and different points.
4. We then created a version without words but just the sound effects and talked about sound effects.
5. We listened to: 'The little train of the Caipira' (https://www.bbc.co.uk/teach/ten-pieces/classical-music-heitor-villa-lobos/z4nsmfr). There was a lot of discussion about why the composer had chosen the different sounds and how they had made them re-create known sounds. It was important for the children to understand that the sounds could actually be used in any sequence and layout, that a soundscape does not need to tell a story but can set a scene, like this https://www.youtube.com/watch?v=XLdreTDZ4Toandt=12s.
6. Following this, we discussed what sounds might be heard around the school. We chose different points around school to use as listening stops to identify what sounds could be heard. We stood in one place and children were encouraged to listen attentively for 20–30 seconds in each place. Children wrote and drew what they could hear and noted the dynamics, tempo and duration of the sound.

   For example: By the kitchen I heard pots and pans and loud voices. It was loud, fast and short sounds. In the playground I heard running feet and lots of shouting voices. It was loud with long sounds.

7. In a following English lesson, the children then worked collaboratively to re-create their version of McGough's 'The Sound Collector' but based on sounds from our school environment taking time to consider the onomatopoeic words which would help with recreating these sounds. See the pupils' example below. They explored how vocal sounds could be used to enhance a performance of the poem.

   Below are the two verses written by the children:

   The thundering of the feet
   The shouting of voices

The thudding of the football
The screech of the whistle

The scratching of the pencils
The scraping of the chairs
The slamming of the classroom door
With talking everywhere

8. Children then explored how to manipulate sounds using either Audacity on PCs or SampleBot on iPads. Sounds from the original 'Sound Collector' had been recorded as samples onto SampleBot and put into the shared drive for use with Audacity. On Audacity we explicitly taught how to cut, copy, shorten and lengthen sounds and ensured children explored the various effect options. As a class, we then created our soundscape to add to the original 'Sound Collector' poem. This became our class model so the children knew what could be achieved using each type of software.
9. Following this they then created their own paired soundscapes to add to the class poem making decisions independently.

Exploring Audacity

These children went to different points around school with sound recorders (iPads, Talking Tins, Dictaphones) and captured small samples of different sounds. The children then added these files to a shared network drive and accessed them using Audacity. Within Audacity they selected a file and then manipulated the recording, for example, by altering the length of the sound. Finally, they created a soundscape by layering different sounds which they used as part of their own 'Sound Collector' performance.

Exploring SampleBot

Using iPads, these children also went to different points around school and captured recordings using SampleBot. They manipulated each sound within the app altering the **pitch**, **tempo** and **dynamics**. Having created the sounds, they considered how to use these to create a performance. Some groups used the app throughout their performance of 'Sound Collector' whilst other groups created a live soundscape before and after the poem was read.

Final outcome

Children used Audacity or SampleBot to create a soundscape for performance interwoven with their new 'Sound Collector' poem.

Evaluation

It was interesting to see how children choose to manipulate their samples within both SampleBot and Audacity. There was a lot of discussion around layering and sequencing and some really thoughtful decisions were made. There were advantages and disadvantages with both types of technology but each led to a successful soundscape. Ensuring the musical learning had real purpose for the performance of the poem really helped to focus the children on their learning and the outcome they needed to create.

Case Study 15.2: Year 5 space composition

Context of learning: *Science topic: earth and space*

Technology explored: Garageband

Musical learning journey

1. The musical learning journey began with a discussion about what music about space might sound like. Children talked about strange 'alien' sounds, 'spooky and weird' sounds. We then listened to theme from 2001: A Space Odyssey (https://www.youtube.com/watch?v=SLuW-GBaJ8k). On the second listening the children made notes in groups about what they could hear. Some drew the shape of the pitch rising at the beginning, others talked about the use of dynamics, long sustained notes, brass instruments, and so on. They were directed to consider how the composer had used the elements of music for effect.

   As a class we discussed what they had noted with the teaching drawing out conversation around the elements of music – pitch, timbre, tempo, dynamics, structure, duration, texture.

   We also talked about the context of the piece, that although it was composed in 1896 it was used for a film about space in 1968. The children were asked to consider why the film maker had chosen this piece of music?

   > *"It was dramatic."*
   > *"It sounded like a rocket taking off."*
   > *"It set the scene for something bad happening."*

   Throughout the rest of the unit of work the listening focus stayed with music for space and included the Planet Suite by Holst, Star Wars theme by John Willians, Space Oddity by David Bowie. Children kept a listening diary to record their thoughts and reflections on the pieces they listened to.

2. The next step in the learning was to consider how music technology can be used to enhance composition. The children studied Delia Derbyshire and the Dr Who theme tune using the resources from BBC 10 Pieces. They learnt how the effects and sounds used in the music were created electronically.

At this point the children were introduced to Garageband. The class had enough iPads for use in pairs with headphones and splitters so noise level was minimalised. Using the 'tracks' menu they explored the Smarts instruments feature; focusing on strings, world, bass, keyboard and percussion.

Given very little instruction, children were able to explore the different menus, effects and sounds. In the classroom there was lots of collaborative work, with children sharing sounds they had found and how they found them.

At the end of the session children were asked to make a note of any particular sounds they had found that they felt might be useful in a space composition.

3. The next step focused on exploring combinations of sounds. Using the keyboard on Garageband children were asked to play three next-door neighbour notes and then 3 notes leaving a space in between each note. We discussed the effect this had and introduced the terms 'concords' and 'discords.'

    Children were then asked to explore concords and discords on the other instrument menus in Garageband and, as an extension task, to find long sustained sounds and short staccato sounds and to consider how these might be used and combined.

    We listened to this example of a composition using Garageband which was written to celebrate the 50th anniversary of the Apollo 11 moon landing (https://www.youtube.com/watch?v=HhQz84o3w5s). We discussed what effects and instruments the composer had used in Garageband and the overall effect of the combination of sounds.

4. In this next session we introduced the children to sampling. The children listened to a track from 80ua https://soundcloud.com/bad-panda-records/sets/80ua/s-UMb8N – a collaborative album of dance music, created by using, manipulating and re-mixing samples from NASAs SoundCloud library https://soundcloud.com/nasa.

    We explored using the sampler on Garageband to record sounds – from speaking short phrases, playing classroom percussion instruments and other sounds around the classroom e.g., slamming doors, flicking rulers, pouring water. Children explored reversing and changing the pitch of the samples they recorded. They kept a record of samples that they wanted to use in their final composition.

    To finish the session, we played a number of samples to the class and asked to consider what the original sound was and what had been done to change it (e.g., my voice very low, a triangle reversed).

5. The next step was to explore how the children might notate their space composition. We explored the concept of graphic notation, first by watching online animations such as Debussy, First Arabesque https://www.youtube.com/watch?v=A6s49OKp6aE and Ligeti, Artikulation https://www.youtube.com/watch?v=71hNl_skTZQ.

    The children were then invited to draw their own graphic score, considering how they might structure their piece as a journey through the space. Figures 15.1 and 15.2 show some examples of the children's graphic score:

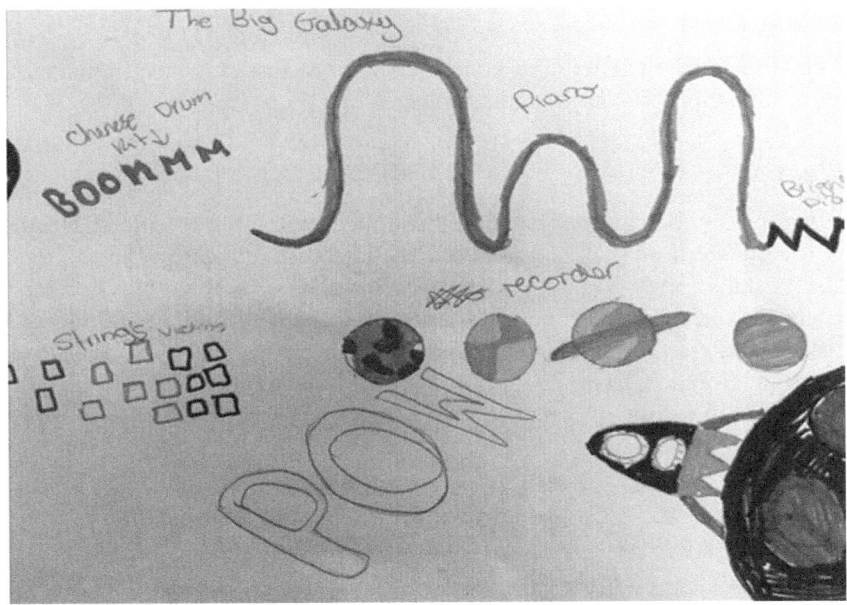

Figure 15.1 Example 1 of children's graphic score

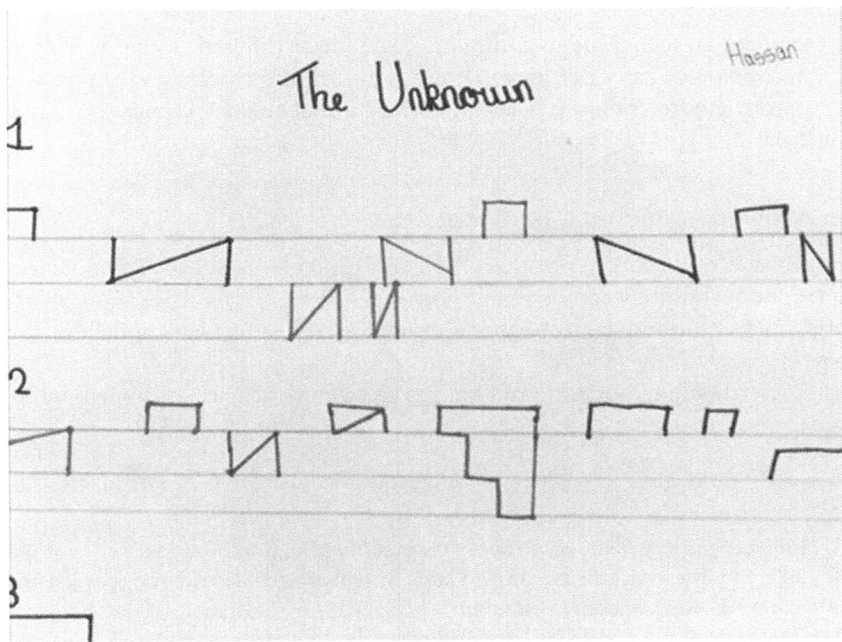

Figure 15.2 Example 2 of children's graphic score

Final outcome

The children used their score to compose their space soundscape in Garageband, using combinations of sounds and samples.

Evaluation

The final pieces the children composed sounded quite abstract and chaotic, but I could clearly see how they had followed their score to structure their music. The children's skills using Garageband grew each week, with some pupils composing independently in their free time and sharing their work with me. The children were motivated and engaged during the sessions and were keen to share their finished pieces using Google Classroom.

The next step will be to compose a song track on Garageband using a drum beat and chord progression.

Summary and key points

Children live in a world filled with digital sounds ready to be recorded, shaped, manipulated, used and combined. The technology they use should either enhance or transform their **musical learning** which above all, is paramount. To select and use technology with purpose is key to its integration and success within music. In summary:

- The use of digital technologies within music connects different sound worlds together.
- Music technologies can open new pathways into music careers and support, enhance and promote children's musical learning using approaches as a teacher you may not have considered.

Further resources

- https://www.ismtrust.org/resources/primary-toolkit – useful advice on general music practice and technology can be found here.
- https://midnightmusic.com/ – many examples of lesson plans and links for online resources.
- https://overthedigitalhorizon.org.uk/ – videos and articles compiled by Wiltshire Music Connect.

References

Craft, A. (2000) *Creativity Across the Primary Curriculum*. London: Routledge.
Craft, A. (2001) "Little c Creativity." In A. Craft, B. Jeffrey and M. Leibling (eds.), *Creativity in Education*, pp. 45–61. London: Continuum.
Craft, A. (2002) *Creativity and Early Years Education*. London: Continuum.
Daubney, A. (2017) *Teaching Primary Music*. London: SAGE.
DfE (Department for Education) (2013) *The National Curriculum*. London: HMSO. https://www.gov.uk/government/collections/national-curriculum.
Higgins, S., Xiao, Z. and Katsipataki, M. (2012) *The Impact of Digital Technology on Learning: A Summary for the Education Endowment Foundation*. https://eric.ed.gov/?id=ED612174.

Kinsella, V., Fautley, M. and Gray, S. (2018) *Musical Inclusion*. Services for Education Music Service. https://bmep.servicesforeducation.co.uk/wp-content/uploads/2019/01/SFE_Inclusion_booklet.pdf.

Lloyd, S., Mead, H. and Audain, J. (2023) "Essential Subject Knowledge for Teaching Primary Music." In N. Majid (ed.), *Essential Subject Knowledge for Primary Teaching*. London: Learning Matters/SAGE.

Major, A. and Cottle, M. (2010) "Learning and Teaching through Talk: Music Composing in the Classroom with Children Aged Six to Seven Years," *British Journal of Music Education*, 27(3), pp. 289–304.

Mills, J. (2009) *Music in the Primary School*. Oxford: Oxford University Press.

16 Technology and computational thinking in early childhood

Emma Goto

Introduction

There has been much focus on computing education over the last decade, with curricula around the world being updated. In many countries, educators are focusing more heavily on computer science, programming and computational thinking. Computer scientist Jeannette Wing's call for computational thinking to be taught to all (Wing, 2006) permeates through curricula, such as the National Curriculum in England, and there is renewed debate about the best ways to prepare young learners for the world they will inhabit in the future. Wing (2006) argues everyone can benefit from thinking like a computer scientist. This is especially important now that technology is ubiquitous in society, and used by children of all ages, in many different ways, to communicate, collaborate, collect ideas and overcome barriers to learning.

Children's learning and development in early childhood is fundamental, as it underpins later learning. Strong foundations built in these early years of development, support strong conceptual understanding and the development of key skills in later education. Therefore, it is essential that we as educators get these early learning experiences right. There is some on-going disagreement over the appropriateness of using technology with our youngest learners in schools and early childhood settings. For some, use of technology in early childhood is seen as wholly wrong and contributing to a toxic and damaging environment (House, 2012); whereas, for others it supports the development of early skills, providing new ways of communicating and representing ideas (Plowman *et al.*, 2012). This chapter explores these ideas and makes suggestions about technology in education for our youngest learners.

Objectives

At the end of this chapter you should be able to:

- have a clear idea of some of the reasons you might choose to use, or not use, technology with young children
- understand some ways you can use technology with young children to good effect
- understand some ways that you could help young children to develop as computational thinkers.

What are the debates around using technology in early childhood?

Concerns about the suitability of the use of technology for children within early childhood are long standing. Sarama and Clements (2019) argue that these debates have

DOI: 10.4324/9781003408925-16

created a bias against the use of technology by some teachers. Of course, we know that young children need to move, physical development is crucial as it underpins so much of the child's later development. We recognise the importance of social and emotional development and the need to develop communication skills; therefore, we want children to play and interact with others learning to, for example, negotiate, share and problem solve together. However, the use of technology does not necessarily oppose these aims. Technology, in itself, is rarely a good thing or a bad thing within education. Rather, it is how it is used that makes the impact positive or negative. Different approaches have different outcomes. For example, consider the difference between giving an individual child an iPad to watch a YouTube video and giving a pair of children an iPad to create a video. One is collaborative, one is not. One will encourage communication, one will not. One focuses on creation, whereas the other is purely about consumption. So how we use technology with children is a very important consideration.

Perhaps reflecting this landscape of differing views about the suitability of technology use in early childhood, since 2021 the curriculum document for early childhood in England (the Statutory Framework for the Early Years Foundation Stage) has had the technology aspect removed (Department for Education, 2023). However, the Understanding the World area of learning within this document does state that, 'listening to a broad selection of stories, non-fiction, rhymes and poems will foster their (*children's*) understanding of our culturally, socially, technologically and ecologically diverse world' (p.10), and this framework certainly does not legislate against the use of technology. Practitioners can still support children's use of technology in their settings, even though this is no longer a statutory aspect of the curriculum. Given the widespread presence of technology within a child's world, it would seem strange to not use technology as a tool within an educational setting, when it can add value to a learning experience.

What are the affordances of technology use in early childhood

Children have different experiences of technology in their formative years. They have opportunities to observe technology being used by adults in their homes and educational settings (McPake *et al.*, 2013). Within their play they mimic how they have seen technology being used and they explore technology for themselves. Technology can be used as tools in early childhood education (Masoumi, 2015) to create and communicate ideas. For example, a child can take a photograph with a camera allowing them to communicate an idea or capture a moment in time (Aubrey and Dahl, 2013; McPake *et al.*, 2013). This can be very empowering, providing ways for children who are not yet able to read and write, to capture and share their ideas with a wider audience. A young child can record their voice to make a book, or annotate a picture, before they can use a pencil to form recognisable letter shapes. For some young children, technology can provide a new way in, to include them and make learning accessible. For example, an iPad can be used to capture a moment, zoom in and reveal aspects of a learning experience to a child with a visual impairment (Goto and Walker, 2014).

Technology can provide tools that can be used in a range of learning experiences. It can provide a context for rich conversations and social learning. It allows opportunities for children to combine ideas and express themselves in new and unusual ways. They can play with ideas creatively, drawing on imagination to bring about new possibilities. For example, in Case Study 16.1, Rachael Coultart shares an experience in which the introduction of some basic digital image skills, using a green screening app in her early years setting, opened up new avenues for creativity and provided a context for a great deal of thought and communication.

Case Study 16.1: Creativity through digital skills

During a Superheroes topic when the children came to school dressed up for the day, I used Green Screen technology and the DoInk app to make them 'fly' around the classroom. First of all, we took a photograph of them in a 'flying' pose as they lay across a table draped in a green shower curtain, then I asked them where they wanted to fly, and we took the photograph together. I then helped them put the two images together in the app and use a pinch motion to shrink/enlarge themselves to fit the scene and fly at the angle they wanted. Some spent a long time deciding where they wanted to be in the scene and were fascinated by the fact they could make themselves larger or smaller. Then one child asked if we could make a photograph with her sitting on a piece of toast! (See Figure 16.1.) This inspired a whole range of imaginative photographs with brilliant captions, as well as giving the children a very real understanding of the fact that you can't always believe what you see in a digital image!

Figure 16.1 Creativity – sitting on toast

Figure 16.2 Creativity – flying

This case study was provided by Rachael Coultart – Teacher and Computing Subject Leader from Stevenage St Nicholas Primary School and Nursery.

Where the decision is taken to enable children to use technology, in addition to considering how it should be used to facilitate learning, it is essential that considerations around digital online safety are at the forefront of our minds. Attention should be given to the avoidance of commercialism as well as protection from inappropriate contact and content (Grey, 2011) (also see Chapter 23 for further information). Schools have an important role to play in supporting young children to develop through their childhood, to become responsible and discerning citizens who use technology safely and appropriately (Livingstone *et al.*, 2017).

How do children learn to use technology?

Play is the means by which children learn about their world and their place within it (Bruce, 2011). Johnson *et al.* (2019) reminds us that whilst play is often child initiated and controlled, there is also a place for educational play that can be initiated and planned by the teacher, if teachers manage interaction sensitively, ensuring to avoid a dominating or controlling approach. By playing with technology, children can explore it and learn about how the technology can be used in meaningful and purposeful ways. Bird and Edwards (2015) differentiate between epistemic play, through which children explore what is possible with the technology, for example by experimenting with the buttons while pretending to take a photograph, and ludic play, where children use technology more deliberately within their play, such as when videoing their friends acting out a story. By allowing children safe access to technology within their play, they can learn about it in natural and enjoyable ways.

Next turn to Task 16.1 to reflect on how you have seen children playing with technology.

Task 16.1: Reflecting on children's play with technology

Think about a time you have seen a child playing with technology. Consider carefully:

- What did you see?
- What were they doing?
- What technology was involved?
- Who was engaged in the play?
- Identify whether this was an example of ludic play or epistemic play.

How does learning in early childhood underpin the development of computational thinking?

Computational thinking has been argued to be an essential skill for all and described as, 'solving problems, designing systems, and understanding human behaviour, by drawing on the concepts fundamental to computer science' (Wing, 2006, p.33). Often when we talk about technology in education, there is a focus upon the technology itself. Using technology and learning through technology becomes the focus. However, Wing (2008, p.3721) reminds us that, 'we do not want the tool to get in the way of understanding the concepts'. Wing (2006) argues that computational thinking skills are beneficial for all and should be taught to children in schools as they can be applied to solve a range of real-world problems.

There has been much debate around what approaches and attributes constitute computational thinking (Barr and Stephenson, 2011; Selby and Woollard 2013). In response to limited primary teacher subject knowledge within computing in England, a project entitled Barefoot Computing was set up which began to address the question of what kinds of thinking are required when solving computational problems. Barefoot Computing proposed a model of computational thinking that has been widely adopted by schools in England (see Figure 16.3). The Barefoot Computing model of Computational Thinking proposes six computational concepts and five approaches as outlined in Table 16.1 (Barefoot Computing, 2014; Csizmadia *et al.*, 2015).

Table 16.1 The computational thinking concepts and approaches from the Barefoot Computing model of Computational Thinking

Concept	Description of this Concept	Approach	Description of this Approach
Logic	Predicting and analysing	Tinkering	Changing things to see what happens
Evaluation	Making judgements	Creating	Designing and making
Algorithms	Making steps and rules	Debugging	Finding and fixing errors
Patterns	Spotting and using similarities	Persevering	Keeping going
Decomposition	Breaking down into parts	Collaborating	Working together
Abstraction	Removing unnecessary detail		

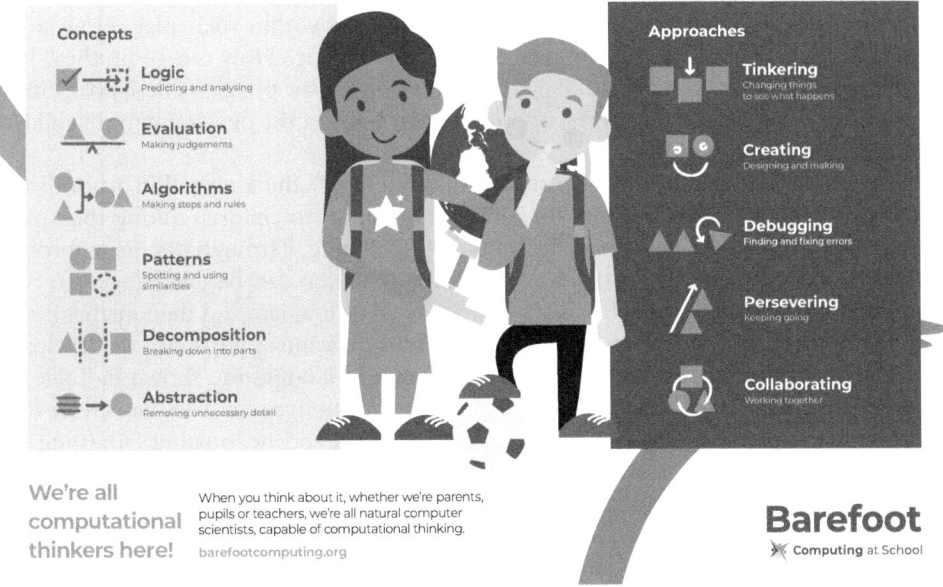

Figure 16.3 'Computational Thinker' poster from Barefoot Computing

(Included with permission. Available to download at www.barefootcomputing.org).

Whilst computational thinking can be developed through practical computer programming, there is also significant potential to teach it through practical problem-solving activities away from the computer and technology. This unplugged approach would seem to provide potential for early childhood professionals.

A curriculum for elementary schooling from the United States of America, K–12 Computer Science (2016), identifies patterns, sequence and problem solving as powerful ideas in early childhood computer science. K–12 Computer Science (2016) argues strongly that these concepts, which would seem to align closely to some of the computational thinking concepts proposed by Barefoot Computing, are learned through play. When looking for, and learning about, patterns we identify similarities and differences as well as noticing repetition. These skills help us to generalise solutions from one situation to many. By thinking through the steps to solve a problem, we are learning about sequence and we learn to recognise that the order in which we do things is important. Through solving a range of problems, we can learn to break things down into manageable chunks (decomposition).

In England, Computational thinking is not part of the Early Years Foundation Stage statutory framework (Department for Education, 2023), which outlines learning expectations for children from birth to five years of age. However, from age five, children follow the National Curriculum within which computing is a statutory subject (Department for Education, 2013). Within the National Curriculum for computing, computational thinking is introduced within the purpose of study, which states, 'A high-quality computing education equips pupils to use computational thinking and creativity to understand and change the world' (Department for Education, 2013, p.178).

Berry and Goto (2015) argue that computational thinking skills can be developed through play-based pedagogies and child-initiated play, within an early childhood educational setting. Children encounter countless problems within their play. How will we move the water from the tap to the bird bath we have made? How can I join these boxes to make a rocket? How can I sort the pieces to solve the jigsaw puzzle? These problems can provide the skilled educator with the opportunity to support the development of children's computational thinking skills.

A key approach that educators can use to develop children's thinking within play is through dialogue (Sylva *et al.*, 2004). Educators can pose questions to children during their play to open up new avenues and prompt different types of thinking. Through discussing problems with peers and engaging in dialogue with teachers, children can be encouraged to reflect upon the processes they used. They can be encouraged to evaluate and then further develop their solutions. This approach to practice provides significant opportunity to develop the computational thinking approaches outlined by Barefoot Computing shown in Table 16.1 above. Through play, children can tinker, explore and try things out. They can create things and make changes. They can play together, collaborating and negotiating, adjusting solutions until they achieve the outcomes they want, fixing errors (debugging) as they go along. Through these experiences, children learn that if they persevere, they can get there in the end.

Additionally, many of these approaches to thinking align very closely with the characteristics of effective learning (playing and exploring; active learning; creating and thinking critically) that are a statutory part of education in early childhood in England (Department for Education, 2023). In Table 16.2 there is a sample list of questions that could be used by practitioners during play, to develop children's computational thinking.

Table 16.2 Questions to develop children's computational thinking

The questions and statements below could be used to develop children's computational thinking during play-based learning

- What do we notice? (patterns)
- What's the same? (patterns)
- What's different? (patterns)
- Can we spot a pattern? (patterns)
- What do we want to do? / What are we trying to do? (abstraction)
- What do we need to think about? (abstraction)
- What comes first? (algorithms / sequence)
- What comes next? (algorithms / sequence)
- What will it do? (logical reasoning)
- How do we know? (logical reasoning)
- Can we break it up? (decomposition)
- Which was best? (evaluation)
- What went well? (evaluation)
- What can we do? (tinkering)
- What can we find? (tinkering)
- What can we make? (creating)
- Did it work? (debugging / evaluation)

- What went wrong? (debugging)
- How can we fix it? (debugging)
- Have we solved a problem like this before? What did we do? (patterns / generalisation)
- Let's play! (tinkering)
- Let's make! (creating)
- Let's fix it! (debugging)
- Let's keep trying! (persevering)
- Let's work together! (collaborating)

Now go to Task 16.2 and consider how you might use these questions in practice.

Task 16.2: Developing your questioning toolbox

Read the questions in Table 16.2 above. Consider the questions. Do any of the questions particularly resonate with you? Are there any others that you could add to the list? Which of the questions do you already naturally use in your practice? Which ones from the list could you add to your repertoire?

Some early childhood practitioners find displaying questions in the learning environment helpful to support adults to develop questioning and dialogue when working with children. Consider whether any of the questions could be used in this way in your classroom. Which questions could you put in which areas of the early years setting?

For early years practitioners, perhaps the key thing is that consideration is given to the stance taken on children's learning in the setting and which pedagogical approaches are seen as effective. If we see problem-solving and thinking skills as important, there would seem to be a great deal of potential for the development of children as computational thinkers within a rich play-based curriculum. Consideration should also be given to the language used to describe approaches to thinking and problem solving. If we teach the children the language of computational thinking and use it when discussing approaches taken to solving problems, there is a possibility that children will be more able to transfer these skills into new contexts in the future. We can use this common language to remind children of approaches they have used in the past and encourage them to reflect upon how these approaches may be useful in new situations that they encounter.

What aspects of the early childhood learning environment should be considered?

To maximise the potential of play-based approaches to develop computational thinking and the use of technology in early childhood education, practitioners need to consider carefully how the learning environment is organised. Firstly, the resources that are made available are important. Children should have access to resources that encourage them to create, explore, tinker and try things out. Building and construction materials (wooden blocks, Lego, recycled materials for junk modelling, marble runs, etc.) can provide many opportunities for children to create and solve problems. Additionally, a range of resources (natural materials like fir cones or stones, beads for threading, small world toys, jigsaw puzzles, etc.) can be used to encourage children to sort, classify, compare and spot patterns. If we want children to develop their understanding of how technology can be used, it would seem important to allow access to technological tools and toys (remote control devices, programmable toys such as Beebot, cameras, microphones, digital devices and computers).

In addition to considering what to provide in the setting, it is important that practitioners consider how resources are made available. If resources are kept away from children and made available occasionally, this can lead to a 'feast or famine' mentality where children are competing to access items (Langston, 2013, p.16). By making these resources easy to get to, in labelled and well-organised storage that children are free to access, children can experience different resources and learn to use them when appropriate in their play. If we keep tools such as cameras away from children and only make these available occasionally, we cannot expect children to become discerning users who use the camera in appropriate ways to communicate aspects of their learning.

Additionally, it is important to give consideration to time. The best solutions often come when we have time to engage with problems, mulling them over and returning to them as thinking progresses. As adults we often break time up into short defined periods, in schools, these are often dictated by timetables and routines, such as lunchtime and playtime. If we want to enable children to engage with things over a longer period, it is worth considering whether there are opportunities to store projects and aspects of learning so children can revisit and build upon what went before.

Summary and key points

This chapter has argued for the use of technology and the place of computational thinking in early childhood. The following points should be considered:

- Early childhood is a crucial stage in a child's development and learning. During this time children learn through play.
- Educators can use dialogue and questions to encourage children to use computational thinking when solving real-world problems in their play.
- The impact that technology can have on young children's learning, will depend on how it is used.
- Used effectively, technology can develop young children's social and communication skills, providing them with a range of tools for communication and creativity, as well as opportunities for collaboration.

Further resources

https://www.barefootcomputing.org/.
   Barefoot Computing provides access via their website to resources to support the development of computational thinking in early childhood and across the primary years of education.
Computing at School (2021) *EYFS Computing*, viewed 1 December 2022 from: https://www.computingatschool.org.uk/teach-computing/teaching-computing-eyfs.
   This resource on early childhood computing provides guidance about links to computing across multiple areas of learning. Additionally, it provides links to other key sources of information.

K–12 Computer Science (2016) *Computer Science in Early Childhood Education*, viewed 10 May 2022 from: https://k12cs.org/pre-k/.

This guidance on computer science in early childhood education is particularly rich and thought-provoking. The discussion around types of pattern activities that educators can use is particularly useful.

References

Aubrey, C. and Dahl, S. (2013) 'The Confidence and Competence in Information and Communication Technologies of Practitioners, Parents and Young Children in the Early Years Foundation Stage'. *Early Years*, 34(1), 94–108, viewed 25 November 2022 from: https://doi.org/10.1080/09575146.2013.792789.

Barefoot Computing (2014) *Computational Thinking Concepts and Approaches*, viewed 18 July 2022 from: http://barefootcas.org.uk/barefoot-primary-computing-resources/concepts/computational-thinking/.

Barr, V. and Stephenson, C. (2011) 'Bringing Computational Thinking to K-12: What Is Involved and What Is the Role of the Computer Science Education Community?' *ACM Inroads*, 2(1), 48–54, viewed 18 July 2022 from: https://doi.org/10.1145/1929887.1929905.

Berry, M. and Goto, E. (2015) 'Laying the Foundations for Computing in the Early Years'. *Switched On*, 19, 6–7, viewed 10 June 2022 from: https://www.computingatschool.org.uk/teaching-resources/2016/january/switched-on-issue-19.

Bird, J. and Edwards, S. (2015) 'Children Learning to Use Technologies through Play: A Digital Play Framework'. *British Journal of Educational Technology*, 46(6), 1149–1160, viewed 15 December 2021 from: https://doi.org/10.1111/bjet.12191.

Bruce, T. (2011) *Learning through Play, for Babies, Toddlers and Young Children*, London: Hodder Education.

Csizmadia, A., Curzon, P., Dorling, M., Humphreys, S., Ng, T., Selby, C. and Woollard, J. (2015) *Computational Thinking: A Guide for Teachers*, viewed 18 July 2022 from: https://eprints.soton.ac.uk/424545/1/150818_Computational_Thinking_1_.pdf.

Department for Education (2013) *The National Curriculum in England: Key Stage 1 and 2 Framework Document*, viewed 18 July 2022 from: https://assets.publishing.service.gov.uk/government/uploads/system/uploads/attachment_data/file/425601/PRIMARY_national_curriculum.pdf.

Department for Education (2023) *Statutory Framework for the Early Years Foundation Stage: Setting the Standards for Learning, Development and Care for Children from Birth to Five*, viewed 21 November 2023 from: https://assets.publishing.service.gov.uk/government/uploads/system/uploads/attachment_data/file/1170108/EYFS_framework_from_September_2023.pdf.

Goto, E. and Walker, M. (2014) 'It's a Little Bit of Magic'. *Nasen Special*, November Edition, 45–47.

Grey, A. (2011) 'Cybersafety in Early Childhood Education'. *Australasian Journal of Early Childhood*, 36(2), 77–81, viewed 1 July 2022 from: https://doi.org/10.1177/183693911103600210.

House, R. (2012) 'The Inappropriateness of ICT in Early Childhood: Arguments from Philosophy, Pedagogy, and Developmental Research'. In: Suggate, S. and Reese, E. (eds.) *Contemporary Debates in Early Childhood Education*, Abingdon, Oxon: Routledge, 105–120.

Johnson, J. E., Sevimli-Celik, S., Al-Mansour, M. A., Tunçdemir, T. B. A. and Dong, P. I. (2019) 'Play in Early Childhood Education'. In: Saracho, O. (ed.) *Handbook of Research on the Education of Young Children*, Abingdon, Oxon: Routledge, 165–175.

K–12 Computer Science (2016) *Computer Science in Early Childhood Education*, viewed 10 May 2022 from: https://k12cs.org/pre-k/.

Langston, A. (2013) 'Learning and Development: ICT - All about … digital journeys'. *Nursery World*, 112, 4328, 16–20, viewed 25 November 2022 from: https://www.nurseryworld.co.uk/features/article/learning-development-ict-all-about-digital-journeys.

Livingstone, S., Davidson, J., Bryce, J., Batool, S., Haughton, C. and Nandi, A. (2017) *Children's Online Activities, Risks and Safety: A Literature Review by the UKCCIS Evidence Group*, viewed 25 November 2022 from: https://assets.publishing.service.gov.uk/government/uploads/system/uploads/attachment_data/file/759005/Literature_Review_Final_October_2017.pdf.

Masoumi, D. (2015) 'Preschool Teachers' use of ICTs: Towards a Typology of Practice'. *Contemporary Issues in Early Childhood*, 16(1), 5–17, viewed 25 November 2022 from: https://doi.org/10.1177/1463949114566753.

McPake, J., Plowman, L. and Stephen, C. (2013) 'Pre-School Children Creating and Communicating with Digital Technologies in the Home'. *British Journal of Educational Technology*, 44, 421–431, viewed 25 November 2022 from: https://doi.org/10.1111/j.1467-8535.2012.01323.16.

Plowman, L., McPake, J. and Stephen, C. (2012) 'Extending Opportunities for Learning: The Role of Digital Media in Early Education'. In: Suggate, S. and Reese, E. (eds.) *Contemporary Debates in Early Childhood Education*, Abingdon, Oxon: Routledge, 95–104.

Sarama, J. and Clements, D. (2019) 'Technology in Early Childhood Education'. In: Saracho, O. (ed.) *Handbook of Research on the Education of Young Children*, Abingdon, Oxon: Routledge, 183–198.

Selby, C. and Woollard, J. (2013) *Computational Thinking: The Developing Definition*, viewed 18 July 2022 from: https://eprints.soton.ac.uk/356481/1/Selby_Woollard_bg_soton_eprints.pdf.

Sylva, K., Melhuish, E., Sammons, P., Siraj-Blatchford, I. and Taggart, B. (2004) *The Effective Provision of Preschool Education (EPPE) Project: Findings from Pre-School to End of Key Stage One*, viewed 28 July 2022 from: https://dera.ioe.ac.uk/18189/2/SSU-SF-2004-01.pdf.

Wing, J. M. (2006) 'Computational Thinking'. *Communications of the ACM*, 49(3), 33–35.

Wing, J. M. (2008) 'Computational Thinking and Thinking about Computing'. *Philosophical Transactions of the Royal Society A: Mathematical, Physical and Engineering Sciences*, 366(1881), 3717–3725, viewed 30 June 2022 from: https://doi.org/10.1098/rsta.2008.0118.

17 Computer programming in the primary school

Lawrence Williams and Beth Mead

Introduction: an approach to computer programming through creative writing

The purpose of this chapter is to provide both a practical and a theoretical introduction to using computer programming creatively in your classroom. The ideas presented here have been tested extensively in classrooms in several countries, and have been successfully adopted in schools (Demo and Williams, 2014). We have found that pupils work most effectively when they have ownership of their work, and the teaching method suggested here rests on their commitment to completing a short story of their own devising. While you might choose to use paper and pen, or a word-processor, this teaching and learning model requires the pupils to present their creative work only through computer coding, using Scratch and Python. Pupils want, generally, to finish their story, and so we have found that the emphasis in the classroom shifts from the teacher directing individual elements of the coding work, to the pupils asking for support in order to fulfil their creative needs.

Objectives

At the end of this chapter, you should be able to:

- understand the constructionist principles underpinning computer programming in primary schools
- create your own short story, using Scratch
- create your own short story, using Python
- plan a short series of lessons to try out with a class
- understand some basic computer programming concepts.

Background to computing

The history of computer programming in schools starts, perhaps surprisingly, with the work of psychologist Jean Piaget (1896–1980). Piaget developed a theory of cognitive development which dealt with epistemology (the nature of knowledge), and how children gradually acquire, construct, and subsequently use it. Known as constructivism, the theory had a wide-ranging impact on teaching, suggesting that play and exploration were important aspects of children's learning. Pupils, he argued, learn by doing, rather than by passively receiving knowledge. Charles Dickens brilliantly parodies this pre-Piaget teaching

DOI: 10.4324/9781003408925-17

and learning method in the famous opening lines of "Hard Times", when Head Teacher, Thomas Gradgrind, explains:

> Now, what I want is Facts. Teach these boys and girls nothing but Facts. Facts alone are wanted in life. Plant nothing else, and root out everything else. You can only form the mind of reasoning animals upon Facts: nothing else will ever be of any service to them.

Piaget's constructivism (1964) thankfully helped to demolish such an arid approach to teaching and learning.

Piaget's work also had a profound influence on one of his pupils in Geneva during the 1950s and 1960s, Seymour Papert (1928–2016), who went on to develop a related theory of learning based on constructivism. Papert's refinement of the theory is called constructionism (Papert, 1980), and it develops Piaget's theory by stressing the notion of learning by making. The learner is consciously engaged in constructing what Papert calls a "public entity". In this chapter the "public entity" recommended for you to try out is that of a short story, as it is a working practice very familiar both to pupils and to teachers.

Logo

The next step in the history of programming is the creation of Logo. Papert used Piaget's work in his development of the Logo programming language. He and his team at the Massachusetts Institute of Technology (MIT) created Logo as a tool to improve the way children think, and to solve problems. These are important general skills. MIT developed a small mobile robot called a "Logo Turtle", and children were shown how to use it in order to solve simple problems, within an environment of play. The first working Logo Turtle robot was created in 1969, and was successfully introduced into schools, where some teachers made good use of the tool.

Scratch

From Papert, the baton of computer programming for young children was passed on to one of his students, Mitch Resnick, who later succeeded Papert as a Professor at MIT. Scratch is a simple, but conceptually valid, block-based programming language, designed to develop coding skills in young children. It is an ideal environment in which children can have fun creating stories and games, while developing authentic concepts in programming. Some of these concepts are presented in story form at the end of this chapter, through another teaching project, Stories for Children, written for teachers by a primary school pupil, and posted on the Literacy from Scratch (LfS) website.

Literacy from scratch

Literacy from Scratch (LfS) began in 2012 as a response to this new computer programming initiative, and has rapidly developed into a cross-curricular, creative, collaborative, and international teaching project. It presents an approach to learning Scratch computer coding through the creation of short stories, in which characters (called "Sprites") are presented against a background (called Backgrounds) and they can speak dialogue with added "voice-over" speech in English or any other language. More recent versions of Scratch offer many more features such as voice-activated movement.

The project has been presented at many international Computing/Informatics conferences, and was quickly adopted by university teachers in the Czech Republic, Germany, Poland, Italy, and South Korea (Passey, 2014). Teaching materials on the Literacy from Scratch website (in English, Czech, Italian, Hindi, Guajarati, French, Russian, and Norwegian) are now quite wide-ranging, and the best starting point is probably the outline PowerPoint presentation, which can be downloaded for use by teachers at home, or shown in the classroom. The LfS teaching model is presented on the main, introductory web page. The PowerPoint gives the basic story-telling plan of the project, as well as exemplifying the introductory Computing skills needed. Once these skills have been mastered, teachers can then use the search engines on the site to find further elements that they may need, such as help sheets, lesson plans for different year groups and subjects, and schemes of work, as well as extensive examples of how Scratch can be creatively developed both by teachers and by their pupils aged from 5 years upwards. There are also some examples of cross-curricular uses of Scratch, created by beginning teachers at Brunel University London, who were exploring the possibilities of using Scratch in their primary classrooms, as part of their professional studies. Their work has inspired teachers across the world (Williams, 2015).

The storytelling method

Scratch can be easily downloaded from the MIT website (http://www.scratch.mit.edu). Scratch 3.0 is the most up-to-date and powerful version, while Scratch Jr is more suitable for younger pupils.

Planning is the key to successful implementation in the classroom. Here is an account by a postgraduate student at Brunel University London, who kindly wrote up her experience of trying to introduce Scratch into her primary classroom for the first time. There is a fuller account of her work in Williams (2014), as well as teaching support materials flowing from this on the Literacy from Scratch website.

Ashley Cox explains:

This project was conducted over three planned lessons, and was piloted using one year 5 class (pupils aged 9–10 years) and one year 6 class (aged 10–11 years). Year 5 and year 6 pupils were taught separately to allow independent learning. (*On the website, you will see her lesson plans and objectives, with further support materials. There are also individual reports of the issues she and her university colleagues experienced.*)

I demonstrated story examples and what I thought were the important Scratch features, including script, stage (Backgrounds) and sprites. I shared some technical vocabulary with the pupils, and encouraged them to use the language throughout the lesson especially when demonstrating completed work to their peers.

Lesson two began in the same way as lesson one, and pupils were immediately excited to learn that we would be continuing with Scratch. I very briefly recapped the key features of Scratch, and instructed pupils to consider using their new skills to create a short story. I decided to allow the learners to choose their own story specifics, due to the varied interests in each group. I also thought this would provide a better overview of individual student knowledge of Scratch. I did, however, demonstrate my own story, and allowed pupils some time to discuss ideas amongst their peers.

In lesson three, Ashley added sounds to the mi17. Newer versions of Scratch now have more sounds and musical elements available for use.

Ashley was able to support her pupils effectively, and to develop Scratch in her Computing classes, with no prior knowledge of computer programming.

The above teaching method was clearly successful, and, encouraged by this, it was subsequently applied to Year 1 and Year 2 pupils (aged 5 years to 7 years) at another local primary school, Swaminarayan, in west London. There, we found that pupils as young as 5 years were easily able to complete a story with two characters (called Sprites), three scenes (called Backgrounds), and add dialogue, in two languages (English speech bubbles, Hindi voice-over files), within only a few lessons.

Pedagogical approaches in England and the Czech Republic

While the Literacy from Scratch project is a joint international venture, it is clear that there are differences emerging between the approaches to the classroom use of Scratch for developing creative narrative work in the two countries.

In London, the programming work undertaken in the classroom was being driven by a teacher of English, and the project is therefore seen from a literacy viewpoint. The Planning Sheet grids are completed in words, for example. In Prague, by contrast, the same project is being driven by a school in which art and creativity are central, and so the classwork developed is seen largely from an artistic viewpoint. This includes the Planning Sheets, which are completed using the pupils' own images. Examples are posted on the website.

Both countries use storyboarding techniques, therefore, but in two very different ways. Both countries agree, however, that these two approaches need to be supported and developed in the future by the addition of music sound files (WAV and MPEG) created in the classroom by pupils, which can provide background, and atmospheric accompaniment to parts of the children's stories they are creating, in their unfolding narratives.

The most important practical aspect of learning how to use Scratch has, in both countries, been to deconstruct existing examples of projects, i.e., to look at successful coding, and to learn from these examples how to solve problems. In Prague, files sent from the UK were used both as a stimulus for creativity, and as examples from which Czech pupils could learn details of successful coding practice. The beginning teacher explained to the language teachers how their pupils would work, and developed study materials (also on the website) for the project. In this way, experienced teachers were able to learn from younger teachers about how to work in Scratch.

At Brunel University London, the Scratch workshop plenary sessions, in which beginning teachers regularly shared their work with each other, proved to be the most valuable parts of the workshops. There were shared solutions to coding problems, and the stimulus of seeing the creative ideas of others also resulted in further creative ideas. The plenary sessions were steadily increased in length, as the project developed.

There is now a world-wide community of Scratch users, and teachers can reinforce and develop their skills, and that of their pupils, by working with others, literally from across the globe. To join, just Google the words: "Join Scratch", create a username and password, and you will have access to an online community of teachers across the world.

Next turn to Task 17.1. and Task 17.2.

Task 17.1: Defining key terms

Look up the following terms using an internet search engine, for example on Google:

Logo, Scratch, Constructivism, Constructionism.

Make a note of what you understand each term to mean.
Next, write an answer to the following question:

What is the point of teaching pupils to write computer coding?

Task 17.2: Using Scratch to write a short story

Using a copy of any version of Scratch (1.4, 2.0, or 3.0), write your own very short story in three scenes (called Backgrounds), with two characters (called Sprites) and some dialogue.

See the website Literacy from Scratch, for worked examples by pupils aged 5 to 11 years, and by beginning teachers at Brunel University London. There are also many short Scratch "YouTube" videos to be found on the web, supporting many aspects of the computer program.

Literacy from Python

Using Python strings for story-telling

Scratch is a simple, block-coding computer program. Python is not. It is a fully professional, high-level coding language, used to power social media and other platforms such as:

- Google (YouTube)
- Facebook
- Dropbox
- Yahoo
- NASA
- IBM
- Mozilla

However, getting started on Python is much easier than it might sound!

The Literacy from Python (LfP) introductory coding project, using Python 3 strings for story-telling, builds on the success of the Literacy from Scratch model outlined above (Passey *et al.*, 2021). The easiest access to the supporting website is through the homepage of the Literacy from Scratch website. The project encourages the development of short story-writing at upper primary level. These stories are then created using Python 3, and in doing so, a series of elementary coding concepts can be developed.

Method of using Python

In English lessons, pupils in Years 5 or 6, write a very short story which includes some dialogue. This story is then taken to the computer room, where, using Python 3, it can be reworked in the IDLE programming window, and printed out in the Shell window as an elementary Python program. This model therefore adds creative and cross-curricular elements to the coding process. Teachers and pupils could later add many more computing elements into the stories, as well.

How to start

Load a (free) copy of Python.

Load IDLE (Called a compiler).

Type in the word PRINT	This will appear as pink writing on your screen.
Type an opening bracket (	This will now appear in black writing.
Type inverted commas "	This will appear in green writing.
Type the Title of Your Story	This will continue in green writing.
Type closing inverted commas"	This will also be in green writing.
Type a closing bracket)	This will revert to black writing.

This is called a Python String, and it is already a very short Python computer program!

Press **Return**

Now on a new line type PRINT () This will print a blank line.
Now type Print ("One day, I wrote a story using Python Strings")
Save and name the file (on the Top Command line)
Run
Your story will appear on the screen as a printout (a "computer output"), this time in blue
   writing.

See the Literacy from Python website (https://sites.google.com/view/literacyfrom python/home) for how to add more Python elements into your story.
   Here is an example from the website:

```
#Programmer and story: Beth Mead, Year 6, aged 10 years
print("MAISY LEARNS TO CODE WITH 'PYTHON'")
print()
print("(Or, how to use 'Python' for story-telling)")
print()
print("Maisy, the Spaniel, was walking past the school.")
print()
print("Hearing the word 'Python', she wondered why the pupils were talking about
   snakes!")
print("She also heard the words 'Times Tables', and wanted to know more.")
print("So, she went to see her wise friend Malika, the cat.")
print("'Malika explained: "It's not a python, it's 'Python', a computer program. It is named
   after a famous TV comedy show"'")
```

print("Maisy wanted to learn about Python, so Malika showed her how to download the free computer program into her computer.")
print("Maisy noticed that different words went different colours depending on what words were used.")
print("Maisy went back to Malika and asked what had happened.")
print("Malika told her that each colour meant something different: 'print' is pinky/purple because it is a function; words in brackets'()' and inverted commas" are green because they are strings.")
print("Even though Malika is very wise, she didn't know what a function was.")
print("Maisy knew that a function is a task that the computer carries out, such as print, or run, and shared her knowledge with Malika.")

The full story and coding, which can be shown (in colour) on a whiteboard to your classes, or downloaded into any recent version of Python, is posted on the Literacy from Python website. There are further teachers' notes on how to do this, and how to include further elements of Python. (We are now working to develop mathematics, in the same way.)

This teaching method, with the coding, was presented as a teaching and learning model at the OCCE/IFIP Conference, Tampere, Finland, 2021, and was later classroom tested with two groups of 30 pupils. As a result, it has recently been incorporated into the permanent computing curriculum of a south London school. Typical pupil responses were:

> *"I enjoyed being able to create my own Python code using the skills we have developed in the lessons." – "I enjoyed everything." – "It didn't feel like work."*

Further classroom testing is planned, with stories focused on mathematics and science topics, and developing the importation of graphs as well as Turtle graphics.

Computational thinking

Computer coding concepts

Some of the coding concepts needed for a fuller understanding of programming have also been written by a primary school pupil, in an accessible story format, using PowerPoint. These coding stories are now housed on the Literacy from Scratch website, under the heading Stories for Children.

The stories can be viewed as PDFs on the Cloud, or downloaded as PowerPoint files, entirely free, for use in your classroom. Class discussion of this material is clearly very important, but it is, we hope, an entertaining way into computer programming concepts. *How about asking your pupils to create their own coding stories?*

There is no single, agreed definition of computational thinking. It depends on whom you ask: programmer, logician, or mathematician. There are, however, several generally agreed elements, and these are explored in the Stories for Children project. These elements include:

- **Algorithmic thinking** (following a set of rules; sequencing skills)
- **Debugging** (detecting and correcting errors)
- **Decomposition** (breaking a complex problem down into simpler parts)

- **Logical thinking** (reasoning skills)
- **Generalisation** (recognising patterns, and using them to find solutions)
- **Abstraction** (sorting relevant information from unnecessary detail)

These skills clearly have a wider value to pupils than within programming itself. Have a look at the range of six stories on the Literacy from Scratch website for examples of their application to real-life scenarios. Figure 17.1 shows a sample title page from one of the animal stories, showing the character, Maisy, and the coding concept that the story illustrates, in this case, Logic.

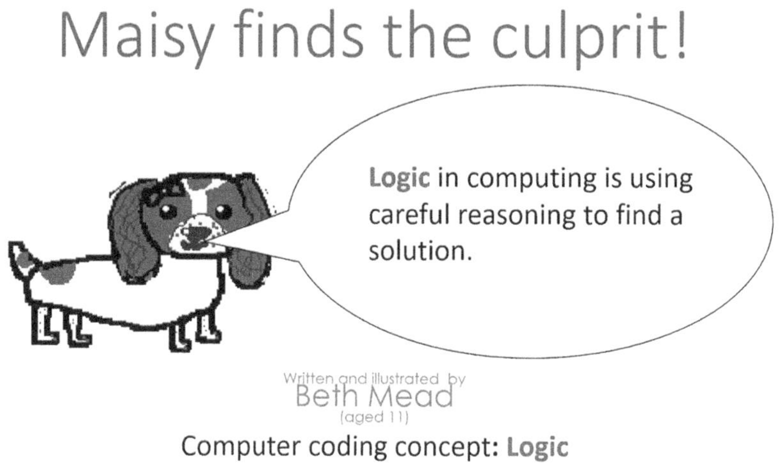

Maisy finds the culprit!

Logic in computing is using careful reasoning to find a solution.

Written and illustrated by
Beth Mead
(aged 11)

Computer coding concept: **Logic**

Figure 17.1 A title page from one of the six stories

Now turn to Tasks 17.3 and 17.4.

Task 17.3: Planning lessons using Scratch for story writing

Plan a set of lessons for your class in order for them to develop their own short stories, using Scratch.

See the Literacy from Scratch website for detailed support.

Task 17.4: Using Python to write a short story

Using a copy of Python and a compiler (e.g., IDLE), write a very short story using Strings.

See the Literacy from Python website for detailed support.

Summary and key points

You should now have a general overview of:

- How computer programming for school pupils has developed over the years.
- Know how to plan and write a short story using Scratch.
- How to write a short story using Python strings.
- How to create a short series of lessons for your own pupils.
- Some basic computer coding concepts such as algorithms, debugging, decomposition, logic, generalisation, and abstraction.

Computer coding can clearly be great fun for pupils, if it is approached through the development of creative writing. With the help of the free online resources presented in this chapter, especially the Literacy from Scratch, and Literacy from Python websites, and other available materials through online educational communities such as MIT Scratch, you can start to develop computational thinking and coding in your own classes.

Further resources

Literacy from Scratch: https://www.literacyfromscratch.org.uk (Accessed August 2022).
   This free website offers examples of teaching materials such as lesson plans and schemes of work, along with examples of pupils' work, 5 years and above.
Literacy from Python: https://sites.google.com/view/literacyfrompython/home
   (Accessed August 2022).
   This free website offers detailed examples of coding in Python, together with an introduction and teaching notes.
Scratch: https://scratch.mit.edu (Accessed August 2022).
   This free website gives access to the different versions of Scratch, with examples of pupils' work, teaching advice, and to a global community of teachers.

References

Demo, G.B., and Williams, L. (2014) A Working Model for Teacher Training in Computing through the "Literacy from Scratch Project" – The Many Facets of Scratch. In: Proceedings of the ISSEP Conference 2014, September, Istanbul, Turkey. Springer, Heidelberg, Germany.
Papert, S. (1980) *Mindstorms. Children, Computers and Powerful Ideas*, New York: Basic Books.
Passey, D., Leahy, D., Williams, L., Holvikivi, J., and Ruohonen M. (2021) Digital Transformation of Education and Learning – Past, Present and Future. IFIP TC 3 Open Conference on Computers in Education, OCCE 2021, Tampere, Finland, August 17–20, 2021, Proceedings pp. 41–53.
Passey, D., and Tatnall, A. (2014) Key Competencies in ICT and Informatics: Implications and Issues for Educational Professionals and Management. IFIP WG 3.4/3.7 International Conferences, KCICTP and ITEM 2014, Potsdam, Germany, July 1–4, 2014, Revised Selected Papers pp. 25–33.
Williams, L. (2014) *Introducing Computing: A Guide for Teachers*. London: Routledge.
Williams, L. (2015) Developing Computational Thinking Skills through the Cross-disciplinary project: Literacy from Scratch. 5th Annual International Conference on Education and e-Learning (EeL 2015), September 14–15, Bangkok, Thailand.

18 Augmented reality (AR) – innovative uses in primary education

Warren Fearn and Jonathan Hook

Introduction

This chapter explains Augmented Reality (AR) and introduces innovative uses of AR in primary education: science is used as an example. One of the main advantages of using AR applications and platforms is the ability to display relevant digital information to support pupils' learning in real time and through specific contexts. I have found, through my research that augmented reality offers exciting opportunities for pupils to digitally interact in ways traditional teaching methods cannot deliver. The chapter is a summary of ideas from my review of published research plus initial findings from my own research (Fearn and Hook, 2023).

Objectives

At the end of this chapter you should:

- understand what is meant by augmented reality
- have developed your understanding of augmented reality tools
- have an awareness of how augmented reality tools might help learning
- have ideas of how to use augmented reality tools in your teaching
- understand the barriers to use of augmented reality in schools.

What is augmented reality?

Augmented and Virtual Reality are not necessarily new inventions; during the 1950s and 60s Morton Heilig known as the 'Father of Virtual Reality' describes in his essay, *The Cinema of the Future* (1955), how our senses can be used to create a defining experience. He later invented the Sensorama Stimulator – an experience theatre – to stimulate a person by using visual image, breeze and vibrations.

Ionitescu and Radu (2015) define AR as 'adding computer-generated content upon the real, physical objects in the world around us, by displaying overlays of information and digital content connected to physical objects and locations'. Augmented Reality (AR) is a live, direct or indirect view of a physical, real-world environment whose elements are augmented by computer-generated 3D graphics, sound, videos or GPS data.

Azuma (1997) and other researchers (Kaufmann, 2003; Zhou *et al.*, 2008) examined the different uses of augmented reality and described it as a variation of VR. Whilst VR entirely immerses a user in a computer-simulated environment, AR allows a user to view the real world with virtual entities layered onto a real-world environment.

DOI: 10.4324/9781003408925-18

An AR system

- combines the real and the virtual
- is interactive in real time, and
- incorporates three-dimensional graphics.

There are so many acronyms associated to 'realities' that it becomes confusing how to differentiate the processes between AR (Augmented Reality), VR (Virtual Reality) and MR (Mixed Reality). Where do they overlap and how do they distinguish themselves from one another? Today, extended reality (XR) is a common acronym. This terminology is frequently being used to encompass all of the emerging technologies under one umbrella. It focuses more upon how new platforms, software and hardware 'cross reality' in an interdisciplinary manner.

Examples of applications for primary education follow.

Augmented reality tools

There are a variety of devices that use AR technologies which can be divided into two categories

- *wearable*
- *handheld*.

Wearable AR technologies generally include head-mounted displays, smart glasses, and gesture-recognition devices. Handheld AR devices are characteristically operated using mobile tablets or smartphones that rely upon screen-based applications.

Wearable AR

Wearable technology describes portable devices with processing power that can record an activity conducted by the user. Head-mounted displays (HMD) are technologically complex devices worn on the head, which allow the learner to see an augmented view of reality through a digitally enhanced viewfinder (Novak *et al.*, 2012). Visual information can be superimposed over a user's field of view, whilst having the benefits of being handsfree (Wang *et al.*, 2018). At present, such AR wearable devices do not provide a full 360-degree field of view. However, as technology advances it is inevitable companies will strive to create an all-round visual experience with less bulky headsets and lighter, slicker and well-designed frames; even now in development are AR contact lenses called 'Mojo Vision'.

A haptic interface (HI) device can essentially capture a sensation on contact and manipulation of an object that is set within a virtual environment or remote setting. Therefore, a user may experience similar characteristics of holding a real object, temperature, texture, weight and shape and so on. In the future, it is envisaged haptic communication will eventually be integrated into virtual experiences.

Today, pupils experience haptic technology through tactile feedback in game consoles, tablets and smartphones. Apple has integrated the *Taptic Engine* that introduces vibrations and levels of interactivity when tapping a device. Advances in technology by Ultrahaptics have led to haptic technology using ultrasound that creates three-dimensional shapes and textures that can be felt, but not visible. This enables haptics to be applied to virtual objects, interfaces and gesture control. Furthermore, companies such as Tesla suits and Bhaptics are now manufacturing suits where your body can feel sensations through immersive experiences. Ultimately, haptic technology offers a new dimension for augmentation and how we interact with our environments and 3D models.

Handheld AR

These include smartphones and tablet devices with good quality touch screen displays and an array of in-built sensors (Onime and Abiona, 2016). Handheld AR can be classified into various categories such as:

1) *Marker-based AR*
2) *Marker-less AR*
3) *Location-based marker-less AR.*

The launch of Apple's ARKit, and Google's ARCore adoption of augmented reality has significantly opened up new opportunities for building creative AR apps for smart devices. There are, of course, many other tools designed to help educators create Augmented Reality content and experiences. More popular AR authoring tools are software applications such as *Zappar, Blippar, Adobe Aero, Vuforia, Wikitude, Niantic Lightship* and so on.

Marker-based AR

The technology uses a device's camera (smart-phone or tablet) to detect a specific target image with recognition automatically triggering an event e.g. via a QR code. Markers can trigger a variety of media from 3D graphics, video, sound and animations.

Marker-less AR

Marker-less Augmented Reality allows the use of specific or all parts of the physical environment to become a target base for the placement of overlayered virtual objects. This type of technology allows a device to understand whereabouts it is situated in space and overlay 3D content on its location. By using both a camera and sensors, it enables a device to map out a structure of any given environment and detect its location.

Location-based marker-less AR

Smartphones and other digital devices make use of an in-built Global Positioning System (GPS) and sensors to locate and interact with an augmented reality application being used. This type of marker-less Augmented Reality is referred to as *location-based* AR. For example, Niantic's mobile game called Pokemon Go uses location-based AR technology to overlayer 3D graphical content onto real-world environments. Furthermore, marker-less systems have the capacity to extract and store information about the characteristics of an environment that can be retrieved later on.

What are the educational benefits for using AR?

Mobile devices such as smartphones and tablets, all have built-in cameras, available to create dynamic context-aware and interactive digital content. Augmented reality no longer requires expensive hardware or restrictions on portability. This presents new opportunities to move away from lecture-style teaching to the use of AR in educational environments to create practical and highly interactive visual forms of learning (Huang *et al.*, 2016). It offers new alternatives for learning materials by making them interactive and providing an incentive for children to directly interact with their environment in creative ways. By over-layering virtual objects onto the real world it can transform rudimentary tasks into creative playgrounds to explore. Mobile augmented reality provides learning designers and educators with a new opportunity to creatively think more deeply about the mobile learner's context and situation. One of AR's key advantages is the ability to create contextual learning experiences (Dede, 2009).

AR can be applied in different educational settings – from young children using magic books, through to schools testing wearable AR applications.

A review of 'Using Augmented Reality in Education from 2011 to 2016' (Chen *et al.*, 2017), concludes that from the 55 studies published, most of the studies reported that AR in educational settings led to better learning and motivation, because AR supplies authentic graphical content and interaction. Deeper pupil engagement, improved perceived enjoyment and positive attitudes were reported as educational benefits of using AR. The technology was reported as attracting and inspiring learners, stimulating their creativity and curiosity. AR provides opportunities for interaction with abstract concepts, experiments and exploration of objects, phenomena and processes that are not always possible or safe (Akçayır and Akçayır, 2017).

Aligning pedagogical theories with practice

Your understanding of pedagogy will play an important role in your employment of augmented reality technology in your teaching. Dunleavy and Dede (2014) refer to theoretical foundations that are based around '*situated*' and '*constructivist*' learning. AR offers an innovative learning space by merging digital learning materials with tools or objects, directly into a physical space and therefore creating 'situated learning'. Furthermore, AR aligns with constructivist notions of education where learners can take control of their own learning, through interactions with real and virtual environments. Bower *et al.* (2014) reinforce these types of practices, referring to AR being compatible with a number of pedagogical approaches like the following ones:

- Constructivist learning: Augmented Reality facilitates pupils to immerse themselves in their tasks and make profound and lasting connections in their knowledge framework by using diverse kinds of information.
- Situated learning: Augmented Reality places the pupil in an actual learning context by incorporating daily life into the classroom.
- Game-based learning: These Augmented Reality games submerge the pupil in a virtual narrative in which s/he must play a given role that prepares him/her to deal with daily life.
- Enquiry-based learning: Augmented Reality makes it possible to experiment with virtual models that are immersed in real-world scenes.

Key questions for you to consider when including AR in your teaching include:

- What impact will using augmented reality have on learning?
- Do you have time to prepare?
- When and where can AR be embedded into your curriculum?

- Do you consider AR to be a regular medium to use or a unique experience?
- Do you have appropriate resources to engage with AR technology?
- Do you envisage group or individual activities? Or both?
- How can AR engage pupils in unique ways in comparison to other media?
- How will you measure the impact of using AR for teaching and learning?

Location-based

The emergence of location-based AR offers great opportunities to interact with public areas as a 'creative playground' where the technology has the potential to overlayer 3D content onto real-world environments. Gaming AR holds the potential to provide a novel kind of interaction with buildings, parks, classrooms and so on, to create innovative experiences. These may involve engaging pupils in quests, with an expectation that users will need to solve AR puzzles in order to progress and eventually be rewarded. It also encourages learning to take place outside of the classroom and lets pupils find new perspectives in their familiar environments.

For example, the AR application called *Magical Park* allows children to be active in a park through gameplay and triggering 3D graphical content.

Game based

Laine (2018) evidences that contemporary educational mobile AR games (EMARGs) are probably best represented by treasure hunts with characteristics of puzzle and adventure genre. Who hasn't ever played Pokemon Go? Puzzle-based EMARGs are also common for example, Metaverse is an AR platform that empowers teachers to author their own interactive experiences, so they can introduce them to their pupils. It has the functionality for creating all types of games including role playing games, choosing your adventure, puzzles, time challenges and others. Dunleavy (2014) says one of his design principles of the affordances of AR is to drive the player interaction and learning through gamified stories or narratives. The story or narrative helps to provide the structure and rationale for the AR experience.

Storytelling

AR brings enriched ways of telling educational stories through visual models. Lessons can now include innovative experiences and interactions through immersive technology never envisaged before. AR technology is capable of augmenting virtual objects over reality, so consequently it allows stories to be placed in a space whether it's on a desk in your classroom, in an outside environment or on your floor at home. 'Wonderscope' uses mobile AR to superimpose characters, scenes and stories onto a user's living room carpet or outside in the garden. The characters can communicate to the user through voice-recognition technology, and the AR-based stories encourage children to engage and move around their environment. Part of the teacher's challenge is to understand the balance of not overwhelming a user with digital content and potentially giving them a cognitive overload.

AR can bring animations and 3D objects to life from print. Billinghurst *et al.* (2001) designed the 'Magic Book' using AR to superimpose 3D rendered models onto books. AR can transform the traditional textbook into an interactive one and where abstract concepts are difficult to comprehend, this technology can help facilitate a learners' understanding delivered in a multilingual mode. AR books are changing the way stories are experienced;

commanding increased awareness from the storyteller. Due to the growing number of smartphones and tablets with in-built cameras and AR capabilities, interactive books are becoming a more attractive proposition in using them to learn.

Augmented creativity

AR can make environments interactive and engaging to a learner in a variety of ways that has never been possible before. The rich content of media lends itself to creating an individual's unique pathway for discovery through the use of 3D environments and models (Lee, 2012). Because AR can be used to superimpose virtual objects and information onto physical environments, it enables users to visualise intangible concepts and therefore supports learners in helping them to understand abstract concepts or unobservable phenomena (Wu *et al.*, 2013).

Augmented creativity aims to combine education and entertainment. It's a response to how humans and machines can work together in synergy between human intelligence (HI) and artificial intelligence (AI). How can machines support and augment our creativity through a more active role?

AR markers have been used to compose music and experiment with various styles of melodies, rhythms, scales, chords and so on. The application is split into a choice of *style* and *instrument* and the user can choose them independently. Moving AR physical markers closer to a device's camera affects the type of sound composition and arrangement of song. In terms of learning, AR offers educational goals through teaching concepts of arrangements and styles as well as encouraging collaboration and understanding of an orchestra.

Children can learn coding skills by programming physical objects such as robots. They use visual programming languages to move the robot, but tracking the programme execution can be difficult to visualise. To help children understand the program, the use of AR via a mobile device can show where and when the program is being executed through visual interaction.

Tangible

Tangible interaction refers to the concept of interacting with the digital world using physical objects, gestures and behaviours in an intuitive manner. It allows pupils to go far beyond the screen and physically interact with objects to support their own learning. Billinghurst (2002) found that the relationship between virtual and tangible items is very personal in AR and these tangible items can be embellished in ways that are impossible in traditional settings. The advantage is that pupils with little to no technology experience will still enjoy a fulfilling interactive experience.

Zhu *et al.* (2017) focused on the use of interaction through a tangible augmented reality toy kit (AR BLOCK) to help 4–7 years old children understand abstract concepts, such as a colour mix, mathematics and 2D-3D geometrical shapes. AR allows users to interact with both onscreen (intangible) and physical objects (tangible) at the same time. AR BLOCK focuses more on the interaction of physical objects with the screen and provides feedback depending on which markers it recognises on the block. They reported that parents widely believed that AR BLOCK creates a fun and interactive learning environment with embedded pedagogical factors. In the context of chemical sciences, DAQRI, an augmented reality company, has designed block faces that can trigger chemical reactions in 4D. The cubes can be made out of paper or laser cut so have the potential to be created within a classroom. Today, schools are using a physical product called MERGE cube where pupils can hold 3D digital objects in the palm of their hands and interact in an entirely different way through the use of AR.

Further studies have explored the use of intelligent virtual characters using AR. Cimen *et al.* (2018) demonstrated how animated models (in this case a character's skeleton as an input), can navigate around real-world environments and react to objects in real time. A virtual character is able to collide with both real and virtual objects by walking over different real-world slopes and changing its behaviour according to the arrangements of predefined physical objects.

The Creative Play Lab – LEGO AR – Studio has been exploring interaction by mixing the virtual and physical LEGO play together. It brings LEGO to life with animations and visual effects when they are placed together. For example, a dragon breathing fire, trains sounding a horn and a fire truck using a fire-hoseare all activated whilst playing with the bricks. The app allows children to control their virtually enhanced animations in real-world environments, so they can create their own stories and adventures. Even virtual golden bricks are hidden around the AR environment for children to search and collect!!

Project-based learning

Project-Based Learning (PBL) is a teaching method in which pupils gain knowledge and skills by working for an extended period of time to investigate and respond to a question, problem or challenge. PBL can demonstrate the importance of 21st century skills such as collaboration, creativity, critical thinking, communication and problem solving. Well-designed authentic projects usually feature real-world context, tasks and tools that a pupil can relate to through their own personal interests and learning needs.

21st-century skills

The exposure of technology throughout our daily lives certainly highlights the need for pupils to be aware and engaged with current practices. The term '21st century skills' offers a framework for digital media skills that are applicable for schools to undertake. These particular skills are condensed into the 4 c's that include: collaboration, creativity, critical thinking, communication and problem solving (Jenkins, 2009). Augmented reality can be used to support both teachers and pupils in all of these areas as 21st-century thinkers and problem solvers. Whether it is sharing technology devices in a classroom to achieve goals, communicating through interaction with 3D models, being challenged by an AR experience or using mobile devices to be creative and innovative. Furthermore, using AR embraces skills aligned to information, media and technology literacy; from understanding visual data, through to teaching pupils about how technology works. According to Dede (2008), AR educational activities can play an important role in helping pupils to be up to date for 21st century education, preparing them for challenges and activities in a rapidly changing technology enhanced world.

Using AR in your teaching: examples for science teaching

Whether it's exploring forces, investigating materials or analysing atomic structures, the use of augmented reality offers the unique affordances of combining the physical and virtual worlds to discover how we can interact with our own environments and make sense of the world around us. Therefore, AR presents unique affordances to engage learners using text, videos, sounds, animations, and so on, to conduct investigations (Dede, 2009). It has the potential to 'enable pupils to see the world around them in new ways and engage with realistic issues in a context with which pupils are already connected' (Klopfer and Sheldon, 2010). Billinghurst (2002), Klopfer and Squire (2008), Wang *et al.* (2018) have found that AR has vast potential implications and numerous benefits for the augmentation of teaching and learning environments through integrating digital learning resource to enable learners to experience scientific phenomena that are not possible in the real world. Furthermore, the use of assistive technologies can enhance the experience of pupils with disabilities or special educational needs.

In 201, the U.S. Department of Education, released a report – *A vision for STEM based learning 2026*. The report outlined the need for flexible and inclusive learning spaces that offer teachers and pupils the structure, equipment and access to materials, including spaces that are located in the classroom, in the natural world, makerspaces, and those that are augmented by virtual and technology-based platforms to enhance learners' STEM experiences. Virtual laboratory technology is becoming more manipulative, interactive and 'real' as time goes on, and the future of these types of technologies will only develop (Brinson, 2015).

Considering the points above, now undertake Task 18.1.

Task 18.1: Making decisions about your own teaching

Having read the ideas above, now make a list of goals that you want to achieve through the use of AR with your own classes. You may need to approach your headteacher or the person responsible for technology in your school to ask for devices to be purchased. You, of course, will need to have sound pedagogical justifications to support your claims for expenditure.

Barriers facing augmented reality in education

Augmented reality can act as a catalyst for major change in education, but as with any technology, there are inherent risks. Because AR blurs the divide between digital and real worlds, it can present threats to a person's physical safety and identity. Barriers include:

- Cost and Investment: Costs might be offset by less need for print materials/books as they are replaced by apps (Andujar *et al.*, 2011).
- Technical Implications: Teachers can spend inappropriate amounts of time on internet connection and software issues (Kiryakova *et al.*, 2018), and the greater number of devices can lead to the higher risk of device failure and maintenance (Wu *et al.*, 2013). AR generally relies on the use of mobile devices (whether handheld or wearable), to require a connection to a wireless internet provider in order to draw down data sources. Information can be stored directly onto a device for retrieval, but internet connectivity allows for users to access real-time information.
- Adoption and Accessibility: The BESA (British Educational Suppliers Association) *EdTech and ICT survey* (2018) revealed that a school state teacher's confidence and

willingness is the most common barrier to using more EdTech (29%) with primary schools more likely to state teacher willingness as a barrier (32%) in comparison to secondary schools (25%). Training on their digital technologies resources is the largest challenge faced by both primary (54%) and secondary (66%) schools. For teachers to incorporate it more often into lessons they need a way to customise the contents and types of activities proposed. Radu (2014) emphasised the need for guidelines for designing effective educational AR experiences, i.e. tools supporting teachers in promoting pupil learning.

- Ethical Implications: Southgate *et al.* (2017) argue there is a strong and moral case for commercial developers, educators and scientists alike to be accountable for ethical issues when designing AR products for children. AR is recognised as being a persuasive application as it can create convincing experiences that can change our thoughts, perceptions and behaviour on how we see and interact with the world around us (Rutledge, 2012).
- Health and Safety: Given a child's development and the potential for headsets to cause potential motion sickness, disorientation, eye strain and other issues, it is strongly advised that young children in primary schools should only interact with handheld devices.
- Privacy: Personal data collection from an end user is a significant ethical concern. The use of AR in public spaces presents challenges in respecting other people's privacy and ensuring a device does not record an environment without consent. Wearable AR technologies in a classroom will need to be regulated to protect privacy.

Summary and key points

If AR is to be used as an effective learning tool within future primary classrooms, the challenge for designers, and for teachers, is to scaffold children's explorations and manipulations of the AR elements within carefully designed parameters to ensure that specific learning aims can be achieved within a relatively short period of time. Teacher's questions need to be less about what the children can see and more about describing the effects of what they have done and what they have learnt from their actions. (Kerawalla *et al.*, 2006). There is evidence from previous studies (Akçayır and Akçayır, 2017; Wang, 2018; Radu, 2014 and Yuen *et al.*, 2011) that educators and learning designers need to collaborate in terms of creating sound pedagogy to develop AR applications that maximise learning outcomes. Some key points about AR are:

- Augmented reality is already making an impact on education by providing unique learning experiences.
- The medium has not set out to replace traditional teaching and nor does it have the capabilities to do that.
- Technologies should supplement not replace 'hands on experience'.
- AR has the ability to overlay virtual content in almost any location. It opens up new domains for location-based AR and how we interact with our environment. This is where the technology can contextualise everyday objects and make science relevant to our lives. There are already existing AR applications where characters are brought to life in your own living room or garden through storytelling. Interactive textbooks provide ways of visualising abstract information. Games can be played in collaboration and AR can playfully interact with real objects. All these variants have great potential to explore new ways of teaching subject matter such as in the sciences to young children.

In terms of using digital technology for education, the Education Endowment Foundation asks fundamental questions regarding what schools need to consider to ensure that effective use of digital technology is driven by learning and teaching goals rather than a specific technology: the technology is not an end in itself. You should be clear about how any new technology will improve teaching and learning interactions. Key points to remember in using AR in the classroom include:

- New technology does not automatically lead to increased attainment.
- How any new technology will support pupils to work harder, for longer, or more efficiently, to improve their learning.
- Pupils' motivation to use technology does not always translate into more effective learning, particularly if the use of the technology and the desired learning outcomes are not closely aligned.
- Teachers need support and time to learn to use new technology effectively. This involves more than just learning how to use the hardware or software; training should also support teachers to understand how it can be used for learning.

Further resources

Adobe Aero, https://www.adobe.com/uk/products/aero.html. Accessed 10 February 2023.
Blippar, https://www.blippar.com. Accessed 10 February 2023.
Creative Play Lab – LEGO AR – Studio, https://kids.lego.com/en-gb/play. Accessed 10 February 2023.
Magical Park, https://www.geoargames.com/magical-park. Accessed 10 February 2023.
Merge Cube, https://mergeedu.com/cube. Accessed 9 February 2023.
Niantic, https://lightship.dev/. Accessed 10 February 2023.
Vuforia, https://library.vuforia.com/getting-started/vuforia-features. Accessed 10 February 2023
Wikitude, https://www.wikitude.com/. Accessed 10 February 2023.
Wonderscope, https://www.commonsensemedia.org/app-reviews/wonderscope. Accessed 10 February 2023.
Zappar, https://www.zappar.com/. Accessed 10 February 2023.

References

Akçayır, M., and Akçayır, G. (2017) Advantages and challenges associated with augmented for education: A systematic review of the literature. *Educ Res Rev*, 20, 1–11.
Andujar, J., Mejias, A., and Marquez., M. (2011, August) Augmented reality for the improvement of remote laboratories: An augmented remote laboratory. *IEEE Transactions on Education*, 54(3), 492–500. doi: 10.1109/TE.2010.2085047.
Azuma, R.T. (1997) A survey of augmented reality. *Presence: Teleoperators and Virtual Environments*, 6, 355–385.
Billinghurst, M., Kato, H., and Poupyrev, I. (2001) e Magic Book – Moving seamlessly between reality and virtuality. *IEEE Computers, Graphics and Applications*, 21(3), 2–4.
Billinghurst, M. (2002) Augmented reality in education. *New Horizons for Learning*, 12(5), 1–5.
Bower, M., Howe, C., McCredie, N., Robinson, A., and Grover, D. (2014) Augmented Reality in education – Cases, places and potentials. *Educational Media International*, 51(1), 1–15.
Brinson, J.R. (2015) Learning outcome achievement in non-traditional (virtual and remote) versus traditional (hands-on) laboratories. A review of the empirical research. *Computers and Education*, 87, 218–237.
British Educational Suppliers Association (BESA) (2018) *EdTech and ICT survey*. Promethean House. https://www.besa.org.uk/insights/technology-supporting-education-2018/.

Chen, P., Liu, X., Cheng, W., and Huang, R. (2017) A review of using Augmented Reality in education from 2011 to 2016. In: *Innovations in Smart Learning*. Lecture Notes in Educational Technology. Singapore: Springer. https://doi.org/10.1007/978-981-10-2419-1_2.

Cimen, G., Yuan, Y., Sumner., R., Coros, S., and Guay, M. (2018, January) Interacting with intelligent characters in AR. *International SERIES on Information Systems and Management in Creative eMedia (CreMedia) [S.l.]*, n. 2017/2, 24–29. ISSN 2341–5576.

Dede, C. (Speaker). (2008) *Immersive interfaces for learning: Opportunities and perils* [motion picture]. The President and Fellows of Harvard College.

Dede, C. (2009). Immersive interfaces for engagement and learning. *Science*, 323(5910), 66–69. doi: 10.1126/science.1167311.

Dunleavy, M., Dede, C., and Mitchell, R. (2009) Affordances and limitations of immersive participatory augmented reality simulations for teaching and learning. *Journal of Science Education and Technology*, 18(1), 7–22.

Dunleavy, M., and Dede, C. (2014) Augmented reality teaching and learning. In Spector, J., Merrill, M., Elen, J., and Bishop, M. (eds) *Handbook of research on educational communications and technology*. New York: Springer. https://doi.org/10.1007/978-1-4614-3185-5_59.

Dunleavy, M. (2014) Design principles for augmented reality learning. *TechTrends*, 58, 28–34. https://doi.org/10.1007/s11528-013-0717-2.

Fearn, W., and Hook., J. (2023) A service design thinking approach: What are the barriers and opportunities of using Augmented Reality for Primary Science Education? *Journal of Technology and Science Education*, 13(1). http://dx.doi.org/10.3926/jotse.1394.

Heilig., M.L. (1992) El cine del futuro: The cinema of the future. *Presence: Teleoperators, and Virtual Environments*, 1, 279–294. (Reprinted from *Espacios*, 23–24, 1955).

Huang., T, Chen, C., and Chou, Y. (2016) Animating eco-education: To see, feel, and discover in an augmented reality-based experiential learning environment. *Computers & Education*, 96(1), 72–82. https://doi.org/10.1016/j.compedu.2016.02.008.

Jenkins, H. (2009) *Confronting the challenges of participatory culture: Media education for the 21st century*. Massachusetts Institute of Technology The MIT Press.

Lee, K. (2012) Augmented reality in education and training. *TechTrends*, 56, 13–21. https://doi.org/10.1007/s11528-012-0559-3.

Kaufmann., H. (2003) Collaborative Augmented Reality in Education. In: *Imagina Conference 2003*. Imagina. Monaco: Monaco Mediax.

Kerawalla, L., Luckin, R., Seljeflot, S., and Woolard, A. (2006) "Making it real": Exploring the potential of augmented reality for teaching primary school science. *Virtual Reality*, 10, 163–174. https://doi.org/10.1007/s10055-006-0036-4.

Kiryakova, G., Yordanova, L., and Nadezhda, A. (2018) The potential of augmented reality to transform education into Smart education. *TEM Journal*, 7(3), 556–565. doi: 10.18421/TEM73-11.

Klopfer, E., and Sheldon J. (2010, Winter) Augmenting your own reality: Student authoring of science-based augmented reality games. *New Dir Youth Dev.* (128), 85–94. doi: 10.1002/yd.378. PMID: 21240956.

Klopfer, E., and Squire, K. (2008) Environmental detectives—The development of an augmented reality platform for environmental simulations. *Educational Technology Research and Development*, 56(2), 203–228.

Laine, T. (2018) Mobile educational augmented reality games: A systematic literature review and two case studies. *Computers*, 7(1), 19. https://doi.org/10.3390/computers7010019.

Novak, D., Wang, M.J., Callaghan, V., and Zhao X.L. (2012) Looking in, looking out: Augmented reality created by LCD heads-up displays and personal projectors. In Jia, J.Y. (ed) *Educational stages and interactive learning: From kindergarten to workplace training*. Hershey: IGI Publishing, 92–106.

Onime, C., and Abiona, O. (2016) 3D mobile augmented reality interface for laboratory experiments. *International Journal of Communications, Network and System Sciences*, 9, 67–76. doi: 10.4236/ijcns.2016.94006.

Radu, L. (2014, August). Augmented reality in education: a meta-review and cross-media analysis. *Personal & Ubiquitous Computing*, 18(6), 1533–1543.

Radu, C., and Ionitescu, S. (2015) *Perspectives on implementing interactive e-learning tools using augmented reality in education.* Bucharest: The International Scientific Conference eLearning and Software for Education, 1, 104–111.

Rutledge, P. (2012) *Augmented reality: Brain-based persuasion model.* Proceedings of the International Conference on e-Learning, e-Business, Enterprise Information Systems, and e-Government (EEE), 1. The Steering Committee of The World Congress in Computer Science, Computer Engineering and Applied Computing (WorldComp).

Southgate, E., Smith, S.P., and Scevak, J. (2017) Asking ethical questions in research using immersive virtual and augmented reality technologies with children and youth. *2017 IEEE Virtual Reality (VR)*, 12–18.

U.S. Department of Education, Office of Innovation and Improvement. (2016) *STEM 2026: A vision for innovation in STEM education.* Washington, DC: Author.

Wang, M., Callaghan, V., Bernhardt, J., White, K., and Peña-Ríos, A. (2018) Augmented reality in education and training: Pedagogical approaches and illustrative case studies. *Journal of Ambient Intelligence and Humanized Computing*, 9, 1391–1402.

Wu, H., Lee, S., Chang, H., and Liang, J. (2013) Current status, opportunities and challenges of augmented reality in education. *Computers and Education*, 62, 41–49. https://doi.org/10.1016/j.compedu.2012.10.024.

Yuen, S., Yaoyuneyong, G., and Johnson, E. (2011) Augmented reality: An overview and five directions for AR in education. *Journal of Educational Technology Development and Exchange* (JETDE), 4(1), Article 11. doi: 10.18785/jetde.0401.10.

Zhou, F., Duh, H., and Billinghurst, M. (2008) Trends in augmented reality tracking, interaction and display: A review of ten years of ISMAR. In: *2008 7th IEEE/ACM International Symposium on Mixed and Augmented Reality.* Cambridge, 193–202. doi: 10.1109/ISMAR.2008.4637362.

Zhu, Y., Yang, X., and Jia Wang, S. (2017) Augmented reality meets tangibility: A new approach for early childhood education. *EAI Endorsed Transactions on Creative Technologies*, 4(11), e2. doi: 10.4108/eai.5–9–2017.153059.

19 Interactive technologies and outdoor learning

Gary Beauchamp, Sammy Chapman, Nick Young and Kristina Kelly

Introduction

The benefits of outdoor learning in the primary school have long been recognised globally and have become increasingly embedded in the different curricula of schools in the four countries of the United Kingdom (UK) and beyond (Adams and Beauchamp, 2019). This is part of the emergence of a movement to reconnect children with nature (Miller *et al.*, 2021). At the same time, interest in the potential for using interactive technologies in outdoor learning in primary schools is growing (Stymne, 2020). In this chapter we will examine the potential, and challenges, of exploiting the potential of technologies in combination with the unique environments available outside of the classroom.

Rickinson *et al.* (2004:16) summarise three main types of outdoor learning activities:

- **'fieldwork and outdoor visits** – where the focus is on undertaking learning activities, often linked with particular curriculum subjects ... in outdoor settings such as field study centres, nature centres, farms, parks or gardens
- **outdoor adventure education** – where the focus is on participation in outdoor adventurous activities ...
- **school grounds and community-based projects** – where learning activities take place in or near to the school, with a range of curricular, cross-curricular and/or extra-curricular purposes ...'.

What they have in common is the centrality of engaging with (including touching, feeling and smelling!), and benefitting from, natural surroundings (both near and far) outside of a building. Throughout this chapter, we will focus on the use of technologies in outdoor visits, in the school grounds and in the community – but the principles remain the same for all these settings.

Objectives

At the end of this chapter you should be able to:

- recognise the potential of interactive technologies for enhancing outdoor learning
- recognise the unique affordances mobile technologies and the natural environment provide for outdoor learning.

DOI: 10.4324/9781003408925-19

Technology and outdoor learning: a paradox?

Outdoor learning is hard to define and can incorporate a multitude of other terms, such as nature-based learning, adventure education, experiential education or environmental education and ecology education. It also includes particular ways of working with nature, or movements which are guided by specific beliefs, with practitioners receiving specific training based on these, such as forest schools (Harris, 2018). In addition, there are also differing views on whether outdoor education should be a means of achieving aspects of a curriculum, or an end in itself, where 'being in nature' can provide 'an engagement with nature that allows us to transcend everyday reality and, in doing so, experience a more authentic existence and an enhanced understanding of life' (Beauchamp, Adams and Smith, 2023:63).

Outdoor learning in its simplest form can be defined as 'education *in, about* and *for* the outdoors' (Donaldson and Donaldson, 1958:17). This definition, however, blurs an important distinction between 'outdoor learning' (*in* and *for*) and 'learning about the outdoors' (*about*). A broader definition is suggested by the Institute for Outdoor Learning (2021), which describes outdoor learning as 'an umbrella term for actively inclusive facilitated approaches that predominately use activities and experiences in the outdoors which lead to learning, increased health and wellbeing, and environmental awareness'. However, the idea that this learning is 'facilitated' neglects spontaneous learning that can occur when primary pupils encounter a natural setting. Nevertheless, this definition does acknowledge the wider benefits of outdoor learning in addition to the academic and does include activities and experiences in the outdoors, as sometimes just being outdoors is a good thing.

Learning through activities and experiences, whether familiar or unfamiliar to the children, can take place in a range of outdoor spaces, such as school grounds, gardens, wetlands (Green and Rayner, 2022), or coastal environments (Barrable and Barrable, 2022). The perceived benefits of outdoor learning include academic attainment and self-confidence (Barrable and Booth, 2020), as well as social, emotional and psychological well-being improvements (Harun and Salamuddin, 2014), even if only using the school grounds (Harvey *et al.*, 2020).

Green and Rayner (2022) suggest that outdoor learning should be focused on the integration of curriculum content and meaningful learning experiences – although we argue there is also a case for just being in a natural setting for its own sake to reconnect with nature and the 'more-than-human' world (Beauchamp, Adams and Smith, 2023). Outdoor learning is *not* simply taking activities designed for the traditional classroom and placing them in the outdoors. It should exploit the potential benefits of learning outdoors, such as interacting with natural resources, increased space and having autonomy to explore this space (Barrable and Barrable, 2022). Therefore, the affordances of outdoor environments should provide the starting point for the learning activities.

Considering the best way of using technology in this context is not totally straightforward, as there has always been the potential for a perceived tension between technology use and outdoor learning. Cuthbertson, Socha and Potter (2004) suggest that using technology outdoors can threaten pupil's engagement with nature. They suggest technology use is thus a 'double-edged sword' as, for example, the concept of being 'present in the moment' can feel threatened by the recording and capturing of such moments using a camera or mobile phone. Thus, an important challenge for primary teachers considering the use of technology outdoors is to be 'more deeply aware of how technology can mediate people's relations to nature' (van Kraalingen, 2021:3). Nevertheless, it is worth it, as 'Digital technology can undermine the aim of being outdoors, but it can also create opportunities to enhance outdoor learning experiences' (Hills and Thomas, 2020:115).

In this chapter we will consider a range of specific activities, but these are to exemplify specific affordances, rather than provide examples of perceived good practice. We would thus encourage you to use these as starting points to stimulate your own pedagogic imaginations of what else *you and your pupils* could do with these and other technologies.

Technologies in outdoor learning

Technologies have been used in outdoor activities for many years. For example, a compass can be used for navigation and paper maps for geographical location. What is new with developing mobile technologies is sophisticated location tracking, geographical orientation and geo-tagging, which can be managed via a mobile device (Bolliger and Shepherd, 2017). Similarly, a clipboard and pen enable pupils to make notes in an outdoor setting, but now with a tablet device they can produce text, and incorporate images and sound, and share in real time with another class in school – or indeed anywhere around the world. Simply substituting the traditional device for a more expensive mobile device, however, is not enough. We need to question *why* we would use the technology in the first place. We suggest a good starting point is to ask the following questions in order:

1. Can the technology do something that cannot be done any other way?
2. Can the technology do it quicker, better or add a new dimension (such as automatic saving, or sharing with others in real time [synchronously] or a recording [asynchronous])?
3. What affordance(s) of the technology am I using and why?
4. Will the technology **enable** or **enhance** engagement with the natural environment?
5. Is the technology suitable for the age group being taught (e.g. too big to hold steady) or can it be simplified or adapted (add a big grip for smaller hands)?
6. What skills (if any) do I need to teach the pupils in advance to use the technology(ies) effectively?
7. Are there any child protection issues that need to be considered (e.g. consent for pictures etc.)?

If the technology can do something nothing else can, or can do it better and quicker, to enhance engagement with the natural environment, it is probably worth using, and/or spending the time teaching the pupils (and yourself) any necessary skills.

TIP: Don't forget the obvious considerations, such as devices need charging or that you need strong enough wi-fi to connect to the internet (e.g. does it cover the whole of the school's grounds or is it available where you are visiting?).

Now undertake Task 19.1.

Task 19.1: What technologies to use outdoors and why?

On your own, or with others, consider a piece of technology you have available in school and think about, or discuss, these questions to decide whether and how to use with the age group you are teaching:

1. Would you use it in outdoor learning?
2. What would it add to the learning?
3. Why, when and how?
4. What preparation (e.g. charging or getting wi-fi passwords) is necessary?
5. Are there any child protection issues that need to be considered (e.g. consent for pictures etc.)?

An important feature of technology is that it can help support 'seamless learning' between in-school and out-of-school contexts (Kali *et al.*, 2018:1145). This means that learning begun in school can continue outdoors and vice versa. In this context, however, it is vital that the outdoor environment, and the use of technology, offer something distinctive, which exploits a unique feature of each – something that cannot be done any other way or is done better through the use of technology.

Affordances

Therefore, in making decisions to use technologies outdoors, it is essential to identify what they are good at and how this can be exploited. In a systematic review of technology in outdoor learning, Van Kraalingen (2021) argues that perceiving and using affordances of technologies (put simply, something which offers the potential for doing something) are vital. In essence this means seeing how a unique feature (e.g. digital video camera on a tablet) can be used in combination with the outdoor environment to achieve meaningful activities (including learning) while engaging with nature. For example, when learning *about* the outdoors, in this case about invasive species (plants and animals), it is possible to use the unique affordance of geo-tagging on a trip to an outdoor setting to 'drop a pin' to record the precise location in a way impossible with traditional maps. This also means that this information can be saved and used for other discussions when back in the classroom – an example of seamless learning. In addition, however, a tablet device could also take photos, videos or even sound recordings of what was seen during explorations. The same process could also be used to note insect life, leaves, birds and types of trees. All of these used the affordances of technology to do something that is very hard, or impossible, to do any other way.

Mobile technologies

The examples above are also uses of mobile technology, which is perhaps the most obvious, and most appropriate, form of technology to discuss when considering using technologies in outdoor settings. Mobile technology is defined as any form of technology that is portable, whilst also providing a clear purpose – such as communication or documentation (Weilenmann, 2001). In addition, increasing internet connection and widespread service providers, alongside greater functionality and user understanding, create a greater argument for the use of mobile technologies in outdoor learning (Hwang, Chou and Huang, 2021). For example, in a discussion about Forest Schools, Garden (2022:3–4) gives an example of children seeing an affordance in the iPad and explains that

> when building a bug den in pairs, the children used an iPad to audio record themselves discussing how the den should be built or made a series of videos over time, showing how they built the den and how the bugs gradually occupied it. In using iPads in this way, the children are doing much more than making a record of their activities; they are learning and creating meaning by interacting with the iPads both individually and as a collaborative pair of learners.

Using technology to support face-to-face collaboration like this is important in outdoor learning, as is trying to include actual physical interaction with the environment, not just more distant activities, such as taking pictures (Eliasson, 2013). For example, mobile technology can be used outdoors to help answer questions, solve problems and help pupils attend to details they may have missed the first time (Siskind *et al.*, 2022).

Having said this, the potential of technology to add information to the environment should not be neglected. Using the affordances, or combination of affordances, of mobile technologies can be done in many existing ways (such as a camera and internet connection with QR codes), but there is also potential, in the near future, to use other technologies (such as Augmented Reality, 360° video and Near Field Communication – the technology involved when using contactless payments).

QR codes have been used for many activities indoors and can also be used outdoors, particularly for learning *about* the environment. They are good for quickly providing links to additional text, images or information (if connected to the internet), which provide further information to learners when used in outdoor learning activities (Lai *et al.*, 2013).

Now undertake Task 19.2.

Task 19.2: Assessing the educational potential of digital tools or games

On your own, or with others, read the example below of a type of technology not originally designed for education being adapted for use in learning. After you have read it, on your own, or with others, decide:

1. Is this outdoor learning?
2. Is this a good use of technology outdoors?
3. Does this trigger any ideas of your own for using types of technology not originally designed for education being adapted for use in learning?

The popular 2016 summer craze of 'Pokémon Go' was, on the face of it, a game of catching creatures and completing what is known as the 'Pokédex'. However, the game also promoted outdoor exploration, regular daily exercise and spending time in nature (Mozelius, Bergström-Eriksson and Jaldemark, 2017). This presents a marriage of mobile technology and outdoor spaces, encouraging children to explore outdoor environments through the medium of an interactive game. Whilst this does demonstrate the benefits of technology to encourage exercise and exploration, it can be argued that the 'feeling of presence' is threatened by a heavy focus on the game itself (Cuthbertson, Socha and Potter, 2004). However, Pokémon Go also demonstrates how the evolving nature of technology can combat these rising issues. Built within the application is an Augmented Reality feature, whereby Pokémon can be photographed within real-world outdoor environments, such as a flowerbed, local forest or in your own garden. This promotes the consumption of both the game functions, but also the nature and outdoor spaces being explored whilst playing. However, Mozelius, Bergström-Eriksson and Jaldemark (2017) suggest that children tend to find enjoyment and distraction in the game itself rather than the learning taking place.

Capturing the outdoors

While it is never possible to authentically capture or recreate the experiences of learning outdoors, technologies do allow pupils to capture some elements of that experience, such as sounds, images and locations. These can be used as ends in themselves (such as an assessment activity) or as a part of ongoing learning. For instance, although using older technology, Ohashi and Makoto (2006) report on an activity in a Japanese primary school, where primary pupils combined different technologies (but now possible within one device) to record sounds and the geographical location of these audio segments. These were then layered onto aerial photographs via Google Maps to create a virtual sound map.

It could be argued, however, that recording the sounds whilst in nature can limit pupils' sense of presence, attention and physical interaction with nature. Nevertheless, through recording and capturing these sounds, children are able to use them within multiple areas of learning to reflect back on the activities experienced whilst outdoors in a way that would be impossible without technology.

Pupil autonomy

What may be apparent by now is that, although there are many affordances of using technology to enhance and inform learning outdoors, there remains a tension between using the technologies and the inevitable way this mediates this interaction by coming between pupils and 'an engagement with nature that allows us to transcend everyday reality and, in doing so, experience a more authentic existence and an enhanced understanding of life' (Beauchamp, Adams and Smith, 2023:63).

Nevertheless, if we accept this compromise, we have seen that the affordances of technology can offer unique potential to enhance and capture aspects of interactions with nature. It is important, however, that these affordances are not just those recognised by the teacher. If we accept that 'mobile technology encourages pupils to take control of their own learning, allowing pupils to establish from their own learning goals' (Domingo and Garganté, 2016:22), then we must also accept that part of pupils taking control is to use the technology in a way *they* perceive is best when learning outdoors.

Summary and key points

Learning through activities and experiences can take place in a range of outdoor spaces, such as school grounds, gardens, wetlands and the seaside, but sometimes just being outdoors, particularly in nature, is enough in itself. Using technologies outdoors can enhance learning, but can also undermine the aim of being outdoors, so there are factors which you should consider before using technology outdoors:

- Outdoor learning is *not* simply taking activities designed for the traditional classroom and placing them in the outdoors, but should exploit the potential benefits of the outdoor environment, such as interacting with nature.
- Using technology in outdoor learning cannot replace unique experiences of touching, smelling and interacting with the natural world.
- Technologies can be a 'double-edged sword', so before using technologies outdoors, you need to question *why* you are using them at all?.
- Technologies should be used to exploit the unique affordances you **and** your pupils see in them to, for example, enhance, augment and capture (e.g. sound and image) experiences.
- Data from these experiences can be used to develop 'seamless learning' between indoors and outdoors.

Further resources

Siskind, D., Conlin, D., Hestenes, L., Kim, S.A., Barnes, A. and Yaya-Bryson, D. (2020) Balancing Technology and Outdoor Learning: Implications for Early Childhood Teacher Educators, *Journal of Early Childhood Teacher Educators*, 389–405.
    This journal discusses the benefits and challenges of different technologies in connection with the outdoors and concludes by discussing technology's place within outdoor learning.
Teach Early Years: Outdoor ICT https://www.teachearlyyears.com/enabling-environments/view/outdoor-ict.
    This website gives examples of different ways in which technology can be implemented for younger pupils. Accessed 14.12.22.
Creative Star https://creativestarlearning.co.uk/.
    Juliet Robertson is an author around outdoor learning and play. Her website has many blog entries with accompanying videos of outdoor play practice. This is a good resource for teachers, who could gain inspiration from the activities and then plan ways to implement technology successfully. Accessed 14.12.22.
Watts, A. (2020) *Outdoor Learning through the Seasons: An Essential Guide for the Early Years*. Oxon, Routledge.
    Watts outlines outdoors activities, with some examples of how technology can be used. There are also case studies throughout to support outdoor learning pedagogy.

References

Adams, D. and Beauchamp, G. (2019) Spiritual moments making music in nature. A study exploring the experiences of children making music outdoors, surrounded by nature, *International Journal of Children's Spirituality*, 24(3), 260–275.
Barrable, A. and Booth, D. (2020) Increasing nature connection in children: A mini review of interventions, *Frontiers in Psychology*, 11(726). Available at: https://doi.org/10.3389/fpsyg.2020.00492.

Barrable, D. and Barrable, A. (2022) Affordances of coastal environments to support teaching and learning: Outdoor learning at the beach in Scotland, *Education 3–13*, 1–12. Available at: https://doi.org/10.1080/03004279.2022.2100440.

Beauchamp, G., Adams, D. and Smith, K. (2023) *Pedagogies for the future: A critical reimagining of education*, The Routledge Education Studies Series. London, Routledge.

Bolliger, D. U. and Shepherd, C. E. (2017) An investigation of mobile technologies and web 2.0 tools use in outdoor education programs, *Journal of Outdoor Recreation, Education, and Leadership*, 9(2), 181–196.

Cuthbertson, B., Socha, T. L. and Potter, T. G. (2004) The double-edged sword: Critical reflections on traditional and modern technology in outdoor education, *Journal of Adventure Education and Outdoor Learning*, 4(2), 133–144.

Domingo, M. G. and Garganté, A. B. (2016) Exploring the use of educational technology in primary education: Teachers' perception of mobile technology learning impacts and applications use in the classroom, *Computers in Human Behavior*, 56, 21–28.

Donaldson, G. W. and Donaldson, L. E. (1958) Outdoor education: A definition, *Journal of Health, Physical Education and Recreation*, 29(5), 17–63.

Eliasson, J. (2013) *Tools for designing mobile interaction with the physical environment in outdoor lessons.* Available at: http://su.diva-portal.org/smash/get/diva2:646160/FULLTEXT01.pdf. Accessed 14.12.22.

Garden, A. (2022) An exploration of children's experiences of the use of digital technology in forest schools. *Journal of Adventure Education and Outdoor Learning*, 1–15. Available at: https://doi.org/10.1080/14729679.2022.2111693.

Green, M. and Rayner, M. (2022) School ground pedagogies for enriching children's outdoor learning, *Education 3–13*, 50(2), 238–251. Available at: https://doi.org/10.1080/03004279.2020.1846578.

Harris, F. (2018) Outdoor learning spaces: The case of forest school, *Area (London 1969)*, 50(2), 222–231.

Harun, M. T. and Salamuddin, N. (2014) Promoting social skills through outdoor education and assessing its effects, *Asian Social Science*, 10(5), 71.

Harvey, D. J., Montgomery, L. N., Harvey, H., Hall, F., Gange, A. C. and Watling, D. (2020) Psychological benefits of a biodiversity-focussed outdoor learning program for primary school children, *Journal of Environmental Psychology*, 67(101381), 1–8.

Hills, D. and Thomas, G. (2020) Digital technology and outdoor experiential learning, *Journal of Adventure Education and Outdoor Learning*, 20(2), 155–169.

Hwang, B.-L., Chou, T.-C. and Huang, C.-H. (2021) Actualizing the affordance of mobile technology for mobile learning: A main path analysis of mobile learning, *Educational Technology and Society*, 24(4), 67–80.

Institute for Outdoor Learning (2021) *Outdoor learning.* Available at: https://www.outdoor-learning.org/Portals/0/IOL%20Documents/About%20Outdoor%20Learning/RR1%20-%20Describing%20Outdoor%20Learning%202-8-21.pdf?ver=2021-08-10-133755-690. Accessed 14.12.22.

Kali, Y., Levy, K.-S., Levin-Peled, R. and Tal, T. (2018) Supporting outdoor inquiry learning (SOIL): Teachers as designers of mobile-assisted seamless learning, *British Journal of Educational Technology*, 49(6), 1145–1161.

Lai, H., Chang, C., Li, W., Fan, Y. and Wu, Y. (2013) The implementation of mobile learning in outdoor education: Application of QR codes, *British Journal of Educational Technology*, 44(2), 57–62.

Miller, N. C., Kumar, S., Pearce, K. L. and Baldock, K. L. (2021) The outcomes of nature-based learning for primary school aged children: A systematic review of quantitative research, *Environmental Education Research*, 27(8), 1115–1140.

Mozelius P., Bergström-Eriksson S. and Jaldemark, J. (2017) *Learning by walking: Pokémon GO and mobile technology in formal education.* In: 10th International Conference of Education, Research and Innovation, Seville, Spain, 16–18 November 2017. The International Academy of Technology, Education and Development, 1172–1179.

Ohashi, Y. and Makoto, A. (2006) Nature talk: A proposed audible database system for environmental learning, *Conference on Interaction Design and Children*, Finland, 167–168. Available at: https://doi.org/10.1145/1139073.1139077.

Rickinson, M., Dillon, J., Teamey, K., Morris, M., Young Choi, M., Sanders, D. and Benefield, P. (2004) *A review of research on outdoor learning*, London: National Foundation for Educational Research and King's College London.

Siskind, D., Conlin, D., Hestenes, L., Kim, S. A., Barnes, A. and Yaya-Bryson, D. (2022) Balancing technology and outdoor learning: Implications for early childhood teacher educators, *Journal of Early Childhood Teacher Education*, 43(3), 389–405.

Stymne, J. (2020) Outdoor learning with mobile technology: A systematic review, *IADIS International Journal on WWW/Internet*, 18(1), 76–106.

van Kraalingen, I. (2021) A systematized review of the use of mobile technology in outdoor learning, *Journal of Adventure Education and Outdoor Learning*, 1–19. Available at: https://doi.org/10.1080/14729679.2021.1984963.

Weilenmann, A. (2001) Negotiating use: Making sense of mobile technology, *Personal Ub Comp*, 5, 137–145.

20 Video conferencing and authentic learning in the primary school classroom

Damian Maher

Introduction

Video conferencing technologies are powerful digital tools that can support the interactions of primary school pupils. These technologies have been available in schools since the early 2000s where the availability of increased bandwidth, lower equipment prices, and standardisation of networks allows for widespread use (Roberts, 2009).

Some of the technological innovations that allow teachers to interact via video conferencing include suites of tablets, installed Wi-fi and bring-your-own-device schemes (Moorhouse and Wong, 2022). Another important technological innovation that enhances communication and collaboration between participants via video conferencing in the classroom is the interactive whiteboard (IWB) (Maher, 2014), which can "encourage the creation of a shared dialogic space within which co-constructed knowledge building can take place" (Warwick *et al.*, 2010, p. 350).

Video conferencing allows pupils to interact with people and places beyond their classroom. In this capacity, video conferencing allows pupils to learn from speakers and take educational tours without leaving their classrooms. As a result, pupils can learn about the people and places rather than by reading outdated textbooks, looking at pictures, or hearing from the teacher (Paderanga, 2014). Through video conferencing, teachers can bring the outside world into the classroom in an authentic and meaningful way. There is also the aspect of immediacy, where students can participate in events with people as they are unfolding. In considering school use, there are many-to-many connections (class to class), one-to-many (individuals interacting with the class), group to group, or one-to-one interactions, which can support learning. Pupils are also able to interact with each other, their teachers, and experts whilst in their classroom, in support of classroom learning.

The focus of this chapter is to examine the contemporary uses of video conferencing, focusing on pupils' interactions with peers and experts. Ways that video conferencing was used to support pupils during Covid-19, where many schools went into lockdowns, are examined. Ways that video conferencing supported pupils' social and emotional needs are also investigated.

Objectives

By the end of this chapter, you should be able to:

- understand the various models that underpin the use of video conferencing
- be aware of some of the pedagogical and logistical considerations of using video conferencing
- further integrate the use of video conferencing into your teaching practices.

DOI: 10.4324/9781003408925-20

The literature on video conferencing – a sociocultural view

Thinking has social origins and social interactions play an important role in the development of higher-order thinking skills (Vygotsky, 1978). Cognitive development cannot be fully understood without understanding the social and historical context within which it is embedded (Polly *et al.*, 2017). As Vygotsky explained: "Every function in the child's cultural development appears twice: first, on the social level, and later, on the individual level; first between people (interpsychological) and then inside the child (intrapsychological)" (Vygotsky, 1978, p. 57). It is through working with others on a variety of tasks that a learner adopts socially shared experiences and acquires useful strategies and knowledge (Scott and Palincsar, 2013). Social interaction is seen as a prerequisite for the growth and development of cognition (Donato and McCormick, 1994), and the physical and symbolic tools that link human interaction cannot be separated from the social environment in which such interactions occur (Wertsch, 1994).

Using video conferencing can be conceptualised within the framework of sociocultural theory (Wiesemes and Wang, 2010). Proponents of sociocultural theory argue that learning is primarily a social process mediated through interactions using tools (Leont'ev, 1981; Vygotsky, 1978). Video conferencing uses sophisticated hardware and software tools to connect learners across the globe using software such as Zoom, Skype, Facebook Live, TikTok Live, Microsoft Teams and Google Hangout.

One of the central tenets associated with sociocultural theory is the concept of authenticity. In undertaking *authentic learning activities*, the types of activities undertaken match as closely as possible the real-world tasks rather than decontextualised classroom-based tasks (Collins, Brown and Newman, 2018). In focusing on real-world experiences, they provide opportunities for more meaningful learning (Bennett, Harper and Hedberg, 2002).

An important component of sociocultural theory is that pupils learn with and from *authentic participants* where interactions are viewed as a process of mutual meaning and knowledge making (Babić, 2017). Interactions can be with classmates, others in the school, family, or community. Authentic participants who are part of the community could include experts, such as scientists and other professionals.

In the context of using video conferencing with experts, some of the skills pupils would be required to learn beyond the content skills include how to communicate with others safely and ethically in an online environment. The role of the teacher is significant here in supporting pupils to understand netiquette, which Pręgowski (2009) explained as having a good online citizen attitude. Attributes such as engagement, responsibility, tolerance, reliability, honesty, and helpfulness are part of netiquette. The role of the teacher also extends to being a moderator ensuring the online safety of pupils. Pupils also need to acquire technical skills, for both school and personal activities. These skills include conducting sound checks, using text chat, dealing with audio problems (Heiser, Stickler and Furnborough, 2013), navigation skills (Chou, 2001), and use of visual images such as emoticons.

The first task is for you to survey the pupils in your class to gain an understanding of their use of video conferencing at home by asking them the questions below. There may be other questions you may like to add. This will give you an indication of the types of activities you can start undertaking with them and with what skills they will need to be supported with. Now move to Task 20.1.

Task 20.1: Surveying the pupils

For this task, survey the students in your class about their use of videoconferencing in relation to the hardware and software they use as well as who they interact with and any restrictions on these interactions.

- what type of video conferencing, if any, do they use?
- what hardware do they use (desktop/laptop/mobile device/other)?
- if pupils are using their phones, what apps do they use for video conferencing?
- who do they interact with?
- what sort of restrictions, if any, do their parents put in place for their use?

Once you have this information consider how video conferencing might be effectively used in your classroom so that you can help to develop learning experiences for your pupils. Ask your pupils what types of activities they would like to undertake using video conferencing related to classroom learning.

Models available for using video conferencing

Various models have been developed to assist researchers and teachers understand how online learning, which can include the use of video conferencing, can add value to the learning experience of young people.

The most common model employing video conferencing involves the pupils and the teacher in classroom interaction with one external person. This other person might be another pupil at the school, a pupil at another school, a parent, or an expert. This type of conferencing provides opportunities for the class to visually experience the location of the external participant. One example might involve a pupil who has gone on vacation and is sharing their location with the class. Another example could be where an expert is invited to talk to the pupils.

The use of video conferencing can reposition the role of the teacher. In a traditional classroom the teacher is generally the sole knowledge provider – the gatekeeper. In using video conferencing, a greater number of experts can be called upon to supplement the knowledge of the teacher and to incorporate different types of expertise. This expansion of experts allows new learning opportunities for both the pupils and the teacher.

One consideration in facilitating conversation with the class is audio. It can be difficult for the internal microphone of a computer to pick up the voice of a pupil at the back of a classroom. Ideally, pupils should have access to a microphone so that their voices can be easily heard by the external participant. This form of video conferencing provides the teacher with control over the conversation and tends to be very teacher-centred with question/answer style conversations.

A variation of a one-to-many interaction is the many-to-many interaction. This can take the form of a class interacting with another class, or a group interacting with a group. The number of participants in a group can be as few as two. According to Knapp (2018), because participants can all see and hear each other and interact spontaneously and informally, these interactions tend to have a similar feel to a face-to-face class discussion.

Group interactions are now possible with software such as Zoom that facilitates the use of breakout rooms. It is also possible to start with the whole class interacting, then move to small group discussions, and then back to a whole-class discussion. These types of interaction groupings mirror the type of groupings that are generally found in face-to-face classroom discussions. In using Zoom, other functions that can be accessed include "chat, screen annotation, polling, non-verbal feedback, … and virtual whiteboards" (Fackler and Sexton, 2020, p. 8). These features allow for interactions that closely resemble face-to-face engagement in a classroom.

The external participant can also use mobile technology via a smartphone or tablet with a video conferencing app, which allows them to share a roving view of their surroundings. An example of this is where a dental assistant showed a surgery to the pupils (Maher, 2022). In using the technology, close ups and panoramic views could be facilitated. One consideration in using video conferencing through a mobile phone is the expense involved in sharing data over a network. Video conferencing involves both audio and video and this can mean large amounts of data, which can be costly.

Another model is the *hybrid learning model*, which Hinterberger, Fässler and Bauer-Messmer (2004) define as the method of educating at a distance using technology, combined with traditional education. In this model, the teachers and some pupils are present in the classroom, while other pupils are participating simultaneously from their home, or another external location. Synchronous hybrid learning has been reported to be a more flexible learning environment compared to fully online or fully on-site instruction (Raes *et al.*, 2020). This model became common in schools during Covid-19, where schools closed, but some of the pupils were required to come physically to the classroom because their parents were working in essential services, for example.

There are differences in video conferencing discussions compared to face-to-face discussions, which has implications for learning. Some of the differences in synchronous online discussions are that they are "fast-paced, socially demanding, and attention consuming…" (Belt and Lowenthal, 2021, p. 422). These differences need to be considered when running hybrid learning sessions. Another consideration is how to give online pupils the same opportunities to contribute to discussions as pupils in the classroom. This requires careful pedagogical and organisational considerations.

Hybrid learning can be used in schools to include pupils who are unable to attend regular classes through illness or incapacity. An example of hybrid learning is where pupils in hospitals participated in classroom learning using video conferencing (Maher, 2022). In one observed lesson, a pupil in a hospital ward was provided with resources and carried out experiments along with peers and the teacher, from the hospital classroom. One of the benefits was that the pupil on the ward was able to participate in the lesson being conducted in the classroom. Through participation in this lesson the pupil was able to learn about physical reactions and converse with the teacher and other pupils. This helped reduce his sense of isolation, which is an issue for pupils who are unable to join their regular classes.

Another opportunity to use video conferencing could be for pupils who are travelling. Keeping pupils connected via video conferencing helps them stay up to date with their work and stay in contact with their school friends. This is particularly important for pupils who may be unable to attend class for a long period of time. The use of video conferencing allows pupils to share their experiences with the rest of the class. This presents the opportunity to design units of work that incorporate the experiences of the pupil. This might include music or food. The travelling pupil can then present their ideas along with the rest of the class. If the pupil is doing a road trip, this presents opportunities for the class to track the progress of the travelling pupil and complete work based on locations, and talk with the travelling pupil about geographical locations. Maths could also be built into the unit where distances travelled, and other related concepts are included.

Another model is the *blended learning model*, which is a pedagogy that combines online teaching methodologies with traditional face-to-face instruction (Hwang, 2019). Blended learning in K-12 education is most likely an adaptation or variation on face-to-face learning (Crippen, Bokor and Evans, 2018). Using this model pupils spend time together in the class and time together online on separate occasions. The online sessions can also be with different teachers or peers. This model was used by some teachers during Covid-19, allowing pupils to attend classes face-to-face some days while receiving instruction via video conferencing and other digital means on other days. A more detailed use of video conferencing during Covid-19 is examined in the next section.

As a form of e-learning, blended learning is the most useful way to integrate technology into education (Kloos *et al.*, 2015). There are advantages to a blended learning model. One advantage is that an active learning environment is created with flexibility in using resources for the pupils, providing more time for teachers to spend with learners in small groups or individually (Oh and Park, 2009). Another advantage is there is the potential to change pupils' experiences and outcomes through learning (Davis and Fill, 2007). One of the limitations in primary schools relates to the supervision of the pupils where duty of care means an adult needs to be responsible.

One example of blended learning occurred in Utah in the United States. The Utah Online School opened with elementary grades in 2004 and developed blended programmes combining online and onsite content and pupil support. The programmes were offered to help pupils master the content (Rice and Dykman, 2018). Another example operated in Singapore. Staker (2022) reports on a project where 22 secondary schools and one primary school teacher have formed a Blended Learning Community of Practice (COP). This group came about in response to Singapore's Ministry of Education (MOE) requiring its teachers to prepare pupils for a new era, seeing blended learning as part of the solution. The program is supported by the Flex model, an online platform that "provides the backbone for students' self-directed work, so students continue to learn, whether they are at home or in person; they are not dependent on an in-person instructor to deliver the lesson live" (Staker, 2022, p. 14).

The blended learning model is one that is likely to be increasingly utilised, driven in part, by Covid-19 experiences. An example of this is where the Australian Productivity Commission has suggested a move to the use of video and online technology to provide access to qualified teachers (Commonwealth of Australia, 2022). This practice is currently in place and mainly aimed at secondary students, but there will be an expanded use of video conferencing supported by a blended learning model.

The use of video conferencing during Covid-19

During 2020, 1.7 billion pupils globally were affected by the closure of schools and higher education institutions and 194 countries implemented nationwide closures. This affected approximately 92% of the world's pupil population (UNESCO, n.d.). In response to the closure of schools, many classes around the world went online where synchronous classes were conducted virtually with the support of video conferencing technology. The four most popular video conferencing applications used were Skype, Zoom, Google Hangouts and Microsoft Teams (Kristóf, 2020). These applications were often used with learning management systems (LMSs).

The use of video conferencing aimed to support pupils' social/emotional needs during Covid-19. According to Taskiran (2021) the social and psychological development of children through interactions during formal education at schools is important. Long-term isolation from school environments can affect psycho-social well-being of children negatively (Gifford-Smith and Brownell, 2003) leading to missed-out formative relationships with peers, and more importantly, missed-out opportunities for play (Levinson, Cevik and Lipsitch, 2020). Some aspects that were reported by parents as being important to support their children during Covid-19 were helping them socialise and build healthy relationships and helping them cope with stress or anxiety (Dudovitz *et al.*, 2022). Psychological distress such as anxiety and depression amongst pupils may increase as they start to lose school connectedness, including a loss or lessening of the belief that both adults and peers in their school care about their learning as well as them as an individual (Pikulski *et al.*, 2020).

Video conferencing served to support pupils by connecting them to their peers and their teachers. The use of break-out rooms was an effective way of supporting pupils so they could socialise with each other through sustaining and building their relationships with each other. The social/emotional needs of pupils are significant for several reasons. Positive emotions can facilitate motivation, self-regulation, and thus improve academic learning (Daniels *et al.*, 2009). Negative emotions, on the other hand, can reduce motivation, consume cognitive resources, and negatively impact self-regulation, and academic learning (Pekrun *et al.*, 2011). Research conducted during Covid-19 indicated that pupils' social/emotional levels were affected; one impact reported was anxiety as a result of missing friends (Pikulski *et al.*, 2020). Through this experience of missing friends, pupils experienced the feeling of disconnection (Ziebell *et al.*, 2020). It was important that teachers understood and addressed the psychosocial challenges of the pandemic (UNESCO, 2020), which should be a priority before teaching. For lessons learned from Covid-19, see Leask and Younie (2022).

For this next task, reflect on your use of video conferencing during Covid-19 lockdowns. If you did not use it, ask a colleague the questions.

Now move to Task 20.2.

Task 20.2: Video conferencing use during Covid-19

For this task, survey the students around their use of video conferencing focusing on school-related work.

- How often was video conferencing used?
- What subjects were focused on during the sessions?
- What subjects were not able to be covered?
- Did peer interactions feature during the sessions? If yes, how did they support pupils' understanding?
- Were there any challenges associated with this use? If yes, what were they? How were they resolved?

The Case Study 20.1 illustrates how the use of video conferencing was incorporated into a project-based learning (PBL) unit of work with students at four different schools in New South Wales, Australia.

Case Study 20.1: PBL project

The research project conducted by the author examined the use of video conferencing to facilitate peer feedback in a community project-based learning (PBL) project conducted with Year 5 and 6 pupils in four schools. The focus of the project for the pupils was to create a product that benefited a group within their community. The overarching question the pupils addressed was how can we create a product that benefits a group within our community?

Questions that guided the pupils' inquiry were:

Who are community groups that we could help?
Who can we get access to?
How will our product help our chosen group?
How can we test the effectiveness of our product?

A video conferencing session between two classes at two schools was conducted where some of the pupils in each class presented their projects and received feedback from the pupils at the other school. Pupils from one school were able to view the website/resource of the pupils from the other school which greatly facilitated understanding and discussion.

This followed on from a session mediated online between the schools where the pupils produced some PowerPoint presentations using Google Slides where they set out the ideas of the project in the early stages as illustrated in Figure 20.1. Pupils from the other school were then able to look at the slides and leave written comments to help the pupils shape their projects.

One of the classes also contacted the local council staff using video conferencing and discussed their ideas with them. The focus of this class's projects was to set up information stations in the local park with which users of the park could interact. One idea was to set up QR stops with different physical activities. The pupils were able to discuss their projects with the council staff and get an understanding of the usefulness of their project and the council guidelines that needed to be followed.

In the final stage of the PBL approach, pupils had the opportunity to present their project to the learning community which included their peers, teachers, family members, and community members. At this point pupils were able to "continue to learn with other pupils by seeing how others approached the problem and from feedback and questions they received from the audience" (English and Kitsantas, 2013, p. 137). Figure 20.2 shows one project presented by a group of students.

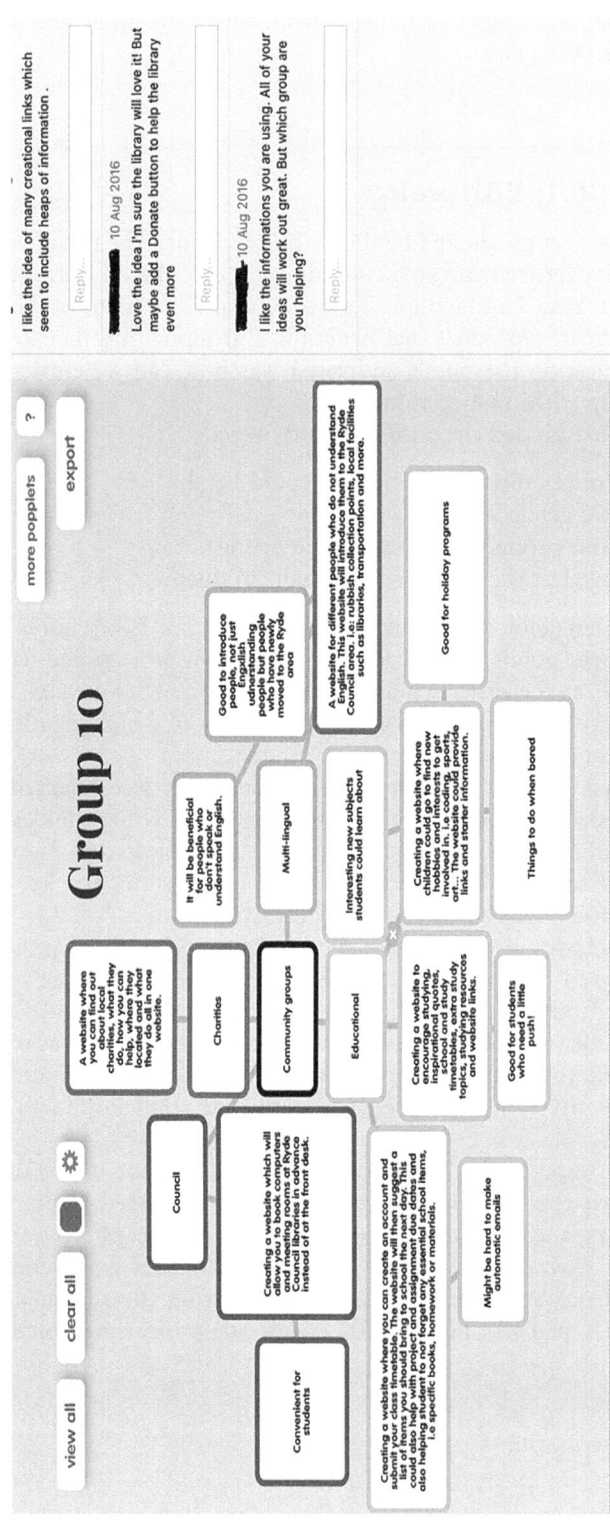

Figure 20.1 Example PowerPoint slide

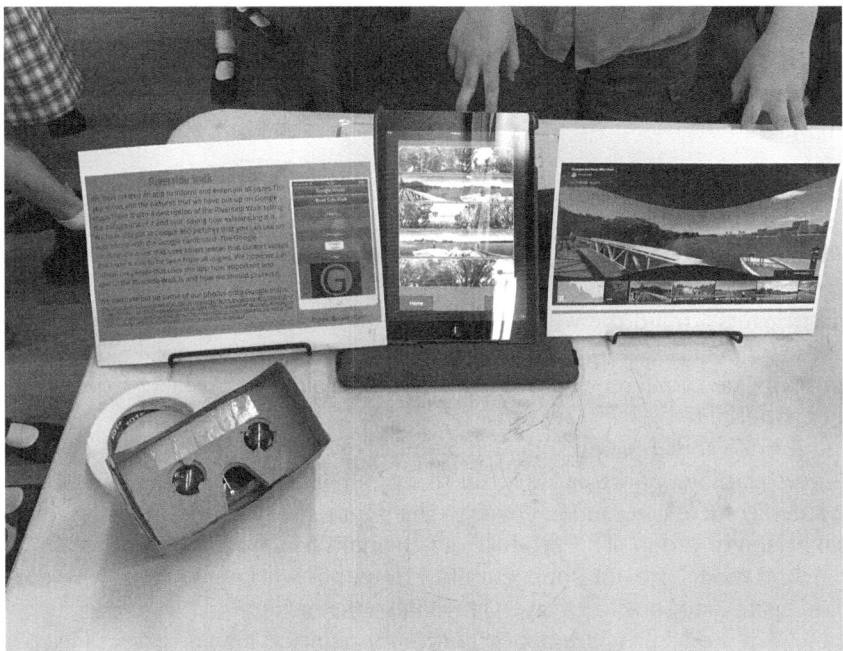

Figure 20.2 Pupils' PBL presentation

Authentic participants with whom the pupils interacted with included pupils at other schools and community members. Providing pupils with access to authentic participants, mediated through video conferencing and then face-to-face, provided context for their work. Pupils were able to give and receive feedback, which helped shape their work and the work of other pupils. Additionally, being involved in authentic learning activities affirmed students' understanding that their work has broader applications and is relevant to current needs and concerns. The pupils appreciated that they were working towards outcomes that had practical applications for themselves and their schools, as well as the broader local community.

Now move to Task 20.3.

Task 20.3: Developing a class-based scenario

In drawing on the ideas you developed from tasks 20.1 and 20.2, develop your own class-based scenario and consider how you would incorporate the use of video conferencing into your own teaching. Use the pupils from Task 20.1 or consider who your next class will be and develop a lesson, or series of lessons, using the video conferencing technologies available in your school.

Summary and key points

As was discussed in this chapter, the use of video conferencing has been steadily growing in schools and is able to facilitate authentic learning opportunities for pupils. Covid-19 accelerated the use of this technology, and it is likely to be used with greater frequency in the coming years.

- The use of video conferencing can be considered from a sociocultural perspective.
- The use of video conferencing technologies facilitates interactions for pupils and their teachers with peers and experts beyond the classroom.
- Video conferencing technologies allow pupils to interact with a wide range of authentic participants around the world, enabling authentic learning experiences in authentic settings.
- The use of video conferencing can reposition the role of the teacher from being a gatekeeper to a facilitator.
- In using video conferencing, a greater number of experts can be called upon, which allows new learning opportunities for both the pupils and the teacher.
- One video conferencing model involves the pupils and teachers interacting with an external person or group. This produces an enlarged community of practice.
- The hybrid model provides opportunities for pupils who might otherwise not be able to participate in lessons to engage via video conferencing.
- The blended model provides opportunities for pupils to engage in extra lessons which can reinforce or extend their understanding of content being learnt in the classroom.
- The use of video conferencing was able to support pupils during Covid-19 to keep them in contact with their teachers and peers.

Further resources

Cavus, N. and Sekyere-Asiedu, D. (2021) A comparison of online video conference platforms: Their contributions to education during COVID-19 pandemic. *World Journal on Educational Technology: Current Issues*, 13(4), Viewed 30 September 2022 from https://files.eric.ed.gov/fulltext/EJ1322873.pdf.
    This article examines the advantages and disadvantages of seven online video conference platforms including Google Meet, Microsoft Teams, GoToMeeting, Cisco WebEx Meetings, Zoom Meetings, ClickMeetings, and BigBlueButton.
Guidelines to support schools using live video with students. Available from https://education.nsw.gov.au/content/dam/main-education/teaching-and-learning/learning-from-home/teachers/documents/using-technology/guidelines-to-support-schools-using-live-video-with-students.pdf.
    This document is prepared by the Australia, New South Wales (NSW) Department of Education. There are some practical suggestions in using video conferencing in the online learning tips section.
Intergenerational learning. Available from https://www.olqpgreystanes.catholic.edu.au/news-and-events/news/2020/03/30/03/23/school-shows-the-way-to-stay-connected-with-elders.
    This web site is produced by Our Lady Queen of Peace primary school in Australia. It contains several short videos and commentary on the process of supporting intergenerational learning through the use of video conferencing.
Technology Enhanced Learning Communities. Available from http://www.meshguides.org/guides/node/880.
    This MESHGuide focuses on online learning for teachers drawing on theories of communities of practice, connectivism, social network theory, and situated learning.

References

Babić, N. (2017) Continuity and discontinuity in education: Example of transition from preschool to school. *Early Child Development and Care, 187*(10), pp.1596–1609.

Belt, E. and Lowenthal, P. (2021) Video use in online and blended courses: A qualitative synthesis. *Distance Education, 42*(3), pp.410–440.

Bennett, S., Harper, B. and Hedberg, J. (2002) Designing real life cases to support authentic design activities. *Australasian Journal of Educational Technology, 18*(1), pp.1–12.

Chou, C.C. (2001) Formative evaluation of synchronous CMC systems for a learner-centered online course. *Journal of Interactive Learning Research, 12*(2), pp.173–192.

Collins, A., Brown, J.S. and Newman, S.E. (2018) Cognitive apprenticeship: Teaching the crafts of reading, writing, and mathematics. In L.B. Resnick (ed.) *Knowing, learning, and instruction* (pp.453–494). Routledge.

Commonwealth of Australia (2022) *Review of the National School Reform Agreement Interim report.* Viewed 8 October 2022 from https://www.pc.gov.au/inquiries/current/school-agreement/interim/school-agreement-interim-overview.pdf.

Crippen, K.J., Bokor, J.R. and Evans, G.N. (2018) A synthesis of the empirical research on blended learning in K-12 science education, 2000-2014. In *Handbook of research on k-12 online and blending learning*, 2nd ed. (p.357). Pittsburgh, PA: Carnegie Mellon University - ETC Press.

Daniels, L.M., Stupnisky, R.H., Pekrun, R., Haynes, T.L., Perry, R.P. and Newall, N.E. (2009) A longitudinal analysis of achievement goals: From affective antecedents to emotional effects and achievement outcomes. *Journal of Educational Psychology, 101*(4), pp.948–963.

Davis, H.C. and Fill, K. (2007) Embedding blended learning in a university's teaching culture: Experiences and reflections. *British Journal of Educational Technology, 38*(5), pp.817–828.

Donato, R. and McCormick, D. (1994) A sociocultural perspective on language learning strategies: The role of mediation. *The Modern Language Journal, 78*(4), pp.453–464.

Dudovitz, R.N., Thomas, K., Shah, M.D., Szilagyi, P.G., Vizueta, N., Vangala, S., Shetgiri, R. and Kapteyn, A. (2022) School-age children's wellbeing and school-related needs during the COVID-19 pandemic. *Academic Pediatrics, 22*(8), pp.1368–1374. https://doi.org/10.1016/j.acap.2022.01.015.

Fackler, A.K. and Sexton, C.M. (2020) Science teacher education in the time of COVID-19. *The Electronic Journal for Research in Science & Mathematics Education, 24*(3), pp.5–13.

Gifford-Smith, M.E. and Brownell, C.A. (2003) Childhood peer relationships: Social acceptance, friendships, and peer networks. *Journal of School Psychology, 41*(4), pp.235–284.

Heiser, S., Stickler, U. and Furnborough, C. (2013) Student training in the use of an online synchronous conferencing tool. *Calico Journal, 30*(2), pp.226–251.

Herrington, J. and Oliver, R. (2000) An instructional design framework for authentic learning environments. *Educational Technology Research and Development, 48*(3), pp.23–48.

Hinterberger, H., Fässler, L. and Bauer-Messmer, B. (2004) *From hybrid courses to blended learning: A case study.* International Conference on New Educational Environments. 27–30 September 2004, pp.1–7.

Hwang, R.H., Lin, H.T., Sun, J.C.Y. and Wu, J.J. (2019) Improving learning achievement in science education for elementary school students via blended learning. *International Journal of Online Pedagogy and Course Design (IJOPCD), 9*(2), pp.44–62.

Kloos, C.D., Muñoz-Merino, P.J., Alario-Hoyos, C., Ayres, I.E. and Fernández-Panadero, C. (2015) Mixing and blending MOOC technologies with face-to-face pedagogies. In *2015 IEEE Global Engineering Education Conference (EDUCON)* (pp.967–971). IEEE.

Knapp, N.F. (2018) Increasing interaction in a flipped online classroom through video conferencing. *TechTrends, 62*(6), pp.618–624.

Kristóf, Z. (2020) International trends of remote teaching ordered in light of the coronavirus (COVID-19) and its most popular video conferencing applications that implement communication. *Central European Journal of Educational Research, 2*(2), pp.84–92.

Leask, M. and Younie, S. (2022) *Education for all in times of crisis: Lessons from Covid-19*. Abingdon: Routledge.

Leont'ev, A. (1981) Language of and in the classroom: Constructing the patterns of social life. *Linguistics and Education*, 5, pp.367–409.

Levinson, M., Cevik, M. and Lipsitch, M. (2020) Reopening primary schools during the pandemic. *New England Journal of Medicine*, 383(10), pp.981–985.

Maher, D. (2014) Learning in the primary school classroom using the interactive whiteboard. In J. Jia (ed.) *Educational stages and interactive learning: From kindergarten to workplace training* (pp.150–162). IGI Global.

Maher, D. (2015) A window to the world: Video conferencing via tablets in schools. In A. Stavros (ed.) *Advances in communications and media research*, Volume 11 (pp.160–175). Nova Science Publishers.

Maher, D. (2022) Connecting students on hospital wards to hospital classrooms and the community using video conferencing technologies. In J. Keengwa (ed.) *Handbook of research on transformative and innovative pedagogies in education* (pp.76–92). IGI Global.

Moorhouse, B.L. and Wong, K.M. (2022) Blending asynchronous and synchronous digital technologies and instructional approaches to facilitate remote learning. *Journal of Computers in Education*, 9(1), pp.51–70.

Oh, E. and Park, S. (2009) How are universities involved in blended instruction? *Educational Technology & Society*, 12(3), pp.327–342.

Paderanga, L.D. (2014) Classroom video conferencing: Its contribution to peace education. *Procedia-Social and Behavioral Sciences*, 123, pp.113–121.

Pekrun, R., Goetz, T., Frenzel, A.C., Barchfeld, P. and Perry, R.P. (2011) Measuring emotions in students' learning and performance: The achievement emotions questionnaire (AEQ). *Contemporary Educational Psychology*, 36(1), pp.36–48.

Pikulski, P.J., Pella, J.E., Casline, E.P., Hale, A.E., Drake, K. and Ginsburg, G.S. (2020) School connectedness and child anxiety. *Journal of Psychologists and Counsellors in Schools*, 30(1), pp.13–24.

Polly, D., Allman, B., Casto, A. and Norwood, J. (2017) Sociocultural perspectives of learning. In R. West (ed.) *Foundations of learning and instructional design technology*. EdTech Books. https://pressbooks.pub/lidtfoundations/chapter/sociocultural-learning/.

Pręgowski, M. (2009) Rediscovering the netiquette: The role of propagated values and personal patterns in defining self-identity of the internet user. *Observatorio*, 3(1), pp.353–367.

Raes, A., Detienne, L., Windey, I. and Depaepe, F. (2020) A systematic literature review on synchronous hybrid learning: Gaps identified. *Learning Environments Research*, 23(3), pp.269–290.

Rice, M. and Dykman, B. (2018) The emerging research base for online learning and students with disabilities. In K. Kennedy and R. Ferdig (eds.) *Handbook of research on K-12 online and blended learning* (pp.189–206).

Roberts, R. (2009) Video conferencing in distance learning: A New Zealand schools' perspective. *Journal of Open, Flexible, and Distance Learning*, 13(1), pp.91–107.

Scott, S. and Palincsar, A. (2013) Sociocultural theory. Viewed 21 November 2023 from http://dr-hatfield.com/theorists/resources/sociocultural_theory.pdf.

Staker, H. (2022) *Singapore teachers design blended learning together*. Viewed 30 September 2022 from https://www.readytoblend.com/_files/ugd/d59f5a_f29ca4ef60364b0586847d4ee7a2d8c9.pdf?index=true.

Taşkiran, A. (2021) Psycho-social and educational dimension of the COVID-19 lockdown for elementary school students. *Journal of Educational Technology and Online Learning*, 4(4), pp.562–575.

UNESCO. (2020) *10 recommendations to ensure that learning remains uninterrupted*. Viewed 30 September 2022 from https://en.unesco.org/sites/default/files/unesco-covid-19-response-toolkit-remote-learning-strategy.pdf.

UNESCO. (n.d.) *Education: From disruption to recovery*. Viewed 30 September 2022 from https://www.unesco.org/en/covid-19/education-disruption-recovery?TSPD_101_R0=080713870fab200055c69582480da3ab45f53de0dd66facc5f7b98de7ae896493dc9938c7fdde541085185d06914300032f2a312a457cf9148b2536c76120f6275af41f2428091973669de31fc25e9a44d1ef82fc94865b8a48257c4b5fe475f.

Vygotsky, L.S. (1978) *Mind in society*. Harvard University Press.

Vygotsky, L.S. (1986) *Thought and Language*. A. Kozulin (Trans.) The MIT Press.

Warwick, P., Mercer, N., Kershner, R. and Kleine Staarman, J. (2010) In the mind and in the technology: The vicarious presence of the teacher in pupil's learning of science in collaborative group activity at the interactive whiteboard. *Computers & Education*, 55(1), pp.350–362.

Wertsch, J.V. (1994) The primacy of mediated action in sociocultural studies. *Mind, Culture, and Activity*, 1(4), pp.202–208.

Wiesemes, R. and Wang, R. (2010) Video conferencing for opening classroom doors in initial teacher education: Sociocultural processes of mimicking and improvisation. *International Journal of Media, Technology and Lifelong Learning*, 6(1), pp.1–15.

Ziebell, N., Acquro, D., Pearn, C. and Seah, W.T. (2020) *Australian education survey: Examining the impact of COVID-19, report summary*. Melbourne Graduate School of Education. Viewed 30 September 2022 from https://findanexpert.unimelb.edu.au/scholarlywork/1456468-australian-education-survey--examining-the-impact-of-covid-19-report-summary.

21 Visual literacy, learning and concept mapping in primary age children – neuro-positive strategies for brain-based learning

Jeffrey Beaudry and Kirsten Gould

Introduction

Early childhood education is a time for learners to continue language development, by making sounds, drawing shapes and pictures, forming letters, adding words to their vocabulary, active listening, speaking, reading, and writing. As learners transition to the world of text-based learning there is strong evidence suggesting that active visual learning strategies like concept mapping, story/picture boards, sketching, graphic organizers, and data graphics contribute to and enhance knowledge development and creativity. As humans we learn through our senses, and sight is one of our most powerful means of engaging in the world around us. If we have our sight, our eyes process visual information quickly and accurately.

There is strong evidence that suggests that for many learners, generating their own concept maps produces deeper learning and large positive effects on memory and knowledge outcomes, attitudes towards learning (Hattie, 2009), and on writing (Sinatra, Beaudry, Pizzo, and Geisert, 1994; Gardner, 2023).

In this chapter we present a variety of visual learning strategies that take learners through stages of visual literacy development, and result in improved vocabulary, better understanding of specific content, and writing.

Objectives

By the end of this chapter you should be able to:

- describe the advantages and effects of visual literacy on learning and achievement outcomes
- understand how to stimulate visual thinking and create visual products like concept maps
- employ a range of strategies to promote visual learning
- differentiate the impact between teacher- and learner-generated concept maps.

Visual thinking and learning

We maintain there are several ways for visual thinking to have an impact on learning. The following examples are ways for teachers to use visual thinking to have an impact or learning:

DOI: 10.4324/9781003408925-21

- Capturing thinking in a rapid and linguistically appropriate, transparent manner honouring the flow of thinking
- Developing a big picture view by formulating questions and setting learning goals, beginning to apply reasoning strategies like sorting ideas into categories and noting similarities and differences
- Grappling with vocabulary, the words and meanings, and how topics, categories, details and examples fit together to organize thinking into cognitive structures
- Using concept maps, sketches, pictures to complement writing genres, storytelling, description, logical discussions, and hip-hop rapping
- Using the visual products to focus discussion with peers and in classroom discussions to support reasoning, the identification of fundamental misconceptions, incomplete knowledge, and flaws in reasoning.

Concept mapping is an instructional strategy that combines with other familiar strategies like classroom discussion, feedback, and metacognition. Research reviews have reported the positive impact of concept mapping and visual learning, see Table 21.1 (Marzano, 2003; Nesbit and Adesope, 2006; Hattie and Clark, 2018). Concept mapping has been studied worldwide (e.g., Taiwan, Nigeria, Turkey, UK, New Zealand, USA, Canada, Saudi Arabia, and Latin America) (Canas *et al.*, 2023), and concept mapping has been used and studied as a culturally responsive practice for African-American pupils (Snead and Young, 2003; Young *et al.*, 2018). A critical review of concept mapping research by Martin *et al.* (2015) found strong evidence that concept mapping may offer adult literacy programs "a significantly positive way to enhance learning" (p.41). A noteworthy connection was made between the text content of rap songs and the structure of concept maps by Young *et al.* (2018), which suggests the importance of building teachers' culturally responsive self-efficacy as a step towards evidence-based, differentiated instruction. We see concept mapping as neuro-positive as well as culturally responsive, giving it even more credibility.

Concept mapping has demonstrated positive effects on learners' attitudes towards learning and tests of knowledge. Additionally, concept maps help reluctant writers complete writing tasks (Gardner, 2023). In a study of semantic mapping, Sinatra *et al.* (1994) determined that the use of mapping for fourth graders showed significant effects on pupils' writing.

Table 21.1 Effect sizes for concept mapping

Effect Sizes	Concept Mapping + Instructional Strategies
0.64	Overall effect size (motivation and achievement (Hattie and Clarke, 2018)
1.57	Concept mapping effects on learner's attitudes when used for brainstorming; effects on pupil motivation of visual facilitation of classroom discussion (Horton *et al.*, 1993)
0.85	Concept maps as a meta-cognitive strategy to transform information to knowledge (Hattie and Clarke, 2018)
0.70	Overall impact of nonlinguistic representations (e.g., concept maps, graphic organizers) (Marano, 2003)

NOTE: These effect size rankings are obtained from Moore and Readence (1994); Marzano (2003); Nesbit and Adesope, (2006); and Hattie and Clarke (2018). Effect sizes are measures of impact, in standard deviation units, of concept mapping compared to other strategies. Effect sizes of 0.60 and above are considered to be high impact (Hattie, 2009).

Ever-increasing exposure to visual products: the context of a visually saturated world

The early childhood experience for children born since 2015 is vastly different from what we adults have experienced. Children born in the last eight years will live in an age crammed with digital images. Enthusiastic amateur photographers AKA mobile phone users are predicted to take 1.72 trillion photos in 2022, a figure which will exceed three trillion in 2030. The shift to mobile phones with high-resolution still photo and video cameras, coupled with massive data storage, and almost ubiquitous internet infrastructure makes us all the more aware of what visual products look like, and of our role as picture-takers and recorders of events, but it does not ensure we understand the deeper significance of visual literacy. With our brains' ever-increasing exposure to more visual information, we teachers need to understand how to transform children's experiences and the role of visual learning tools like concept maps.

One might wonder, with all the images readily available, how quickly our pupils are able to process images. Our visual systems are being constantly overloaded and we are able to detect basic information in images in as little as 13 milliseconds! Processing and interpreting images is complex and time consuming; first they are processed in units which are hierarchically arranged within the brain. Small units of information travel along visual pathways to the temporal cortex, and then the prefrontal cortex. Importantly, repeated visual experiences strengthen these pathways, and frequent interactions with visuals is expected, and should prompt our teaching to include both the proper habits to consume as well as create visual products. Our goal is to create smart consumers, and creative, innovative producers of visual content. We strongly believe that children must develop their agency for visual literacy and learning, as it represents both a positive process and product for learners across cultures, languages, and ethnic origins.

Neuropositive learning strategies: dual-coding and schema theories

Why do our brains appreciate the use of visual learning strategies? One way to explain this is to understand the role of cognitive load in making learning "stick." Cognitive load refers to the amount of resources being used by the working memory, which is the cognitive system that allows one to temporarily hold a limited amount of information. While long-term memory is virtually limitless, working memory typically has the capacity to hold around seven chunks of information for just 5–10 seconds. How exactly does cognitive load work in the context of long-term learning? There are three types of cognitive load: intrinsic, extraneous, and germane.

Intrinsic load is the effort required to complete a specific task or focus on a topic. In the classroom, intrinsic load amounts to the interactions of short-term and working memory. We call it active learning. Effective instruction simplifies and consolidates this load by using strategies like chunking information, use of dual-coding, and schema (defined below). Next is the *extraneous load*, which we should seek to manage and keep at a reasonable level as much as possible. Extraneous load is unnecessary or unrelated information that may come from the individual's emotions or random thoughts; it also could be impacted by teacher actions, such as long-winded directions, discussion about unrelated topics, or frivolous decorations around the classroom. The final type of cognitive load is *germane*, which is the effort required for deep processing and the construction of schema.

Effective instruction maximizes pupils' opportunities to relate new information to old, form new neural connections, and organize (or reorganize) schema.

Often, when pupils struggle to retain new information or form connections to prior learning, it is because there was not ample germane load available. Visuals, such as graphic organizers and concept maps, alleviate this obstacle by reducing intrinsic load and providing constructs that allow for deep connections to be made between new learning and prior knowledge, a function of germane load.

In addition to reducing cognitive load, teachers must consider visual learning strategies to support pupils' memory through two other modes: *dual-coding* and *schema*.

Dual-coding, coined by Allan Paivio, involves the use of verbal associations (words and language) and imagery. Because verbal and visual memories are processed and retained in different areas of the brain, both channels can be used to recall information, increasing the likelihood of pupils' ability to retrieve learning at a later time. The key to dual-coding success is that the imagery used is relevant and meaningful. Careful use of visuals, as described in this chapter, align strongly with Dual-Coding Theory, and in turn, are highly effective for increasing pupils' retention of learning.

As soon as we can put drawing tools in children's hands they make their marks on paper, and, just about anything if given the chance. In the early stages of this written communication, before you erase their markings, ask for their meaning. The dynamic interplay between visual images and words is the vital link between the dual schema, words, and images. Together these become neuro-enhancing strategies, simultaneously activating words and complex neural connections. Our examples demonstrate how mapping adds to vocabulary, builds upon prior knowledge, and scaffolds sentence construction, as well as a product for teachers' feedback to improve writing.

Schema Theory, first proposed by Jean Piaget, is a branch of cognitive science that focuses on how the brain organizes, or structures, knowledge. Schemata are dynamic, organized units of knowledge that are always changing based on prior learning and experiences. They guide how we interpret new information, and they focus our attention on relevant information for coding. As our learning around a topic grows, so too, does our schema, becoming highly complex over time. The more complex our schema, the easier it is to remember information because of all the connections we are able to make. However, unless pupils are actively thinking about that schema during learning, it is unlikely that those important connections will be made. Visual learning strategies support pupils in building their schemata as they provide both the structure and cognitive capacity for that critical neural updating to occur.

Visual literacy: for content creators and content users

What is visual literacy? Why is it important to preserve and strengthen visual literacy in young learners? Visual literacy is about what we see, and how our sight-based learning feeds into the ecosystem of literacies we possess as humans. Visual literacy is about how we observe the world that surrounds us, and the pictures we draw to interpret and represent the world around us. Early childhood is a world of neuro-development and differentiation.

Learning to write in our native language, in this case English, or in any language, is an acquired skill. In the USA we adopt a curriculum, the Common Core that focuses our teaching on writing at the earliest possible age and grade level. Most models of writing depict a series of phases, from the earliest age, usually 2–6 year-olds, as a time of transition from marking and drawing to full sentences and paragraphs. The progression is portrayed as a one-way, linear sequence in which early childhood learners pass through the markings and draw to a more desirable outcome, words, sentences, and paragraphs. It seems like a retelling of the evolutionary story, the dominant place of text and words is reinforced in this hierarchy. In the push for growth and progress, conformity to curriculum like the Common Core in the USA seems like the logical, and efficient way to go.

But wait!!

A vision of the world as funnelling into text and writing does not reflect the visual culture that is rapidly changing our world. Our brains and our eyes, once the exquisite tools for seeing the physical world are now exposed to visual imagery on the internet through our mobile devices and computers. If we use the year 2015 as a demarcation, it is the brains of early childhood who are most affected. These young learners are already using mobile devices and computers, no surprise there. What is surprising is the content, the volume of visual imagery and data that is being produced and viewed, the newly emerging visual culture of pictures (snaps), selfies, and videos. The headline to *The Guardian* online newspaper read "In 2014 we took 1tn [trillion] photos: Welcome to our new visual culture." Put another way, "Americans take more photographs every two minutes than were taken worldwide in the 19th century." Videos follow the same trend, but as a phenomenon of the 21st century, generations of *YouTube* users are blazing new learning territory.

What does this mean for visual learning and, specifically for concept mapping? One thing for sure, our learners need to be visual content creators as well as content consumers. In the USA Common Core standards we have put learners at a disadvantage by emphasizing graphicacy, the ability to comprehend maps, plans, and visual messages. Putting learners in control of their visual learning is what we advocate, and this means that visual learning, especially creating, is as important as reading, writing, and math. In 2022 a survey of advertisers found that original graphics out-performed video presentations, charts, and stock photos for successful communications. This is not an endorsement of advertising nor is it a call to create a new workforce of graphic artists. This finding does align with the kind of visual agency we want to preserve and develop in our young learners. One of the likely consequences for 21st-century learning is that concept mapping is a connecting strategy, word-to-word, word-to-many words.

Examples of concept mapping

Let's turn to our examples, the kinds of things elementary teachers can pick up, and implement with a high degree of success.

Scenario and student #1

Preschool learner working on vocabulary and categorization.

Figures 21.1 and 21.2: One standard (L.K.5.A) in the Common Core State Standards (CCSS) for kindergarten asks pupils to categorize common objects into categories in order to gain an understanding of concepts within each category. This teacher-assisted concept mapping "How Animals Move" was created by a preschool pupil who arranged into three categories how animals move: swim, fly, and walk.

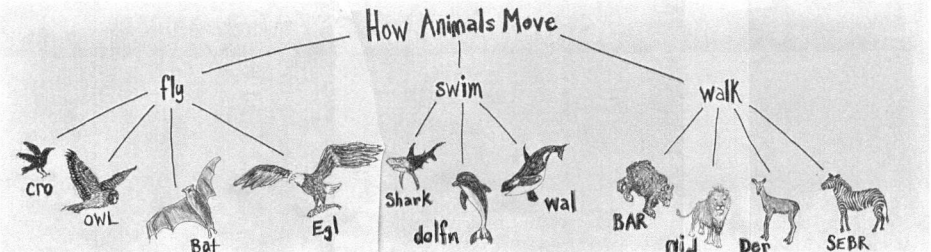

Figure 21.1 "How Animals Move" – connect map

Figure 21.2 Close-up of "How Animals Move" showing details of the pupil's writing and invented spelling about animals that fly

What you can do: Begin with a list of animals to be studied, a list prepared by the teacher to reflect the standards and goals of the lesson. In small groups, have pupils work together to sort these ideas into categories and name each category. Allow the pupils to make observations based on evidence to support their claims.

Scenario and student #2

Kindergarten pupil's concept map of a reading passage about seasons of the year.

Figure 21.3: CCSS RI.K.2 asks kindergarteners to identify the main topic and retell key details from a text, with prompting and support. This is a map developed by a kindergarten pupil, Piper, using information from a brief text read aloud. The printed words and images used in the map are details from the text. Following the "read aloud," with teacher assistance, Piper organized the information into a map, then used the map to retell the details from the text. Finally, to build meaning, she added her own background knowledge in red.

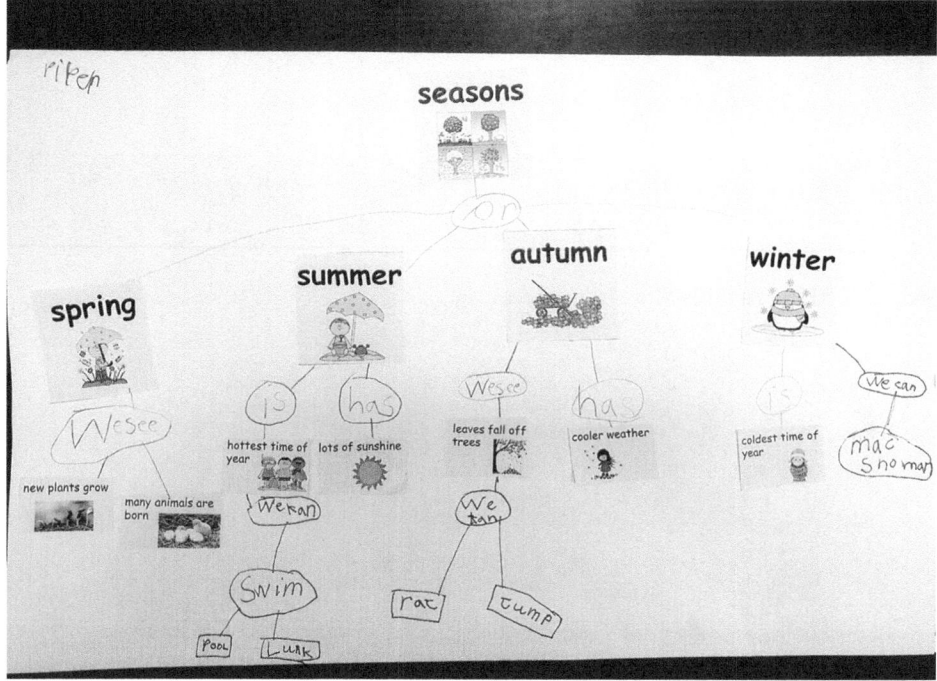

Figure 21.3 Creating a concept map with pupils

What you can do: Have pupils read a block of text, information relevant to your lesson. Have them select the big ideas, the supporting concepts, and the details and specific examples, and make a list. In groups of between three and four, have the pupils write out each concept and detail on a small piece of paper and collectively sort them into a hierarchical semantic structure. Each one takes turns explaining the concept map to each other, and then use jigsaw grouping to put pupils in different groups to practice explaining the meaning of the text using their concept map. Have learning targets that state you must have 15–20 concepts. For deeper learning of key vocabulary, have pupils fill in the lines with linking verbs.

Scenario and student #3

A first-grade pupil created a concept map to deepen understanding around how animals use their parts to help them survive. First-grader pupil created a concept map to connect information learned throughout a unit on animal parts, a standard from the Next Generation Science Standards (NGSS).

Figure 21.4: A first-grade pupil created a concept map to connect information learned throughout a unit on animal parts, a standard from the Next Generation Science Standards (NGSS). Each colour represents learning from different lessons or clusters of lessons, an approach used to help kids visualize how their learning is building and connecting over time.

What you can do: Identify a focus question for a lesson(s), how do animals' different body parts help them survive? Have pupils work individually, in pairs, or small groups, depending on how much confidence they have with concept mapping. Have pupils sort concepts into a concept map structure, and explain their concept map to their peers, and to you (the teacher), with protocols for providing timely, focused feedback. Use colours each time pupils add to their map, either from further study, reflection, or from feedback.

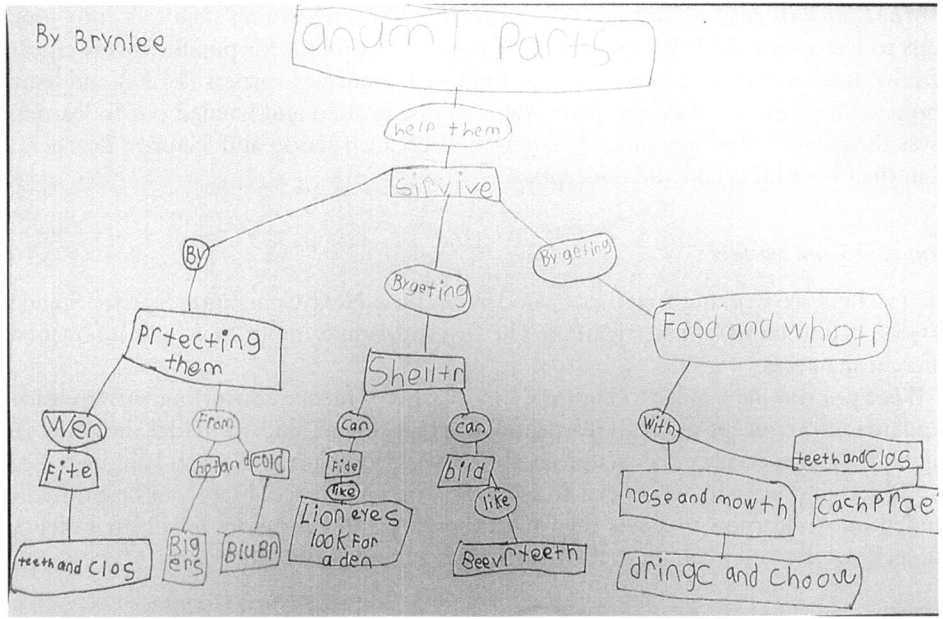

Figure 21.4 A first-grade pupil creation of a concept map

Scenario #4 and teachers

These teachers are working together on clear learning targets in mathematics. Their task is to create different visual representations of the math standards to assist in planning instructional units and to help learners identify concepts and the relationships between concepts, see Figure 21.5.

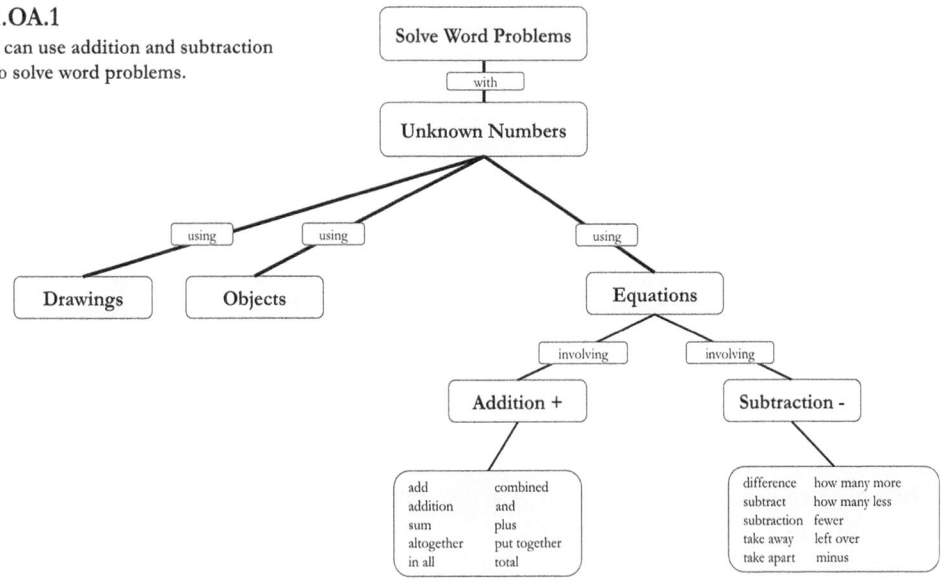

Figure 21.5 Concept map of math standards for math problem-solving for unknown numbers

What you can do: Teachers practice converting written learning standards into concept maps to learn how to create them, and to model the process for pupils. This is especially effective for vocabulary development of English Language Learners (ELLs) and learners who need to learn at a different pace. Maps can be printed and handed out to learners to assess their understanding, and as guides for direct instruction and lectures. Learners can fill in their own ideas and add concepts.

Scenario #5 and teachers

The teachers are working together to understand the Next Generation Science Standards (NGSS) definition of an investigation. The investigation is about how light interacts with different materials.

What you can do: Similar to Figure 21.6. Teachers practice converting written learning standards into concept maps to learn how to create them, and to model the process for pupils. This is especially effective for vocabulary development of English Language Learners (ELLs) and learners who need to learn at a different pace. Maps can be printed and handed out to learners to assess their understanding, and as guides for direct instruction and lectures. Learners can fill in their own ideas and add concepts.

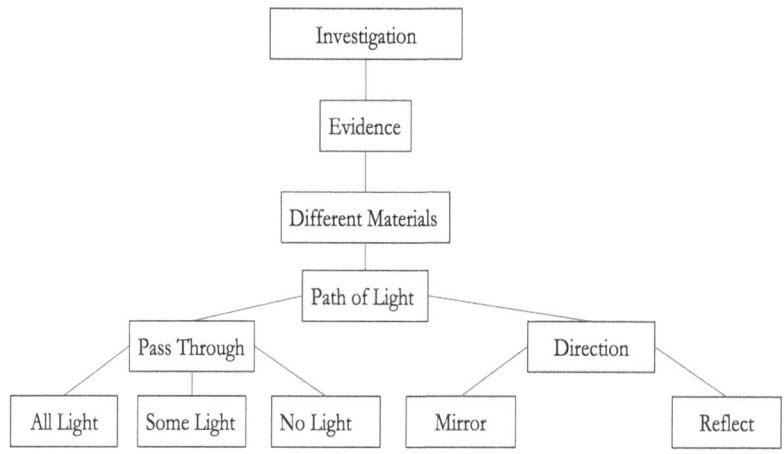

Figure 21.6 Concept map of an NGSS standard on investigating how light interacts with different materials

Scenario #6 and writing

Teachers embed mapping as a step in the writing process for first-grade learners. Learners begin with a focus question, "What does Fall mean to you?" Mapping helps learners combine pictures and words to make meaning, as we see in Figure 21.7.

What you can do: Students who develop concept maps do so in order to organize their thinking and as a pre-writing strategy. With any of the pupil examples, the concept maps can serve as a guide for writing. Students' self-assessment and your feedback can then focus on three aspects of their writing: 1) What is the main idea or central theme?, 2) How does

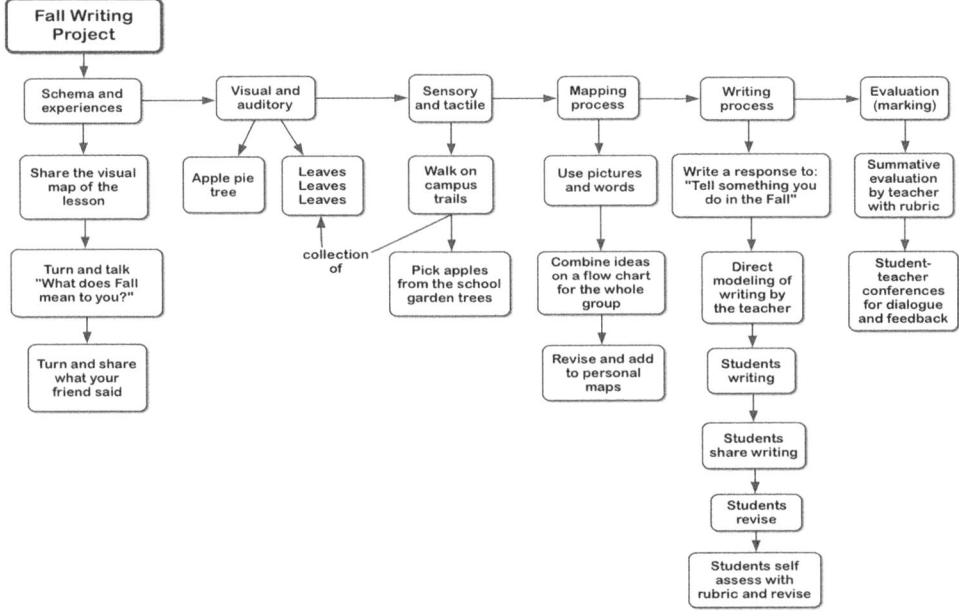

Figure 21.7 Writing process with concept mapping – Timeline for fall writing project

your concept map assist your organization? Is it a sequential narrative? A descriptive essay with multiple themes?, and 3) What specific details will you use in your writing?

Summary and key points

Expanding the visual literacy of elementary learners by using concept mapping is a worthwhile goal. Concept mapping and similar instructional strategies are best developed in early childhood to get the most gains in reading comprehension, deeper thinking, and improved writing. A case study of visual representations found a hidden efficiency with the use of concept mapping, teachers spent 85% to 90% less time reading fully-developed concept maps than reading essays with equivalent information (Gomez, Griffiths, and Navathe, 2014: 252). The effects of concept mapping are most likely when learners have sufficient practice creating concept maps.

Here are some final considerations:

- Visual learning strategies like concept mapping, while effective, are still marginalized strategies in teaching and learning.
- Early childhood educators need to invest the time in learners so that they can infuse concept mapping into their development.
- We see concept mapping as an effective tool for culturally responsive teaching, learning, and assessing, as well as for multi-language learners.

If you think that concept maps are a matter of learning style, think again. Don't mistake your prior learning experiences and familiarities for an intrinsic learning attribution.

Our brains are not binary when it comes to thinking and learning. Concept mapping in the context of visual literacy is learned over time, in different learning content areas, for different thinking skills. Neuropositive teaching means that we expand our repertoire of strategies.

Further resources

MESHGuides. Creative Commons. http://www.meshguides.org/guides/node/38. Accessed 6 February 2023.

References

Beaudry, J. and Wilson, P. (2009) Concept mapping and formative assessment: Elements supporting literacy and learning. In Marriott, R., and Torres, P. (Eds.) *Handbook of research on collaborative learning using concept mapping.* Hershey, PA: IGI Publications.

Beaudry, J. (2014) Visual literacy for teaching and learning: Essential knowledge and skills to create, use and assess concept maps and graphic organizers. In Leask, M., Burden, K., and Younie, S. (Eds.) *Learning to teach using ICT in the primary school.* London, UK: Routledge.

Canas, A., Ford, K., Novak, J., Hayes, P., Reichherzer, T., and Suri, N. *Using concept maps with technology to enhance collaborative learning in Latin America.* Retrieved from Institute for Machine and Human Cognition, https://www.ihmc.us/users/acanas/Publications/QuorumSoupST/SoupsST.htm#_ftn1. Accessed 4 December 2023.

Gardner, P. (2023) Writing: Reluctant writers. *MESHGuides.* Creative Commons. http://www.meshguides.org/guides/node/38. Accessed 6 February 2023.

Gomez, G., Griffiths, R., and Navathe, P. (2014) Concept maps as replacements of written essays in efficient assessment of complex medical knowledge. In Shedletsky, L., and Beaudry, J. (Eds.) *Cases on teaching critical thinking through visual representation strategies*, pp. 223–271. Information Science Reference (IGI).

Hattie, J. (2009) *Visible learning: A synthesis of over 800 meta-analyses related to achievement.* London: Routledge.

Hattie, J., and Clarke, S. (2018) *Visible learning: Feedback* (1st ed.). Abingdon: Routledge. https://doi.org/10.4324/9780429485480.

Kinchin, I. (2001) If concept mapping is so helpful to learning biology, why aren't we all doing it? *International Journal of Science Education*, 23(12), 1257–1269.

Kuechel, T., Beaudry, J., and Ritz-Swain, S. (2023) Visual literacy. *MESHGuides.* Creative Commons. http://www.meshguides.org/guides/node/214. Accessed 6 February 2023.

Martin, L. G., Martin, F. A., and Southworth, E. (2015) A critical review of concept mapping research literature: Informing teaching and learning practices in GED preparation programs. *New Horizons in Adult Education and Human Resource Development*, 27(3), 27–45. https://doi.org/10.1002/nha3.20109.

Marzano, R. (2003) *What works in schools: Translating research into action.* Reston, VA: Association for Supervision and Curriculum Development.

National Reading Panel. (2000) *Teaching children to read: An evidence-based assessment of the scientific literature on reading and its implications for reading instruction.* Washington: National Institute of Child Health and Human Development. https://www.nichd.nih.gov/sites/default/files/publications/pubs/nrp/Documents/report.pdf. Accessed 6 February 2023.

Nesbit, J., and Adesope, O. (2006) Learning with concept and knowledge maps: A meta-analysis. *Review of Educational Research*, 76(3), 413–448.

Norton, P., McConney, A., Gallo, M., Woods, A., Senn, G., and Hamelin, D. (1993) An investigation of the effectiveness of concept mapping as an instructional tool. *Science Education*, 75, 95–111.

Novak, J. and Gowin, D. (1984) *Learning how to learn*. New York: Cambridge University Press.

Shedletsky, L., and Beaudry, J. (2014) *Cases on teaching critical thinking through visual representation strategies*. Hershey, PA: IGI Publications.

Sinatra, R. (1986) *Visual literacy connections to thinking, reading, and writing*. Springfield, IL: Charles Thomas Press.

Sinatra, R. (2000) Teaching learners to think, read, and write more effectively in content areas. *The Clearing House*, 73(5), 266–273.

Sinatra, R., Beaudry, J., Pizzo, J., and Geisert, G. (1994) Using computer-based semantic mapping, reading, and writing approach with at-risk fourth graders. *Journal of Computing in Childhood Education*, 5(11), 93–112.

Snead, D., and Young, B. (2003) Using concept mapping to aid African-American students' understanding of middle school science. *Journal of Negro Education*, 72(3), 333–343.

Stewart McCafferty, A., and Beaudry, J. (2018) *Teaching strategies to create assessment-literate learners*. Thousand Oaks, CA: Corwin Press.

Ware, C. (2013) *Information visualization*. Elsevier.

Young, J., Young, J., Cason, M., Ortiz, N., Foster, M., and Hamilton, C. (2018) Concept raps versus concept maps: A culturally responsive approach to STEM vocabulary development. *Education Sciences*, 8, 1–10.

Terminology

Concept mapping: A strategy in which verbal and visual thinking are integrated and displayed in a way distinctive from traditional writing. Concept maps are constructed by the individual learner, in collaboration with other learners, or created and shared by teacher-experts. Key concepts are arranged in space (not in a linear, grammatically structured form), and may be accompanied by icons and graphic images. Novak and Gowin (1984) defined concept maps as specified maps constructed in a hierarchical format, in which big ideas are linked with verbs or key words to supporting concepts and details. The National Reading Panel (2000) issued a definition of literacy for reading in which concept mapping is included as a key strategy to assist learners in the comprehension of text.

Culturally responsive teaching: Characteristics of culturally-responsive teaching include the following: it activates prior knowledge, makes learning contextual, considers differences in learners, incorporates popular culture, and employs pupils' social and cultural capital. Concept mapping can make an explicit connection with prior knowledge, contextualizes learning by asking learners to build their own understanding and seek feedback from peers and teachers, and incorporates the dominant visual culture of the 21st century.

Neuropositive strategies: Also called brain-based teaching, learning, and assessment, this means that we are employing a variety of learning strategies, in order to maximize each individual's learning need, knowing that their needs may differ from our own learning experiences and preferences. For example, we may want to teach letters and words, and use experiences, visuals, stories, singing, and dancing; more than just oral dictation.

Visual literacy: The first stage of literacy development for learners with all five senses, visual literacy, is followed by language and then written literacy (Sinatra, 1986). Humans with sight actively view and seek information as hearing develops. It is the responsibility of educators to create learning environments for all learners to develop cognitive skills. "Language, then, becomes the natural extension of symbolic thought, and symbolic thoughts help form the mental schemata of a visually literate person" (Sinatra, 1986: 11). Visual learning strategies support pupils in building their schemata as they provide both the structure and cognitive capacity for that critical neural updating to occur.

22 Global citizenship

Education in an interconnected global space

Sharon Tonner-Saunders

Figure 22.1 Image of the globe with the word 'globalisation' prominent

Introduction

Today's pupils live in an interconnected globalised world where they can connect, communicate, collaborate and create with their global peers. Time and location are no longer barriers to learning with pupils in other communities and countries due to digital platforms

DOI: 10.4324/9781003408925-22

providing online global spaces that enable collaborative learning. In education, pupils engaging in online collaborative learning with their global peers have two main benefits: developing the necessary skills for their future employability and developing an understanding of interculturalism, diversity and inclusion to enable them to interact harmoniously in multicultural societies. It also enables pupils to work towards achieving aspects of the United Nations' (2021) Sustainable Development Goals (SDG) through providing an inclusive and equitable quality education (SDG4) that promotes peace, justice and inclusion (SDG16) where inequalities are reduced across countries (SDG10) and where partnerships are enabled (SDG17). Through collaborative learning online, pupils develop their intercultural awareness of the world they live in by exploring similarities and differences between their own lives and those of their global peers alongside engaging with complex global issues.

Intercultural competence incorporates knowledge, skills and attitudes that are embedded in the European Commission's (2019) eight key competences for lifelong learning, with 'cultural awareness and expression', 'citizenship', 'personal, social and learning to learn' and 'digital' given prominence. The importance of pupils being competent users of digital technology for work and life has been a priority of the European Policy Agenda for many years with the creation of a Digital Competence Framework (DigComp 2.2) for educators that outlines five key digital competences that teachers should teach:

1. information and data literacy
2. communication and collaboration
3. digital content creation
4. safety
5. problem solving (Vuorikari *et al.*, 2022).

The EU vision for education, therefore, requires teachers to take a global view ensuring their pupils learn ___**in**___ and ___**about**___ global spaces. Learning ___**in**___ a global space is where pupils use online social platforms to connect with their global peers and work collaboratively, whereas learning ___**about**___ global spaces focuses on pupils developing their intercultural awareness.

Over the past twenty years, I have been involved in small- and large-scale projects whilst a primary teacher and now as a lecturer in education and a British Council Ambassador for intercultural learning. For the past five years I have been managing and coordinating an award-winning global project, called Hands of the World (HOTW): Can You See What I Say? with over 2000 pupils and student teachers from over 50 schools and teacher training institutions around the world (Tonner-Saunders, 2020). The project primarily uses music and Makaton signing to preserve linguistic identities and create an inclusive learning environment to enable pupils to 'work collaboratively to develop an understanding and appreciation of identities, cultures and languages' (Tonner-Saunders, 2020). This aligns with the United Nations' (2022) view of the importance of preserving linguistic identities to ensure that some linguistic identities do not become extinct alongside preserving a sense of belonging. The HOTW project strives to celebrate and share the pupils' linguistic differences through providing a platform for all these rich, wonderful language sounds to be heard by all rather than muted (Leproni, Canals-Botines and Tonner-Saunders, 2021).

This chapter provides an introduction to the notion of what it means to learn **in** and **about** global spaces through the use of digital technologies. Three case studies are presented that illustrate innovative and creative examples of projects undertaken by pupils who were involved in my HOTW global project alongside a step-by-step guide on how to create effective collaborative projects using a range of digital applications.

Objectives

At the end of this chapter you should be able to:

- demonstrate an awareness of the importance of embedding intercultural learning and sustainability into education
- explain different ways to connect your class with other schools across the world through digital technologies
- develop your digital pedagogy in creative ways to connect pupils with their global peers.

Learning about a global space

Learning **about** a global space is where pupils develop knowledge and skills to be able to 'examine local, global and intercultural issues, understand and appreciate different perspectives and worldviews, interact successfully and respectfully with others, and take responsible action toward sustainability and collective well-being' (OECD, 2018). The importance of pupils developing an understanding of the wider world around them and making connections with global issues is promoted by various organisations, for example Think Global (2023), which states that education plays a vital role in preparing pupils to live, engage, interact and work in a global society. Embedding a global dimension into pupils' education provides opportunities for what the UK Department for International Development and the Department for Education and Skills (DFID/ DES, 2005) defined, in their document *Developing the Global Dimension in the School Curriculum*, as 'exploring the world's interconnections' where they can make links with their own lives and others and explore issues from other countries in the world. This DFID/DFES document (2005) states that education plays a key role in helping pupils become responsible global citizens who 'make informed decisions and take responsible actions.'

Think Global (2023) defines learning *__about__* a global space as education that fosters:

- critical and creative thinking
- self-awareness and open-mindedness towards difference
- understanding of global issues and power relationships
- optimism and action for a better world.

The OECD (2018) expands on this by providing a global competence framework with four target dimensions that are illustrated in Figure 22.2.

Research over decades has shown the positive effect on teachers' professional development and pupils' learning, motivation and enthusiasm through embedding a global dimension into education that provides opportunities for active and participatory learning with real audiences and contexts alongside questioning and critical thinking of cultures and stereotypes (Bocconi *et al.*, 2012; Bourn, 2011; Hunt, 2012; Shah and Brown, 2009).

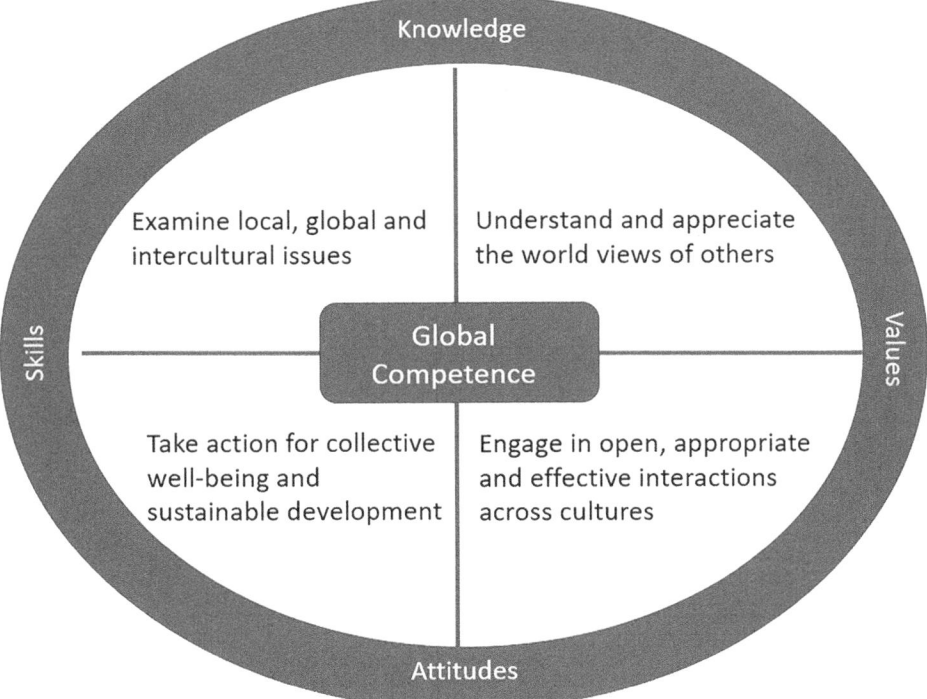

Figure 22.2 The dimensions of global competence (adapted from OECD, 2018:11)

Learning **about** a global space, therefore, provides pupils with opportunities to develop as global citizens and requires a commitment by teachers to ensure that learning is not 'bolted on' but is meaningful, relevant and active.

Now undertake Task 22.1.

Task 22.1: Learning about global spaces

To develop your understanding of what it means to learn **about** a global space, read the OECD's (2018) Global Competence Framework and reflect on what aspects of the four dimensions are currently embedded in your school's practice and what could possibly be integrated into practice. The document can be accessed at: https://bit.ly/3jbBmiI.

Learning *in* a global space

Learning ***about*** a global space can be achieved through using digital technology to learn ***in*** a global space, for example, online social platforms can be used to connect pupils with their global peers and enable collaborative learning. The importance of extending the collaborative aspect of learning to a wider audience beyond the local environment to a global one is not a new one. Back in 2006, Thomas Freidman warned that technology was flattening the world to enable people to work together no matter their locality. He provided an excellent example of collaborative working across locations when he described how Disney™ made an animated movie: the script was created in one country, the animation in another, the voice over and music in yet another location with the final production in Disney Studios (Friedman, 2006). Location, culture, language and time zones are no longer barriers to collaboration as technology enables people to work together anytime, anyplace, anywhere. The use of online social platforms in the form of virtual 'spaces' or 'studios', as Loveless (2007) called them, enables pupils to create and share work and, more importantly, it enables learning from one another and with one another. These benefits are also applicable to teachers, as was evident in the HOTW project where teachers and student teachers learnt pedagogical approaches and content knowledge from each other (Tonner-Saunders and Shimi, 2021).

The importance of teachers having a digital competence to use online spaces for teaching and learning became apparent during the Covid-19 pandemic when by the end of April 2020, pupils in 180 countries were no longer attending school (World Bank, 2020). Teachers therefore had to learn new skills, using digital tools, to ensure that learning continued and pupils felt connected to one another (Education Scotland, 2021). This was possible through implementing five key ingredients, participation, recognition, collaboration, cooperation and facilitation, which Leadbeater (2008) and Tapscott (2008) advocated many years ago.

Global spaces online afford opportunities for creative learning through using a range of multimedia tools to communicate shared learning experiences. There are many examples online of teachers using digital technologies creatively and innovatively to enable pupils to learn about global issues. Some projects are organised and managed on a small scale as a one-to-one project using one or two digital tools, whilst others are more ambitious, on a larger scale, with multiple schools involved, and with a wide range of digital tools incorporated into the project. The HOTW project provides examples of small- and large-scale projects that incorporate a range of digital tools in a global space.

Building on Task 22.1, now undertake Task 22.2.

Task 22.2: Introduction to intercultural learning: using the Hello song

The first part of this task, pertaining to learning **in** and **about** a global space, is to develop an understanding of how my HOTW project aligns with developing teachers and pupils' intercultural and digital competences. First go to the HOTW website (https://bit.ly/3H4evNG) and read the first two presentations (*Introduction* and *Aims, Goals and Journey*) to develop an understanding of learning **about** a global space through the project's:

- goals, aims, background and pedagogical innovation and creativity, and
- the curricular integration, interdisciplinary learning and pedagogical approaches used.

Now make links with theory and practice by reflecting on how the project links with the United Nations' SDGs and the theory referred to in the section pertaining to learning **about** a global space above. Share your reflection as a comment on my blog post: https://bit.ly/3Y1TnPe.The second part of this task is to read another four presentations on the same HOTW website to develop an understanding of learning **in** a global space through the project's:

- collaboration between schools
- digital technologies used
- impact on pupils' learning, and
- dissemination through a range of digital applications.

What links can you make between the project and the DigiCom competencies as well as the policies noted in the section pertaining to learning **in** a global space? Reflect on the connections you make and share these on my blog post at: https://bit.ly/3DFQImH.

Now undertake Task 22.3.

Task 22.3: Introduction to intercultural learning that is situated <u>in</u> and <u>about</u> global spaces

Your next task provides an opportunity for your class to now take an active role **in** the HOTW project to learn **about** different cultures. This task focuses on a Hello Song that was used in the HOTW project for the schools to introduce themselves in their own language. Due to each school singing the song in their own language and signing the song in Makaton, pupils were able to preserve their linguistic identities and develop an awareness of other languages and for some, learning a new language.

First, watch the instruction video to learn the song and how to use Makaton signs for specific words: https://bit.ly/3kA2nwn. You can watch the video alone and learn the song and words to teach your pupils or you could watch the video with your pupils and learn with them. Learn the signs slowly at first; remember to say the words in your own language. Now practise the song with the signs in your own language. You can have a musical accompaniment if you wish. The chords are simply C, F and G. Once your class can sing and sign the song competently, you are ready to incorporate digital tools as follows:

1. Using a device that can record videos and share easily, teach your pupils basic videography skills, for example, landscape mode, zoom, focus, lighting and so on. The following website provides some simple advice to assist you with what skills a videographer requires: https://indeedhi.re/3Y07pkd. I would suggest that you record your pupils singing and signing and model the skills for this step and the next.
2. Allow pupils time to work in pairs or small groups to video each other in different locations to enable them to experiment with the different functions and learn new skills.
3. Assign groups to video a short video, maximum 10 seconds, of an area of their classroom/ school that they would like to share to show their global location.

4. Pupils can now be taught video editing skills, for example, trimming, lighting, adding captions. Depending on the device used, this will be as simple as using the tools and applications on the device or uploading or sharing the video to another device that has video editing tools.
5. The final stage is to put all the videos together. If the class is young, you may wish to undertake this task, however, if your pupils are capable of learning how to do this, then allow all to create their "Hello" cultural movie.

You can now upload these to your school's online platform, however, if you have written permissions from parents and the school to allow your pupils' videos to be placed online in a public space, you could upload these to the HOTW Hello Song Padlet page at: https://padlet.com/sharon_tonner2/Hello.

Once uploaded, why not get your pupils to watch other schools sing and sign the song to develop their awareness of other languages. Can they sing the song in another language? This activity will open up dialogue about other countries with regards to place and culture.

Now undertake Task 22.4 which gives examples of other joint projects.

Task 22.4: The 'bear' necessities of learning in and about global spaces

This task focuses on using teddy bears or soft toys to learn about other cultures. In Table 22.1 there is a small selection of projects that use a range of digital tools in a creative way to enable pupils to learn in and about a global space. These projects were successful due to incorporating the five ingredients of success for collaborative projects:

- participation of all pupils and teachers involved
- recognition through publishing content online
- collaboration through working together on a common goal
- rules for cooperation agreed by all members of the project, and
- a facilitator who organised, managed, supported and motivated everyone to be active participants.

Spend time exploring the following projects to develop an understanding of how technology can be used to enable learning **in** a global space. Whilst viewing the examples, look at how digital technology was used in creative ways to communicate and collaborate. Now try one of the projects with just your pupils, for example, you could change *Ted Bear Travels the World* to *Ted Bear Travels Around our School* where the bear becomes the school mascot sharing good news with parents and carers. The other three projects work well with a partner school. The school does not need to be in another country as another local school or a different stage in your own school provides a real context for developing digital literacy skills alongside literacy skills.

Table 22.1 Examples of learning in a global space using bears

PROJECT	*Ted Bear Travels the World*
LINK URL	https://bit.ly/3XIm0Bh
DESCRIPTION	Ted Bear accompanied the famous adventurer Mark Beaumont on his challenge to cycle around the world in 194 days. The upper stage pupils read Mark's daily blog, then they created their own weekly blog post to tell the story of Ted's adventures for the rest of the school to read or listen to.
TECHNOLOGY	Blog, Voki, Microphone
PROJECT	*Bear Exchange*
LINK URL	http://tecnoteddy.blogspot.co.uk
DESCRIPTION	Student teachers learn about other cultures through a bear exchange similar to what pupils participate in.
TECHNOLOGY	Blog, Digital Camera
PROJECT	*Culture in a Box*
LINK URL	https://bit.ly/3Hdu6La
DESCRIPTION	An extension of a bear exchange where children create a culture box and send it to another school. Go to the link near the end of the document to see the examples.
TECHNOLOGY	Digital Camera, Various online media tools
PROJECT	*Ted Teaches the World to Sing*
LINK URL	https://bit.ly/3wxMQjr
DESCRIPTION	Using QR Codes, Ted bear teaches schools a song.
TECHNOLOGY	QR Codes, Blog, Response application

It should be noted that working collaboratively with schools around the world can sometimes not run as smoothly as a lesson in the classroom due to various factors:

- language barriers
- lack of communication
- time differences
- available time
- limited participation from partner school
- expectations not being the same
- digital level of competence of partner teacher
- digital resources available
- different ways of teaching
- cultural misunderstandings.

For learning in a global space to be successful it therefore requires three further ingredients:

- patience,
- understanding, and
- simplicity.

The final case study exemplifies innovative and creative ways of learning **in** a global space to develop pupils' knowledge and understanding **about** a global space.

Case Study 22.1: Schoolovision

Website: http://schoolovision.eu/
Project type: eTwinning since 2009 https://school-education.ec.europa.eu/en/etwinning
Lead practitioner: Michael Purves primary teacher at Yester Primary School, Scotland, UK
Schools involved: Primary schools from 38 different countries mainly across Europe: from Iceland in the north west to Azerbaijan in the south east. Schools are from different socio-economic settings and comprise mainstream and rural schools.
Age: 5–12 years
Overview of project: Schoolovision is an annual eTwinning project for primary schools based on the Eurovision Song Contest. The majority of teachers involved are members of the eTwinning network which is the European Commission's partner finding and collaboration website in which UK schools can be invited by a European school to participate.

Schoolovision was created by a Scottish primary school teacher, Michael Purves, in 2009 as a creative way to use music to connect European schools together. Since the project started, it has won many highly acclaimed awards, for example, first place in the 2009 Global Junior Challenge, the eLearning Awards 2009 and the 2010 European eTwinning Awards to note a few. In an award, by the MEDEA Awards (MEDEA, 2013), the judges commented very highly on the creative aspect of the project using ICT. The following comments are illustrative of the judges' views:

> The pupils clearly enjoy the experience and gather some interesting insights into different European cultures ... Very good choice of media – video for what it is good at and a blog site to support – it is easy and can be done by everybody ... it shows that song can connect people in all Europe ... and it develops creativity of students
>
> (MEDEA, 2013: n.p.)

Creativity and collaborative working are at the heart of the project. The pupils need to work together and be creative to ensure the end product is representative of their school and country and captures the imaginations of others. Prior to the project commencing, each teacher plans how they will embed the project into their teaching and learning. This will be different in each country; however, all schools are required to submit a video of their chosen song. Over the duration of the project schools meet virtually online to develop their understanding of different cultures, geography skills and practise their language skills.

Schoolovision: what happens

The project had over 1,000 pupils from primary schools across Europe each year in the Schoolovision contest. The requirements of the project are for participating schools to upload a video to the Schoolovision blog of pupils singing a song that represents their country. Schools then attend an online virtual meeting where participating pupils can cast their votes for their favourite songs. The following provides a step-by-step guide to how this project is organised and managed:

1. The facilitator of the project creates the online blog where all videos will be uploaded then communicates with schools involved using a variety of social network platforms, ranging from the eTwinning collaborative area, to Facebook, Google chat, Google Hangoutsand other video conferencing tools such as Zoom or Google Classroom. Throughout the project the facilitator manages this community.
2. The facilitator shares the rules of participation in the teacher online community and on the blog. Each partner must agree to these rules each year.
3. The pupils in each school choose a song to represent their country and incorporate it into their music curriculum where they practise the vocals: this could be solos, small groups and choirs and in some cases accompanying music. Auditions are held in many of the participating countries!
4. The pupils then discuss how the song will be filmed. This requires a collaborative whole class or school effort to ensure that the song is representative of everyone involved. For some schools this might be as simple as all pupils being filmed singing their chosen song in their classroom or on a more creative level pupils plan their video with regards to the setting, costumes, who will be involved, camera angles, song recorded separately and added to the video. This is an opportunity for the pupil, and the teachers, to be innovative and creative.
5. Videos are edited using video editing software then uploaded to the Schoolovision blog which only participating schools have upload access to; the blog can, however, be viewed by anyone.
6. All schools then view all contributions to decide which countries they will cast their votes for.
7. On the day before the Eurovision Song Contest, every participating school from each country meets online at an agreed time using a video conferencing tool. They then take turns to cast their votes for the songs that were their favourites. All scores are collated and displayed live during the video conference with winners announced once the final votes have been cast. In order to ensure that the winning country can always be announced on the final day of the project, all partners must also email their results to the facilitator by the night before the live vote, so that they can be collated. Thus, in the event of a failure of an online network at the time of the live vote, the winners can still be notified via the blog.
8. The Schoolovision trophy is then engraved with the new winners' details and sent to the winning country.

Now undertake Task 22.5.

Task 22.5: Reviewing an intercultural project

Spend a little time viewing the interesting entries to Schoolovision from the current year and previous years, specifically the original entries in 2009 to enable you to see how the digital movie-making skills have developed over the years: http://schoolovision.eu/. Next, with your class choose a song to represent your country and once learnt, the children can create a storyboard to decide how their song will be filmed. This activity is similar to the first task; however, it is on a larger scale. You could create a whole school, local authority or country Schoolovision project, using the same management and organisation steps above, to connect pupils together through music.

Case Study 22.2: Traditional postcard with a modern twist

Website: https://bit.ly/3ZYiUdM.
Lead practitioners: Sharon Tonner-Saunders from University of Dundee, Scotland, Elaine Manton retired secondary teacher from Loretta Grammar School, England, and Sarah Ashborn, a primary teacher in Oregon, USA.
Project type: Hands of the World
Schools involved: Schools from around the world are involved in the HOTW project.
Age: 3–18 years
Overview of study: The Traditional Postcard with a Modern Twist was created in response to a teacher wishing to send traditional postcards to a few schools in the project. I therefore decided to create a project that would bring the postcards alive and preserve linguistic identities using digital technologies, for example, QR Codes and a Padlet page. The project also created a meaningful context for writing and developing pupils' awareness of learning **about** a global space.
What happened: Pupils would purchase or create postcards to represent their local area. A short message was written on the postcard in the pupils' own language and an accompanying QR code was added that linked to a video of the pupils saying in their own language what was written. A second QR code was placed on the postcard that linked to the class's Padlet page where a translation of the text into English was provided alongside information about the school and community. All schools involved in the project would send three schools a postcard and, each month, those that had time would be provided with three more schools. When the pupils received a postcard, this opened opportunities to learn more about the location of the sender's school through communicating and collaborating with the school online.

Now undertake Task 22.6.

Task 22.6: Bringing learning alive through traditional postcards

The final task is to create interactive postcards with your class. First, read the post-card instructions that are on the HOTW postcard page: https://bit.ly/3HAtUXN. Once your class has created their postcards, they can be displayed in the school to share information with visitors, to send to local people to provide them with information about the school, or to send to a partner school. If you do not have a partner school, I would advise joining the HOTW Facebook group (https://bit.ly/3HzLbAb) where there are schools from around the world who would happily participate in a postcard exchange with your class.

Summary and key points

- Learning **in** a global space online enables collaborative and participatory learning with a global audience rather than the confined nature of learning in a physical classroom or geographical location.
- These spaces provide opportunities for rich learning to take place that is relevant and in a real-life context. As McLuhan stated, 'technological environments are not merely passive containers of people but provide active processes that reshape people and other technologies alike' (1962: 7).

This chapter has provided a small insight into how digital technologies can facilitate learning **about** a global space through innovative projects that use a range of simple digital tools. The role of teachers is to prepare pupils for the future where they will need the skills to navigate an interconnected world and an understanding of their role as a global citizen. Learning **in** and **about** a global space is about making your pupils mindful of their actions and how they will affect others locally and globally. It is therefore worth remembering one of Albert Einstein's quotes that he was reputed to have said where the world we have created is a product of our thinking; it cannot be changed without changing our thinking.

Further resources

The following documents provide a deeper insight into learning in and about a global space:

Bacigalupo, M. and Cachia, R. (2011) *Teacher Collaboration Networks in 2025. What is the Role of Teacher Networks for Professional Development in Europe?* Luxembourg: Publications Office of the European Union.

DFID/DES. (2005) *Developing the Global Dimension in the School Curriculum*. London: DES.

Mansilla, V. B. and Schleicher, A. (2022) *Big Picture Thinking: How to Educate the Whole Person for an Interconnected World*, accessed on 16 January 2023. Available at: https://pz.harvard.edu/resources/big-picture-thinking-how-to-educate-the-whole-person-for-an-interconnected-world.

Websites

University of Dundee – HOTW: https://www.dundee.ac.uk/stories/makaton-project-goes-global
British Council: https://www.britishcouncil.org/school-resources
Edublogs: http://edublogs.org/
European Commission: https://pz.harvard.edu/resources/big-picture-thinking-how-to-educate-the-whole-person-for-an-interconnected-world
eTwinning: http://www.etwinning.net/en/pub/index.htm
Global School Alliance: https://www.globalschoolalliance.com/
Oxfam: https://www.oxfam.org.uk/education/
Think Global: https://think-global.org.uk/ and http://globaldimension.org.uk/
Voki: http://voki.com/

References

Bocconi, S., Kampylis, P. and Punie, Y. (2012) *Innovating Teaching and Learning Practices: Key Elements for Developing Creative Classrooms in Europe.* Available at: https://publications.jrc.ec.europa.eu/repository/handle/JRC72278. Accessed on 16 January 2023.

Bourn, D. (2011) Discourses and Practices around Development Education: From Learning about Development to Critical Global Pedagogy, *Policy & Practice: A Development Education Review*, 13, 11–29.

DFID/DES. (2005) *Developing the Global Dimension in the School Curriculum.* London, DES.

Education Scotland. (2021) *What Scotland Learned: Building Back Together.* Livingstone, Education Scotland.

European Commission, Directorate-General for Education, Youth, Sport and Culture. (2019) *Key Competences for Lifelong Learning.* Available at: https://data.europa.eu/doi/10.2766/569540. Accessed on 16 January 2023.

Friedman, T. (2006) *The World is Flat.* Washington, Picador Publishers.

Hunt, F. (2012) *Global Learning in Primary Schools in England: Practices And Impacts.* London, Development Education Research Centre.

Leadbeater, C. (2008) *We Think: Mass Innovation not Mass Production.* Washington, Profile Books.

Leproni, R., Canals-Botines, M. and Tonner-Saunders, S. (2021) Web-Building Connections: A Best-Practice Example of Using International Resources in Online Intercultural Didactics for Teachers, *Textus*, 28(2), 121–138.

Loveless, A. M. (2007) *Creativity, Technology and Learning, A Review of Recent Literature.* Bristol, Futurelab.

McLuhan, M. (1962) *The Gutenberg Galaxy: The Making of Typographic Man.* New York, Signet.

MEDEA. (2013) *MEDEA Awards.* Available at: http://www.medea-awards.com/home. Accessed on 16 January 2023.

OECD. (2018) *Preparing Our Youth for an Inclusive and Sustainable World. The OECD PISA Global Competence Framework.* Available at: https://www.oecd.org/education/Global-competency-for-an-inclusive-world.pdf. Accessed on 16 January 2023.

Shah, H. and Brown, K. (2009) *Critical Thinking in the Context of Global Learning.* London, DEA.

Tapscott, D. (2008) *Growing up Digital. How the Net Generation are Changing the World.* London, McGraw-Hill Publications.

Think Global. (2023) *Promoting Education for a Just and Sustainable World.* Available at: http://think-global.org.uk/pages/3865/. Accessed on 24 November 2023.

Tonner-Saunders, S. A. (2020) *Hands of the World: Can You See What I Say?.* Available at: https://twinspace.etwinning.net/94991/pages/page/741925. Accessed on 16 January 2023.

Tonner-Saunders, S. A. and Shimi, J. (2021) Exploring Student Teachers' Experiences of Engaging in Hands of the World, a Contextualised Global Intercultural eTwinning Project, *International Journal of Higher Education Pedagogies*, 2(4), 10–20.

United Nations. (2022) *International Mother Languages Day: 21 February.* Available at: https://www.un.org/en/observances/mother-language-day. Accessed on 16 January 2023.

United Nations. (2021) *The 17 Goals.* Available at: https://sdgs.un.org/goals. Accessed on 16 January 2023.

Vuorikari, R., Kluzer, S. and Punie, Y. (2022) *DigComp 2.2: The Digital Competence Framework for Citizens – With New Examples of Knowledge, Skills and Attitudes.* Luxembourg, Publications Office of the European Union.

World Bank. (2020) *The Covid-19 Pandemic: Shocks to Education and Policy Responses.* Available at: The Covid-19 Pandemic : Shocks to Education and Policy Responses (worldbank.org). Accessed on 16 January 2023.

23 School policy and online safety

Rachael Peckover

Introduction

The digital world continues to develop at a rapid pace, providing a range of new possibilities and ways of working. Partly as a result of the Covid-19 pandemic in 2020, there has been a significant increase in children's online presence and changes in online habits and behaviour (ONS, 2021). We have seen an increasing number of new software apps; parents have reported a significant increase in the amount of time that children are playing online games (Ofcom, 2022b); and it is reported that 99% of all children went online in 2021 (Ofcom, 2022a). Looking ahead, development has also begun on Web 3.0, which will see greater decentralisation, openness, and user utility but which may also result in increased cybercrime, hate speech, and misinformation.

Therefore, online safety continues to be a focus for our work in schools. Government guidance makes it clear that, as teachers, we have a responsibility to ensure that our pupils are safe online. The Department for Education introduced *Keeping Children Safe in Education* (KCSIE) in 2014, setting out the statutory guidance which schools should follow. With each iteration, there appears to be a greater emphasis on online safety, with the requirements that all staff understand the role that technology plays in many safeguarding and wellbeing issues; that staff receive appropriate training to ensure that they are able to identify risks; and that staff know a range of strategies to keep children safe (DfE, 2023b). Schools also have a statutory duty to teach pupils how to navigate the digital world (DfE, 2023a).

Objectives

By the end of this chapter, you should be able to:

- demonstrate an understanding of online safety and how this relates to primary-aged pupils
- know where to locate information for your professional practice
- know how to access resources specifically developed for primary-aged pupils relating to online safety.

Background

As Pinto and Younie (2015) note, the publication of *Safer Children in a Digital World* (also known as the Byron Report, 2008), was a major milestone in considering how best

DOI: 10.4324/9781003408925-23

children could be supported to access the digital world safely when using the internet or playing video games. It called for a 'shared culture of responsibility with families, industry, government and others in the public and third sectors all playing their part to reduce the availability of potentially harmful material, restrict access to it by children and to increase children's resilience' (Byron, 2008, p.2). It resulted in an action plan with recommendations which included the launch of the UK Council for Child Internet Safety (now UK-CIS) to lead on national strategy; strengthened regulations; better education for children and families through public information and safety awareness; and reforming video game classification systems with better enforcement.

Following a change in government in 2010, work on these priorities slowed and many of the recommendations were not implemented: of the original 38, only 16 were fully completed (NSPCC, 2018, p.4). There were accusations that, at the highest level, not enough was being done to protect children online. However, online safety was added to the Ofsted remit in 2015. A recent refocusing on these issues included a call for consideration of when and how online safety should be taught in schools, which has seen the introduction of the new statutory Relationships and Sex Education curriculum (DfE, 2019a), as well as a range of Government guidance to support schools in dealing with online risks, (DfE, 2014; 2017; 2019b) and action on the long-awaited Online Safety Bill (DCMS, 2022).

The outcome of the Online Safety Bill is likely to see social media companies (including TikTok, Snapchat, Facebook, and Instagram) held legally responsible for the content on their sites, facing significant fines or potential blocking for any breaches. This Bill will aim to:

- Protect children from harmful and inappropriate content and remove illegal content;
- Place legal duties onto social media companies to use age-checking measures and enforce their own age limits;
- Make illegal any posts that encourage self-harm;
- Ensure greater transparency in explaining the risks posed to children when using social media platforms.

Online safety policy in schools

Byron (2008) provided a conceptual framework (developed by the EUKids Online project) for understanding the complexities of online risks, now updated. See Table 23.1.

Data from Ofcom (2022b, p.8) reports that a third of children aged 8–15 have seen 'worrying or upsetting content' in the past 12 months. There has also been a significant rise in bullying which, among children who have experienced it, is now more prevalent online (83%, compared to 60% who had experienced it face-to-face). ONS data from 2020, also found that during the previous 12 months, around one in six 10–15-year-olds spoke online with someone they had never met before, it was estimated that 5% had met up in person (212,000 children) and of those, 21% met up alone. The NSPCC (2020, p.11) has found that these risks have been exacerbated during the Covid-19 lockdown with children spending more time online, but subject to less supervision. The Internet Watch Foundation (2023) has published disturbing data highlighting that, since the pandemic, there has been a 1,058% increase in webpages containing images and videos of children aged 7–10 coerced into sexual abuse on camera (63,050 reports in 2022,

Table 23.1 4Cs of online risk (Livingstone and Stoilova, 2021)

	Content (Child as recipient)	Contact (Child as participant)	Conduct (Child as actor)	Contract (Child as consumer)
Aggressive	Violent, gory, graphic, racist, hateful, and extremist content	Harassment, stalking, hateful behaviour, unwanted surveillance	Bullying, hateful or hostile peer activity e.g. trolling, exclusion, shaming	Identity theft, fraud, phishing, scams, gambling, blackmail, security risks
Sexual	Pornography (legal and illegal), sexualization of culture, body image norms	Sexual harassment, sexual grooming, generation and sharing of child sexual abuse material	Sexual harassment, non-consensual sexual messages, sexual pressures	Sextortion, trafficking for purposes of sexual exploitation, streaming child sexual abuse
Values	Age-inappropriate user-generated or marketing content, mis/disinformation	Ideological persuasion, radicalization and extremist recruitment	Potentially harmful user communities e.g. self-harm, anti-vaccine, peer pressures	Information filtering, profiling bias, polarisation, persuasive design
Cross-cutting	Privacy and data protection abuses, physical and mental health risks, forms of discrimination			

compared to 5,443 in 2019). Even before the pandemic, it wasn't unusual for the police to alert schools to children who were in contact with adults who were being monitored for illegal activity.

It is therefore important that online safety policies are robust, ensuring that they provide consistent practice across the school for safeguarding against, and dealing with, online incidents, and paying particular attention to how we can best support our vulnerable pupils.

Policies should pay due heed to national guidance, including KCSIE (DfE, 2023b) and the *Early Years Foundation Stage Statutory Framework* (2023a), and should link to existing school policies, including behaviour, anti-bullying, and safeguarding. Whilst the SWGfL report (2021) continues to show that policy documents remain an area of strength across schools, and there are many good examples to support your school in writing your own, schools should not simply use a model version, 'badged' from another organisation. It needs to be a live, bespoke document, which reflects your school's specific context, vision, and values. It should also consider all devices that are able to connect to the internet, such as wearable technology, games consoles, and internet-connected toys. As technologies are ever evolving, there should be regular opportunities for review and updating, which should be done at least annually (NSPCC, 2022). It is useful to note that measuring the impact of these policies is still an area of weakness in many schools; however, the SWGfL (2023) provides a free online safety self-review tool to support with this.

Pinto and Younie (2015) also ask us to consider the emotional aspects of using technology. Ofcom reports (2022a; 2022b) highlight that children were broadly positive about the benefits of being online. Six in ten children aged 8–17 who used social media or messaging sites reported that they felt happier (59%) or closer to their friends (61%) when using them. But children are also aware of the negative aspects of using these platforms. Eight in ten children said they had felt that, at some point, people could be mean or unkind to each other when using social media. Research by D'Lima and Higgins (2021) highlights that children may be vulnerable when using social media due to increased susceptibility to peer pressure and less developed self-regulation and that 'fear of missing out' and a desire to belong may be a driver in under-age social media use. Children are often very competent with the technology, but are still developing critical thinking skills and can make unwise decisions. Whilst we think we know what our children feel and need, it is important to reflect the voices of our pupils (and wider stakeholders) when creating policies and procedures and ensure that these are understood by all. Views can be sought through School Council meetings, Digital Leader sessions (see Case Study 23.2) or whole-school pupil attitude surveys.

Case Study 23.1 details how one primary school addressed a recent safeguarding incident.

Case Study 23.1: Dealing with online safeguarding concerns – an example from practice

One of the more complex issues we have faced recently was when a Year 6 pupil disclosed that a boy in her class had sent her several sexually explicit WhatsApp messages, which included personal comments about her and her mum. Whilst this happened online and outside of school, all members of staff are clear about our duty to deal with this. The class teacher immediately reassured the victim that these were serious and distressing messages, and that she had done the right thing in disclosing them. She was, understandably, worried about telling her mum and we also reassured her that we would do this for her, supporting them both in their ongoing conversations.

Whilst we felt that this matter should be dealt with through our behaviour policy and anti-bullying procedures, there were concerns over the explicit nature of the messages. We used Brook's *Sexual Behaviours Traffic Light Tool* (2020) to help us ascertain whether there were also safeguarding concerns in relation to the alleged perpetrator.

In line with KCSIE (DfE, 2023b), we risk assessed the situation and made the decision to move the alleged perpetrator to a parallel class. This allowed us to place a team around each child which consisted of their class teachers and teaching assistants, but also a different member of the school's pastoral team, with support extending to break, lunchtimes, and before and after school where necessary.

The boy's carers were contacted the same morning, and during discussions it was found that he was in an emotionally vulnerable position, which was difficult to manage at home. A referral was made to Early Help so that further family support could be put in place. As much as we made a promise that we would do all we could to support the alleged perpetrator, we made it clear that this behaviour was unacceptable, that we take a zero-tolerance approach, and consequences were given in line with the school behaviour policy. Time was spent in working with the child to help him understand the impact of his actions on the victim and her family.

We arranged for our IT technicians to meet with carers to help them to set up parental controls to monitor and support their child to behave appropriately online.

We also referred the case for review to our Local Authority Designated Officer (LADO) to ensure that our procedures were robust and that there was nothing further we could have done to support these families.

Whilst our response required a considerable amount of time and resources, it enabled both pupils to complete the year in a positive way.

This case study was from a Deputy Headteacher of a primary school in England who shared their experience of dealing with online safeguarding concerns and outlined the responses that were taken.

Now undertake Task 23.1

Task 23.1: Understanding online safety

Read the latest KCSIE guidance.

- What do you understand by the terms e-safety and safeguarding children online?
- What do you consider to be the key issues relating to online safety for primary aged pupils?
- What are your responsibilities as a teacher?
- How confident do you feel in fulfilling these?

Digital leaders – pupils supporting online safety

One way in which schools can ensure that they are recognising the importance of pupil voice is by recruiting pupil digital leaders, whose role is not only to support teachers to showcase a range of digital skills, but also to be advocates for good behaviour with technology, shaping online safety strategy. There are a number of free resources which give advice on setting up digital leaders in school (which may have a similar structure to a school council, with, for example, pupils from each group applying for the role and meeting termly), such as those offered by Natterhub (2023) and Knowsley City Learning Centres (2022). There are also organisations which, for a cost, provide training on peer-to-peer digital support, such as Childnet (2022b) and 2Simple (2023), which is free for subscribers to Purple Mash. Impact research is promising, with school staff reporting safer online behaviours and current digital leaders sharing that, as well as supporting their peers, they were also able to support their parents in understanding the issues children face online (Childnet, 2022a).

Case Study 23.2 gives an overview of how one school successfully set up a Digital Leaders programme.

Case Study 23.2: How to develop pupil Digital Leaders in school

All of our Key Stage 2 pupils have an individual iPad device to support their learning whilst also developing their digital literacy skills. The Covid-19 pandemic, and the need for remote provision, accelerated our journey in this area, and technology is now integrated across the curriculum as a tool to scaffold and enhance our children's learning experience.

After noticing the impact it was having on our pupils, we felt that it would be valuable to set up Digital Leaders, as our children have a real interest in digital learning, and wanted to share so many great ideas. We were also very aware that pupils' understanding and skills can often be more advanced than those of some of the adults and we wanted to utilise this.

The children were selected for various reasons. For some, it was an opportunity to develop their confidence and their oracy skills outside of the usual day-to-day teaching and learning. For others, it was because they were very competent with technology and were keen to share that knowledge with others. We saw a different side to those children who were really passionate about the use of technology; it was their chance to shine.

Over the course of the last two years, our Digital Leaders have been involved in a variety of different activities, ideally meeting twice a term, in a similar way to a school council, to decide their focus. They've been responsible for delivering sessions to other year groups and supported in lessons where a new skill has been taught, providing hands-on help for individual children (as well as for the teachers!). They've also delivered well-attended lunchtime workshops, deciding which apps and areas of technology they wanted to share.

Additionally, they have helped to observe lessons and identify strengths and areas for development in this subject, giving them a genuine pupil voice. They love this leadership experience and take real ownership of their work.

In terms of online safety, they have helped to measure the impact of our new scheme by monitoring examples of work that have been produced across the school and feeding this back to the Senior Leadership Team.

Our vision is that our pupils will use their developing digital literacy to become confident, creative, and responsible digital citizens, weighing and managing online risks, but also using technology as a form of expression and a way of doing things differently, to remove barriers to the whole curriculum.

This case study was provided by Jenny Hinton, Digital and Computing Lead at Parkdale Primary in Nottingham, who discussed the development of pupil Digital Leaders within her school.

Now undertake Task 23.2.

Task 23.2: School policies on e-safety

Read your school online safety and acceptable use policies.

Make a note of how they are specific to your context and reflective of your vision and values.

- Is there evidence of pupil voice and the contribution of other stakeholders?
- Do they cover the broad range of risks, as detailed in Table 23.1?
- Are there any amendments you would recommend in the school policy? If there are, discuss them with your school-designated safeguarding lead (DSL) and computing lead.

Devices, infrastructure and data protection

As a teacher, you need to be aware of the guidance and regulations around devices, infrastructure, and data protection as well as your specific responsibilities. These should be shared with you on a regular basis, along with other safeguarding updates, by your DSL and Data Protection Officer.

Filtering and monitoring

Schools need to ensure that appropriate levels of filtering and monitoring protect pupils from harmful, inappropriate, and extremist material when using school devices and, as part of this, also have due regard for the Prevent duty (DfE, 2021). The UK Safer Internet Centre (2022) provides a guide on appropriate filtering and monitoring. It notes that school strategy should: be age appropriate; cover Bring Your Own Devices (BYOD); be compliant with data retention regulations; be informed by the school context and risk assessment; and be flexible and understood by all.

However, schools should also be wary of 'over blocking'. In 2019, UKCIS published its *Digital Resilience Framework* (see Figure 23.1) which was designed to help organisations support digital resilience through a focus on 'experience, rather than learning' in a 'safe and managed' environment in order to prepare pupils when using technology outside of school. Ofsted (2010) found that pupils in schools with 'managed systems' (fewer inaccessible sites), rather than those in schools that locked down most of the network, were more knowledgeable and better able to manage online risks.

Figure 23.1 Features of digital resilience (adapted from UKCIS, 2019)

Data protection

Schools also have a duty to comply with Data Protection legislation covering how personal data is handled, stored, or published.

DfE guidance (2020) provides information on compliance, following the introduction of the Data Protection Act, 2018, which saw all schools become data controllers. Schools will hold a range of sensitive data, including contact information for pupils, carers, and staff; health information; school census data detailing SEND, pupil premium, and free school meal information; safeguarding information; pupil progress and attainment data; and employee references. General Data Protection Regulations (GDPR) require all organisations to appoint a data protection officer to advise on protection, and obligations as well as monitor internal compliance. You should know who this is within your own school. Anyone who handles data, including storing, collecting, or analysing it, is regarded as a data processor under the regulations. Any breaches of GDPR, such as information being inadvertently sent to the wrong person, should be reported to the data protection officer, however minor they appear, who can decide the best course of action.

As cloud-based data management systems are now widely used, procedures should clearly address concerns when any personal information is taken from school in electronic format or when staff are using their own devices. These procedures and practices are an inherent part of teachers' roles and responsibilities, and schools require an ongoing commitment to data protection compliance. However, SWGfL (2021) notes that this remains a weakness in schools, with 30% having no practice in place around data protection and, therefore, failing in regulatory duties. You should find details of your school's approach in your Acceptable Use policy, as discussed in Task 23.2.

Mobile and bring your own devices

There may be times when it is appropriate to lend or give school devices to individual pupils, for example those in receipt of Looked After Children (LAC) Pupil Premium funding. During the Covid-19 pandemic, 36% of primary school-age children did not always have access to an adequate device for online learning at home (Ofcom, 2022a). Schools were able to apply for new devices from the DfE which they could then loan on a larger scale. Whenever devices are provided in this way, there is a responsibility to ensure that pupils and their carers have adequate advice on safer internet use.

With the increase in the number of pupils being given mobile phones during the pandemic, robust policies also need to cover procedures for when they are brought into school. Pupils should be educated on the importance of electronic security and made aware of how to create robust passwords, as well as track and report missing devices. Options for staff to bring their own laptops, tablets, and phones also come with challenges, as senior leaders must ensure that the integrity of safeguarding procedures is maintained. At the time of writing, the DfE has not published any set guidance on procedures. It is up to headteachers and governing bodies to decide the best approach which works for their school context. However, it is likely that guidelines will form part of your Staff Code of Conduct and include rules around never taking images on a personal device and information on where within school you are able to use your mobile. These should have been shared with you at induction, and usually annually thereafter. Failure to adhere to this code of conduct is considered a serious breach and may result in disciplinary action being taken.

Now undertake Task 23.3.

Task 23.3: Building digital resilience

Use the Digital Resilience Framework (UKCIS, 2019) as a self-assessment tool to reflect on how well you are supporting your pupils to build digital resilience.

Share your results with your school's computing lead.

Curriculum resources for online safety

Relationship Education became compulsory in all state-funded primary schools in England in September 2020. Through this new curriculum (DfE, 2019a), pupils are taught about online safety and harms, online relationships, and respectful online behaviour, as well as how to evaluate what they see online and recognise techniques for persuasion. It complements the content in the computing curriculum which includes how to use technology responsibly and how and when to seek support.

Alongside this, the DfE (2019b) also released the non-statutory *Teaching Online Safety in Schools*, which highlights the importance of focusing on knowledge and behaviour to navigate the online world, regardless of which platform is being used. It aims to help schools to deliver a 'fully rounded' online safety education by identifying potential risks and how these could be addressed within the curriculum. Throughout, it references *Education for a Connected World* (UKCIS, 2020), which describes the knowledge and skills that pupils should develop at each key stage, as well as information on current technology. The guidance also signposts a wide range of resources, including those to support learning for the most vulnerable pupils.

There are a vast range of resources that can support you in delivering online safety lessons. Those listed in the Further Resources section at the end of this chapter are a useful starting point and can be filtered by both topic and age.

Whilst guidance makes it clear that learning and online safety should be reinforced across the curriculum throughout the year (UKCIS, 2022), some schools have found it beneficial to add additional sessions in the run up to the summer holidays in preparation for the likelihood that pupils may have more unsupervised access to the internet and online games, but fewer places to turn to for support.

Also worth considering is research by Macaulay *et al.* (2020) which suggests that, whilst children believe that they have a good awareness of online dangers and how to avoid them (subjective knowledge), when asked open-ended questions, they find it difficult to articulate exactly what those dangers are and how they could elude them (objective knowledge). Within this objective knowledge, the research found that children may have a good understanding of online risks per se, but do not know what practical measures to take to stay safe in the face of those risks; for example, pupils may know that they should report anything that worries them online, but do not know the mechanisms for doing this.

Opstad and Williams (2020) argue that many of the conventional teaching resources available use a didactic approach and that alternative, interactive, and dialogic options are available. Therefore, opportunities to gain this practical knowledge should be sought. There are experiences that bridge the gap between subjective and objective knowledge which provide a different context for what is being taught, alongside practical tools; for example, safety centres such as Leicester's Warning Zone. See Case Study 23.3 and Figure 23.2.

Case Study 23.3: Warning Zone

Warning Zone, housed in an industrial building on the outskirts of the city, is a life skills centre which provides educational experiences for 80% of Year 6 pupils in Leicester, Leicestershire, and Rutland, reaching over 20,000 children and young people per year through its work.

It provides incredibly realistic safety zones, allowing children to discuss risky scenarios related to fire in the home, electricity and building sites, alcohol and anti-social behaviour, arson and criminal damage, and county lines.

In 2015, it opened its e-safety zone. With a fairground theme, and interactive activities, it covers subjects such as online grooming, cyberbullying, trolling, sharing images, and online phishing.

Staff acknowledge that many children who visit will play games with an older age rating and use social media. There is no judgement; the aim is to teach children to use technology responsibly. Warning Zone promotes self-confidence, self-esteem, and self-worth. Pupils are told that they have a right to feel safe and that it's never their fault if something goes wrong. They are encouraged to identify a trusted adult that they can talk to if they have any concerns, with the message to keep talking until they get the help they need.

Current projects aim to make further links between the safety zones and the online activities; for example, helping pupils to understand that being coerced into county lines could start with meeting someone while playing online games.

The success of Warning Zone in supporting children's risk perception are reported by Boam and Pulford who note that, 'those in the most at-risk sector of society are showing an increase in risk perception by visiting Warning Zone, and retaining this increase most effectively' (2019, p.186).

Online safety and parent responsibility

Data surrounding parental understanding of online safety presents a mixed picture. Most parents had some involvement in their child's internet use, with 38% of children stating that their parents knew a lot about what they do online, and 47% saying a fair amount. 12% didn't feel that their parents knew very much, with 3% believing that they knew nothing at all (ONS, 2021). Additionally, the majority of children under 13 had their own profile on at least one social media app or site, with just four in ten parents knowing that this was contrary to the minimum age requirement (Ofcom, 2022a).

As D'Lima and Higgins argue, 'these findings exhibit the futility of age restrictions on social media, which could be interpreted as tokenistic in ensuring children are happy and safe online' (2021, p.320). It may be worth noting that the majority of the most popular social media platforms only have the seemingly arbitrary 13+ age restriction due to the US Children's Online Privacy Protection Act, 1998 (COPPA), which was introduced to

Figure 23.2 Warning Zone – life skills centre

protect the personal information of children under 13 long before the wide-spread use of social media.

As schools are likely to be in regular contact with parents and carers, they are in a good position to provide information and guidance. Schools are now required to publish online safety information within the safeguarding tab of their school website and this should signpost parents to online toolkits (see Further Resources), as well as ensure that there is access to the CEOP report button.

It can be difficult to engage some carers in online safety, particularly if they are concerned about their own skill in using digital technologies. As Byron (2008) notes, there remains a 'generational divide' between parents and their children, often leaving parents unsure as to how they can support their children in the digital world. As Avery (2021) advises, it is important to be clear that online safety is not about technology, but about keeping children safe, putting parenting skills ahead of computing skills. Events run for, or by, children often encourage a greater parental turnout. Including online safety events as part of wider open evenings, transition evenings or parents' evenings, or even running them whilst parents wait for children during the school disco, may all help to boost your audience.

Offering drop-in sessions with school technicians provides opportunities for carers to gain support in setting parental controls on children's devices (these are not automatically set to a 'safety' standard when purchased); investigate a wide range of parental control apps such as Microsoft's Family Safety app, Qustodio, and Circle Home Plus; and explore useful websites.

Now undertake Task 23.4.

Task 23.4: Resources

Read the DfE (2019b) guidance *Teaching Online Safety in Schools*, look through some of the websites in the Further Resources section and search for external providers offering online safety education in your area.

Bookmark or download any resources that could enhance your current provision.

Summary and key points

The digital world brings many different opportunities for our pupils. Your role as a teacher is to empower them to engage with these creatively and safely, and guide them to become responsible digital citizens.

From the information provided in this chapter you should have:

- Developed a general overview of your roles and responsibilities in respect to online safety.
- Identified guidance and resources to support your delivery of online safety.
- Understood the need to consider the wider school context in relation to online safety.

Further resources

360° Safe: https://360safe.org.uk
This website provides an 'online safety self-review tool'.
Childnet: https://www.childnet.com/resources?paged=3
Childnet's resource page provides a range of stories, videos, lesson plans, and toolkits that can be filtered by age and topic. There is also a calendar overview suggesting ways in which online safety can be incorporated into the curriculum.
Teaching Online Safety in School: https://www.gov.uk/government/publications/teaching-online-safety-in-schools
This resource provides support in mapping identified risks to curriculum areas. It also provides a range of links to additional guidance and resources.
CEOP: https://www.thinkuknow.co.uk
This website provides resources for professionals, pupils, and parents.
Digital Resilience Framework: https://assets.publishing.service.gov.uk/government/uploads/system/uploads/attachment_data/file/831217/UKCIS_Digital_Resilience_Framework.pdf
This resource provides a self-evaluation framework for organisations to assess how well they are supporting users to build digital resilience.
Appropriate filtering and monitoring: A guide for education settings and filtering providers: https://saferinternet.org.uk/guide-and-resource/teachers-and-school-staff/appropriate-filtering-and-monitoring

UK Safer Internet Centre provides support for schools on appropriate filtering and monitoring.

Acknowledgments

Thank you to Jenny Hinton, Digital and Computing Lead at Parkdale Primary School in Nottingham, and Elaine Stevenson, CEO of Warning Zone, for sharing their time and expertise, which has contributed to this chapter.

References

2simple (2023) Digital Leader Scheme. Available at: https://www.2simple.com/purple-mash/digital-leaders/ (Accessed: 3 January 2023).

Avery, R. (2021) *How can we get families more involved in Online Safety?* Available at: https://www.theeducationpeople.org/blog/online-safety-faq-how-can-we-get-families-more-involved-in-online-safety/ (Accessed: 1 January 2023).

Boam, S. and Pulford, B. D. (2019) Experiencing risk: the effect of the experiential life-skills centre 'Warning Zone' on children's risk perception. *Journal of Risk Research.* **22**(2), pp.177–190.

Brook (2020) *Sexual behaviours traffic light tool.* Available at: https://www.brook.org.uk/training/wider-professional-training/sexual-behaviours-traffic-light-tool/ (Accessed: 1 January 2023).

Byron, T. (2008) *Safer children in a digital world: the report of the Byron Review.* Nottingham: DCSF Publications.

Childnet (2022a) *Childnet Digital Leaders impact report.* Available at: https://digital-leaders.childnet.com/annual-impact-report/ (Accessed: 3 January 2023).

Childnet (2022b) *The new Childnet Digital Leaders training platform is here.* Available at: https://www.childnet.com/blog/the-new-childnet-digital-leaders-training-platform-is-here/ (Accessed: 3 January 2023).

Children and Social Work Act 2017, c.4. Available at: https://www.legislation.gov.uk/ukpga/2017/16/contents/enacted (Accessed: 31 December 2022).

D'Lima, P. and Higgins, A. (2021) Social media engagement and Fear of Missing Out (FOMO) in primary school children. *Educational Psychology in Practice.* **37**(3), pp.320–338.

Department for Digital, Culture, Media and Sport (DCMS) (2022) *Michelle Donelan writes to parents, setting out how the Online Safety Bill will keep children safe.* Available at: https://www.gov.uk/government/publications/michelle-donelan-writes-to-parents-setting-out-how-the-online-safety-bill-will-keep-children-safe/read-the-secretary-of-states-open-letter-to-parents-carers-and-guardians (Accessed: 2 January 2023).

Department for Education (DfE) (2014) *Cyberbullying: advice for headteachers and school staff.* Available at: https://assets.publishing.service.gov.uk/government/uploads/system/uploads/attachment_data/file/1069987/Cyberbullying_Advice_for_Headteachers_and_School_Staff_121114.pdf (Accessed: 31 December 2022).

Department for Education (DfE) (2017) *Preventing and tackling bullying: advice for headteachers, staff and governing bodies.* Available at: https://assets.publishing.service.gov.uk/government/uploads/system/uploads/attachment_data/file/1069688/Preventing_and_tackling_bullying_advice.pdf (Accessed: 31 December 2022).

Department for Education (DfE) (2019a) *Relationships education, relationships and sex education (RSE) and health education: statutory guidance for governing bodies, proprietors, head teachers, principals, senior leadership teams, teachers.* Available at: https://assets.publishing.service.gov.uk/government/uploads/system/uploads/attachment_data/file/1090195/Relationships_Education_RSE_and_Health_Education.pdf (Accessed: 21 December 2022).

Department for Education (DfE) (2019b) *Teaching online safety in school: guidance supporting schools to teach their pupils how to stay safe online, within new and existing school subjects.* Available at: https://www.gov.uk/government/publications/teaching-online-safety-in-schools (Accessed: 21 December 2022).

Department for Education (DfE) (2020) *Data protection for education providers*. Available at: https://www.gov.uk/guidance/eu-exit-guide-data-protection-for-education-providers(Accessed: 27 December 2022).

Department for Education (DfE) (2021) *Revised Prevent duty guidance: for England and Wales*. Available at: https://www.gov.uk/government/publications/prevent-duty-guidance/revised-prevent-duty-guidance-for-england-and-wales (Accessed: 26 November 2023).

Department for Education (DfE) (2023a) *Early years foundation stage statutory framework*. Available at: https://assets.publishing.service.gov.uk/government/uploads/system/uploads/attachment_data/file/1170108/EYFS_framework_from_September_2023.pdf (Accessed: 26 November 2023).

Department for Education (DfE) (2023b) *Keeping children safe in education 2023*. Available at: https://assets.publishing.service.gov.uk/government/uploads/system/uploads/attachment_data/file/1181955/Keeping_children_safe_in_education_2023.pdf(Accessed: 27 November 2023).

Internet Watch Foundation (2023) *Sexual abuse imagery of primary school children 1,000 per cent worse since lockdown*. Available at: https://www.iwf.org.uk/news-media/news/sexual-abuse-imagery-of-primary-school-children-1-000-per-cent-worse-since-lockdown/ (Accessed: 30 January 2023).

Knowsley City Learning Centres (2022) *Getting started with Digital Leaders*. Available at: https://www.knowsleyclcs.org.uk/wp-content/uploads/2020/07/Digital-Leaders-Starters-Toolkit.pdf (Accessed: 22 December 2022).

Livingstone, S. and Stoilova, M. (2021) *The 4Cs: classifying online risk to children*. Available at: https://core-evidence.eu/posts/4-cs-of-online-risk (Accessed: 3 January 2023).

Macauley, P. J. R., Boulton, M. J., Betts, L. R., Boulton, L., Camerone, E., Down, J., Hughes, J., Kirkbride, C. and Kirkham, R. (2020) Subjective versus objective knowledge of online safety/dangers as predicators of children's perceived online safety and attitudes towards e-safety education in the United Kingdom. *Children and Media*. **14**(3), pp.376–395.

Natterhub (2023) *Digital Leaders pack*. Available at: https://natterhub.com/resources/digital-leaders-pack (Accessed: 3 January 2023).

NSPCC (2018) *Ten years since the Byron Review: are children safer in the digital world?* Available at: https://learning.nspcc.org.uk/media/1045/byron-review-10-years-on-report.pdf (Accessed: 21 December 2022).

NSPCC (2020) *How safe are our children?* Available at: https://learning.nspcc.org.uk/media/2287/how-safe-are-our-children-2020.pdf (Accessed: 3 January 2023).

NSPCC (2022) *E-safety for schools*. Available at: https://learning.nspcc.org.uk/research-resources/schools/e-safety-for-schools (Accessed: 21 December 2022).

Ofcom (2022a) *Children and parents: media use and attitudes report 2022*. Available at: https://www.ofcom.org.uk/__data/assets/pdf_file/0024/234609/childrens-media-use-and-attitudes-report-2022.pdf (Accessed: 29 December 2022).

Ofcom (2022b) *Online nation: 2022 report*. Available at: https://www.ofcom.org.uk/__data/assets/pdf_file/0023/238361/online-nation-2022-report.pdf (Accessed: 29 December 2022).

Ofsted (2010) *The safe use of new technologies*. Available at: https://www.nen.gov.uk/wp-content/uploads/2020/05/The-safe-use-of-new-technologies.pdf (Accessed: 29 December 2022).

ONS (2021) *Children's online behaviour in England and Wales: year ending March 2020*. Available at: https://www.ons.gov.uk/peoplepopulationandcommunity/crimeandjustice/bulletins/childrensonlinebehaviourinenglandandwales/yearendingmarch2020 (Accessed: 4 January 2023).

Opstad, H. and Williams, C. (2020) Fifteen-minute consultation: keeping young school children safe online using the 'SOCKS' workshop. *Archives of Disease in Childhood. Education and Practice Edition*. **105**(6), pp.322–325.

Pinto, T. and Younie, S. (2015) Developing e-safety in the primary school. In Younie, S., Leask, M. and Burden, K. (eds.) *Teaching and learning with ICT in the primary school*. London: Routledge, pp. 241–253.

South West Grid for Learning (SWGfL) (2021) *UK Schools Online Safety Policy and Practice Assessment 2021*. Available at: https://swgfl.org.uk/assets/documents/uk-schools-online-safety-policy-and-practice-assessment-2021.pdf (Accessed: 29 December 2022).

South West Grid for Learning (SWGfL) (2023) *Reviewing Online Safety Policy and Practice*. Available at: https://swgfl.org.uk/topics/back-to-school/important-reminder-for-online-safety-review/ (Accessed: 4 January 2023).

UK Council for Internet Safety (UKCIS) (2019) *Digital resilience framework: a framework and tool for organisations, communities and groups to help people build resilience in their digital life*. Available at: https://assets.publishing.service.gov.uk/government/uploads/system/uploads/attachment_data/file/831217/UKCIS_Digital_Resilience_Framework.pdf (Accessed 3 January 2023).

UK Council for Internet Safety (UKCIS) (2020) *Education for a connected world – 2020 edition*. Available at: https://assets.publishing.service.gov.uk/government/uploads/system/uploads/attachment_data/file/896323/UKCIS_Education_for_a_Connected_World_.pdf (Accessed: 2 January 2023).

UK Council for Internet Safety (UKCIS) (2022) *Using external expertise to enhance online safety education*. Available at: https://assets.publishing.service.gov.uk/government/uploads/system/uploads/attachment_data/file/1105567/OS_UKCIS_Draft_External_Visitors_to_Support_Online_Safety_Final.pdf (Accessed 11 December 2022).

UK Safer Internet Centre (2022) *Appropriate filtering and monitoring: a guide for education settings and filtering providers*. Available at: https://saferinternet.org.uk/guide-and-resource/teachers-and-school-staff/appropriate-filtering-and-monitoring (Accessed: 29 December 2022).

Warning Zone (2022) Available at: https://warningzone.org.uk (Accessed: 29 December 2022).

24 Family learning in the context of computer science education

Nina Bresnihan, Richard Millwood, Glenn Strong and Louise Caldwell

Introduction

This chapter outlines an innovative way of working with families with the aim of having a positive impact on parental attitudes to computing. To achieve this, the authors have developed and rolled out a workshop programme called 'OurKidsCode' which involves families working together on creative computing projects. This chapter explains the foundations and design principles for this programme so that you can adapt it to your context.

Parents are key advisers to children when making subject and career choices, but many are ill-prepared to offer advice about computing's potential and struggle to facilitate the learning experiences of a child who has an interest in computer science. Also, parents and children alike have expressed a desire to learn together, but rarely get a chance to do so (Bresnihan *et al.,* 2019a, 2019b). The method proposed here has been successful in the Republic of Ireland and offers family workshops where children and parents work together as equals and collaborate with other families. They create fun artefacts that demonstrate how they can learn together and be successful in engaging with creative computing (see Figure 24.1). This chapter reports on the design principles used for the programme and advises on how these can be used by you in preparing your own initiatives to engage families in computer science education.

Objectives

At the end of this chapter you should be able to:

- explain the benefits of family learning with regard to computer science education
- explain the significance of parental attitudes regarding computer science education
- design and evaluate your own school's response to engaging parents in computer science education using research-informed design principles.

Family learning

The importance of parental involvement

The role of parents in their children's education has long been of interest to researchers, educators and policy makers, but it is a complex field. For example, parents' socio-economic status, cultural background, gender and education levels are all significant factors (Desforges and Abouchaar, 2003). In addition, Epstein's (2001) influential model emphasises

DOI: 10.4324/9781003408925-24

Figure 24.1 Making of a wearable wristband to play Rock-Paper-Scissors

In the foreground, girls from different families share the making of a wearable wristband to play Rock-Paper-Scissors while other children work with parents to program the game. Photo attribution: Richard Millwood

the shared responsibilities of schools, families and communities, and Hornby and Lafaele (2011) identify individual parent and family factors; child factors; parent-teacher factors; and societal factors as being important.

Despite this complexity, findings consistently provide evidence that parental involvement is strongly associated with higher cognitive and non-cognitive outcomes (Borgonovi and Montt, 2012; Desforges and Abouchaar, 2003; Emerson *et al.*, 2012; Goodall and Vorhaus, 2011; Harris and Goodall, 2008). Moreover, there is evidence that specific interventions to improve parental involvement can have a positive effect on reading, writing and mathematics skills (Epstein *et al.*, 1997; Jordan *et al.*, 2000; Starkey and Klein, 2000); homework completion (Cancio *et al.*, 2004); and behaviour (Kratochwill *et al.*, 2004; Pantin *et al.*, 2003). This is despite the difficulties involved in the design of such interventions, including delivery, uptake and sustainability (Goodall and Vorhaus, 2011). The OECD (Borgonovi and Montt, 2012) argue that promoting higher levels of parental involvement may increase student outcomes, and that high-quality parental involvement may help reduce performance differences across socio-economic groups.

Importance of parental involvement in computer science education

There has been extensive research on how family interaction influences children's learning in traditional academic areas, but less about how families contribute to building computer science competencies. Research has tended to look at broader Information and Communications Technology (ICT) issues and focus on concerns such as internet safety and digital literacy with the attention on parents managing and mediating children's internet use (Goh, *et al.*, 2015; Livingstone *et al.*, 2015, 2017). While some studies have found a positive relationship between childrens' ICT competences and the support they receive at home (Aesaert *et al.*, 2015; Vekiri, 2010; Vekiri and Chronaki, 2008; Yuen *et al.*, 2018), computing in the home tends to be viewed as a passive or consuming activity rather than something that is active or creative. In the family context, children's computing use is often perceived as a contentious issue that needs to be carefully regulated and controlled by parents (Chaudron *et al.*, 2015; Hollingworth *et al.*, 2011).

Many parents' own education has left them with little experience in programming or computational thinking with the result that they can experience anxiety, lack of confidence and make gendered assumptions about technology (McClure *et al.*, 2017). More broadly than that, Hollingworth *et al.* argue:

> that parents' orientation and practices are determined not only by their experiences of education and learning and their access to material resources (technology assets), but also the ways in which parents engage with and become familiar with ICT – or not – in their daily lives.
>
> (2011:358)

While parents may struggle to facilitate the learning experiences of a child who has an interest in computer science, there is strong evidence that parents are interested in computer science education: Wang *et al.* (2016) found that 91% of US parents want their children to learn more computer science and two-thirds think it should be required learning in school. In Ireland, where it is not yet part of the primary school curriculum, our investigation found that 95% believed that it should be (Bresnihan *et al.*, 2019b). Parents are also key to choosing non-formal activities for their children (Crowley and Jacobs, 2002) and their willingness to support computer science education is also clearly demonstrated by the huge success of non-formal coding clubs such as CoderDojo and Code Club.

Parental support is found to be significantly associated with general 'career decidedness and career self-efficacy' (Clarke-Midura *et al.*, 2019; Wang *et al.*, 2015). However, while 73% of Irish parents recognise themselves as the biggest influencers of subject choice 68% reported feeling uninformed on STEM career opportunities and industry needs (Accenture, 2013). In England, in 2023 the government announced an initiative to provide careers education to primary children (Department for Education, 2023). However, parents feel limited in their ability to talk to their children about computer science, conversations that can be vital for recruiting youth (Clarke-Midura *et al.*, 2019).

There is also some evidence to suggest that parents can directly influence learning when they choose to engage in coactivity with their children (Brahms, 2014; Roque, 2016; Sadka and Zuckerman, 2017; Takeuchi and Stevens, 2011). In addition, Maruyama (2019) found attitudes toward and confidence in supporting children at home improved as a result of participation in a parent-children workshop. The potential for learning together as a family has also been recognised by Barron who argues that '[g]iven that families are central sites for learning interactions, working to help expand their opportunities to co-learn may be one of the more important things we can do to fulfil the potential promise of technology as a resource for the greater good' (2009:351).

With the growing importance of computer science education in schools, there is a clear potential for parents to play a significant role in initiating and supporting their children, whether it be helping a pupil with their homework or with subject and career choices.

What is lacking is support for those who wish to undertake this role but feel they lack confidence, knowledge and skills. However, questions remain over what form this support should take, and how to maximise its impact on the quantity and quality of parental involvement.

The need for design principles

These questions inspired our research in support of developing a set of design principles for interventions to provide such support. The design principles are intended to help you develop interventions aiming to support parental involvement in Computer Science Education. This section outlines their theoretical basis. The principles were further refined through their implementation and evaluation.

We began by surveying a large sample of parents of children aged 5–13 (n=1228) to explore their computing attitudes, behaviours and current involvement in computer science education. We identified that computing confidence, availability, experience and creative usage were factors that had an impact on parental involvement and concluded that these factors should be targeted by any interventions (Bresnihan *et al.*, 2021). A further consideration was to promote autonomy and self-directed learning as it is crucial for participants to take ownership of their learning if they are to persist. We therefore decided that interventions should create sustainable opportunities to foster confidence and creativity through experience of computer programming and making.

This understanding, along with a literature review to identify appropriate pedagogy (described below), informed the design principles, and these were used to underpin the iterative development of the programme for the family creative coding workshops.

Literature review

Much of the discussion of learning within the family has been informed by the insights of constructivist theorists such as Piaget, Vygotsky and Freire (Mackenzie, 2010). Piaget argued that the way in which one acquires, or constructs, knowledge is equally, if not more important, than the knowledge attained (Kamii and Ewing, 1996). Vygotsky had earlier brought a social dimension to this process, particularly with his concept of the 'zone of proximal development' (ZPD) which is concerned with how social interaction can help to bridge the gap between a learner's current, and potential levels of, cognitive development. He posited that a person's learning, development and knowledge are all rooted in the particular social and cultural context in which they exist. The idea of teaching and learning as less of a transmissionist and more of a connected, learner-centred, model manifests in an approach where teachers are not simply information providers, but facilitators of pupils' knowledge construction (Vygotsky, 1980).

As parental involvement can clearly be located within situated approaches to learning that acknowledge the importance of socio-cultural issues in learning relationships, the development of the design principles can be usefully grounded in such social-constructivist theories. A literature review was therefore conducted to identify and understand the nature of social interactions that surround and support family learning and to foreground how to best support such learning in the context of family-based computer science education. It aimed to take such theories of learning, where knowledge construction is viewed as a social and cultural process and social interaction is crucial to the learning outcomes, and examine them for their practical pedagogical implications in this context.

Intra-family collaboration

Rogoff's theory is particularly relevant to the family context (Rogoff, 1998). Inspired by Vygotsky's concept of the zone of proximal development (ZPD), she describes a form of apprenticeship where learning occurs through 'guided participation' in specific cultural activities and cognition is 'situated' in specific contexts. These interactions

> allow children to participate in activities that would be impossible for them alone, using cultural tools that must be adapted to the specific practical activities at hand, and thus passed on to as well as transformed by new members of the community.
>
> (1998:682)

Within the family learning context, examples of this type of learning are provided in Tizard and Hughes' transcripts, where children initiated discussions to satisfy their curiosity, with parents providing a 'scaffold' for their conversation (Tizard and Hughes, 2008). Mackenzie (2010) gives examples of normal family activities that create learning: 'enjoying a book, taking a walk, visiting the Post Office, baking a cake, fixing a puncture and playing a computer game all provide contexts for family learning' (2010:7) and stresses the importance of dialogue in this process.

While Rogoff's focus is on how parents influence their children's learning through their everyday, informal interaction (1998), Barron (2009) describes how more purposeful inter-family coactivity can also contribute to learning. Such activity gives an opportunity for observation and for spontaneous questions and explanations as well as parents providing support as the 'more knowledgeable other' within the child's ZPD (Vygotsky, 1980).

The relevance of this theory to computer science education is reinforced in related interventions which have shown that there are potential benefits for parental involvement when parents and children engage together in collaborative computer science activities. Von Wangenheim *et al.* (2017) argue that family computing workshops provide an opportunity for families to share ideas, explore computing as a career and create important time for intergenerational learning. Roque *et al.* (2015) suggest that learning computing as a family reinforces sharing behaviours and attitudes, adding that 'parents can benefit from first-hand engagement with the design practices of computing and with the practices of supporting their children in computing experiences' (p.687).

The implications of this for the design principles include:

Implication 1 – Interventions should take the form of coactivity, with families engaging together in collaborative computer science activities.
Implication 2 – Dialogue about the activity should be supported and encouraged.

Inter-family collaboration

The importance of the broader community outside of the family to learning is explored by Lave and Wenger (1991) who also see learning as a social process, characterised by what they term 'legitimate peripheral participation'. This 'situated learning', which takes place in a specific context and a particular social and physical environment, involves the learner becoming a member of a 'community of practice' and moving toward full participation in that community. Bers (2007) points out the importance of a shared goal or 'joint enterprise' in the development of such communities and adds that workshops are 'natural spaces for forming communities of practice in which people engage with each other and with new knowledge and skills by producing artefacts, relationships and ideas' (Bers, 2007:552).

The importance of inviting participants' input into the development of such communities is emphasised by Summer and Summer (2014). Recognising their existing expertise, and building on skills and competencies that they already possess draws on Gonzales *et al.*'s influential concept of 'funds of knowledge' which presupposes that 'people are competent' (2006:x). This idea, that people have knowledge that they have gained through life experience and that it is possible to harness this knowledge for positive learning experiences, fits comfortably within our social constructivist framework and, more specifically, provides a strong argument for co-creation. Inviting families to contribute to the learning environment through such activities as setting learning goals and choosing topics with other families may work to strengthen inter-family collaboration and dialogue.

Interventions should therefore:

Implication 3 – invite participants' input and recognise their existing knowledge and expertise;

Implication 4 – encourage families to engage with other participating families for help and support.

Structure and scaffolding

Constructivist theories of learning, where knowledge construction is viewed as a social and cultural process and social interaction is crucial to the learning outcomes (Steffe and Gale, 1995) have sometimes been criticised as being overly child-directed, or as regulating the teacher or facilitator to a passive role (Baines and Stanley, 2000; Matthews, 2003; McPhail, 2016). However, in practice, constructivist learning environments can often be highly structured with teachers or facilitators carefully designing and promoting experiences that, in turn, require pupils to become active participants in the learning process. Bruner's concept of 'scaffolding' is useful here (Wood *et al.*, 1976). Taking Vygotsky's ZPD theory, which says we can learn more in the presence of a knowledgeable other person, as a starting point, Bruner argues that when learners encounter new concepts they need purposeful meaningful interaction with a skilled instructor or more proficient peers. At the early stage, they are reliant on that active support, but as they become more independent in their thinking and gain competence and knowledge, the support can be gradually removed. Rather than directly presenting or providing content, the instructor supports or 'scaffolds' the learning experience by providing the information and resources necessary for the learner to construct or discover it either individually or collaboratively.

However, ZPD and scaffolding are not equivalent. ZPD is a broader concept which includes the contribution of the novice to the shared endeavour of learning. This idea is at the heart of the community-of-learners model (Brown and Campione, 2002; Newman *et al.*, 1989; Rogoff, 1994; Tharp and Gallimore, 1991) which emphasises the active and participatory nature of *all* parties in the learning process. Rogoff captures this idea well:

> In a community of learners, […]; no role has all the responsibility for knowing or directing, and no role is by definition passive. Children and adults together are active in structuring shared endeavours…
>
> (1994:213)

Structure and purpose are clearly important in this model; but it is conversational in nature with all parties contributing to the direction.

From the discussion above, the following implications are relevant to the formation of the principles:

Implication 5 – Interventions should consist of clearly structured activities.
Implication 6 – Participants should be given the opportunity to become progressively more active in planning and structuring the activities.

These conclusions necessitate a closer look at what form such structured activity should take.

Creativity and constructionism

A family-learning activity will often result in a product that enhances the wider community; traditionally that may have been a musical or theatrical production, a festival or storytelling event. Mackenzie (2010) conducted extensive questionnaires, interviews and field visits exploring family learning in Scotland. A key theme that emerged was the power of the arts to provide contexts in which families can experience personal and social transformation. She found that bringing families together to prepare a shared creative output such as drama, dance or music developed a sense of connectedness as well as providing fun, promoting inclusivity and building self-esteem.

Alongside the power of creative activities lies the importance of their outputs. Papert's theory of constructionism argues that learners can actively create, interpret and reorganise knowledge in a particularly effective manner through the construction of a meaningful tangible artefact (Papert, 1980). This argument has had a powerful legacy in the sphere of computer science education, with constructionism gaining wide acceptance as a classroom approach to teach children computing (Lye and Koh, 2014).

The interventions should then:

Implication 7 – involve participants working towards the creation of a meaningful tangible artefact;
Implication 8 – formalise the sharing and celebration of activity outcomes between families.

Reflection

Finally, we need to explore how participation in these activities can effectively lead to development of family learning and more positive parental attitudes towards Computer Science. For Dewey, reflection is:

the thread that makes the continuity of learning possible (Rodgers, 2002).

He understood reflection as a process of making meaning through the learner connecting their current experience with past experiences and ideas in a systematic fashion, so as to develop a deeper understanding. Freire (1996) also placed importance on people's consciousness of learning and change aided by reflection. Interestingly, in this context, Dewey also proposed that ideally reflection be undertaken in interaction with others (1997).

Facilitating collaborative reflection can also demonstrate the value of a wider community by providing greater clarity to issues than can be individually perceived in order to strengthen the connection between families (Rearick and Feldman, 1999). The importance of reflection in turning experiences into learning means that:

Implication 10 – interventions should be structured to include time and space for ongoing dialogue about what is being learned;
Implication 11 – time should be reserved for collaborative reflection at the end of the learning experience.

Design principles based on literature review

The review of the literature supported the adoption for the OurKidsCode project of a social-constructivist based framework, with scaffolding and reflection activities. Within this framework and drawing on the implications listed above, the Design Principles outlined in Table 24.1 were identified and applied to the OurKidsCode programme:

Table 24.1 Design Principles for the design of interventions to support parental involvement in computer science education

	Principle	Theory
DP1	The interventions should be collaborative within families and include suitable roles for different family members to play.	Social-constructivism Family learning
DP2	The interventions must bring multiple families together to encourage inter-family support and communication.	Communities of Practice Learning Communities
DP3	The interventions should consist of structured activities.	Scaffolding Guided Participation
DP4	Parents' and children's input should be invited, and their existing knowledge and expertise recognised. They should be given the opportunity to become more active in planning and structuring the activities as the intervention progresses.	'Funds of Knowledge' Scaffolding Communities of learning
DP5	The interventions should use computers as creative tools and lead to the making of a meaningful artefact.	Constructionism Family learning
DP6	The outcomes of the intervention should be celebrated and shared.	Constructionism
DP7	The interventions should be structured to include ongoing dialogue about what is being learned. Time should be reserved for collaborative reflection to complete the learning experience.	Reflection
DP8	The interventions should encourage and support the pursuit of further activity, as a family unit or along with other families.	Communities of practice Communities of learning
DP9	Interventions need to consider the availability and design of a suitable learning environment and technical infrastructure for their implementation and for any future ongoing activity.	(This principle arose from a survey of families and the project's practice.)

Implementation and lessons learnt from OurKidsCode

The Design Principles pointed to the importance of structured collaborative learning for the design of the workshops that we were planning. While most of the reports of related interventions did not provide detail on workshop structures, both Family Creative Learning (Roque,

2016) and Project Interactions (Bers, 2007) provided some guidance. In addition, the Bridge 21 activity model was considered, a team-based, technology-mediated learning model shown to be pragmatic for effective twenty-first-century learning (Lawlor *et al.*, 2018). Our research team had already had a successful experience adapting it for use with teachers (Oldham *et al.*, 2018). In particular, Bridge 21 provided an example of the kind of clear and consistent workshop structure that could assist in keeping families on track (Byrne *et al.*, 2019).

Following a consideration of how elements of these models could be adapted to better implement the draft design principles, an activity model for the workshops was developed consisting of timed phases of activities (see Further Resources from www.ourkidscode.ie). Sometimes, phases were 'overloaded' i.e. addressed more than one aim. For example, the phase 'Icebreaker' would be designed not only to build ease in interrelationships, but also focus on the task at hand by adopting an 'unplugged' task. 'Unplugged' meant carrying out a computing process by hand, without the actual computer, which helped introduce the workshop concept through playful collaboration.

Table 24.2 lists the workshop phases and notes how each addresses relevant principles:

Table 24.2 The Activity Model – workshop phases and their rationale

Phase	Description	Rationale and Relevant Design Principles (DP)
Setup	The physical environment is set up to enable the rest of the workshop. The facilitator makes refreshments available to the participants, distributes materials, and helps ensure the equipment is working.	Debugging issues such as wi-fi connectivity in this phase avoids interfering with the workshop activities. Meanwhile participants begin to talk casually over refreshments [DP2, DP4].
Introduction	The facilitator briefly explains the workshop model to orient the families.	This sets the scene and helps focus the participants on the process as well as the content [DP3, DP7].
Icebreaker	All participants take part in an 'unplugged' icebreaker activity specific to the creative activity planned for the session. These activities are physical (participants stand up and move around) and both inter- and intra-family in nature.	This phase introduces the creative task and allows families to be more at-ease with each other, thus facilitating peer assistance during the next phase [DP1, DP2, DP5].
Create	A creative technical challenge is given, forming the main part of the workshop. The challenges combine coding and 'making' activities and are designed to encourage family members to take on different roles during the completion of the challenge.	Families are encouraged to collaborate both within and between family groups, and to take on varying roles as they work on the challenges [DP1, DP2, DP3, DP4, DP5].
Share	Families share their creations in a structured way (a tournament or showcase).	Bringing the families together at the end gives a sense of achievement and fulfilment [DP2, DP5, DP6].
Reflect	All participants sit in a circle and share what they have enjoyed and learned, encouraging discussion of future plans. Participants are provided with OurKidsCode guides and materials for another of the workshops to complete at home.	Improves the learning by offering an opportunity to say out loud what was learnt and evaluate strengths and weaknesses. Setting an agenda for further work and making a commitment for future engagement is a part of this phase [DP7, DP8].

The Workshops

Three separate stand-alone workshops were developed along with support materials. Each workshop follows the activity model, with workshop-specific content being provided for the 'Icebreaker', 'Create' and 'Share' phases. A facilitator trained by the project team guides the families through the workshops – a role for you to consider in initiating an intervention, but ripe for an enthusiastic family to take on as confidence grows.

Figure 24.2 The wearable artefact to play Rock-Paper-Scissors by randomly displaying a symbol after shaking the wrist.

One workshop, 'Rock-Paper-Scissors', involves making and decorating a wearable (see Figure 24.2) using the BBC Micro:bit that can be used to play the well-known game, adapting content from the MakeCode site. A second, 'Conductor', uses Scratch to make an orchestra of 'players' which can then be 'conducted' using a 'baton' fashioned out of craft materials detected by the computer's camera. A third workshop, 'Dance Mat', is described below in detail to show how the activity model works in practice.

All workshops involve the creation of an artefact using both physical and digital materials, and all endeavour to give families a sense of fun, achievement and confidence in their own abilities.

An example workshop design – 'Dance Mat'

Table 24.3 describes one of the OurKidsCode workshops, 'Dance Mat' (see Figure 24.3). The workshop is based on creating music and dance. It uses the Makey Makey (Collective and Shaw, 2012), a tool for constructing physical interfaces, and the Scratch programming language (Resnick *et al.*, 2009). A series of switches using paper plates and aluminium kitchen foil are connected to the Makey Makey and are used to trigger sound effects from a computer via the Scratch programming language. Families are then invited to choreograph a set of dance moves to play a short tune, activating the switches by stepping on the plates. Families exchange dances to experience each other's work. The workshop is designed to be completed within a 60–90 minute timeframe, but in organising workshops, two hours

Figure 24.3 A six-year-old participant tests the dance mat she has constructed from paper plates and aluminium foil and programmed in collaboration with her father, by following the choreography for 'Old MacDonald's Farm' in County Mayo

were allocated to allow flexibility and ensure everyone went home in time and having fulfilled the challenge. Table 24.3 sets out the plan for this workshop.

Table 24.3 Sample OurKidsCode one-off workshop

Phase	Description
Setup (**10 mins**)	The families settle in, and the facilitator makes sure everyone has refreshments, that the participants' laptops can access the necessary online resources for the workshop and that they have the necessary support materials.
Introduction (5 mins)	The facilitator briefly introduces the overall workshop model and explains the timeline for the rest of the session.
Icebreaker (**c. 10 mins**)	The facilitator introduces the dance mat idea and shares the basic rules of the challenge. The families work on paper to design a set of dance steps and then challenge another family to perform the dance by following instructions. This is intended to reduce inhibitions between families so that they are more likely to share knowledge and support during the following 'Create' phase. This phase also introduces the idea of giving instructions to be followed in a specific sequence.
Create (**c. 45 mins**)	This is the longest phase of the workshop. The facilitator gives a short introduction to the Makey Makey, explaining the basic idea of closing a circuit. A simple hand-holding activity gives participants a concrete demonstration of how circuits work with the Makey Makey.
	The families are encouraged to explicitly identify 'Maker', 'Programmer', and 'Organiser' roles, giving them some guidance in structuring the family effort. Family members are encouraged to exchange roles during the activity, so participants do not become stuck in a single role.

(*Continued*)

Table 24.3 (Continued)

Phase	Description
	Families then make a set of paper-plate 'switches' and connect them to the Makey Makey. They decorate and personalise the 'switches' as they make them. This offers creativity and play during the workshop, and also provides opportunities for family members of all ages to make enjoyable and meaningful contributions.
	A program is built in Scratch which plays selected musical notes on key presses triggered using the Makey Makey. This is generally characterised by exploratory coding and physical activity as families investigate the capabilities and needs of the Makey Makey platform. Simple musical composition and choreography are included in the design of the challenge allowing families to integrate a range of creative interests.
Share (c. 10 mins)	Families are invited to try each other's dances, typically with a 'caller' from the family who designed the challenge giving instruction to a participant from another family activating the switches, in a mirror of the Icebreaker activity.
Reflect (c. 5 mins)	Families discuss and share experiences, and the facilitator encourages discussion and planning for future activities.

Support materials

We identified a need for support materials for the organisation and running of the workshops, as well as for continuing activities outside the workshops. In response to this, paperwork was developed to support the workshop facilitators and families.

We first designed cards to guide participants, but later moved to A4 booklets (see Figure 24.3), which simplified reproduction and manageability in use. The booklet acted as a narrative to help participants organise themselves, understand the challenge and to follow the activity.

Colourful diagrams were mixed with text to make the booklet aesthetically delightful. The instructions were accompanied by pictures, taken from the application used for programming (Scratch and MakeCode) and photographs of the artefacts as they were made. The workshop overview (see Figure 24.3) employed a block programming style which matched the visual style of the application.

The instructions for programming employed a 'copy code' pedagogy (Waite, 2021) optimised for obtaining results and indeed a full version of the final code was included in the booklet for those who preferred to make the 'jigsaw' rather than follow step-by-step instructions. In either case, we did not anticipate a full conceptual understanding, and the approach can be likened to making a Lego giraffe from a kit which includes just the pieces necessary, and demands little existing competence. Competence in computer science may well be developed later, but this was not the foremost goal of our work, which was to have an impact on parental attitudes.

To further assist participants, we created brief 'explainer videos' which were accessed by short URL or by QR code using mobile phone. These were also offered to participants in advance of the workshop to enhance their opportunity for preparation.

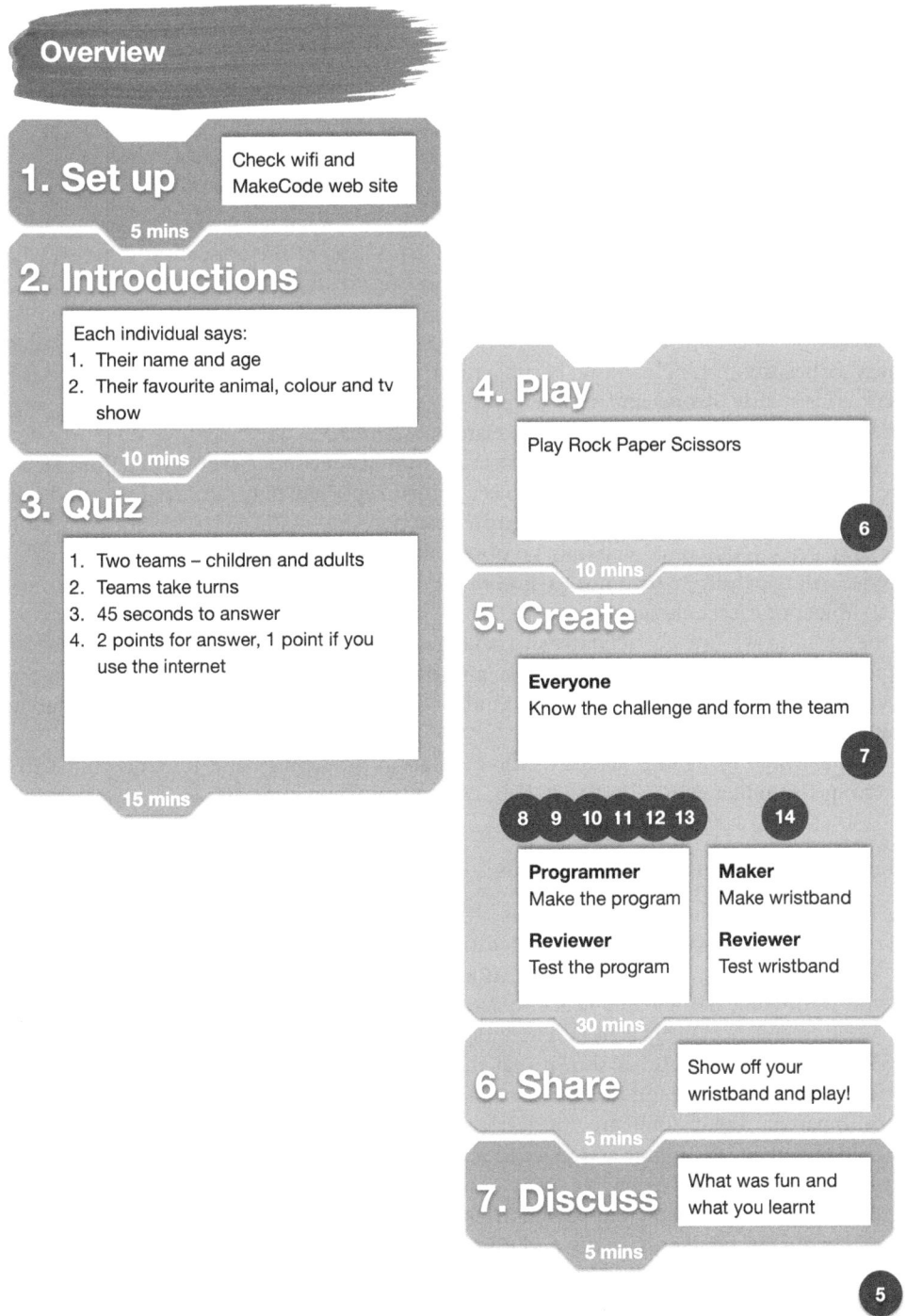

Figure 24.4 Rock-Paper-Scissors workshop – overview page

Participants and facilitators also had access to a supporting website (ourkidscode.ie), which contains descriptions of the workshop model, and downloadable copies of the materials and provides support and encouragement for families to undertake follow-on activities. In order to further encourage future activities, the project gave each family a Micro:bit to take home with them.

Evaluation

This chapter has no space to go into a detailed exposition of the evaluation strategy, which we based on Kirkpatrick's identification of assessing 'reaction', 'behaviour' and 'learning' (Millwood, 2018).

'Reaction' was built into every workshop using an online form to capture the participants' beliefs about fun, learning, participation, confidence and desire to continue. Results were consistently strong and responses to an open question to report their experience revealed some exciting, positive and revelatory experiences.

Data on 'behaviour' and 'learning' was captured in a second survey several months after the experience. Not unexpectedly, a lower return reported that participants could recall what they had learnt, but more importantly, had become strong advocates for computing.

Kirkpatrick's 'outcome' will only be observable in a decade or so, when the parent's attitudes will hopefully be seen not to discourage their children from considering computing as a subject or career choice.

In addition we invited facilitators to reflect on each workshop by observing what happened and identifying opportunities for improvement. This data helped their own competence, but also has given some clear guidance to the team in improving our design and materials.

If you would like more details of the evaluation procedures and findings they can be found in Bresnihan *et al.* (2019a, 2019b, 2021) and Bresnihan (2022).

Practical recommendations to schools

1. This project has shown how you could create successful family learning through a theoretical and evidence-based approach distilled into design principles.
2. To make family learning work, you should adopt a playful approach, emphasising fun and reminding participants that the activity is not school, will not be tested and that working collaboratively is to be encouraged, not seen as cheating.
3. Although our research has shown that the vast majority of parents will say they want to learn with their child, and that the vast majority of children love to learn with their parents, both parents and children are not necessarily clear on how they go about it. You will succeed if you give them time and space to reflect on themselves, identify roles, adopt responsibility and benefit from the company of other families embarking on the same activities.
4. By building confidence, and paying attention to the design principles, you may be able to encourage families, parents and children, to organise and run their own activities independently in the form of a club, with an obvious payoff in reduced load on the teacher.
5. Based on the evidence of our evaluation (to be published), we believe that you will increase interest in school computing through this approach.

The following tasks are intended to help you plan your own workshops.

Task 24.1: Facilitate a family workshop

Organising a family workshop using the OurKidsCode materials is easy and they are fun to do. The families do the work, your role is to bring them together and host. Start by downloading the Facilitator's Guide on the OurKidsCode website at www.ourkidscode.ie and read its advice.

1.1   Look at the workshop guides on the OurKidsCode website and select an activity that you have the resources for. If your school has access to Makey Makeys or Micro:bits you could do the workshops that need those. Invite parents to bring their own laptops so that they can continue informally at home.

1.2   Select a venue – can you use a classroom after school has ended?

1.3   Contact some willing families, a minimum of 3 and a maximum of 6. You need enough room for the families – imagine each family sits around a table, count enough space for as many tables again so that you have floor space for the activity.

1.4   Get the families to commit to the time. You can ask each family to bring something for the refreshments table, you don't have to supply it all yourself!

1.5   Make sure the materials you need for the workshop are ready for the day (craft supplies and tools, computers, WiFi access details).

1.6   On the day, follow the Facilitator's Guide to keep things running smoothly. Make sure you have familiarised yourself with it first!

1.7   Follow-up with families afterwards to learn what worked and find out if they would like to take part in further activities.

Task 24.2: Design a new workshop using the design principles

Once you are familiar with the OurKidsCode design principles, you can use them to develop new ideas. Having a range of workshop ideas that follow the OurKidsCode scaffolded model allows families to have further meetings until they are confident enough to choose their own activities from ideas they find online or elsewhere.

2.1   Choose a creative computing task from the internet – see Further Resources

2.2   Create phases/scaffolds according to the Design Principles outlined here, and the Activity Model in Table 24.2 that supports those principles (icebreaker/create/share, etc.)

Summary and key points

- Family learning outside school hours has much to commend itself for influencing parental attitudes.
- Families can, with initial facilitation and a principled approach, develop confidence in computing without formal assessment, curriculum or teaching.
- The goal is not to learn Computer Science but simply to show that Computer Science is not a dry technical activity but can be a hugely creative and craft activity.

- In the process, both parents and children will be able to fulfil their art, craft and computing ambitions, regardless of learning outcomes. This increases their confidence in their ability to pursue similar activities in the future.

Further resources and websites

OurKidsCode family workshop and facilitation guides www.ourkidscode.ie Accessed 5 February 2023.
Coderdojo https://coderdojo.com Accessed 5 February 2023.
Codeclub https://codeclub.org Accessed 8 February 2023.
Scratch https://scratch.mit.edu/ Accessed 8 February 2023.
Micro:bit / MakeCode https://microbit.org/ Accessed 8 February 2023.
MakeyMakey https://makeymakey.com/ Accessed 8 February 2023.
LibraryMakers https://librarymakers.net/ Accessed 8 February 2023.
Raspberry Pi Foundation https://projects.raspberrypi.org/ Accessed 8 February 2023.

References

Accenture (2013) *Powering economic growth: Attracting more young women into science and technology*, Accenture.

Aesaert, K., van Braak, J., Van Nijlen, D., and Vanderlinde, R. (2015) Primary school pupils' ICT competences: Extensive model and scale development, *Computers and Education*, 81, 326–344, https://doi.org/10.1016/j.compedu.2014.10.021.

Baines, L.A., and Stanley, G. (2000) 'We want to see the teacher' constructivism and the rage against expertise, *Phi Delta Kappan*, 82, 327–330.

Barron, B., Martin, C.K., Takeuchi, L., and Fithian, R. (2009) Parents as learning partners in the development of technological fluency, *International Journal of Learning and Media*, 1, 55–77.

Bers, M.U. (2007) Project InterActions: A multigenerational robotic learning environment, *Journal of Science Education and Technology*, 16, 537–552.

Borgonovi, F., and Montt, G. (2012) *Parental involvement in selected PISA countries and economies*, OECD Education Working Papers, No. 73, https://doi.org/10.1787/5k990rk0jsjj-en.

Brahms, L. (2014) *Making as a learning process: Identifying and supporting family learning in informal settings* (Unpublished doctoral dissertation), Pittsburgh, PA, University of Pittsburgh.

Bresnihan, N. (2022) *Designing to support parental involvement in computer science education: An exploratory study*, Doctoral dissertation, Trinity College Dublin. School of Computer Science and Statistics. Discipline of Computer Science.

Bresnihan, N., Bray, A., Fisher, L., Strong, G., Millwood, R., and Tangney, B. (2021) Parental involvement in computer science education and computing attitudes and behaviours in the home: Model and scale development, *ACM Transactions on Computing Education*, 21, 1–24.

Bresnihan, N., Strong, G., Fisher, L., Millwood, R., and Lynch, Á. (2019a) *OurKidsCode: Facilitating families to be creative with computing*, Presented at the CSEDU (1), 519–530.

Bresnihan, N., Strong, G., Fisher, L., Millwood, R., and Lynch, Á. (2019b) *OurKidsCode: Facilitating families to be creative with computing*, in: Proceedings of the 11th International Conference on Computer Supported Education. Presented at the 11th International Conference on Computer Supported Education (CSEDU), Crete, 519–530, https://doi.org/10.5220/0007729405190530.

Brown, A.L., and Campione, J.C. (2002) Communities of learning and thinking, or a context by any other name, in: P. Woods (Ed.), *Contemporary issues in teaching and learning*, Routledge, 120–126.

Byrne, J.R., Kearney, S., and Sullivan, K. (2019) Technology-mediated collaborative learning: The Bridge21 activity model in theory and practice, in: Linda Daniela (Ed.), *Didactics of Smart Pedagogy*, Springer, 309–330.

Cancio, E.J., West, R.P., and Young, K.R. (2004) Improving mathematics homework completion and accuracy of students with EBD through self-management and parent participation, *Journal of Emotional and Behavioral Disorders*, 12, 9–22, https://doi.org/10.1177/10634266040 120010201.

Chaudron, S., Beutel, M., Donoso Navarrete, V., Dreier, M., Fletcher-Watson, B., Heikkilä, A., Kontríková, V., Korkeamäki, R., Livingstone, S., and Marsh, J. (2015) *Young children (0–8) and digital technology: A qualitative exploratory study across seven countries*, Luxembourg, Joint Research Centre of the European Commission.

Clarke-Midura, J., Sun, C., Pantic, K., Poole, F., and Allan, V. (2019) Using informed design in informal computer science programs to increase youths' interest, self-efficacy, and perceptions of parental support, *ACM Transactions on Computing Education* (TOCE), 19, 1–24, https://doi.org/10.1145/3319445.

Collective, B.M., and Shaw, D. (2012) *Makey Makey: Improvising tangible and nature-based user interfaces*, in: Proceedings of the Sixth International Conference on Tangible, Embedded and Embodied Interaction, Kingston, Ontario, Canada, 19–22 February 2012, 367–370.

Crowley, K., and Jacobs, M. (2002) Building islands of expertise in everyday family activity, in: G. Leinhardt, K. Crowley, and K. Knutson (Eds.), *Learning conversations in museums*, New York, Routledge, 333–356.

Department for Education, (2023) *Careers boost for young people* [WWW Document]. GOV.UK, https://www.gov.uk/government/news/careers-boost-for-young-people. Accessed on 5 February 2023.

Desforges, C., and Abouchaar, A. (2003) *The impact of parental involvement, parental support and family education on pupil achievement and adjustment: A literature review (Research Report)*, Nottingham, DfES publications.

Dewey, J. (1997) *How we think*. Mass, Courier Corporation.

Emerson, L., Fear, J., Fox, S., and Sanders, E. (2012) *Parental engagement in learning and schooling: Lessons from research (Research Report)*, Canberra, Australian Research Alliance for Children and Youth (ARACY) for the Family-School and Community Partnerships Bureau.

Epstein, J.L. (2001) *School, family and community partnerships: Preparing educators and improving schools*, Boulder, CO, Westview Press.

Epstein, J.L., Simon, B., and Salinas, K.C. (1997) Involving parents in homework in the middle grades, *Research Bulletin*, 18, 4.

Finn, C. (2014, October 17) A third of people think coding is more important than learning Irish, *thejournal.ie*, https://www.thejournal.ie/coding-children-school-1729832-Oct2014/.

Freire, P. (1996) *Pedagogy of the oppressed* (revised), New York, Continuum.

Goh, W.L., Bay, S., and Chen, V.H.-H. (2015) Young school children's use of digital devices and parental rules, *Telematics and Informatics*, 32, 787–795, https://doi.org/10.1016/j.tele.2015.04.002.

González, N., Moll, L.C., and Amanti, C. (2006) *Funds of knowledge: Theorizing practices in households, communities, and classrooms*, Abingdon, Routledge.

Goodall, J., and Vorhaus, J. (2011) *Review of best practice in parental engagement*, DfE Research Report No. RR156, London, Department for Education.

Harris, A., and Goodall, J. (2008) Do parents know they matter? Engaging all parents in learning, *Educational Research*, 50, 277–289, https://doi.org/10.1080/00131880802309424.

Hollingworth, S., Mansaray, A., Allen, K., and Rose, A. (2011) Parents' perspectives on technology and children's learning in the home: Social class and the role of the habitus, *Journal of Computer Assisted Learning*, 27, 347–360.

Hornby, G., and Lafaele, R. (2011) Barriers to parental involvement in education: An explanatory model, *Educational Review*, 63, 37–52, https://doi.org/10.1080/00131911.2010.488049.

Jordan, G.E., Snow, C.E., and Porche, M.V. (2000) Project EASE: The effect of a family literacy project on kindergarten students' early literacy skills, *Reading Research Quarterly*, 35, 524–546, https://doi.org/10.1598/RRQ.35.4.5.

Kamii, C., and Ewing, J.K. (1996) Basing teaching on Piaget's constructivism, *Childhood Education*, 72, 260–264.

Kratochwill, T.R., McDonald, L., Levin, J.R., Bear-Tibbetts, H.Y., and Demaray, M.K. (2004) Families and schools together: An experimental analysis of a parent-mediated multi-family group program for American Indian children, *Journal of School Psychology*, 42, 359–383, https://doi.org/10.1016/j.jsp.2004.08.001.

Lave, J., and Wenger, E. (1991) *Situated learning: Legitimate peripheral participation*, Cambridge, Cambridge University Press.

Lawlor, J., Conneely, C., Oldham, E., Marshall, K., Tangney, B. (2018) Bridge21: Teamwork, technology and learning. A pragmatic model for effective twenty-first-century team-based learning, *Technology, Pedagogy and Education*, 27, 211–232.

Livingstone, S., Mascheroni, G., Dreier, M., Chaudron, S., and Lagae, K. (2015) *How parents of young children manage digital devices at home: The role of income, education and parental style*, London, EU Kids Online, LSE.

Livingstone, S., Ólafsson, K., Helsper, E.J., Lupiáñez-Villanueva, F., Veltri, G.A., and Folkvord, F. (2017) Maximizing opportunities and minimizing risks for children online: The role of digital skills in emerging strategies of parental mediation, *Journal of Communication*, 67, 82–105.

Lye, S. Y., and Koh, J. H. L. (2014) Review on teaching and learning of computational thinking through programming: What is next for K-12? *Computers in Human Behavior*, 41, 51–61.

Mackenzie, J. (2010) *Family learning: Engaging with parents*, Edinburgh, Dunedin Academic.

Maruyama, Y. (2019) *An investigation into the effects of programming workshop experiences on parents' concerns about programming education in elementary school*, in: Proceedings of the International Conference on Educational Technologies. Presented at the International Conference on Educational Technologies, Hong Kong, International Association for Development of the Information Society (IADIS), 55–64, https://doi.org/10.33965/icedutech2019_201902l007.

Matthews, W.J. (2003) Constructivism in the classroom: Epistemology, history, and empirical evidence, *Teacher Education Quarterly*, 30, 51–64.

McClure, E.R., Guernsey, L., Clements, D.H., Bales, S.N., Nichols, J., Kendall-Taylor, N., and Levine, M.H. (2017) *STEM starts early: Grounding science, technology, engineering, and math education in early childhood*, New York, Joan Ganz Cooney Center at Sesame Workshop.

McPhail, G. (2016) The fault lines of recontextualisation: The limits of constructivism in education, *British Educational Research Journal*, 42, 294–313.

Millwood, R. (2018) *Evaluating the impact of learning – Kirkpatrick* https://blog.richardmillwood.net/2018/05/24/evaluating-the-impact-of-learning-kirkpatrick/. Accessed on 14 February 2023.

Newman, D., Griffin, P., and Cole, M. (1989) *The construction zone: Working for cognitive change in school*, Cambridge, Cambridge University Press.

Oldham, E., Cowan, P., Millwood, R., Strong, G., Bresnihan, N., Amond, M., and Hegarty, L. (2018) Developing confident computational thinking through teacher twinning online, *International Journal of Smart Education and Urban Society* (IJSEUS), 9, 61–75.

Pantin, H., Coatsworth, J.D., Feaster, D.J., Newman, F.L., Briones, E., Prado, G., Schwartz, S.J., and Szapocznik, J. (2003) Familias Unidas: The efficacy of an intervention to promote parental investment in Hispanic immigrant families, *Prevention Science*, 4, 189–201, https://doi.org/10.1023/A:1024601906942.

Rearick, M.L., and Feldman, A. (1999) Orientations, purposes and reflection: A framework for understanding action research, *Teaching and Teacher Education*, 15, 333–349.

Resnick, M., Maloney, J., Monroy-Hernández, A., Rusk, N., Eastmond, E., Brennan, K., Millner, A., Rosenbaum, E., Silver, J., and Silverman, B. (2009) Scratch: Programming for all, *Communications of the ACM*, 52, 60–67.

Rodgers, C. (2002) Defining reflection: Another look at John Dewey and reflective thinking, *Teachers College Record*, 104, 842–866.

Rogoff, B. (1994) Developing understanding of the idea of communities of learners, *Mind, Culture, and Activity*, 1, 209–229.

Rogoff, B. (1998) Cognition as a collaborative process, in: W. Damon, D. Kuhn, and R.S. Siegler (Eds.), *Cognition, perception, and language. Vol.2: Handbook of child psychology, cognition, perception, and language*, 5th ed., New York, John Wiley and Sons, 679–744.

Roque, R. (2016) Family creative learning, in: K. Peppler, E. Halverson, and Y.B. Kafai (Eds.), *Makeology: Makerspaces as learning environments*, New York, Routledge, 47–63.

Roque, R., Lin, K., and Liuzzi, R. (2015) Engaging parents as creative learning partners in computing, *Exploring the Material Conditions of Learning*, 2, 687–688.

Sadka, O., and Zuckerman, O. (2017) *From parents to mentors: Parent-child interaction in co-making activities*, in: Proceedings of the 2017 Conference on Interaction Design and Children. Presented at the 2017 Conference on Interaction Design and Children, ACM, 609–615, https://doi.org/10.1145/3078072.3084332.

Starkey, P., and Klein, A. (2000) Fostering parental support for children's mathematical development: An intervention with Head Start families, *Early Education and Development*, 11, 659–680, https://doi.org/10.1207/s15566935eed1105_7.

Steffe, L.P., and Gale, J.E. (1995) *Constructivism in education*, London, Psychology Press.

Summer, M., and Summer, G.L. (2014) Creating family learning communities, *Young Children*, 69, 8–14.

Takeuchi, L., and Stevens, R. (2011) *The new coviewing: Designing for learning through joint media engagement (Research Report)*. New York, NY, The Joan Ganz Cooney Center at Sesame Workshop.

Tharp, R.G., and Gallimore, R. (1991) *Rousing minds to life: Teaching, learning, and schooling in social context*, Cambridge, Cambridge University Press.

Tizard, B., and Hughes, M. (2008) *Young children are learning*, New Jersey, John Wiley and Sons.

Vekiri, I. (2010) Boys' and girls' ICT beliefs: Do teachers matter? *Computers and Education*, 55, 16–23, https://doi.org/10.1016/j.compedu.2009.11.013.

Vekiri, I., and Chronaki, A. (2008) Gender issues in technology use: Perceived social support, computer self-efficacy and value beliefs, and computer use beyond school, *Computers and Education*, 51, 1392–1404, https://doi.org/10.1016/j.compedu.2008.01.003.

von Wangenheim, C.G., von Wangenheim, A., Pacheco, F.S., Hauck, J.C., and Ferreira, M.N.F. (2017) Teaching physical computing in family workshops, *ACM Inroads*, 8, 48–51.

Vygotsky, L.S. (1980) *Mind in society: The development of higher psychological processes*, Boston, Harvard University Press.

Waite, J., and Liebe, C. (2021) *Computer science student-centred instructional continuum*, in: Proceedings of the 52nd ACM Technical Symposium on Computer Science Education, 1246–1246.

Wang, J., Hong, H., Ravitz, J., and Hejazi Moghadam, S. (2016) *Landscape of K-12 computer science education in the US: Perceptions, access, and barriers*, in: Proceedings of the 47th ACM Technical Symposium on Computing Science Education, 645–650.

Wang, J., Hong, H., Ravitz, J., and Ivory, M. (2015) *Gender differences in factors influencing pursuit of computer science and related fields*, in: Proceedings of the 2015 ACM Conference on Innovation and Technology in Computer Science Education, 117–122, https://doi.org/10.1145/2729094.2742611. Accessed on 14 February 2023.

Wood, D., Bruner, J.S., and Ross, G. (1976) The role of tutoring in problem solving, *Journal of Child Psychology and Psychiatry*, 17, 89–100.

Yuen, A.H., Park, J., Chen, L., and Cheng, M. (2018) The significance of cultural capital and parental mediation for digital inequity, *New Media and Society*, 20, 599–617.

25 Case study

Sustainable strategies for ICT/digital technology use in schools

Mario Marais

Introduction

Attempts to continue educational provision using digital tools during the Covid pandemic starkly revealed barriers to the use of digital tools for learning by teachers, families and pupils in both developed and developing countries. Two specific problems which need to be overcome if all learners are to have the benefits of access to digital tools are:

- Problem 1: local community access to the technical knowhow to keep digital devices functional, and
- Problem 2: upskilling teachers

This case study describes initiatives funded between 2008 and 2016 by the Department of Science and Technology in South Africa to provide solutions to these problems. These solutions may work in other countries in rural areas in particular.

Problem 1: building technical knowhow in rural communities

The 'village operators model': Young entrepreneurs who can build social capital

South Africa's Council for Scientific and Industrial Research (CSIR) has researched sustainable development of South African schools from two perspectives related to improving digital access, namely:

- the provision of internet access to clusters of rural schools using a novel technical support model (the Broadband-for-All project), and
- the challenge of introducing the use of Information and Communication Technology for Development (ICT4D) for enhancing teaching and learning as part of a sustained systemic change in a provincial education department (ICT for Rural Education Development – ICT4RED).

A support model was developed by selecting local post-school youth for entrepreneurial attitudes and then training these so-called "Village Operators" (VOs) as on-site technical support (Marais *et al.*, 2022). Their job was to maintain wireless-mesh networks (WMNs) serving clusters of schools and in-school internet access. Schools have several connection paths in a WMN to retain access when a wireless link goes down. The VOs were selected

DOI: 10.4324/9781003408925-25

from youth recommended by the principals of the schools they had attended. They received intensive small business training and mentoring from experts to prepare them for growing their own businesses. Their business was to provide technical support and training to the schools to ensure high availability of internet access and to support teachers to develop computer literacy. VOs had their own offices to provide services to teachers and learners to use the internet for educational purposes, such as research, but they also served the public to adopt internet use to benefit themselves and their businesses.

All the VOs received the same support from the project, however there were large variations in their business performance. A Social Capital perspective was used to research all sources of support and the business strategies used. The relationship networks of the VOs were mapped out in interviews to obtain detailed information. It was found that successful VOs had parents who had the resources to supply loans to buy more PCs. The support from their family included assistance from their siblings who served local clients in the office while VOs were providing services at schools. An additional motivation was their desire to learn computer skills. The building of close relationships with clients led to innovation with clients to fit their needs and their level of digital skills and ICT use. An example was the setting up of email accounts for builders who only used cell phones to give them access to tender documents and assisting the creation of tender documents and CVs.

VOs assisted learners to do research on the internet and lowered the cost of internet access by caching research results on their laptops which the learners could search first before searching on the internet. Teachers were also trained in using applications. Members of the community, such as elderly women, received computer training early in the morning from a lady VO since this time fitted them and she understood their needs well. VOs were known in these communities and hence support networks existed already and could be grown rapidly.

The transition from a project funded by the national Department of Science and Technology to a business contracted by the Provincial Department of Education was a challenging process and in the end the department did not have the funds to support internet access to schools and hence VOs lost the school internet support business, but some have continued due to their services to the business and citizens in their communities. One important lesson is that it is vital that service models are designed and implemented with the direct involvement of the legally responsible institution to enhance adoption.

Marais *et al.* (2022) provides further information about this initiative.

Problem 2: upskilling teachers

The information and communication technology for rural education development (ICT4RED) project

The experience gained and problems encountered in the Broadband-for-All project (described above) led to the ICT4RED project adopting a strategy of engagement with a provincial education department to partner in a sustained systemic change approach (Herselman, Botha and Ford, 2014b; Meyer *et al.*, 2017).

To realise the potential benefit from ICT implementation in an education system, long-term sustainability must be designed into the strategy. Sustainability was defined as the ability to sustain the anticipated benefits of a project, over an appropriate period, for pre-defined project participants. A systems perspective simply means considering how well the system (the participating organisation or community) can absorb a project into normal operations. ICT4RED introduced a "teaching with tablets" approach in a circuit of 26 schools in a rural area. It was designed to uncover the fundamental relationships between entities in the system in order to understand the readiness and maturity of the system to absorb and sustain a fundamental change to teacher and learner-centric use of ICTs/digital tools.

A purposeful systems approach was used, initially identifying six implementation modules that needed to be focused on in order to ensure sustainability and integration of the schools into the education ecosystem (Herselman, Botha and Ford, 2014a). This implementation model was tested, extended, and improved throughout the project, resulting in an eventual twelve modules (ibid.), categorised under "Governance and Processes", "Technology" and "People and Practices" as indicated in Figure 25.1.

The learning from this project was generalised for all ICT4D projects, by creating a matrix of the 12 modules. When planning interventions each module can be shaded according to the intensity of effort needed to adequately make provision for weaknesses of various entities and their relationships. Thus, the modules can be adjusted to fit the needs within a target environment, therefore resulting in a balanced system of appropriate intervention.

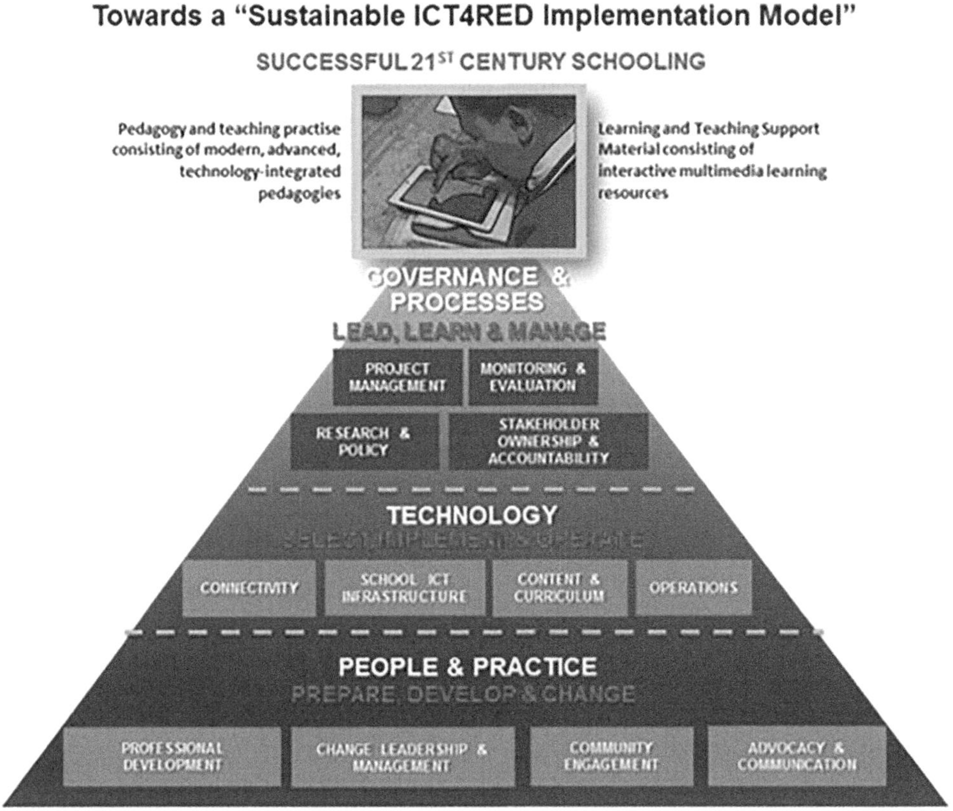

Towards a "Sustainable ICT4RED Implementation Model"

SUCCESSFUL 21ST CENTURY SCHOOLING

Pedagogy and teaching practise consisting of modern, advanced, technology-integrated pedagogies

Learning and Teaching Support Material consisting of interactive multimedia learning resources

GOVERNANCE & PROCESSES
LEAD, LEARN & MANAGE

PROJECT MANAGEMENT   MONITORING & EVALUATION

RESEARCH & POLICY   STAKEHOLDER OWNERSHIP & ACCOUNTABILITY

TECHNOLOGY
SELECT, IMPLEMENT & OPERATE

CONNECTIVITY   SCHOOL ICT INFRASTRUCTURE   CONTENT & CURRICULUM   OPERATIONS

PEOPLE & PRACTICE
PREPARE, DEVELOP & CHANGE

PROFESSIONAL DEVELOPMENT   CHANGE LEADERSHIP & MANAGEMENT   COMMUNITY ENGAGEMENT   ADVOCACY & COMMUNICATION

Figure 25.1 ICT4RED 12 component implementation model – a systems approach towards sustainability of ICT in schools (Meyer *et al.*, 2022)

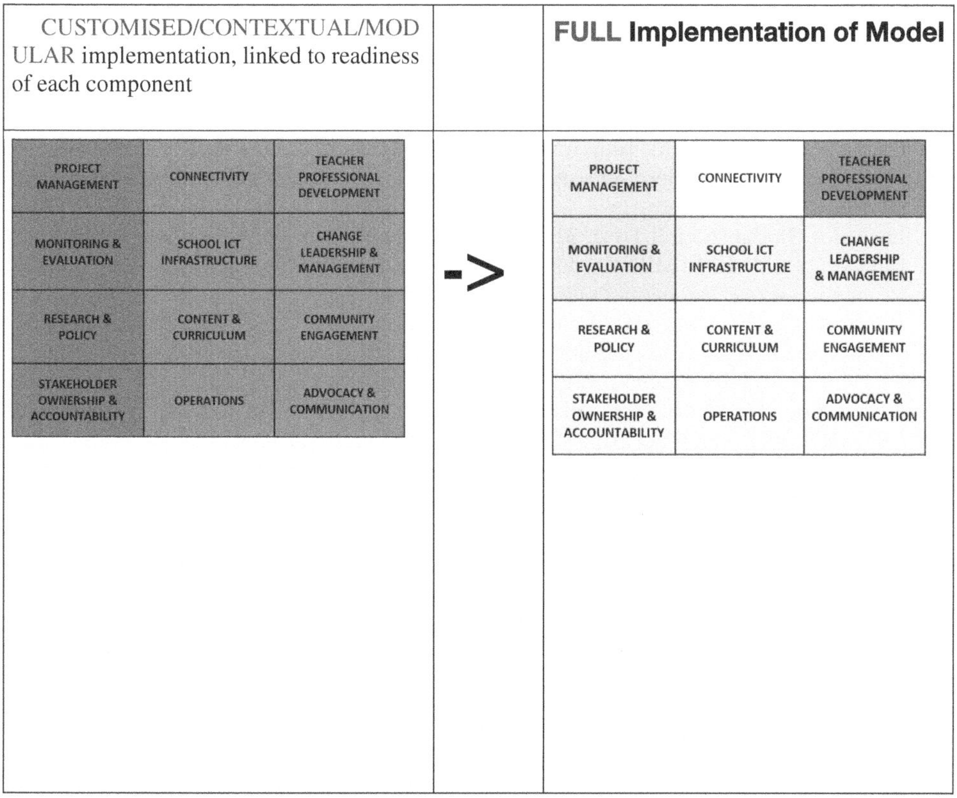

CUSTOMISED/CONTEXTUAL/MODULAR implementation, linked to readiness of each component		FULL Implementation of Model	

PROJECT MANAGEMENT	CONNECTIVITY	TEACHER PROFESSIONAL DEVELOPMENT
MONITORING & EVALUATION	SCHOOL ICT INFRASTRUCTURE	CHANGE LEADERSHIP & MANAGEMENT
RESEARCH & POLICY	CONTENT & CURRICULUM	COMMUNITY ENGAGEMENT
STAKEHOLDER OWNERSHIP & ACCOUNTABILITY	OPERATIONS	ADVOCACY & COMMUNICATION

->

PROJECT MANAGEMENT	CONNECTIVITY	TEACHER PROFESSIONAL DEVELOPMENT
MONITORING & EVALUATION	SCHOOL ICT INFRASTRUCTURE	CHANGE LEADERSHIP & MANAGEMENT
RESEARCH & POLICY	CONTENT & CURRICULUM	COMMUNITY ENGAGEMENT
STAKEHOLDER OWNERSHIP & ACCOUNTABILITY	OPERATIONS	ADVOCACY & COMMUNICATION

Figure 25.2 ICT4RED 12 component implementation model – customised focus according to the strengths and weaknesses in the target environment (adapted from Meyer *et al.*, 2022)

An example of the use of this customised implementation model is a Teacher Professional Development-focused implementation in the Northern Cape Province by a company. The shade of a block indicates the level of effort, investment and focus as can be seen in Figure 25.2.

Customised implementation deals with the following issues of a full implementation:

- One size does not fit all – different contexts, needs and levels of readiness/maturity
- Unnecessary costs by not building on what is already available
- Not using a phased implementation
- A "Big bang approach" is risky.

Summary and key points

- These two models provide a means for addressing family and school internet connection and adoption challenges.
- Sustainable solutions to these problems are essential if the use of digital technologies is to be embedded in practices in all schools.

References

Herselman, M., Botha, A. and Ford, M. (2014a) *ICT4RED 12-component implementation framework: A conceptual framework for integrating mobile technology into resource-constrained rural schools.* IST-Africa, Mauritius. https://www.researchgate.net/publication/263922686_ICT4RED_12-Component_Implementation_Framework_A_conceptual_framework_for_integrating_mobile_technology_into_resource-constrained_rural_schools, Accessed on 6 February 2023.

Herselman, M., Botha, A. and Ford, M. (2014b) Section 1: Introduction, background and the evolvement of the ICT4RED framework, in *Designing and implementing an Information and Communication Technology for Rural Education Development (ICT4RED) initiative in a resource-constrained environment: Nciba school district, Eastern Cape, South Africa.* Herselman, M.E. and Botha, A. (Eds.) 1–69, Edition: 1 published by CSIR, Pretoria. ISBN 978-0-7988-5618-8 (hbk). DOI: 10.13140/2.1.4932.5121.

Marais, M., Lotriet, H., Matthee, M. and de Moor, A. (2022) *The role of Social Capital in sustainable ICT4D.* Submitted conference paper. 20th Annual Community Informatics Research Network Conference (CIRN): Examining the past, present and future of communities and technology, 9–11 November 2022, Monash University, Prato, Italy. https://1drv.ms/b/s!AipM2vmmMnODgtp8Sr_7nhvvHevwKQ?e=K0FBTZ.

Meyer, I., Marais, M., Ford, M. and Dlamini, S. (2017) *An exploration of the integration challenges inherent in the adoption of ICT in an education system, information and communication technologies for development,* 14th IFIP WG 9.4 International Conference on Social Implications of Computers in Developing Countries, ICT4D 2017, Yogyakarta, Indonesia, May 22–24, 2017, in: Choudrie, J., Sirajul Islam, Wahid, F., Bass, J.M, and Priyatma, J.E. (Eds.) *IFIP advances in information and communication technology,* 504, 463–474. DOI:10.1007/978-3-319-59111-7_38. https://www.researchgate.net/publication/317183252_An_Exploration_of_the_Integration_Challenges_Inherent_in_the_Adoption_of_ICT_in_an_Education_System, Accessed on 6 February 2023.

26 Using digital technologies to support continuing professional development

Christina Preston and Sarah Younie

Introduction

The quote which follows is used in the introduction to this book because it sets out starkly the risk to your pupils if you do not keep up to date with new knowledge and new practices.

> If we teach today as we taught yesterday, we rob our children of tomorrow
>
> (Dewey, 1944: 167)

This chapter outlines different forms of teacher continuing professional development (CPD) that you may have access to and introduces ways that digital technologies can be used to support you to develop your professional knowledge. We consider a range of strategies for supporting your learning as it is your responsibility, as a teacher, to keep your professional knowledge and practice up to date.

While digital technologies can be used to support teachers' continuing professional development CPD, teachers also need CPD in how to use and appropriate digital technologies for their own pedagogic practice. The previous chapters in this book focus on your pedagogic practice. In this chapter we focus on the use of digital technologies to support your CPD.

Objectives

At the end of this chapter you should be able to:

- understand what CPD opportunities are available to you now and be motivated to join relevant professional organisations
- engage in the forms of continuing teacher education outlined in this chapter if you are not already using them
- set up your own regional, local or school-based organisations where you can share your experience and knowledge with a view to growing collaborative professional development
- develop an understanding of the opportunities to access research through quick and easily available routes
- understand how to deploy relevant digital technologies to improve your own professional practice.

DOI: 10.4324/9781003408925-26

Current forms of CPD opportunities

There are many different routes for teachers to use to keep up to date, from formal routes such as

- traditional CPD courses provided by regional/national government bodies, subject associations, charities, unions and for-profit organisations through to
- accredited programmes (Masters, PhDs) as university higher-level degree qualifications and
- sector-led employability qualifications such as in England, NPQs (national professional qualifications, for senior and middle leaders).

Alongside these formal routes are more grassroots approaches set up by teachers, in which teachers meet up and share knowledge, such as

- teachmeets,
- school conferences, and
- virtual CPD via online communities of practice utilising social media and video conferencing.

National and international teacher-led professional organisations or charities independent of governments also support teachers' CPD beyond the provision of formal CPD courses often providing knowledge exchange and research opportunities via conferences, online platforms for knowledge exchange and hubs for research, such as:

- Subject associations – for the UK, see the Council for Subject Associations list. Many of the authors of this book are from the Technology, Pedagogy and Education Association (TPEA).
- For the national teaching – there are four in the UK – see the Further Resources list.
- Charities and research institutes such as in the UK, the Dyslexia Association, the MESHGuides research summaries charitable initiative (which the editors of this book initiated), the Education Endowment Fund (EEF) and many others which provide expertise, knowledge, research reports and networking opportunities.

There are also many many *for-profit* organisations providing services to the education market and we advise you to check the qualifications of those offering such training, and to ask yourself are they providing services based on research into effective practice? Ideas put forward may be promoting particular products, ideologies or approaches which do not have a solid research foundation.

This chapter now explores collaborative learning between teachers in online communities of practice, which use the affordances of digital technologies as a way to create new professional knowledge; where every teacher is recognised as an expert with important knowledge and experience to share. The outcomes are stored digitally on the internet where they are easily accessible and updatable.

Your school

How do teachers currently access CPD opportunities? At a local level these are often, first and foremost, offered through your own school. CPD sessions are provided after school for teachers and run internally by schools, alongside schools providing whole training days, usually before term starts. These predominantly have a focus on the individual school's priorities as set out in the school's improvement plan (SIP). Also there may be further opportunities that are offered by local school networks such as in England, multiple academy trusts (MATs). Collaborations between schools can scale up the professional development opportunities offered by an individual school and can provide work shadowing, secondments, specialised training programmes like coaching, subject knowledge enhancements through subject leads, as well as CPD run by external providers.

National/regional opportunities

In many countries the national government plays a role in ensuring teachers have access to continuing professional development. In the UK, this is different between the four home nations. There are also national professional organisations which support teachers, such as the Chartered College of Teaching (CoT) in England and the General Teaching Council for Scotland (GTCS), the Education Workforce Council (Wales) and the General Teaching Council for Northern Ireland (GTCNI).

At the regional level, there are advisory teachers who may focus on particular subjects, like STEM or be used to target particular needs like SEND (special education needs and disability) or EAL (English as an additional language).

There are also opportunities to gain accredited CPD, with recognised courses such as the National Professional Qualifications (NPQs) for senior leaders and middle leaders, from different external providers paid for by the school. Also, the Chartered College of Teaching provides pathways and certificates for all teachers giving accredited CPD.

Universities

Higher Education institutions also provide CPD for teachers through courses that allow for teachers to undertake further study and gain higher qualifications, such as Masters programmes, the professional doctorate Ed.D and PhD research. There is a move to translate individual's doctoral research into accessible online research summaries for teachers to inform their practice. Whilst a traditional PhD is too long for any busy teacher to read, by providing a shortened knowledge map from the research that highlights what is applicable for other teachers, this research knowledge can be translated into usable summaries for others, thereby widening the knowledge base of the profession. See more on this below under MESHGuides.

Your professional subject association/educational charities

Each curriculum subject has an associated professional organisation that provides expert knowledge on specific disciplines, see the CfSA (Council for Subject Associations) list. Each subject association provides specialist support for that specific curriculum area, including research and professional practice-informed approaches thereby supporting continuing teacher development.

Also, educational charities can provide specialist knowledge to help inform teachers' practice. For example, see SEND-related charities linked to dyslexia, dyspraxia, dyscalculia and teaching for the hearing impaired. We advise you to learn more about the range of education charities that can support your work with your learners.

There are also a growing number of private providers, however it is beyond the scope of this chapter to provide further detail here, though your CPD lead for your school should be able to inform you of what is available.

Lack of EdTech CPD is an international problem

The Organisation for Economic Cooperation and Development (OECD) represents the wealthier nations and undertakes regular surveys to compare practices between countries. Lack of access to CPD is a recurring problem reported across countries. For example, they report the following data for England: the percentage of teachers who received IT skills training for practical teaching in their initial teacher education was 75%, but only 40% of teachers in England reported receiving any CPD based on IT skills for classroom practices thereafter (OECD, 2019). Thus, there is a discrepancy between CPD opportunities at different stages of a teacher's career.

How does digital technology affect and change the professional development landscape for teachers?

Issues arise when the approaches to CPD are specified as skills 'deficits', as opposed to enabling a more in-depth understanding of how these skills can be applied through a focus on pedagogical practices (Daly, Pachler and Pelletier, 2009). This in turn causes issues in how time and provision of technological resources are utilised. Prior research has shown that technology-focused CPD, which is provided through external means as a one-off event, has led to dissatisfaction, as has internal school provision where CPD has not been differentiated to support the differing levels of technical understanding or subject pedagogical application (Atkins, 2018; Daly, Pachler and Pelletier, 2009; Younie, 2007).

The General Teaching Council for England (GTCE, 2006, 2007, cited in Leask and Younie, 2013) reported on four factors that contribute to effective CPD:

- Instead of having disparate one-off courses, CPD should be meaningful and consistent.
- The effectiveness of any programme is dependent upon whether teachers have the ability to tailor the CPD to address their own needs and how relevant it is to their own teaching practices.
- Teachers are at various points within their careers and thus there is a requirement to recognise and cater for these differences.
- Schools should provide opportunities to become 'professional learning communities', for teachers to learn from and with each other, and other staff including teaching assistants.

With the increased use of technology, online platforms play a vital role in supporting teachers' professional development; as seen during the Covid-19 pandemic and shift to online learning when schools were closed (Leask and Younie, 2022). Teachers quickly learnt from one another.

Technology ultimately provides teachers with the opportunities to access holistic development opportunities from a distance, as sessions can be recorded for viewing thereafter and resources made readily available to access (IRIS, 2022). These resources can be used multiple times, whenever it is necessary to do so and can be viewed simultaneously by members of a learning community. Online platforms can bring together research that is underpinned by theory and practice as well as providing space for teachers to share ideas and resources to learn from each other, for each other, as identified by the theory of communal constructivism (Leask and Younie, 2001), in which knowledge is collaboratively developed.

Within these online communities of practice teachers may have access to knowledgeable coaches, which many teachers have indicated is a preferable option (Kraft, Blazar and Hogan, 2018).

How can teachers use digital technologies to support their continuing professional development?

In addition to traditional CPD programmes in which teachers can undertake Masters and professional doctorates (Ed.D or PhD), which are university-accredited qualifications, there is a move to microcredits via short courses delivered online. The development of MOOCs (massive open online courses) is a model for delivering learning content online to anyone who wants to take a course, see, for example, Futurelearn courses (https://www.futurelearn.com/). However, both these models are still predicated on learning content as defined by the provider and by undertaking accredited assessment, whereas a more grassroots model has emerged where teachers share and create new knowledge amongst themselves, and use digital technologies to facilitate this process.

In this section we outline how teachers can make use of online communities of practice to support their own development, which is predicated on theories of learning linked to constructivism. Also, we explore online research-knowledge-exchange initiatives, which facilitate teachers creating and sharing new knowledge for professional practice, like MESHGuides and TPEA (Technology Pedagogy Education Association) with which we are personally familiar.

Rhizomatic learning

Continual professional development can effectively take place with teachers adopting an active role in the creation and sharing of ideas. Individuals construct the meanings that are then associated with representations of knowledge (Piaget, 1953, 1972). Social constructivism suggests that these meanings are ultimately constructed through social interactions with expert others in the surrounding environment (Vygotsky, 1986). From this, stems the term communal constructivism which argues that learners' construction of knowledge is a collaborative effort 'with and for each other' (Leask and Younie, 2001). Practice-Based Research (PBR) and Lesson Study (see below and Further resources) provide examples of these theories applied in practice.

Communal constructivism also relates to the concept of rhizomatic learning which has been inspired by the connections within plants. The older roots of a plant have the ability to grow new shoots that connect back to the original plant. These connections are recognised as rhizomes. The outward, seemingly obvious connections in plants are often outnumbered by these interconnected underground networks. This concept can be applied to learning; where learning is co-constructed through professional networks, and learning can occur through interdisciplinary connections where knowledge is continually shared and added to (Cromier, 2008). The affordances of technology allow this collaborative process of constructing, exchanging and transferring knowledge to be taken further

(Cuthell *et al.*, 2022). See *MESHGuides: Online Collaborative Learning: A rhizomatic approach* (2022) which is illustrated in Figure 26.1.

Online communities of practice (CoPs)

Wenger (1998) notes that within communities of practice individuals can interact continually with one another and share their knowledge. Successful CPD programmes have been identified on the basis that they are founded on communities of practice (CoPs) such as the MirandaNet Fellowship which is (now in partnership with the Technology, Pedagogy and Education Association (TPEA) a national subject association. Such CoPs are holders of research knowledge, which is important given that when governments change, such research may be archived and no longer easily accessible (Blamires, 2015). This emphasises the need for teachers CoPs to ensure that previous research is always available on their websites.

Communities of practice allow for teachers to share their understanding in a practical and informative manner, as they have opportunities to build relationships within the school and the wider teaching community (Preston and Younie, 2016). When teachers feel supported, they feel confident to take risks, to implement their ideas and disseminate their findings. Thus, headteachers have a vital role to enable teachers to support one another in developing pedagogic practices around the use of technology, and to inspire teachers to experiment and attempt new approaches within their practice.

Digital technologies can support these groups through social media, such as Twitter, using education hashtags, Facebook specialist groups, Google Hangouts and MS Teams channels as 'fast and effective communication channels, which inform teachers of evolving [practices], often written by teachers to share and disseminate ideas' (Hynes and Younie, 2018: 156). These are also referred to as professional learning networks (PLNs), which enable teachers to reach out, support and learn from one another.

The following recommendations for CPD have been identified as the most effective:

* CPD should be founded on collaboration, where headteachers are providing opportunities, time and resources for teachers to discuss, critically engage and plan activities.
* Observations and regular feedback is crucial, in both informal and formal settings as both can be considered as CPD opportunities.
* Leadership should also ensure that there are plentiful opportunities for external technical CPD through exchanges in knowledge between schools where teachers can observe and attain alternative ideas on the uses of technology.
* School leaders should engage with the latest research on creating learning communities.
* Investing in technology is required and necessary to support teachers in their practice.

MESHGuides – *Mapping Education Specialist knowHow*

Given that there has been a focus on teachers using research evidence to inform their practice, the ability to access research easily is essential for CPD. However, often research cannot be reached, primarily due to prerequisites such as needing to be a member of an academic organisation like a university, or having to provide payments to read certain articles. Another barrier that should also be considered is that teachers require time to read in-depth research and to engage in the processes of analysing the implications of the research for their professional practice (Jones, Procter and Younie, 2015).

A beneficial alternative to this is access to summaries of the research, based on evidence and practice, which allows teachers to understand how research can be translated to a classroom environment. This is referred to as 'translational research' and is often seen within the disciplines of medicine and the sciences rather than in education. To address this need the Mapping Educational Specialist knowHow (MESH) initiative was created (Burden, Younie and Leask, 2013). This freely available resource translates education-based research into summaries in the form of online knowledge maps. Underpinned by pedagogical understanding, the MESHGuides appear as flowcharts or snapshots where any teacher can simply identify the aspects that are relevant to them. Access to such resources has had beneficial impact, for instance the use of the Early Years MESHGuide in the Rohingya refugee camps in Cox Bazar Bangladesh, where education workers could access research on effective pedagogy to support learning with very young children (Laxton, *et al.*, 2020).

Understanding teachers' need for different types of knowledge demonstrates that there is a continual need for professional development throughout a teacher's career. CPD needs to capture and address the range of differing knowledge required, including the following: pedagogic knowledge (overarching aspects of teaching and learning that are not specific to the curriculum) (Shulman, 1986); pedagogical content knowledge (teaching and learning practices that relate to specific subjects) (Meyer and Land, 2003); troublesome knowledge (knowledge that is difficult to understand or is new in comparison to previous knowledge) (Perkins, 1999) and learner knowledge (knowledge based on the characteristics, abilities and needs of individual learners) (Shulman, 1986). These aspects provide teachers with extensive and diverse choices for their CPD opportunities.

TeachMeets

The interplay between teachers' understanding of curriculum subject content and pedagogy is related to teachers' understanding of technology. Mishra and Koehler (2006) suggest that teachers require all three components and the integration of specific technical tools can enhance practice. A way in which teachers can access continual professional development opportunities is through joining and organising TeachMeets. These are open access meetings where teachers present their ideas, often through a series of presentations or open discussions to share effective practices and innovative processes. These can be face-to-face meetings or online. Presentations within these TeachMeets are often for either two minutes, where a short burst of information is provided in a 'nano' form, or for seven minutes in a 'micro' approach. These TeachMeets can be organised by any group of teachers, at any time and use an online platform of their choice.

MirandaMods

In traditional CPD events and conference settings, the teacher would take notes from expert presenters. In an extrapolation of this model, the speaker or coach would explain their ideas to the audience. Apart from a short Q&A at the end, the teacher would not only have a limited opportunity to question the speaker but would also have limited opportunity to share their own ideas. A MirandaMod is a version of an 'unconference', where all individuals are on an equal footing when contributing their ideas within a face-to-face or online conference (Preston and Cuthell, 2012). Digital technologies create a different opportunity; during a talk from an expert, by using large screens and software like Twitter Walls, the audience can see what others are thinking (Cuthell, Cych and Preston, 2011).

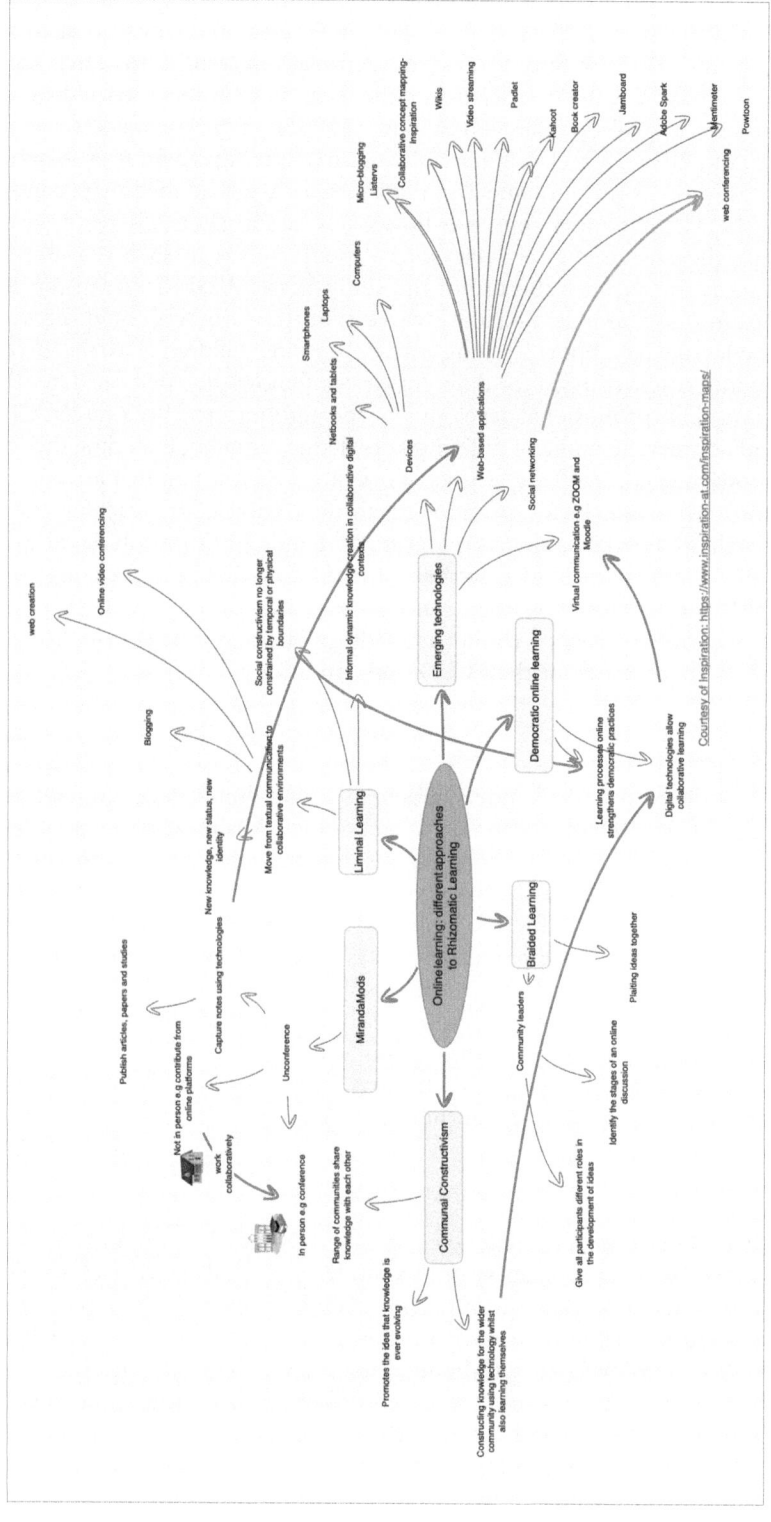

Figure 26.1 MESHGuide on rhizomatic learning (www.meshguides.org)

This notion is taken further in a MirandaMod where a topic of interest is selected by the professional organisation members. Then members present their ideas whilst the others build a multi-authored concept map, creating new approaches to the issues being discussed. Concept mapping is a tool through which individuals are able to share, create and connect their ideas (Cuthell and Preston, 2012). As this is a non-linear process, individuals have the opportunity to think creatively, be flexible in making connections and can explore the complex relationships between different aspects of a chosen topic (Davies, 2011). Concept maps can be handwritten or digitally created using visual depictions of knowledge to communicate ideas, either through written words, images or a combination of both (Tinkler, 2022). Examples of concept mapping tools include Inspiration and Miro.

Figure 26.1 is an example of a concept map that was created at an unconference that discussed approaches to Rhizomatic Learning, which also has an accompanying MESHGuide.

Case Study 26.1: A school approach

From discussions with teachers about CPD opportunities and the resources available online, the following case study was developed. Teachers acknowledged that CPD is a proactive process, usually driven and led by the teachers themselves. Despite the fact that there may be some time available in staff meetings, teachers felt the pressure of other responsibilities and, therefore, felt that they could not dedicate enough time to CPD. In the case study primary school, subject leads would use staff meetings for CPD, however, this meant that they were all competing to gain a 'slot' of time with the staff. Primary school teachers teach a wide range of subjects and thus, not all the subjects could be covered in this CPD time adequately as there are only a certain number of meetings dedicated to CPD per year.

Practice-based research

> *We've had years of implementation, but now it's time to get into enquiry.*
> Primary school teacher.
> *Research puts the 'wow moments' back into teaching. We'll do the things that we're interested in and we know that it will have a pay off for our school.*
> Primary school teacher.
>
> (The General Teaching Council, 2006: prelim.)

A generic way to make use of the different strategies for engaging teachers that have been described above is to implement a form of CPD which is called Practice-Based Research (PBR). PBR is an original investigation undertaken in order to gain new knowledge. It is a term for the process which encourages teachers to conduct a small-scale inquiry in their own classrooms with their own pupils. In the most effective examples teachers decide on the basis of their findings to implement changes into their practice. Schools may do this as part of *Lesson Study*, or undertaking action research, or forming impact teams in their own schools.

It is an important principle of practice-based research that teachers as researchers should control the process of change and development by fact-finding, planning, implementing a course of action, evaluating that action, reassessment and modification. This iterative cycle helps learners take risks, experiment and adapt because they are not constrained by the need to be right the first time (Somekh and Davis, 1998; Elliott, 1991; Hopkins, 2002).

This has developed from action research as a process developed by Schön (1992) as a means of empowering teachers, facilitating their participation in professionalism, encouraging them to share their stories and to rethink what they know (Thomas, 1995; Preston, 1998, 2000).

However, Barnett (1997) is critical of action research methods based on Schön's (1992) work because it can be uncritical. Barnett (1997) argues that teachers must further engage with professional issues and practise their critical skills. Brown and Dowling (1998) make the same case for teachers being given the space to pursue an apprenticeship in research methods, rather than concentrating entirely on their own classroom or school. Armitage *et al.* (2003) also deplore the decrease of the teaching of theory in teacher education and contend that, as a result of reflective practice approaches, practice and theory have become confused. In her view 'theory' often means nothing more than 'talking about practice' (Armitage *et al.*, 2003: 22).

The General Teaching Council for England's policy adviser for research, Saunders (2002) spoke eloquently of an evidence base which is not a body of infinite knowledge to be prescribed and imposed on teachers but rather as a living process built around and tested on practical experience in classrooms, developed from and adapted to particular teaching and learning settings. Encouraging teachers to publish their studies for the rest of their learning community meant that the results could be far reaching. This facilitates the opportunity for teachers to gain a 'strong and principled voice' and learn how to use it effectively (Freidson, 1994).

Lamb and Simpson (2003) claim that practice-based research is a vital ingredient of continuing professional development in order to give teachers the opportunities for learning and, in addition, for them to have the space and capacity to build critically on theoretical knowledge in order to think the unthinkable. The critical phrase here is 'to build critically on theoretical knowledge' (Lamb and Simpson, 2003: 62).

The educationalist Lawrence Stenhouse defined research as 'systematic enquiry, made public', arguing that research inquiry aims to solve problems by achieving deeper understanding (Stenhouse, 1980: 1). The GTCE report (2006) refers to the development of this concept by Graham Handscomb of Essex County Council and John MacBeath, professor at Cambridge University. They propose that schools can become research-engaged by placing research activity 'at the heart of the school, its outlook, systems and activity' (Handscomb and MacBeath, 2003). They suggest that a research-engaged school has four main features:

- It has a research orientation
- It has a research-rich pedagogy
- It promotes research communities
- It puts research at the heart of school policy and practice

How does this help the school, the teacher and the learner? A school that is research-engaged uses that engagement to sharpen its focus on school improvement and enhance teaching and learning. The school becomes involved in both large- and small-scale projects. Supported by school leaders and governors, research engagement is shared among all staff, and gives opportunities for professional development. It becomes embedded in school culture and so is used for decision-making. It helps forge a link between schools and education policy. Research engagement provides a platform for the development of learning communities, both within and outside the school, and enables and sustains learning conversations. It helps people in school reflect together about pedagogy, assessment, curriculum and leadership.

The GTCE report (2006: 12) goes on to say that people undertake research in order to find things out.

There isn't a great deal of point in doing research if you already know the answer. But this very 'open-ended' nature of research can make it unsettling – how do you know you're getting it right? The answer lies not in trying to make research predictable, but in approaching it as if you are setting out on a journey of discovery. Be very clear about your research questions and systematic in your processes, but remain open to new information and different points of view. Have people on hand to offer support and advice and help you decide which direction to take. They can also help you think of ways to test your findings, as this can add validity to the research. Finding the time is perhaps the biggest challenge. Not only that, if you want to reap the benefits of collaborative working, your school needs to find a way of facilitating at least two members of staff to work together. Most school leaders can find a way to make time available – if the issue is sufficiently high on their agenda, which in a research engaged school it should be. Time for teachers to work together can be found, for example, through team teaching, peer observation and/ or planning and preparation time....

But how to achieve this aim? Teachers are very busy and need quick access to research and theoretical ideas. Schools can engage a university education researcher or support a member of staff in completing a PhD or Masters in the topic. Another way is to find an e-learning course with a research module that can help the participants to use practitioner research to lead to a greater sense of professional autonomy. MESHGuides are particularly designed to give teachers an insight into current thinking and research in their field. Teacher-researchers also developed subject links, where a primary school can work alongside local secondary schools, especially regarding science. For example, the science lead of a primary school can set up meetings with the STEM lead in the local secondary school to provide CPD opportunities. Professional associations in national curriculum subjects can also be helpful in supporting schools through annual conferences, TeachMeets and MirandaMods, which can be encouraged so that insights are shared between schools, regions and even across international borders.

In this mode of CPD, schools can benefit from wider professional networking, for instance, creating subject hubs. This is exemplified in national and regional 'maths hubs' to support the pedagogy and mastery approach to teaching maths in primary and also music hubs to provide expertise.

A key reason to encourage all staff to engage in this process is so that the teachers themselves can use the evidence they have developed to promote changes in teaching and learning that they have ownership of. Publication of teachers' practice-based research case studies and the rationale behind their projects through professional bodies also takes this concept to a logical conclusion for sharing findings and building the knowledge base of the profession. See the Chartered College's Impact magazine, the MESHGuides website and other trusted sources of published research.

Another area is the development of apps specifically for teachers. For example, the Erasmus+ funded app BRIST (Building a Research Infrastructure for School Teachers), responds to the central question: 'How do we support teachers to become teacher-researchers and evidence-informed practitioners?'. The free app develops teachers' research skills and networking practices, with case studies available to inform professional development. See Building a Research Infrastructure for School Teachers (BRIST) | University of Hull.

Now turn to Task 26.1 on developing your own professional practice through undertaking school-based research, to inform your own work and to share with other teachers, to grow the knowledge base of the profession.

Task 26.1: Conducting your own research to inform your professional development

In this task we will examine how you can conduct a practice-based study in a school/s. There are many guides on the internet about how to conduct practice-based research that can be modified to suit you and the needs of the school. Here are some basic suggestions:

What is the question? Decide on the questions you want to ask. For example:

- What are the learning gains for pupils when they use digital technologies?
- What are the most effective ways of supporting SEND pupils with technology?
- How can digital technologies help our pupils to be more confident?

Previous research: When you have decided what you want to explore, find out what has already been done in this area. Potential routes for this are to engage an expert in the area to work with you; contact subject specialist organisations; explore MESHGuides for information. One suggestion is to explore the MESHGuide (2022) *Introducing RISE: Research-Informed School self-Evaluation: A tool kit for teachers.*

Sample: You will want to decide which pupils or groups of pupils will be involved in your research. A reasonable sample size helps with the validity of the results. However qualitative research with small groups can also provide valuable insights for practice. At this stage you must also think carefully about the ethics of your research. All participants need to give consent (if working with adults/staff) and assent (if pupils); all must give permission to be studied, including permission from your line manager and/or head teacher.

Methodology: How will you find the evidence? You can use a range of data collection methods, like questionnaires, observations, interviews and focus groups.

Findings: You will need to explain your findings, whether they are quantitative statistics from questionnaires or qualitative findings from observations and interviews.

Conclusions: This is where you discuss the implications for practice of what has been discovered. This section can also contain recommendations for both practice and policy.

Dissemination: To share your findings, you can create an executive summary of your research for wider dissemination and also write an article of about 500–2,000 words. Teachers, governors and parents will be interested and you can also use this article to send to education publications, write blogs and contact subject organisations. You could contribute to conferences and/or set up your own specialist TeachMeets or MirandaMods to share and to gain more evidence from other teachers. You may have tackled the subject in enough detail to write your own MESHGuide to support members of the profession in the future.

Accreditation: The Chartered College of Teaching offers a Certificate in Education Research and Inquiry, which enables a teacher to engage in purposeful inquiry to evaluate a key area of policy or practice in their school. This provides support to teachers to engage in the process of practitioner research, supporting teachers to plan and implement a piece of evidence-informed inquiry that focuses on a specific area of classroom practice. This will include undertaking a comprehensive literature review to support the inquiry and to build an understanding of a range of research methods and approaches to collecting and analysing data, as outlined in this task.

More research: The MirandaNet Fellowship (www.mirandanet.ac.uk) has been archived by the British Library so that you can still read case studies. Although you do not need funding to do your own research, in the MirandaNet context, funding was procured from EdTech companies who wanted to know how they could make their products more useful to schools.

Summary and key points

This chapter has outlined a variety of strategies for facilitating professional development that enable you, as a teacher, to take ownership of your own learning to enhance your practice. Specifically we hope that you can now:

- Be motivated to join relevant professional organisations and networks to support your own development.
- Engagee technologies to set up your own regional, local or school-based network where you can share your experience and knowledge with a view to growing collaborative professional development.
- Understand the opportunities to access research through quick and easily available routes.

Further resources

Building a Research Infrastructure for School Teachers (BRIST) https://www.hull.ac.uk/work-with-us/research/case-studies/building-a-research-infrastructure-for-school-teachers-brist
This website develops teachers' research skills and networking practices, with case studies available to inform professional development.

Computing at school (undated) https://www.computingatschool.org.uk/teach-computing/teaching-computing-primary
This site has many resources for schools on the topic of computing in school.

CfSA – https://www.subjectassociations.org.uk
The Council for Subject Associations supplies links to national subject associations for each specialist curriculum area, to provide research and professional practice-informed approaches to the curriculum, pedagogy and supports continuing teacher development.

Chartered College for Teaching – https://chartered.college
This is the professional body for teachers in England. This connects teachers and provides support for bridging the gap between practice and research. Accredited CPD programme certificates are available, for example in Education Research and Inquiry.

Education Workforce Council (Wales) – https://www.ewc.wales
The Education Workforce Council (EWC) is the independent, professional regulator for the education workforce in Wales, covering teachers and learning support staff in school and further education settings.

The General Teaching Council for Northern Ireland (GTCNI) – https://gtcni.org.uk
This is the professional body for teachers in Northern Ireland.

Lesson Study– https://lessonstudy.co.uk/about-us/
>   This organisation provides a model for reviewing the effectiveness of teaching which some schools use for CPD.

MESHGuides – www.meshguides.org
>   This freely available resource translates education-based research into summaries in the form of online knowledge maps, which can be accessed by teachers.

Mirandanet –http://mirandanet.ac.uk/the-knowledge-hub
>   This is a community of practice for education professionals interested in technology that has been archived by the British Library so you can still access members' publications via their website (see http://mirandanet.ac.uk/knowledgehub/publications/) and also reviews of books by members (see http://mirandanet.ac.uk/knowledgehub/book-reviews/). Mirandanet is now merged with TPEA below.

Technology, Pedagogy and Education Association (TPEA) – https://tpea.ac.uk
>   This is the UK national subject association which supports teachers' use of technology for professional practice. It has an associated research journal, *Technology, Pedagogy and Education* which publishes peer-reviewed academic papers. Many of the contributors to this book are TPEA members.

References

Armitage, A., Bryant, R., Dunnill, R., Hayes, D., Hudson, A., Kent, J., Lawes, S. and Renwick, M. (2003) *Teaching and Training in Post-Compulsory Education* (2nd edn). Maidenhead: Open University Press.

Atkins, L. (2018) *Exploring Teachers' Professional Development and Digital Literacy: A Grounded Theory Study*. Ph.D Thesis, Leicester: De Montfort University.

Barnett, R. (1997) *Higher Education: A Critical Business*. Maidenhead: Open University Press.

Blamires, M. (2015) Building Portals for Evidence-Informed Education: Lessons from the Dead. A Case Study of the Development of a National Portal Intended to Enhance Evidence Informed Professionalism in Education, *Journal of Education for Teaching*, 41(5), 597–607.

Brown, D. and Dowling, P. (1998) *Doing Research/Reading Research: A Mode of Interrogation for Education*. London: Falmer Press.

Burden, K., Younie, S. and Leask, M. (2013) Translational Research Principles Applied to Education: The Mapping of Educational Specialist Knowhow (MESH) Initiative, *Journal of Education for Teaching: International Research and Pedagogy*, 39(4), 459–463.

Cromier, D. (2008) Rhizomatic Education: Community as Curriculum, *Innovate: Journal of Online Education*, 4(5). https://nsuworks.nova.edu/innovate/vol4/iss5/2/ [Accessed 24/11/2023].

Cuthell, J., Cych, L. and Preston, C. (2011) *Learning in Liminal Spaces* [Presentation]. Mobile Learning: Crossing boundaries in convergent environments Conference, University of Bremen. http://www.virtuallearning.org.uk/wp-content/uploads/2011/03/Liminal-Spaces-Bremen.pdf [Accessed 12/12/2022].

Cuthell, J.P. and Preston, C. (2012) Tracking the Stages of Learning: Concept Maps as Representations of Liminal Space, *Themes in Science and Technology Education*, 5(1/2), 79–94.

Cuthell, J., Hall, S., Osman, H., Preston, C., Younie, S., Blamires, M., Leask, M., Procter, R., French, N., Hawkins, G. and Boulter, L. (2022) *Everyone's an Expert: Rhizomatic Learning in Professional Learning Contexts*. London: Mirandanet. http://u3e.55d.mywebsitetransfer.com/wp-content/uploads/2022/09/draft-chapter.pdf [Accessed 24/11/2023].

Daly, C., Pachler, N. and Pelletier, C. (2009) *Continuing Professional Development in IT for Teachers: A Literature Review*. Coventry: Becta.

Davies, M. (2011) Concept Mapping, Mind Mapping and Argument Mapping: What are the Differences and Do They Matter?, *Higher Education*, 62(3), 279–301.

Department for Education [DfE]. (2019a) *Teacher Recruitment and Retention Strategy*. London: DfE. Retrieved from gov.uk website: https://assets.publishing.service.gov.uk/government/uploads/system/uploads/attachment_data/file/786856/DFE_Teacher_Retention_Strategy_Report.pdf [Accessed 12/12/2022].

Department for Education [DfE]. (2019b) *Realising the Potential of Technology in Education: A Strategy for Education Providers and the Technology Industry*. London: DfE. Retrieved from gov.uk website: https://assets.publishing.service.gov.uk/government/uploads/system/uploads/attachment_data/file/791931/DfE-Education_Technology_Strategy.pdf [Accessed 12/12/2022].

Education Endowment Foundation (2021) *Effective Professional Development: Guidance Report*. https://d2tic4wvo1iusb.cloudfront.net/eef-guidance-reports/effective-professional-development/EEF-Effective-Professional-Development-Guidance-Report.pdf?v=1673030254 [Accessed 12/12/2022].

Elliott J. (1991) *Action Research for Educational Change*. Maidenhead: Open University Press, Buckingham.

Fletcher-Wood, H. and Zuccollo, J. (2020) *The Effects of High-quality Professional Development on Teachers and Students: A Rapid Review and Meta-analysis*. London: Education Policy Institute. Retrieved from: https://epi.org.uk/wp-content/uploads/2020/02/EPI-Wellcome_CPD-Review__2020.pdf [Accessed 12/12/2022].

Freidson, E. (1994) *Professionalism Reborn: Theory, Prophecy, and Policy*. Chicago: University of Chicago Press.

GTCE (General Teaching Council for England) (2006) *Using Research in Your School and Your Teaching: Research-engaged Professional Practice*. UCL Institute of Education. https://dera.ioe.ac.uk/19213/1/tplf_research_tp060106.pdf.

Handscomb, G. and MacBeath, J. (2003) *The Research-engaged School*. Chelmsford: Essex County Council.

Hopkins, D. (2002) *A Teacher's Guide to Classroom Research*. Maidenhead: Open University Press.

House of Commons Library (2022) *Teacher Recruitment and Retention in England*. London. Retrieved from: https://researchbriefings.files.parliament.uk/documents/CBP-7222/CBP-7222.pdf [Accessed 12/12/2022].

Hynes, P. and Younie, S. (2018) BYOD: Bring Your Own Device, in S. Younie and P. Bradshaw (Eds.), *Debates in Computing and ICT Education*, Abingdon: Routledge.

IRIS (2022) *Towards Unity: Professional Development for the Next Generation*. Retrieved from: https://1603217.fs1.hubspotusercontent-na1.net/hubfs/1603217/CPD_Guides/IRIS%20Connect-White%20Paper-Towards%20Unity_2022.pdf [Accessed 12/12/2022].

Jones, S., Procter, R. and Younie, S. (2015) Participatory Knowledge Mobilization: An Emerging Model for Translational Research in Education, *Journal of Education for Teaching: International Research and pedagogy; Translational Research and Knowledge Mobilisation in Teacher Education*, 41(5), 555–574.

Kraft, M.A., Blazar, D. and Hogan, D. (2018) The Effect of Teacher Coaching on Instruction and Achievement: A Meta-analysis of the Causal Evidence, *Review of Educational Research*, 88(4), 547–588.

Krumsvik, R.J. (2008) Situated Learning and Teachers' Digital Competence, *Education and Information Technologies*, 13(4), 279–290.

Lamb, T.E. and Simpson, M. (2003) Escaping from the Treadmill: Practitioner Research and Professional Autonomy, *Language Learning Journal*, 28(Winter 2003), 55–63.

Laxton, D., Cooper, L., Shrestha, P. and Younie, S. (2020) Translational Research to Support Early Childhood Education in Crisis Settings: A Case Study of Collaborative Working with Rohingya Refugees in Cox's Bazar, *Education 3–13, International Journal of Primary, Elementary and Early Years Education*, 49(5), 1–19.

Leask, M. and Younie, S. (2001) Communal Constructivist Theory: Information and Communications Technology Pedagogy and Internationalisation of the Curriculum, *Journal of Information Technology for Teacher Education*, 10(1–2), 117–134.

Leask, M. and Younie, S. (2013) National Models for Continuing Professional Development: The Challenges of Twenty-First-Century Knowledge Management, *Journal of Professional Development in Education*, 39(2), 273–287.

Leask, M. and Younie, S. (2022) *Education for All in Times of Crisis: Lessons from Covid-19*. Abingdon: Routledge.

MESHGuides (2022a) *Online Collaborative Learning: A Rhizomatic Approach.* http://www. meshguides.org/guides/node/2422.

MESHGuides (2022b) *Introducing RISE: Research-Informed School Self-Evaluation: A Tool Kit for Teachers.* https://www.new.meshguides.org/introducing-rise-research-informed-school-self-evaluation/.

Meyer, J.H.F. and Land, R. (2003) Threshold Concepts and Troublesome Knowledge 1 – Linkages to Ways of Thinking and Practising, in C. Rust (Ed.), *Improving Student Learning – Ten Years On*, Oxford: OCSLD.

Mishra, P. and Koehler, M.J. (2006) Technical Pedagogical Content Knowledge: A Framework for Teacher Knowledge, *Teachers College Record*, 108(6), 1017–1054.

OECD (2019) *TALIS 2018 Results (Volume 1): Teachers and School Leaders as Lifelong Learners.* TALIS, Paris: OECD Publishing. Retrieved from: https://www.oecd-ilibrary.org/ sites/1d0bc92a-en/1/2/2/index.html?itemId=/content/publication/1d0bc92a-en&_csp_= 1418ec5a16ddb9919c5bc207486a271c&itemIGO=oecd&itemContentType=book#bs53 [Accessed 12/12/2022].

Perkins, D. (1999) The Many Faces of Constructivism, *Educational Leadership*, 57(3), 6–11.

Piaget, J. (1953) *The Origin of Intelligence in the Child.* Abingdon: Routledge and Kegan Paul.

Piaget, J. (1972) *The Principles of Genetic Epistemology.* Abingdon: Routledge and Kegan Paul.

Preston, C. (1998) Swept by the Tide of Technology, *National Association of Advisers and IT Co-ordinators (ACITT) Journal*, April.

Preston, C. (2000) Industry Education Partnership, in M. Leask and N. Pachler (Eds.), *IT Issues in Schools*, London: Routledge.

Preston, C. and Cuthell, J.P. (2012) MirandaMods: From Practice to Praxis in Informal Professional Learning Contexts, in C. Jimoyiannis (Ed.), *Research on e-Learning and IT in Education*, New York: Springer.

Preston, C. and Younie, S. (2016) Taking the Tablets: Engaging the Professional Community in Systemic Change Impacting on the Pupils, the Teachers and School Policy, in A. Quinn and T. Hourigan (Eds.), *Handbook for Digital Learning in K-12 Schools*, New York: Springer, 147–171.

Saunders, L. (2002) *Evidence-led Professional Creativity.* GTC/IOE Joint Conference, Teachers on Teaching and Learning, London.

Schön, D. (1992) *The Reflective Practitioner: How Professionals Think in Action.* Abingdon: Routledge.

Shulman, L.S. (1986) Those Who Understand: Knowledge Growth in Teaching, *Educational Researcher*, 57, 4–14.

Somekh, B. and Davis, N. (Eds.) (1998) *Using IT Effectively in Teaching and Learning Studies in Pre-Service and In-Service Teacher Education.* Abingdon: Routledge.

Stenhouse, L. (1980) The Study of Samples and the Study of Cases, *British Educational Research Journal*, 6(1), 1–6.

Thomas, J. (1995) *Meaning in Interaction: An Introduction to Pragmatics.* London: Longman.

Tinkler, J. (2022) Hand-drawn Concept-mapping as a Participatory Visual Method, *Visual Studies*, 1–17. Routledge. https://doi.org/10.1080/1472586X.2022.2143417.

Vygotsky, L. (1986) *Thought and Language.* Cambridge, MA: The MIT Press.

Wenger, E. (1998) *Communities of Practice: Learning, Meaning, and Identity.* Cambridge, MA: Cambridge University Press.

Younie, S. (2007) *Integrating Technology into Teachers Professional Practice.* Ph.D Thesis, Leicester: De Montfort University.

Younie, S. and Leask, M. (2013) *Teaching with Technologies: The Essential Guide.* Maidenhead: Open University Press.

Younie, S. and Preston, C. (2020) Understanding the Contribution of Professional Communities of Practice in Education Technology in Influencing Teacher Recruitment and Retention, in T. Ovenden-Hope and R. Passey (Eds.), *Exploring Teacher Recruitment and Retention*, Abingdon: Routledge.

Appendix

Emerging trends: artificial intelligence and education

Wayne Holmes

Over many years, a growing range of digital technologies has been used in and beyond classrooms, especially during the Covid-19 pandemic, by teachers to support both their teaching and their students' learning. Many of these technologies have been designed specifically for use in education (EdTech), while others have been repurposed for use in education (e.g., Google Docs, Zoom, Instagram). This is also true for the application of Artificial Intelligence (AI) in classrooms, which has mushroomed in recent years: AI-assisted tools designed for education (AIED) and non-educational AI-assisted tools repurposed for or adopted in education (such as the text-generating AI tool ChatGPT, which burst onto the world stage in early 2023). So, what actually is AI, and what are the connections with education?

Since it was named, in 1956, AI has been defined in too many ways to count. Nonetheless, here we may summarise it as computer software that uses complex rules and/or pattern-finding in large amounts of data to automate processes that would usually require human intelligence. In fact, we encounter AI almost every day – whenever we use our mobile phones, navigate with GPS to our destination, order something from an online store, choose what to watch on a streaming service, talk to customer support, and so on. The list is endless. AI has also been used in biology research (to predict protein folding), to automatically create images (e.g., Stable Diffusion), for facial recognition (e.g., at passport control), and in autonomous vehicles. However, while the many achievements are impressive, AI is also full of myths and exaggerations. For example, despite its name, no AI tool or system is actually intelligent. They might appear to be but they are not. In particular, with clear implications for education, they do not understand either the text that they can generate or the speech that they can recognise.

Nonetheless, as we have mentioned, AI has entered the classroom. In fact, around the world, there are as many as 40 multi-million-dollar-funded AIED companies selling their products to schools and sometimes to whole education ministries (all too often following little consultation with teachers). So, what are these connections between AI and education (AI&ED)? In fact, there are so many that it is not sensible to make generalised claims about the impact or the effectiveness of AI. Instead, we should consider each connection in its own terms and context. Accordingly, at the first level, we need to distinguish between the **application** of AI in education (AIED), and the **teaching** of AI in education (AI Literacy).

The **application of AI in education**, which has been researched for more than 40 years and is now increasingly being commercialised, may be further categorised as institution-focused, student-focused, and teacher-focused. Institution-focused AIED tools include those for admissions, timetabling, and identifying students at risk. Meanwhile, student-focused AIED tools, probably the largest category, include adaptive tutoring systems (which have received the most funding and are the most widely commercialised), AI-assisted apps (e.g., for mathematics problem solving or translation between languages), AI-assisted Virtual Reality and Augmented Reality simulations, and support chatbots, as well as the text generation (for creating teaching plans and possibly writing essays) and image generation AI tools not designed for education mentioned earlier. Finally, teacher-focused AIED tools include plagiarism detection, automatic curation of learning materials, and teacher-supporting grading systems. These are only the most common examples, and things are moving quickly – such that by the time you read this, many other AIED applications are likely to have emerged.

As has been noted, when deciding whether and how to use one of these AIED tools, each one must be considered on its own terms. Some might be useful, while others might not be; and even some tools that have been shown to work in some classrooms, might not be appropriate for yours. But there are some general things to consider. First, what evidence is there for the effectiveness of the tool in question? All too often, there is very little, and the evidence that is available is either very limited or not widely applicable. Mostly, all we have to go on is the developer's own research (there is rarely any independent research at scale) and the marketing blurb. Second, does the evidence that does exist consider the wider impact of the particular tool on teachers (e.g., Are teachers empowered or disempowered by the tool?), classroom practices (e.g., What is the effect of the individualised tool on the social nature of classrooms?), or children's rights (e.g., Are the children being used to generate data in order to develop a commercial tool?)?

And then there's the **teaching of AI in education**: AI Literacy. At first glance, it might seem that this should be the responsibility of IT or computing teachers. However, while these teachers should without doubt be involved, AI and AI Literacy are relevant far more widely. In fact, we ought to consider AI Literacy in two dimensions: the **technological dimension** (how AI works and how it can be created) and the **human dimension** (the social and ethical impact of AI on humans). While IT and computing teachers have an important role to play in teaching the technological dimension (at appropriate levels for young people of different capacities), all teachers should have some involvement in teaching the human dimension. For example, teachers of geography might consider the impact of AI on climate change and the environment (due to its requirements for massive amounts of energy and rare earth metals). Meanwhile, teachers of economics and politics might consider the impact of AI on jobs and the effects of AI-generated fake news. And teachers of literature might look at AI-generated poetry, to explore with their pupils' implications for what it means to be human. Teachers should also aim to achieve an appropriate level of AI Literacy, so that they can fully support all their pupils in a world that is increasingly being impacted by AI, and so that they can have a properly informed understanding of the real benefits and challenges.

Whether any of us like it or not, AI is here now, in classrooms and beyond, and it is not going anywhere. Instead, it is likely to only become more common and more sophisticated over time. If only for these reasons, the **application and teaching of AI** in classrooms is relevant and of importance to all schools, all teachers, all students, and all other education stakeholders (which means all of us). Accordingly, all of us need to achieve an appropriate level of AI Literacy, to ensure that we understand how these technologies are being used, what they can do, what they cannot do, and their implications for humans and human society. Meanwhile, teachers also need to better understand the wide range of available AIED, the efficacy and impact evidence, and their strengths and risks, so that they can see through the marketing claims and make the best use of appropriate AIED in their classrooms.

Index